Music Business

FOR DUMMIES®
A Wiley Brand

by Loren Weisman

FOR DUMMIES®
A Wiley Brand

Music Business **For Dummies**®

Published by: **John Wiley & Sons, Inc.,** 111 River Street, Hoboken, NJ 07030-5774, www.wiley.com

Copyright © 2015 by John Wiley & Sons, Inc., Hoboken, New Jersey

Published simultaneously in Canada

No part of this publication may be reproduced, stored in a retrieval system or transmitted in any form or by any means, electronic, mechanical, photocopying, recording, scanning or otherwise, except as permitted under Sections 107 or 108 of the 1976 United States Copyright Act, without the prior written permission of the Publisher. Requests to the Publisher for permission should be addressed to the Permissions Department, John Wiley & Sons, Inc., 111 River Street, Hoboken, NJ 07030, (201) 748-6011, fax (201) 748-6008, or online at http://www.wiley.com/go/permissions.

Trademarks: Wiley, For Dummies, the Dummies Man logo, Dummies.com, Making Everything Easier, and related trade dress are trademarks or registered trademarks of John Wiley & Sons, Inc., and may not be used without written permission. All other trademarks are the property of their respective owners. John Wiley & Sons, Inc., is not associated with any product or vendor mentioned in this book.

For general information on our other products and services, please contact our Customer Care Department within the U.S. at 877-762-2974, outside the U.S. at 317-572-3993, or fax 317-572-4002.

For technical support, please visit www.wiley.com/techsupport.

Wiley publishes in a variety of print and electronic formats and by print-on-demand. Some material included with standard print versions of this book may not be included in e-books or in print-on-demand. If this book refers to media such as a CD or DVD that is not included in the version you purchased, you may download this material at http://booksupport.wiley.com. For more information about Wiley products, visit www.wiley.com.

Library of Congress Control Number: 2015941027

ISBN: 97-811-1904965-4

ISBN: 97-811-1904946-3 (ePub); ISBN: 97-811-1904944-9 (ePDF)

Manufactured in the United States of America

SKY10095158_010525

Contents at a Glance

Table of Contents

Part II: Making Music and Creating Your Brand 75

Chapter 5: Writing, Rehearsing, Recording, and Performing 77

Chapter 6: Creating and Following a Production Plan 99

Introduction

· ·

There's nothing else quite as incredible as being able to make a living in music. Mixing up a schedule that includes making music, recording music, performing music, and handling the business side of music is more obtainable than ever. Whether writing, performing, recording, marketing, studying, or just listening to music, as a fan, a hobbyist, or an aspiring full-time musician, make the most out of every element.

By taking the most responsible steps on the business side of music as you experience all the fun and enjoyment the creative side can bring you, you can find a true joy and a security in the world of music.

Becoming a full-time musician or working in the music business today is easier than ever with recent changes. It's now easier to record music more affordably. You can reach people through social media on a daily basis where you never could before. And there are simple ways to connect and network, as well as promote and market yourself to venues, investors, and record labels.

All you need is a basic understanding of the different elements of the business of music. And that's exactly what this book is about. I cover the array of all the fundamentals for a successful career in the music business of today.

About this Book

This book contains the tools and the basic blueprints to help you build the specific and personalized career you want. This book isn't a lecture, however. You don't have to read it from beginning to end unless you want to. The chapters are organized in a way that most music business careers progress — in other words, what needs to be done first before continuing to the next step.

This book

✔ Encourages you to explore the many different aspects of the music business

✔ Gives you ideas on where the music business is going

✔ Deals with the branding, promotional, and marketing requirements both online and off

✔ Helps you decide on the right logo, font, bio, and basic branding content to describe you and your music

✔ Discusses the security concerns around copyrights, publishing, contracts, and agreements

✔ Shows how to create content and market it to connect with new audiences while you maintain the relationship with your existing fans

✔ Provides different pieces and line items to include in a recording production plan

✔ Takes a detailed look at music business plans with the costs and the profits

✔ Teaches you the basics of securing sponsorships and endorsements

✔ Gives you a step-by-step approach for tracking and analyzing your progress to better understand what's working and what needs to be changed

✔ Covers an array of problem-solving ideas and basic information on how to persevere, thrive, and survive in today's music business

I also include the best habits to build and maintain success as well as the top ways to present yourself so you can impress industry professionals.

Icons Used in This Book

Peppered throughout this book are helpful icons that present special types of information to enhance your reading experience and help with your forward motion in the music business.

Think of these tips as words of wisdom that — when applied — can make the music business that much easier and less stressful.

These warnings alert you to potential music business problems that could make your experiences unpleasant, rough, and troublesome. Take note and take them to heart!

I use this icon to point out things that need to be kept in the forefront of your mind when making decisions about your career, the music business as a whole, and the choices you make. Remember these aspects before making decisions to help you make the best choices.

Foolish Assumptions

If you have never looked at the business side of music, this book covers all the different aspects that need to be addressed, considered, and applied for success. I assume you have no prior knowledge on the business side of music . . . the contracts, the terms, the marketing, and the business techniques.

However, if you want to be a musician and are ready to jump into the business side of music, this book is a great resource for you. You'll find concepts and ideas to apply so you can protect yourself, your music, and your career. In short, this book is for any musician who realizes there's a business side to music, and it's a business that you want to learn.

Beyond the Book

There is much more information available from your author, and from the Dummies brand, for your learning pleasure. Check out these resources to learn more about the music business:

- ✔ Find the Dummies Cheat Sheet for this book www.dummies.com/cheatsheet/musicbusiness

- ✔ Dummies Extras are available at www.dummies.com/extras/musicbusiness

- ✔ And, although this book includes information about the basics of the music business, this author gives you more in depth from *The Artist's Guide to Success in the Music Business*, published by Greenleaf Book Group.

Where to Go from Here

You can start anywhere with Dummies books, but there's a logic to the motion of the book. If that's not in your personality, consider starting with Chapter 4 to see what your music business plan needs to look like. Then head to Chapter 7 to learn about the basic branding steps you need to take and what you will be presenting both artistically and content wise.

You might have some apprehension about the business side of music. Check out Chapter 2 to get some ideas on what has changed in recent years and how that can help you.

Chapter 14 takes a deep look into the touring and performing elements of the music business, which for many people is the best part. This chapter gives you ideas and angles on how to get out there that much more so you can play that much more often.

Chapter 10 digs in to the website and social media presence elements, which are a very large part of your marketing and promotion. Read this chapter to get the best ideas for creating the best content, and learn how to post it to reach, engage, and stay connected with your current fans as you connect with new ones.

My advice is not to rush through the book, but let the different ideas set in. There's a lot of information here, and all of it will help you have a greater understanding of the music business. Look a little deeper, don't buy into the rumors or hearsay, and look at the bigger picture of the music business. You don't have to be a business expert, but the more you understand, follow, and comprehend the business side of your creativity, the more success you can find.

Part I

Getting Started in the Music Business

getting started
in the

Music Business

In This Part . . .

- ✔ Learn the difference between the music and the music business, and discover how to separate the two to get a greater understanding of how they both work together.

- ✔ Understand recent changes in the music business and how they affect the industry as a whole.

- ✔ Examine all the different options — such as musician, recording engineer, manager, and more — to find the perfect fit for you.

- ✔ Learn about different options for funding your career, and how to create a music business plan to wow investors.

Chapter 1

Getting on the Path to Results

In This Chapter

▶ Discovering the best musical path for you

▶ Jump-starting your plan to get what you want

▶ Knowing who to listen to and who to avoid

▶ Differentiating between the music and the music business

The journey into the music business starts with two steps. The first step moves you forward toward the creativity, writing, performing, and love of the music and the art. The second step takes you toward the organization, optimization, planning, and structure of the business side. The best path to achieving the greatest results in the music business mixes the creativity of the music with the budgeting and organizational nature of the business side. It combines the spontaneity of the music with the planning and contractual structuring of the legal side; a yin and yang mix of freedom to create with the conformity of recordkeeping.

This chapter gives you an overall look at the two sides of the music business. I talk about social media and a little about the legal stuff you need to know about conversions and your music business plan. Odds have it, you're already familiar with the creative side of this industry, and you now need an insight into the business aspects. Throughout this chapter (and the book, actually), I stress that the music business is a career. Hopefully it's your career.

Differentiating between the Music and the Music Business

There's a big difference between your music and the music business. That might sound like a "big duh" statement, but take a minute to think about it.

As much as you're already established on the creative side of music, you might have little to no experience in the business world or the business side of music. A great musician might have no knowledge about or experience in business — one discipline encourages freedom to create; the other demands left-brain practical thinking. Music and business are truly two entirely different forms and practices.

All too often, the lines blur between the two and cause musicians to make big career mistakes that cost them in the moment and often in the long term. As much as the lines get blurred, always remember that your music is your art. Whereas you might be in the beginning stages of business, never let anyone make you doubt the music you create and love. That's the creative part, not the business part.

Some claim there are formulas to writing hit songs, and million-dollar successes bring all the fame in the world. But the reality is that for every formula presented or example of how the ten best songs of any given year were hits, there are millions of other songs that went nowhere that followed the same exact structure and at least another ten songs that did just as well in completely different molds.

Even though you need to know the business side of the music industry, regardless of the job or role you take, trust in your art and your creative side so you can learn and grow in your craft. Don't make the music all about business, or there will be nothing creative to it.

Many different tasks are presented to and required from you throughout your career, but those activities make up the business side. When you separate and differentiate the two, both are much easier to do and give you a greater understanding of how they both work together.

Why you need to grasp the business

You don't need to go to business school and get an MBA, just like you don't need to learn every aspect of the music business to succeed. Still, taking business and accounting classes as well as intellectual property, copyright, and marketing courses can help to supplement your knowledge. Learning about each position, each expense, each revenue, basic legal and copyright information as well as the fundamentals of contracts inside and outside of your music, your band and the people involved with you gives you a better understanding of everything happening around you. Also, networking and connecting with the right people can also help. Never feel bad about asking questions regarding contracts, copyrights, and other legal aspects.

When you have a basic knowledge of what goes on in your career, you have a better idea if you're going in the right or wrong direction. In turn, you can make better decisions when things are going wrong and make things grow even larger when things are going right.

When you let others take care of your career, you have no idea if your business matters are being handled in your favor or to benefit others. Many artists who have lost money and prestige, more often than not, let it happen to themselves by being ignorant or uninvolved in decisions that directly affected them.

Understanding the basics of the music biz buffet

The music business can be compared to a buffet composed of tables with platters of copyrights, publishing, sync licensing to television and movies, CDs, performances, digital downloads, download cards, T-shirts, hats, glassware, posters, bags, performance royalties, mechanical royalties, online advertising revenues, and many other revenue-generating and tasty choices.

Sitting at these tables with you are producers, mixing engineers, managers, publicists, publishers, promoters, graphic designers, SEO people, mastering engineers, lawyers, investors, web designers, distributors, photographers, videographers, consultants, songwriters, talent buyers, venue owners, booking agents, insurance agents, radio promoters, fundraisers, and others who want their share of each dish.

It can seem overwhelming and intimidating; many avoid it all together. But the best way to simplify everything while still addressing every detail is to make sure the following five elements are covered for every person and every product.

- ✔ **Understanding and planning:** Make sure everyone has a clear understanding of what each person is doing, what they're getting, and how long they're involved. Also make clear how monies are spent and how work is being done. I discuss more of this in Chapter 9.

- ✔ **Protection and contractual obligation:** This is where you and your legal team draw up and sign binding contracts that clarify each role and what each gains from revenues also discussed in Chapter 9.

- ✔ **Problem solving and preventative maintenance:** Make certain that you have an emergency preparedness and readiness plan in place and that you have solutions ready to resolve the issues. I go deeper into this in Chapter 18.

✔ **Education and updating your learning:** Stay up to date with new products, old contracts, and changes in the law for entertainment, intellectual property, and other related issues.

✔ **Due diligence and fact checking:** Before working with anyone or signing any agreement, making sure to verify your information, and check up on the people giving you that info before you go into business with them. From calling references to checking reviews and past clients, make sure the people you're working with and the path they want to walk leads you where you want to go.

You don't need to know every aspect of every job and every detail, but the more familiar you are with the basics of all the different people, jobs, companies, and requirements, the better the decisions you make and the more you're able to take for yourself at the music biz buffet.

Disconnecting the business from the music

Understand that on any given day, you have to focus time on the business side of things to make your music thrive and succeed. This takes time and effort away from actually making music. Just keep in mind why you're in the music business and the business side will be less stressful and tedious.

It's okay to get lost in the creative side of your music and let it take you to another place, somewhere carefree, inspiring, and almost like you're lifting off and flying. But don't let that happen with the business side. Keep a firm grip on all things and all people around you, and you won't have to feel the sensation of your legs being swept out from under you.

Practicing Responsible Career Tactics

Creating the plan for your career or any career in any business is a great first step, but if you aren't using responsible tactics in your plan as you begin to execute that plan, it could cost you a lot in the long run. By asking all the questions that you need to know, preparing for the best and worst-case scenarios and getting everyone working with you on the same page, both conceptually and legally (signed contracts), you can keep the confusion, misunderstandings, and potentially devastating problems to a minimum. At the same time, you reinforce the clear expectations you have with others and what they can have with you. More about the plans and the planning in Chapter 4.

Planning for the plan and creating the blueprint

A great number of musicians work from the mindset that after they connect with the right people, agent, manager, label, or investor, everything gets taken care of as far as the business side is concerned and they get to live the rock-star life.

Not to completely discredit that view, but less than half a percent live that dream, which actually is a nightmare. Never forget that when you have someone doing everything for you, they can take everything from you.

Your music, art, and creative vision are priceless to you. When you bring that to the music business, however, what it takes to get you, your music, and your brand out to the world without your help means the bulk of profits end up with those who had control. Plan to stay involved in the business side of your career.

Create a basic music business plan that you can begin to implement immediately, regardless of where you are in your career. This blueprint helps to map the path of where you want to go while showing others just how far you can go. The organization early on helps you start on the best path to lead you to the most opportunities and the most connections to get you where you want to be. More details about music business plans are discussed in Chapter 4.

Building your own foundation first

The more you can put together and the more you can take care of yourself, the less you require from others. Sounds simple, right? But think about it — if you can create the basics for others to work from, you create and have the rights to that much more of your branding, graphics, and foundational elements. You've done that much more work that you don't have to pay others to create.

The more you do, the less you need others to do, and the more you can keep for you. When you handle the basic business structure, as well as the basic plan, the logos, content, one liners, bios, and preliminary branding elements, you can move forward that much faster with people who can work with what's already been put in place. More about this is Chapter 7.

Focusing on conversions and rules of engagement

Many musicians get so wrapped up in the idea of numbers that they don't create any real or pertinent numbers for them or their careers. The amount of friends, followers, likes, views, plays, and shares builds nothing other than numbers if there's no conversion. Would you rather have 100,000 followers on Twitter or $100,000.00 in conversions to revenues for albums, downloads, product sales and so on? More about your conversions as well as tracking them in Chapter 17.

Social media has helped reach many people and yet at the same time has taken some musicians backward with the idea of how to engage all those people and convert them to fans who buy music, merchandise, and show tickets. In the past few years alone, artists boast and brag about the number of views on YouTube, the number of followers on Twitter, or the number of likes on Instagram like they measure success. When they're asked, however, how much music has been sold, how many gigs they have lined up, or what opportunities are coming from those numbers, most give a blank look and answer with very low numbers.

How to use social media summary

Simply summed up for the music or any other business, regardless of having the biggest budget in the world or not having a penny in the bank, it's the same — using social media for marketing and promotion is a requirement that most understand. Still, using social media with the most responsible tactics to create the best engagement and conversions comes from thinking of every post as a marketing and promotional tool that helps you today, and reinforces and compounds what you posted yesterday as it helps to push tomorrow's post and solidifies all posts in the future.

Those who just sell, sell, sell and bore their existing fans with the same pitch over and over, with the same videos or posts over and over, end up losing their existing audience as they reach to grow it larger. The content is key and with the addition of an editorial calendar and basic posting plan for online marketing, you can keep the existing fans engaged, reach for new fans, and continue to sell without spamming, boring, or pressuring your existing or new audiences. Chapter 11 goes deeper into organizing and posting content.

Acting and behaving in the music business

Responsible tactics also include how you behave and present yourself in emails, phone calls, and in person. An arrogant approach and a rock-star persona attitude are all too often presented to music industry people who have seen it all too much and are sick of it.

Take that extra second before you post online or send that email to make sure your Is are dotted and your Ts are crossed. Thinking about not only what you are presenting, asking for, or looking to discuss, but also thinking about your communication, the volume of your voice, the confidence in your tone by mixing humility, integrity, and respect helps you be seen as that much more of a professional. From how you dress to your posture, and even your eye contact, a great deal of your first impression creates that many more opportunities for you.

What you're asking for or what you want in most cases has been heard a million times before by the people you're pitching to. Keep that in mind and formulate a pitch that's strong in its delivery and shows that you understand the people you're talking to. This individualized approach helps industry personnel see you as more of an individual, instead of just another musician thinking they're the best thing since sliced bread.

Taking the high road on your music path

Even as things go wrong or when others do wrong by you, take the high road. Going online to bash whoever you feel did you wrong is usually not going to help you get what you need. It also presents an immature and reactive image and a lack of professionalism that may drive away potential music business professionals and companies. No one wants to work with those who hang their dirty laundry out to be seen by everyone.

Keep that stuff offline and out of marketing, and handle your business like a professional business person. That doesn't mean being taken advantage of or letting the business steamroll you. It means that you will contact the right people the right way to try to make things right and stay offline and quiet about it. Your existing fan base and the new fans you are reaching out to don't need to see this side, so don't show it to them.

Letting go of the things that aren't going to change

There are times when letting go is the better option over continuing after something that will never get fixed, never get you paid, and never be right. It's good to right the wrongs; righting a wrong from someone who wronged you is even more desirable. Still, if you spend a hours, money, and energy to chase after something from the past, it can end up stalling you from moving forward.

Pick and choose your battles wisely. You can't win them all; if you try, you could end up losing everything.

Keeping your online info in check

Responsible marketing and sharing both online and in interviews can help keep your fans interested in you. Social media has turned into a cesspool of over-sharing, however, both with celebrities and normal people alike. Then bring in the paparazzi, TMZ, and rumor trains, and you have way too much over-saturated information that has infected the online world.

Keep your pages about your music and your business. Whereas sharing personal aspects about yourself can work in your favor, make sure the info ties directly to something that can lead these people to want to find out more about you. Just sharing, "I like scrambled eggs" and showing a picture of scrambled eggs is pretty boring, mundane, and pointless.

From doctor's appointments to private jokes to other pictures of food, keep the personal stuff personal, and keep the marketing for your music pages. Think before you post and stay responsible! Is this post going to be good for market-ing, promotion, and helping to reinforce your branding for new and old fans, reviewers, booking agents, investors, and other music business professionals? Can this post be effective in two years? If the answer is no to these questions, don't post it and keep it private, or put it up through personal channels.

Create personal pages for personal information or the over-sharing information if you really want to put it out there, but make sure that those pages are named something other than your stage name. For example, if your real name and stage name is Nerol Namsie, and you already have http://nerolnamsie. com/ as well as a number of pages on social media tied in to that name, try using a nickname for your personal page and make it private. This helps to avoid confusion from both new and old fans searching you.

Keeping the personal stuff private and not sharing too much can also add to a mystery and a mystique about you. It's that much more refreshing for new and old fans to know that when you post, it's something they might want to see, as opposed to being inundated with too many posts that don't give them the information to build better engagement.

Think of the brand new fans who have come upon you by accident. Do you want to have to make them scroll through page after page of meaningless posts that have no tie to your music or marketing? Or should they immediately get a sense of your music and you?

Marketing for musicians: Basic anatomy of a good post

Jumping back to the scrambled eggs update (see the earlier section, "Keeping your online info in check"), each social media site has different best practice rules for posting.

As shown in the earlier section, the post was eggs and just "I like scrambled eggs" for content. And, yes I have seen this come across my feed from a musician in the past. This isn't made up. Now, if you shared a picture of scrambled eggs shaped in your band's logo, the logo next to scrambled eggs, or on a plate with your logo super-imposed over it, then band's the caption, you get what's seen in Figure 1-1. Nice, hm?

Figure 1-1: This attention-grabbing social media post gives the reader all the info they need.

Here is the breakdown:

1. You start with a headline that jumps out, even if it comes off a bit weird.

2. The band name is clearly mentioned — Kitty Likes Avocado.

3. You give a vivid description of the track.

4. You include the call to action and accompanying URL where fans can listen to the track and access your main web page.

5. The image upload of the eggs is named (scrambled-eggs, funk-music, kitty-likes-avocado.jpeg).

6. You finish with a couple hash tags that tie into the topic and the post.

In Google+, you can get some pretty amazing optimization on words and photos if you post correctly. They offer this as a push to get more people on Google+, so take advantage of that! The post can still be shared to all your other pages, as well.

The post can draw in a new fan, keep an existing one engaged, and help with search engine optimization (SEO) and the uniform branding that needs to be there. Taking those extra steps to come up with a post and then tailoring it for the best results gives you a serious leg up in social media.

Weeding out the Myths, Scams, and Scammers

There are a lot of people with a lot of claims that promise you the world, fame, riches, and success as long as you listen to them. Unfortunately, the truth usually boils down to anyone who's promising the world, fame, riches, and success right out of the gate is most likely a scammer or part of a scam. There's money to be made in the legitimate music business, but it doesn't come close to the totals that have been made off fake record labels, consultants, coaches, producers, studios, managers, and agents who prey on the sensitivity, lack of experience, and ego of many artists.

From taking money to getting these artists signed into contracts that can have a negative effect for years to come, one of the most important elements of thriving and sustaining in the music business is to clarify and watch out for the scams/scammers who are all over it and a major part of it.

Take it all in, but choose wisely who you listen to and what advice you choose to follow. From research to references to due diligence, things can still go wrong, but the chances are much more in your favor that they'll go right if you know what to look for.

The old quote "Born on third base and you think you hit a triple" has been credited to a number of different people, but it's absolutely true. When you choose to buy into the hype of someone who has a very successful career but delivers information from second guesses instead of backing it up with the numbers and the proof, you are headed toward a model that will hurt more than help.

These people present themselves by feeding in to a musician's dreams, their weaknesses, and their desires as they look to make money off them. There are some with the best intentions to make things go that big, but their lack of experience, knowledge, and problem solving mixed with their abundance of ego, ignorance, and foolishness set themselves and the artists up for failure.

You don't need a life coach or cheerleader

Let me repeat this section heading — you don't need a life coach or cheerleader. If you need someone to help you find the drive to do the work that's required to be successful in music, you might be in the wrong profession. You do need those who can guide you, who have the experience and proof to help in today's music business. You need to track the results of what you're doing to see what's working and what isn't. You need you more than anyone else to ask the questions, follow up on the claims, do your due diligence, and be patient with what you're creating.

Opinions, facts, theories, and proof

Watch for the morphing of opinions that turn into facts, just as you keep an eye on those who discuss theories that somehow shift into proof. You're smarter than you give yourself credit for. By taking simple steps to ask questions and then question the answers you get, you can to surround yourself with honest people and make better choices about the direction to take your career.

The music business has changed dramatically over the decades and continues to change each year. Certain facts that were once true are now expired; certain proven theories that were once right are now wrong. Differentiating between what was and what is needs to take place with every decision you make for your career and every piece of advice you choose to follow or take. With so many people sharing so much information — from the creative elements of what it takes to write a hit song to the budgeting elements of how much it costs to record that song to the performance elements of what kind of team it will take to put you on tour performing that song and everything in between — make sure for each concept, tip, approach, or piece of advice you get, ask the following:

- ✔ What made it work?
- ✔ When did it work?
- ✔ What was the budget?
- ✔ Who made up the team?
- ✔ How long did it take?
- ✔ What are the similarities to you and your situation?
- ✔ What are the differences?
- ✔ What direction do things seem to be going to make it work or not make it work again?

Looking up and addressing those elements and finding out the details can help you in any business, but especially in the music business. Think of yourself as a card-carrying red-flag holder who's ready to raise that red flag as soon as something sounds too good to be true or hits you the wrong way. And realize there are so many different personal approaches. This is not a one-size-fits-all business.

Find out as much as you can whether an opinion is worth its weight in gold and truly can be justified as a fact or is just an opinion with nothing to truly substantiate it.

Not every opinion can be proven as a fact, but in that case look at the track record of who's supplying that opinion and other facts they have supplied in the recent past. Although facts and proof are best, the opinions and theories from those who truly know the music business can give you reason to believe them to be true.

It's okay to say I don't know

It's actually one of the best things you can say and one of the best things you can hear. If you don't know something, then don't pretend to know it, and don't make something up. It's not cool. Would you want someone to make up something to try to come off cool? Probably not.

Take a path of honor and honesty by being honorable and honest about what you know and what you don't know. I wasn't the greatest drummer by far, and I wasn't the best music producer either. I never claimed to have all the answers and I still don't claim to. One of the things that got me a lot of work and connections, though, was being the first to say I didn't know something. That humility you carry in the music business will take you far.

As I shifted to becoming a music industry consultant, speaker, and author, being able to say "I don't know" got me even more opportunities. It reinforced the belief from others that when I said I knew something, I really did, and it built trust that I wasn't making things up when I said I didn't know but I would find out.

Don't try to be cool by pretending to know something. Be cool by being the first to say that you don't know, but you'll find the answer.

Committing to, Reinforcing, and Running a Career

After you get your plan in motion and your music the best it can be, and you supplement it with the efforts to make the music-business side run as smoothly as possible, you're in the longest stage of your career in the music business: the continuity stage.

This stage consists of the ongoing commitment to both your craft and the business of your craft that allows for sustaining success and continued growth. This commitment is key and needed in both hard times as well as good times. The continued commitment allows for certain aspects of the business to be that much more streamlined and allow for the business and creative sides to flow that much easier. By understanding what worked well, you can repeat it, just as having the understanding of what didn't work so that you won't repeat it helps you survive, thrive, and succeed for years to come.

The humility of your business and creative sides

Humility is one of the last pieces of the puzzle that helps you build the best map as you create the smoothest roads and most productive path for your music business career. The humility in the art you write and perform, the business you partake in, and the artists you work with gives you a leg up in a world of arrogance and excessive egos.

Stay centered, stay humble, and understand that not everyone is going to like you, believe in you, or want to work with you. You can always grow in all elements of your craft from the business to the creative sides. Whether it's handling criticism a little better to keeping that level head when someone is hyping you up, the way you act in front of the biggest fan to the person you're the biggest fan of should be similar if not the very same. The humility, respect, and drive to stay grounded as you fly high helps you stand out among a sea of egos.

You're an original, but you aren't the only one

As new as it is to you, whether your marketing, music, approach, look, lyrics, performance, or anything else you can think of, it has been described before, asked for before, and done before. Maybe not exactly like what you're doing, but close or at least in the same ballpark.

Don't get discouraged, and don't go changing who you are, the music you write, or the way you perform it. That creative side is you. It's just a key point to keep in mind as you approach booking agents, talent buyers, record labels, investors, agents, and whoever else when you're looking for support, a connection, or an opportunity. That pause you take and that breath before the send, the ask, or the request can make all the difference. It also helps with your connections and networking with others in and out of the music industry ten fold.

Your endurance and patience

The music business is made for those with the endurance and the patience to make sure that all the pieces are created the right way and presented in the right fashion. From recording the music, to the graphics on the album, the touring plan, marketing, and so on, your endurance to build it the right way yields the best results. Managing your time, multitasking, practicing patience, and realizing there are enough hours in the day is part of the winning formula; how you allocate those hours makes the difference.

Understanding your audience, fans, and customers

There's a big different between *reaching* a potential fan and *converting* them to a fan who comes to see you play, buys your music, and truly stays connected and engaged. As you think about the engagement and connection of each fan over the friend, like, view, listen, or follow, you create the best fan base that stays with you for a long time to come.

Chapter 2

A Change is Gonna Come: Changes in the Music Business

*W*ith ever-changing technology, the music business is more confusing than ever. Many businesses have changed and adapted over the years, but as technology brought affordable and accessible computers, the Internet, and social media, the music business has seen some of the most dramatic changes of them all. From the economy to social media, from music piracy to file sharing, and from a limited number of local radio stations to millions of online music networks, the music business is still shifting each day.

On a positive note, the changes have been less drastic in the past few years, and the dust is settling as new opportunities and options present themselves. At the same time, some of those rules and basic blueprints of the industry are still there. They've just been updated and adjusted for the present as well as the direction of the future.

Whether you're a musician just starting out or a seasoned pro, a business manager or promoter, or you have another role in this fast-paced but ever-changing business, you need to roll with the changes. This chapter takes a look at how the music industry is changing.

Changes for the Better

Could you imagine what Woodstock would have been like if we had social media and the Internet back in 1969? What if the Beatles could have recorded in a studio like The Sound Kitchen in Nashville, Tennessee, on a digital board with endless tracking capabilities? From a marketing standpoint, wouldn't it have been amazing for an artist to be able to write an email to an existing fan base to tell them about a show or event back in the 1950s?

Beyond all the different websites, social media pages, sales pages, and the Internet as a whole, the biggest positive change in the music business is the increase in the ability for connection, communication, networking opportunities, engagement, organization, and education. Now more than ever, musicians, artists, record labels, booking agents, representatives, and so on have the ability, technology, and platforms to connect instantaneously and immediately.

The communication and exchange of information and materials that used to take sometimes weeks to send back and forth can now be done in a matter of seconds. Recordings can be zipped and uploaded onto websites like Dropbox and sent as a simple link to a mixing engineer. High-quality posters and marketing materials can be sent with a click and then printed out locally. The ability to expedite and deliver everything from fully digital promotional packages to contracts that once took weeks can now be done in minutes.

Recording

Professional recording engineers, home studio mavens, and everyone in between have been positively affected by recent changes in technology. Gone are the days of needing to travel far and pay a great deal to get in to a recording studio. Gear is much more affordable and delivers high-quality results. This has allowed artists to record great-sounding music for much less money.

With the digital age, the excessive cost of recording on tape and the hefty costs of tape machines have been replaced by a variety of inexpensive programs that can be run on most computers. Both the recording equipment advances as well as the simplified and more affordable methods have opened the door for that many more people to be able to record. The ability to soundproof, the access to microphones, and the variety of digital effects have allowed the recording industry to cut industry-level recordings in home studios and even bedrooms.

Email

Email databases and email newsletters save a fortune on paper and stamps, and allow the task to be simplified and streamlined much faster than all the printing and physical mailing. Record labels, publicists, and promoters can reach out to reviewers, fans, and media with the click of a button. From artist updates to band announcements as well as press releases and email newsletters, artists, bands, promoters, and other music industry professionals save more time and money announcing the new single, the tour, or the album release.

Gear

Musical gear has come a long way, baby! Take a look at musical instruments like guitars, drums, and keyboards as well as recording gear such as microphones, mixing boards, and software programs. Amazing-sounding guitars can be manhandled a little more; hardware used to hold up and position drums exactly where you want them is more durable; in fact, gear as a whole is more durable both sound- and technology-wise.

The advancement in the tools, toys, and items to help keep the vintage instruments sounding their best is outstanding. From the quality of the drum sets to the technology of the new keyboards, even at the beginner levels, artists can afford and purchase musical instruments that have advanced in their quality light years from where they were just a couple decades ago. On the same note, the tools and parts to be able to fix the vintage instruments and be able to maintain or bring some instrument back from the dead are available now, too. For example, guitarists have the option to purchase their own guitar-making kits. They can order them online with all the pieces to custom-build their own with personal touches. For older gear, there are electronic devices you can use to check the angle of a neck and the radius of the fret board. Luthier tools (tools to adjust and fix guitars) have come down in price and are more affordable. And check out online instructional videos on YouTube that can guide you through do-it-yourself maintenance.

Merchandise

Gone are the days when you had to order a bazillion promotional items and then wait weeks for them to be delivered. Now, a couple of clicks, a few days, and your new stuff arrives at your doorstep. What used to cost a fortune and force artists to order in bulk through larger, more expensive sources now is cheaper and faster with promotional merchandise and marketing accessories sites like Vistaprint, 4Print, and Branders.com. These companies, as well as the larger merchandise businesses, have newer equipment that allows for smaller runs of merchandise, and your order can be turned around and shipped that much faster. Then back to email, with the ability to email or FTP designs to a manufacturer as well as review the proofs online, the process has sped up exponentially.

The ability to order CDs, T-shirts, coffee cups, stickers, posters, pens, hats, bags, and all sorts of other merchandise items at a fair cost now enables musicians to expand their products, their product sales, and allows for more profits. Artists, designers, merchandise producers, and distributors all benefit and profit that much more. You're also able to order these products in smaller runs; for example, you can purchase 25 T-shirts instead of being required to buy 250. Digital downloads of individual tracks to full albums, streaming live shows to previously recorded performances, and even giving away free downloads, have allowed for more music to be made, sold, or shared that much quicker and that much easier.

Distribution

Distribution (which is how you physically get your music to all the stores possible) used to cost a fortune and was mainly used for the highest-level and major-label artists. Now, however, it's shifted to online distribution and favors the little guy. The iTunes store, Amazon, and Bandcamp (sites that you can upload your music to and sell from their digital stores directly to fans) as well as distribution sites like TuneCore (which can help you to put your music up on iTunes, Amazon, and a number of others digital music selling sites) give musicians a choice of where and how to distribute their music. And musicians now have the ability to sell directly from their own websites. The world of distribution has become better and smaller for individual artists; they can now extend their reach globally while maintaining just one location. Although record labels still use both online (downloads) and physical distribution methods (CDs, vinyl), now independent artists and smaller labels can directly sell their music through these channels. The ability for an artist to use a distributor like TuneCore allows them to pay a smaller percentage for the distribution because they are cutting out the label and profiting that much more.

Record labels have also offered distribution deals to artists where they don't have a recording contract with a band, but they distribute their music across many channels. This allows for an independent artist to be found and have their music for sale on numerous online sites, but also to have physical product distributed to physical stores such as Best Buy, Target, Walmart, and other places where you can buy music. Labels focus more on the online distribution, but by putting up the money to create product and physically placing that product in stores, it helps the brand and the visibility of artists.

Internet and social media

When talking about advances in the music business, no discussion is complete without talking about the Internet and social media. Sites like YouTube enable artists to highlight music videos, live performances, and interviews that can be seen around the world 24/7/365. Photo-related sites like Instagram, Flickr, and Pinterest allow for band photos, live photos, road photos, and more fan accessibility (and more accessibility for family members, too . . . Mom always wants to know where you are). Reviewer sites and blogs that introduce new artists are everywhere. SoundCloud, iTunes, and other streaming sites now enable people to listen to the music and buy it at will.

The Internet has helped to make a very large world just a little bit smaller. It's also made marketing and promotion much more personalized while giving potential investors, labels, and representatives a wider reach. They can now connect with, invest in, and work with artists all around the world many times in real time for a nominal amount of money. The engagement of fans has made them a part of marketing since the world came online. Pictures taken by fans are posted across social media; album or concert reviews are shared immediately; social media pages like Facebook and hash tags have brought the importance of a fan that much more to the forefront.

The ability to share what people like with their friends has allowed a level of exposure never seen before. It's part of why just three years ago, over 4.6 billion dollars was spent on social media advertising and it is expected to see over double that spent in 2016. From promoted posts and ads on sites like Facebook and Twitter to Google Adwords campaigns and impression ads that can show up on any site from Yahoo! to CNN, the new name of the game is recognition of the brand as it's pushed and presented to you every day.

Even the product part of the music business has been affected by the Internet and social media. Artists can send unfinished music files by FTP to have others play on those songs, mix those songs, and master those songs as they send everything back and forth by email links. The Internet has allowed contracts to be signed in the same day and then announcements about those deals to go out minutes later.

Changes for the Worse

The music business has also had its share of changes for the worse, and I can't go all shiny-happy without mentioning some of the negatives. With all that technology has brought, it's also caused some damage.

Fewer sales

Cassettes are gone, CDs are just about gone, and vinyl is a niche market in which most music aficionados don't own a turntable or record player. Fewer fans are going out to concerts, choosing to stay home and not spend the money for the concert, the ticket charge, the facility fee, the parking costs, and so on. With the price of concert tickets on the rise, it's not as affordable as it used to be to see a live show. And when at a live show, fewer fans are buying T-shirts, CDs, and other merchandise items. Falling sales equals falling revenue.

The vast majority of music buyers have turned to digital where file sharing and music piracy have created fewer sales. When you can stream music online and are able to download on numerous sites for free, it takes a very large chunk out of profits for artists.

Music piracy is loosely defined as copying, downloading, and distributing (or sharing) music without the copyright holder's consent. With it being easier than ever to download a song illegally and share it with a friend, or ten, this cuts in to the profits that the artist may have made. While it may not be as big a deal for larger-scale artists, this piracy can hurt smaller, independent artists.

Pandora and other streaming channels available on computers, in cars, and on smartphones enable consumers to purchase subscriptions services, which allow for music to be heard, streamed, and in some cases downloaded in bulk. This also means less for the artist.

Reality and competitive TV shows

There are musicians who think their YouTube video will magically launch them to fame, riches, and stardom, being the greatest thing since sliced bread and all. Others feel that producers from American Idol, XFactor, The Voice, and other star-maker shows will be calling any day. But here are the facts: Of the millions of talented musicians, dancers, singers, and so on who've tried out, less than 20 have created careers in the music business. The majority who get a shot to audition for a producer never make it in front of a camera.

And then there's the legal issue of signing a contract with show producers. Contracts can take away artist control, causing the artist to lose ownership of their name, likeness, and career choices for years to come.

 When signing any contract with anyone, always have a music or entertainment attorney look over the agreement. The "fine print" has caused many an artist to regret what should be the happiest day of their life. An attorney not familiar with music is not the one to use.

The bad guys, the fakes, and the con artists

So-called social media gurus, graphic designers, fake labels, managers, agents, and consultants with no experiences, no success, and no knowledge are out to make a fast buck and take advantage of artists. Mix that with a select few who have the knowledge and money to woo an artist into an impossible and detrimental contract that will take advantage of them in the moment and take percentages for life, and that small trusting error can end up as a big catastrophe. It's crucial to practice your due diligence with anyone you work with, pay, or sign a contract with by not only asking and checking for references but looking at the work or services performed for others and the end results.

These scammer types were always around, but now with graphic designers and the Internet many more of these types have been able to troll and prey on dreams of those that do not know enough to put up red flags. Looking sharper, more professional, and better than you expect from a scammer are key factors buying into what they're saying.

The business side requirements of artists

There was a time when music and being a musician were a little less about the business and more about the music and the quality of music. Now, however, musicians who are neither savvy about nor proactive in the business find success.

Artists at any level have to be in tune with the business side of the industry so they can protect themselves and their careers. And this isn't limited to musicians; the same goes for engineers, managers, publishers, booking agents, producers, and songwriters, too.

College courses and online video searches that both describe the different jobs and job descriptions, along with learning about the roles in the business can help you understand what has to be done and who usually performing what task. In Chapter 3, I highlight a series of different jobs and their basic descriptions.

It's easier these days for people to call themselves agents, managers, and publishers, and seem legitimate as they make intentional and unintentional moves that can hurt those around them. It was an issue in the past, but now with the Internet and the ability to check in and check up on someone mixed with artists learning the roles from classes, online videos, and books like this one, better choices and wiser decisions can be made.

Pitch adjusters and over-production

Sadly, you don't need talent in a world where a simple push of a button can fix your off-key voice out-of-rhythm beat. You can now add a series of extra background voices or backing vocals to reinforce a weaker lead vocal, or you can throw in additional layers of instruments and supplemental sounds that would be very hard to replicate live on stage. All of this can bring up the overall professionalism of a song that wouldn't otherwise be there.

Pitch perfect, almost

With software like Auto-Tune from Antares, it's possible to slide an out-of-tune note to a note that's pitch perfect. If a singer can get close enough, a small bend or adjustment with Auto-Tune is not even recognizable. If the singer is further off, though, that adjustment will make the note sound digital and robotic. Remember Cher's hit "I Believe" in 1998? Some still refer to Auto-Tuning as adding the Cher effect. More recently it's been called the T-Pain effect, because T-Pain has used a great deal of Auto-Tune. Less extreme examples include anything from Maroon 5 in recent years.

Supporting cast

Almost like a supporting cast, overproduction (where an excess of sounds, instrumentation, or a heavy adjustment to the tone or mix of a given instrument) is used to beef up a song and fill it out. In some cases it can be a positive, but for an artist who has an excess of instruments and sounds that can't be created on stage, the use of overproduction can disappoint fans.

Embellishments can be a wonderful thing, such as an extra harmony added to a section for a musical effect. But adding a 60-person choir, a horn section, and a whole bunch of strings to a song by a band with only three members performing live can be too much.

Auto-Tune and overproduction shows up in those who just can't sing or have a solid song. With this growing trend, there are so many artists out there who can barely sing live without it, too. And yes, technology has hit the point, where you can Auto-Tune while someone is on stage these days. Just as backing tracks can be added to support a live band, there are both the good sides and the bad sides of pitching correction and overproduction. In the end, it comes down to personal choice.

Not to be completely negative, there are those out there who still believe in the raw, authentic sound and true talent. I remember producing an album back in 2006 where we added a note on the back of the disc cover that no Auto-Tune was used on the lead vocalist at all, but also at the same time, we had a section with a pitchy backup singer, and it only took two minutes to pitch her perfect instead of spending the time to bring her back in and cut it again.

Promotion oversaturation

More and more musicians are recording more and more music and putting it out on more and more websites, social media pages, and sales sites. Then, add in the marketing, the spamming, the emails, the texts, the posts and the requests . . . oh the requests:

- Like my page
- Download my song
- Buy my album
- Follow me on this site
- Pre-order the t-shirt, hat, other merchandise item
- Donate to my crowd funding campaign
- Come to my show
- Tell others about my music
- Review my album
- Vote for me in this contest
- Share my video
- Gimme, gimme, gimme . . .

With millions of musicians making millions of requests in a nonstop fashion, the industry has become oversaturated and filled with artists who might not even realize that they're part of a barrage of an oversaturated business that's pressuring fans way too often.

When you inundate your existing audience with nonstop requests and asks, you turn them off and turn them away. Find the balance with your requests as you focus on creating and delivering engaging content to keep the existing fans happy and draw interest from new ones.

Promoting and Marketing Gone Bad

Many musicians unintentionally find themselves in the mindset that what they are sending out is original and new. Actually, however, the average fan sees these types of promoting and marketing items from bands they have been fans of for a long time, from bands they have just connected with recently, and even from bands that have bought advertisements to show up in their feeds and as ads on websites they visit.

Then, when you add the spammers and artists that hire very shady promotional and public relations people to grab your email and sign you up on a list you never wanted to be on, to pushy, pressuring posts, requests and ads, promotion and marketing have taken a turn for the worse in the recent years of the music business. There's always been a negative push of promotion that goes far back. Still, with the Internet and social media as well as the ability to send out these free pitches at the click of a button it has, as a whole, gone from bad to worse.

From the physical marketing of people stapling posters onto trees or the disrespectful covering of another poster, some musicians and promoters have reached an arrogant-type level of thinking they are the only band, the only promoter, and the only artist who's worth looking at.

Negative promoting and marketing by insulting other bands and artists is also at an all-time high. Combine all these elements and bring them online to the over-the-top arrogant posts such as, "There is no one better than us." the passive-aggressive content such as "if you don't like this page, then just un-friend me," and spam, where the same sales pitches, messages and links are sent on a regular basis, and you have the perfect storm of a marketing and promotion disaster.

To combat this and stand out with the audience you have as well as the audience you're trying to reach, take a humble approach and keep the self-aggrandizing and spam to a minimum, if any at all.

Even if you are promoting or marketing with the best intentions, think of how it can come off to someone else. Others may have laid a negative foundation that automatically puts a bad taste in their mouths. By staying aware of what others are doing and taking that extra second before you post or market something, you will have a better chance to avoid being seen in a worse light.

As you grow and look to reputable marketing professionals, publicists, and promoters, make sure that you're building and creating solid content that makes you that much easier to market and promote over waiting for the funds or the personnel to do it for you.

Making Change Work for You

By taking a close look at the changes in the industry, you can avoid making the mistakes of the past but also avoid making moves that once worked and were effective, but are no longer applicable.

Look at what has happened when you are building your plan and keep the past, present, and future in mind. Keep in mind not only the changes that have occurred but also the trends of where the music business is heading.

Keep an eye on new products and ways to distribute your music, such as releasing more music over time instead of releasing an album every few years. Look to the opportunities of music placement and licensing in your home country, but also elsewhere around the world.

Streaming live shows for downloads, booking house concerts, setting up subscription services with additional exclusive products, putting your logo on the next hot fad (like a band beach towel or beach ball for summer), and more will keep you on top of what's changed and where things are heading. Look to the past to stay connected with what worked, and keep a sense of what changes have happened. This enables you to see changing future trends.

Changing the definitions

Just as the changes have happened in the music, changes have happened in the definitions of the business. Here are three key definitions that have changed and how they can benefit you and your career:

- ✔ **Music to music business:** Change the definition of the music business from only being about the art, the music, and the love to a definition of having to handle the business side of things so you can share the art, the music, and the love you have for it.

- ✔ **Caught up to catch up:** Don't get caught up in blame or how dirty the business is. Catch up on the basics of the business so you can avoid those pitfalls and protect your self.

- ✔ **Big time to big success:** Don't look at winning a Grammy, being a millionaire or selling a million albums as success. You can keep that as a goal, but change the definition of big time to big success, by working to create a sustainable career that can support you, your dreams, and your future.

Just as the music business has rapidly changed, the economy has changed, technology has changed, and music has changed, so have the definitions.

Keeping that connection with the past, the awareness of the present, and a solid eye on where the future is heading, you will be able to move and change with it as you thrive and succeed at it.

Changes in the future

Stay aware of new trends, products, social media pages, and different ways that artists are creating and making revenue, just as you should stay aware of the things that are no longer working, working less, or all together going away.

By staying connected to the changes of the past, what is changing before your eyes in the present, and the trends that are leading toward changes in the future, it will be that much more easier for you to change with the ever-changing music business. Many businesses have a cyclical motion to them. By learning how parts of the business once worked, you find themes; for example, right now, vinyl records are becoming popular again, albeit on a small level.

Look to websites like the Recording Industry Association of America (www.riaa.com) to find the numbers and key industry announcements. Other sites such as Music Industry News Network (www.mi2n.com) are worth the subscription so that you can stay on top of current trends. Magazines like Billboard (www.bilboard.com) also have a great deal of information about any changes in the industry. Take everything with a grain of salt, however, and look deeper than the headline to find out what's really going on.

Do your research on bands that seemed to appear out of nowhere. Look at what type of items they're selling and what type of marketing they're doing. The more you keep your finger on the pulse of the industry from the biggest names to the newest artists, the more you can make the changes that change your results for the better in the business.

Chapter 3

Getting Your Music Business Job Options On

In This Chapter

▶ Discovering your options in the music business

▶ Choosing to be in or out of the spotlight

▶ Understanding the job requirements

▶ Finding the best fit for you

The bulk of the music business is made up of people, jobs, companies, and positions that have nothing directly to do with the creative side of music itself. Just because you can't sing a tune, play an instrument, or write a song doesn't mean you can't still be part of the music business. Think about the ending credits of a movie, where you see the names, titles, companies, and services that were all needed to make the movie.

Whether you want to be a songwriter, a performer, or a session musician, or the idea of being behind the scenes is more appealing to you, there are many options available in the music business. By educating yourself not only through music classes but also through business and accounting courses, you have a greater understanding of the music business and a broader idea your career options in it.

If your goal is to be that musician on the stage, but you have those parents who tell you that you need to have a backup plan (which is really a good idea!), consider one of the other music biz options while you continue to go after that dream of stage and fame. This allows you to stay involved with the music business, regardless of what happens, and still get the tools and the know-how to advance your career. Plus, you learn about a different side of the business, and as everyone knows, knowledge is power.

Finding Your Best Fit

The best fit for you is where you are happiest. Doing what you love and what you're good at is a dream worth going after. When it comes to the music business, many are unaware of how many options are available. Many see being in the music business as just being a musician, but from the production to the writing, the managing to the promoting, there are many different career options in this fast-paced and fun business.

The best fit for you in the music business includes not only what makes you happy, but also what drives you to work hard for success. If all you dream of is fame and stardom, but find the idea of marketing and working all the other business aspects absolutely horrific, it will be a long hard road. And if you don't like dealing with people and aren't a people person, being a manager or a booking agent would be a bad choice. You might be better suited for a job like recording engineer or accountant.

Self-Assessment Questions

A great way to figure out what you want to do as well as what you would never do in the music business is to ask some important questions of yourself in a self-assessment format. Looking in the mirror and really being honest with yourself is the best way to know what's best for you.

Don't lie to yourself or answer these questions any other way than with brutal honesty. This assessment is for you, to help you see how certain aspects of your career could work better than others.

While the goal is to find the best fit and even a backup job in music, there is no job out there that is all roses and candy. Plan on hard times, struggles, and issues with any path you choose. But, if you resonate more with one job or position than another, it makes those hard times, difficult tasks, and other issues much easier to handle and get through.

Backup jobs and options aren't just for those trying to be in the spotlight (but they may be necessary). As you narrow down your list of the best fit for you, realize that studying and learning about some of the options that show up as your second, third, and fourth choices don't only give you a leg up in your first choice, but expand your knowledge in other areas that you may be able to work in before, during, or after you work toward your primary job.

The first self-assessment questions are from the more creative side and more pointed to the artist who wants to be a musician in the music business.

✔ **Who should you play with?** Think of and find the people who share your common instrumentation lineups and have the type of personalities you can work with both on and off stage.

✔ **Who shouldn't you play with?** Avoid personalities that ignite and upset you. Think about how much time you're going to spend with someone off the stage. You could make the best chemistry on stage, but you have to work with this person for most of the day off stage. Keep that in mind.

✔ **Who do you want to work with and not want to work with?** Some artists want to go completely DIY, whereas others want to get signed or supported. Some look to do home recordings; others want to go to larger studios. Work with those who are on the same page with their approach.

✔ **What are your most favorite and least favorite genres?** This is something to share with others, but also can help to understand the versatility of yourself and the potential options that are available in the music business for you. This helps to describe your sound and influences to reach more potential fans down the road.

✔ **Who are your biggest influences both inside and outside of music?** Listing, sharing, and comparing what you love, where you came from and what you are about can help to connect you with others who have similar influences as well as creating great marketing content down the line to entice fans and followers.

✔ **Who are your biggest comparisons?** Sharing your comparisons with other musicians to narrow down who to play with while also sharing this information with fans and in your marketing connects you to that many more people.

The next questions are biggies for everybody wanting to go into the music business.

✔ **What does success look like to you?** Define your vision and what success means to you; then decide with whom you want to work and play. Success comes in many forms and can mean many things to different people. Working with those who are on the same page makes for a better working environment for everyone.

✔ **Where do you want to live?** Where you want or have to live should be addressed. Whether you have family commitments or need be live in a specific city or area of the country, addressing this with others early on can keep location problems from showing up later.

When posing questions to band mates or other business associates, don't look for them to provide perfect answers. You don't need to all think or feel the same to be a good fit. Friction and difference can help with creativity and business both. Just make sure that the differences still allow you all to go after the same goals together . . . and without really getting on each other's nerves.

Looking at Your Options in the Music Business

So you asked yourself a number of questions, you did the research about what each job consists of, and now it's come down to three options: the full-time professional, the part-timer, and the amateur or hobbyist.

The options can change. Your position or job in the music business can change. Still, the better you can plan and begin on a path toward a goal or a dream with the best approach and the right organization, the easier it will be to shift your path and transition to another area if you choose to do so down the line. Some music business professionals learned to play instruments and then crossed over to becoming musicians. Many musicians have switched over to the business side. The opportunities are endless, and transitioning is easier when you start with the most solid foundation. With that foundation in place, it can allow for formerly professional musicians to return to full time later on in life.

Amateur hour

Being an amateur isn't a bad thing, and the negative connotations don't need to be there for you and what you love to do.

The root of being an amateur comes from doing what you love. Maybe you aren't interested in making music your full-time career, or maybe you would rather not put in all the time that it takes to become a professional musician. There's no failure in that. It's your dream and what you want to do, and it shouldn't be defined by someone else's terms or views.

I know a lot of happy amateur (or hobbyist) musicians. Just because you aren't professional doesn't take away from your love of it. I've

watched amateur drummers that blew me away (as in were a hundred times better than I was or will ever be). Just because I did it full-time and was a professional didn't make me better than them. It just meant that was what I did for a living.

When you weigh all of the options of your place in the music business, whether in the spotlight or behind the scene, as a full-time professional, a part-timer, or a hobbyist, don't let the word *amateur* bother you. Though I was a professional drummer and a professional full-time music producer, I was also an amateur, because I did it and I loved doing it.

Becoming a hobbyist

So you've gone through all the questions in the previous section, and you've decided that you like your existing path of playing music strictly for fun. Then becoming a hobbyist is the best direction for you. Again, it's okay to be an amateur, a lover of music, or a person who doesn't make the music business a priority in their lives. There is no shame in it, and it's actually what a lot of other musicians in denial should be doing!

If you can't be honest with yourself about what you want to do and where you want to be, you're not going to be a very happy person. Don't lie to yourself about your goals and your dreams. If you come to the decision of wanting it to be about the music and not about the music business, you will be so much happier as a hobbyist and have so much more fun.

Being a hobbyist doesn't mean you can't play with professionals or even do professional events, recordings, or do professional work. It just means you are doing it as a hobby and not as a profession.

One of my favorite back-up vocalists had a professional housecleaning service. She decided to build up a great company and leave the music as more of a hobby. She attended a lot of open mic nights to have fun, and she also had a gig a couple times a year where her friends as well as her clients would come out to see her.

I loved her voice, and she loved singing in the studio. She could take a lead line and build really warm and cool harmonies on top of the lead vocals . . . in most cases, in a single take. Whenever I had a need for her tone and sound, I would always get in touch as early as I could to get her to take a few days off to work with me. She was not a professional, but she was on my list of go-to people for professional albums.

So don't get lost in the idea that if you are a hobbyist, you're only allowed to play with other hobbyists. Some hobbyists take the time off of work or use vacation time to do short tours, too. At the end of the day, it can make music that much more fun and still give you a sense of security in a day job that affords you the lifestyle you want to live.

The same goes if you want to be involved in the businesses side of the music industry. From marketing and promotion of a band, to advertising and producing, there are always musicians and businesses that need help and want your involvement even if your primary job is something that doesn't involve the music industry at all.

Becoming a part-timer

This is in that place between the hobbyist and a full-time professional. If you feel comfortable doing some of the work and the business that needs to be done, and you adjust your world to be able to give a solid percentage of time and effort to a part-time career, you may find that the part-time angle might be best for you.

Perhaps you're on the fence about going all in and giving the full dedication to having a full-time career in music. This can be a testing phase and for others it can just be a solid place for a simple foundation to be involved in the music business, but not going all in.

Most part-timers look to find the type of supporting jobs that allow them the ability to live the lifestyle they desire while leaving more time for music than just the hobbyist. The part-timer derives income from music, from licensing songs, and has the flexibility in their day job to be able to play out some as well as travel and tour a little and write music as well.

If you are looking for a regular day job as a part-timer or someone who has to work a little longer before you can quit the day gig to become a full-time musician, look for jobs that don't require you to work too early in the morning or too late at night. These part time jobs that require weekends can get in the way of being able to play gigs as well. Try to find the work outside of the music business that can pay your way and your bills but doesn't hamper or block your forward motion inside of the music business.

Being in the music business on a part-time level allows a great deal of musicians and those in the business side of things an additional stream of income while following a dream that they want but are not sure if they want it 24 hours a day and 7 days a week.

If you are working on the business side or on the musician side as a part-timer, make it clear to those around you that you are not full-time. Don't get a bad reputation as someone who claims to be professional and then not being able to do what's expected. Your honesty about being a part-timer can help to build more part-time clients and connect with the right professionals or aspiring professionals that might need your help.

Becoming a professional

That amazing song, that great look, that band that sounds like no other: These are only parts of the music business. To thrive, sustain, and succeed in the music business — the singer on the front of the stage, the drummer in the back of the stage, the manager on side stage, or the production company that built that stage — you need to know the 16 Ps that help you move further in all the aspects of the music business or any type of business today. In becoming a professional, have the 16 Ps in Place!

P is the 16th letter in the alphabet, and these 16 skills that start with the letter P can help you move further, faster, and higher in business than anything else:

- ✔ **Personality and the ability to engaging others:** So much of the music business is communication and engagement with different personalities. Learn the best ways to resonate and connect with other personalities.

- ✔ **Patience:** So many have failed because of lack of patience — rushing, posting, reacting, or racing to put something out before its ready, signing on the dotted line before having a third party or lawyer review it, or launching something before the marketing, promotion, and distribution is in place. Be patient to prosper!

- ✔ **Perseverance:** Continuity and continuing to do the work in the best of times, in the worst of times, and every time in between is a skill that you want to practice in the music business.

- ✔ **Practice your skill:** Practicing your instrument and making the time to constantly learn and grow is key. Always make time to practice.

- ✔ **Professional work ethic:** It sounds obvious, but a strong, centered, and professional work ethic makes all the difference.

- ✔ **Problem solving:** Make sure your problem-solving skills are focused on fixing the problem instead of assigning the blame.

- ✔ **Preventative maintenance:** After a problem has been fixed, apply the skills and methods to make sure it doesn't happen again.

- ✔ **Planning and attention to detail:** Looking at every number, every option and every cost allows you to handle every question and every possible thing, good or bad that comes at you.

- ✔ **Preparation:** Get your ducks in a row, whether you are going in to the studio, sitting down for an interview, or getting ready to solicit an investor.

- ✔ **Production:** From producing your music to producing your music business plan, the skill of knowing how to allocate time and the attention to each production element is key.

- ✔ **Promotion:** Promotion never stops. This skill is required to continue to keep revenues and profits coming your way. Whether promoting a studio in which people record to a venue for people to see you perform in, to the songs you want people to buy, promoting and marketing is part of the rest of your career.

- **Phone:** Your phone skills need to be up to par. No mumbling, and don't talk too fast or too slow. Work to avoid the "uhhs" and "umms." Make sure your verbal delivery on the phone is professional, personable, and prepared.

- **Proficiency:** From your instrument to the phone skills, from your promoting skills to your presentation, and everywhere in between, the proficiency skill set, mixed with practice, helps you to maintain and grow all your abilities and all your skill sets.

- **Practical communication:** Knowing the right time to talk, the right time to be quiet, and the right way to connect with people is a great skill to have. That old Kenny Rodgers song, says it best. . . "Know when to hold 'em, know when to fold 'em, know when to walk away and know when to run." Think practically, logically, and considerately in your communication, and many more people will listen.

- **Playing well with others:** Don't hog the sandbox. Your skill set of knowing how to play well, communicate well, connect well, and even argue well, will leave you very well off.

- **Presentation:** It's all about the delivery. With all the other skill sets you have, with all the work you do and details you add, it all culminates in the delivery and presentation. Make it pretty, make it sharp, and make it represent all the Ps in harmony.

Whether you're a performer, in the spotlight or out, the business person, or the creative type, these key skill sets will take you further than the best song, the best look, and the best band. The music business of today is much more open to the professionals that care and consider others than the egotistical and selfish stars and stories of yesterday.

Eyeing Options Out of the Spotlights

The most familiar jobs in the music business are the stars, the singers, guitarists, keyboardists, and other players as well as the DJs, and even the conductors. These are the spotlight jobs and positions in the music business. Still there are dozens of other jobs that are part of the music business that you might not realize.

The list can go in to further detail, but here are the most popular 65 jobs out there. This can be an eye opener for realizing just how many people and positions are needed in the music business to keep things moving, growing, profiting, and sustaining. I break it down to the following eight key categories:

- Staying behind the spotlights
- Building the spotlights

✔ Selling the spotlights

✔ Protecting the spotlight

✔ Paying the spotlights

✔ Reviewing the spotlights

✔ Educating the spotlights

Search online to find out more detailed job descriptions for each title and position.

Behind the spotlights

These are the musician jobs that don't have the brightest spotlights shining on them, but keep you playing, performing, recording, and writing the music that is out there shining.

Session musician, substitute musician, and backup musician: The highest caliber musician job for musicians; these musicians are the first call to the studio, the last-minute call to cover for another, or one of the backup singers or players for a tour, session date, or gig.

Songwriter, composer, jingle writer, movie and television scoring: These are the writing and composition job options.

Chart writer and transcriber: Writing charts for live musicians and for studio sessions also includes transcribing parts.

Theatre musician and regular/repeating gig musician: The solid continuity gig that has some great security to it.

Cruise ship musician and or wedding/cover band: Short-term but also good-paying gigs and jobs. Wedding and cover bands or general business groups can be very lucrative in certain cities and towns.

The cruise ships can be rough if you are a larger or taller person because the accommodations can be tight.

Though safe and somewhat secure, the cruise ship, theatre, and wedding band or cover band options can become monotonous, boring, and repetitive. Some musicians love this work, whereas it can really drive others insane after a while. It's a personal thing. I couldn't handle a theatre subbing gig that had me playing the same thing, every day, over and over and over and . . . well, you get the idea.

Building the spotlights

Are you the architect type? Do you like the kind of work that builds from the ground up and the type that is all about creating the right foundations? Maybe the building-careers job options strike your fancy.

Music business consultant: A professional and experienced music business consultant has a wide array of experience and knowledge about the music business and helps artists, labels, managers, and others organize and outline plans for successful ventures.

 The consultant job takes a great deal of music business experience under your belt before jumping into this field. More than 90 percent of music business consultants hurt more than help clients because they take a life coach approach to make up for lack of experience, knowledge, or up-to-date information.

Graphic designer: Designing logos, merchandise, promotional posters, social media, headers and everything else graphic!

Web designer: Designing artist's websites, merchant pages, landing pages and other web-based music sites.

Search engine optimizer/branding content planner: These folks help plan, design, and optimize the content that artists post on blogs, social media sites, and their own websites to build up their rankings in searches and grow the social media fan bases. They're also referred to as *content providers*. This is a new and growing field.

Recording studio employee: Working at a recording studio from administrative to assistant engineer. This can be a great position to work your way up in the production field.

Music producer: The person who oversees the recording project as a whole. The job description of music producer can be wide, or in some cases very narrow.

Recording engineer: In some cases, the producer is also the engineer; in other cases, the recording engineer is handling all the aspects from setting up the microphones to getting the basic sounds and working with the producer to capture the songs and the takes.

Mixing and mastering engineer(s): Setting the volumes, effects, sounds, equalization, and manipulating the song to where you want it. The mastering engineer takes the final mix and gives it a final two-track review along with setting up the order of the songs, the fades, and the last touch.

Photographer: Taking the pictures for branding, web, postings, marketing, and everything else.

Videographer: From music videos to interviews, short promotional videos to YouTube video shorts.

Fashion consultant: Some artists need help with their look and image. From working individually with the artists or working through a manager or a record label, this job helps create the overall appearance and branded image of an artist or band.

Hair and makeup: This job option includes photo shoots and specific gigs, but many larger-scale artists travel with hair and makeup personnel.

Sound, light, and stage designer: Designing the lights or the stages for tours and artists with large budgets.

Choreographer: Many artists need dancers, and dancers need a choreographer.

Instrument builder: Building the instruments for the musicians.

A&R (artist and repertoire): Finding musicians and artists is less of a job due to the Internet, but if you have a good ear, an eye for development, and an understanding of what it would cost to develop an artist, you could be in A&R.

Whereas internships can be a great thing, make sure you learn from them. Many internships, especially in the music business, take advantage of those trying to learn by having them do menial tasks that don't help the intern grow. You have to do some basic tasks, but an internship is about learning, growing, and developing for a potential job or experience. Make sure you get that experience, and you're not being used as a free worker.

Selling the spotlights

Do you like the idea of the pitch? The idea of selling? Is advertising and sales your game? Here are a number of the selling job options in music:

Booking agent: Booking the gigs, the festivals, the events, and every other show.

Distributor: Distributing the physical and digital product to brick-and-mortar stores and online sales sites everywhere; also setting up the contracts to get the best percentages for those sales.

Solicitor: Soliciting to record labels, managers, investors, and others for financing, sponsorships, endorsements, opportunities, and partnerships. This is the true sales part of the music business — always out there asking and selling to get the support and the backing.

Music publisher: Publishing music, inserting and licensing music, collecting the royalties, and tracking where the music is being used and how often.

Marketer and advertiser: Setting up the advertising budgets for physical and online ads. Tracking the conversions and following the trends to save the most time and get the most bang for your buck in creating to most exposure possible.

Music store employee: Selling equipment to musicians, from guitars to amps, from strings to bows.

Online promoter: Specifically promoting online through websites, social media pages, and networking with bloggers, reviewers, and other sites to expand promotion as far and wide on the net as possible.

Street or physical promoter: The crew that puts up stickers and posters as well as has a physical presence in stores and outside of shows. Often times working for a series of different bands and artists coming into the area where that promoter is based.

Translator: Translating content into other languages to reach international audiences.

Running the spotlights

The hands-on jobs make the lights shine, the sound move, and the money flow. These are the direct job options for the music business.

Manager, representative, personal assistant: The chief operating officer (COO) for an artist, overseeing and running all the operations.

Personal assistant: Taking care of all direct needs of a star or group. Tasks include everything from running errands to keeping the schedule and calendar.

Publicist: A crucial job building the biggest media awareness for an artist or band.

Talent buyers: Planning shows and buying the right acts for the right times.

Merchandise: Creating, selling, ordering, and customizing promotional merchandise (T-shirts, CDs, keychains, and so on).

Driver or travel agent: From driving the tour bus to organizing the travel plans. This person handles all point A to B operations.

Venue owner or manager: Handling a venue that brings in the talent.

Stage manager: Running the stage, side stage, front of house, and all the crew.

Lighting tech (literally running the spotlights at times): Handling the visuals from the on stage effects lights to lighting for the artists.

Sound engineers: Mixing at the front of the house or running monitors on the side of the house; delivering the best sound for the artist and creating the best sound for the audience.

Touring manager: Overseeing and handling all planning, contacts, and schedules for a tour.

Instrument technician: Setting up, breaking down, and maintaining the instruments for musicians.

Website/social media manager/content creator: Running the website and social media; ensuring the best content is being posted.

Backline: Renters, suppliers, and owners of backline gear available as and when needed. Backline gear makes up anything you need for a show, from a drum set to an amplifier, a piano to a keyboard, and anything else that an artist might need to perform.

Roadie: The people who move the gear from A to B and back to A, as well as handling the lifting and basic issues.

Protecting the spotlights

From the legal contracts internally and externally, from insurance to instrument repairs and restoration to taking care of the music, and the wellbeing of musicians, these are the protection job options in the music business.

Lawyer (entertainment, intellectual property, and business law): One of the key areas that musicians in the music business need.

Accountant, bookkeeper, and auditor: Tracking the expenses, revenues, profits, and percentages so that everyone knows exactly what is being made, what is being spent, and where it is going.

Insurance professional (personal and gear): Insuring gear and people. What happens when a musician can't play? If you're the insurance professional, you make sure both the artist and venue are protected.

Instrument repair and restorations: Repairing and restoring instruments from the present and the past is a great job for the detailed craftsman.

Healthcare professional (chiropractic, massage, dental, physician): From being a personal physician to a massage therapist on tour to being budgeted by recording studios and some venues for massage, chiropractic care, acupuncture, and other healthcare-related needs. This is a growing option that may cost investors and labels to hire you, but can save them tens of thousands on the other end when their artists stay healthy and fit.

Bodyguard: Bodyguards are in high demand with higher-echelon artists who gain popularity quickly.

Music librarian: A challenging job to get, but a musicologist of sorts that organizes, catalogs, tracks, and in some cases even transcribes music from the past and present.

Protection is key. Lawyers, accountants, and insurance agents are some of the most important jobs for musicians, labels, managers, and agents to use and hire. The ones that don't find out the hard way in the end.

Paying for the spotlights

Key parts of the music business are the money jobs. From finding it, to investing it, to donating it, to raising it, to getting paid back. Here are some areas if you have an interest in the money side of the business.

Record Label: Often times the record label is the financer and the organizer of many of the jobs listed above, just placed in to a one-stop shop of sorts. Working for a label that has financing and actually finances its artists is more and more rare. Yet that really is the base of a label. Working for a label can include all the above in building, protecting, and running the spotlights jobs.

There are a lot of fake record labels out there. Be very careful with whom you get involved and what they actually do and don't do. If a label is not financing or finding the financing for an artist to create, distribute, and promote a product, they are only covering the job descriptions of representative, manager, or agent, but taking percentages that they don't deserve. Always do your due diligence and check out everyone and everything.

Banker/allocator: Handling the banking and allocation of funds from investors, labels, or wherever money came from. This is one of those positions that's sometimes covered by the manager or representative, but having a third party that allocates the money going out and tracks the money being spent can make investors and the label feel more secure.

Private/personal investor: Being an investor or working with investors to find individual entertainment investments can pay well on referrals and percentages. Also, being the middle person between an artist and investor can save others time as it pays you money.

Venture capitalist/angel investor: This job is usually set aside for those with a great deal of money or companies that invest in entertainment. Although music and entertainment can be a risky investment, a great deal can be made in percentages and profits by those who invest wisely.

Grant writer: If you have or want to develop skills in grant writing, many artists, labels, music businesses, and music-based businesses are always looking for money. This is a great field if you have interest.

Fundraiser: Raising funds for projects with music business plans, assisting with grant proposals, and reaching out to both profit and nonprofit avenues to raise money can be a solid career. Setting up combinations of crowd funding, sponsorship campaigns, and other types of fundraising approaches can be beneficial and lucrative.

Royalty and payment collector: Working with a performing rights organization or one of the royalty collection groups can be a bit like being a detective. To find out if, when, or where music has been used and who should be paid can be a great job option and also be morally fulfilling to help those who should be paid and haven't had the ability or tools to find out how.

Reviewing the spotlights

The reviewers, writers, and critics of the music business can be a great area if your writing skills are what you love to use the most. Also, serving as an editor for a label, an artist, management groups, or others in the field can be rewarding.

Editor and content editor/proofreader: The English teacher, of sorts. The editor makes sure that the content is well optimized, that correct grammar and spelling are used, and that a second set of professional eyes has gone over it. From product content to web content, from music business plans to press releases, being that editor can make all the difference between a professional release and something that looks amateurish.

Music reviewer: A challenging job to get because, in a way, everyone's a critic. But, if you have the drive and work to connect with various magazines, websites, and both entertainment- non-entertainment–based publications, being a music reviewer can be a lot of fun.

Music journalist or blogger: Whether working for a magazine, a website, or as an independent writer, music journalism can be a great option. Mixing payment for your articles with online ads on a website around your article can draw supplemental revenues.

Educating the spotlights

These jobs are for the person who might be leaning toward teaching or supplementing another area in music with a job in education. These are jobs in which you want to build up experience and knowledge before coming out of the gate.

Teach for the love of it and not for the money. Teach after you have learned and after you have enough experience to guide others. Way too often, musicians needing extra income turn to teaching even if they aren't ready to teach. Don't hurt the growth and fundamentals of another if you aren't really ready to teach. Also understand that you need a degree for most of these as well as a good number of years of study.

Music educator (teacher, professor, private instructor): In classrooms to online as full-time professors to private instructors and everywhere in between, music teachers, instructors, and professors are needed from elementary schools to colleges and music stores to online video conferencing.

Speaker or clinician: From speaking or delivering clinics for musical instruments, composition, business aspects, and many other areas of the music business, the speaker or clinician presents education formats to larger audiences. This is also a job option where years of experience should be in place prior to entering. While a degree is not required, many want to see one or see a vast amount of experience in the industry with a résumé that reflects the knowledge of an expert.

Music therapist: A music therapist applies elements of music to therapeutic situations for non-musicians as well as for an array of both physical and mental disorders. Though the history of music as therapy has been around for a long time, this is a newer field. This is a field that requires a degree.

Chapter 4

Creating a Music Business Plan

Do you remember the stories about the two squirrels facing a coming winter? One plans and prepares as he collects nuts for the cold winter, and the other squirrel just frolics (does anyone frolic anymore?), procrastinates, and doesn't do anything to prepare. Then fast forward, he's cold, no food, and watches the other squirrel in jealousy.

Mapping your career path and creating a music business plan for every step from recording to release to touring and any other venture is one of the most fundamental steps to take early in your career. By building your first plan with the right details, the right organization, and the right people, it helps in the moment and can be the starting template for future plans.

This chapter helps you organize and put together a consolidated music business plan that hits on all the primary needs to approach an investor. These plans can go into much longer, lengthier, and expanded formats, but for here, you get the nuts and bolts of what you need for your condensed plan and the main parts of what an investor is looking at and not looking at in a business plan.

"Planning is bringing the future into the present so that you can do something about it now." – *Alan Lakein*

Defining Your Success

Before you begin building your roadmap and your first music business plan, first define what you want to do in music and what success means to you.

From basic goals of sales to basic goals of gigs, and the realistic numbers of paying yourself to what you are able to pay others to help you are all considerations to take. You need to understand the expenses that may be required to make your plan successful, and this also enables investors to have a clear sense of who you are and what your project is about.

The basic numbers can help accountants, music business consultants, and others help you formulate a plan that can work. If you want to create a music business plan to open a recording studio, how much will it cost to get all the gear? How many clients do you need to cover your basic expenses? How much should you charge per hour or per session? How much are your monthly operating expenses? These are all questions that help you create the best plan possible and showcase your professionalism and organization to those who might be able to fund it.

Addressing questions like how much you want to pay yourself in the short term and then what you'd like to make in the long run is also key. How often you want to work, and how many people you want to work with can range from doing as much by yourself to trying to hire as many others to help as possible.

You don't need to have exact answers, and you don't need to know every detail, but as you begin to map out your route to success in music and begin to lay the groundwork for a music business plan, these bullet points, numbers, and justifications for yourself and others can be added easily and quickly.

Work to define what success means to you and what it looks like from the financial, lifestyle, and working standpoint.

More humble, realistic, and conservative needs are funded more often and cost worlds less. You may think it's cool to ask for a salary of $50,000 a year to record and launch, but that $50,000 will have to be returned with percentages, and the higher the budget needed, the higher the risk that it won't be returned, much less see profit from it.

The more you can define what success means to you, what you're willing to do to be successful, and where you'll make compromises, the easier it is to organize a plan to become successful.

Projecting Your Time Frame

From penning the plan to penning your first royalty check is going to take a little while. Many of the overnight successes you hear about that magically seem like they just came out of thin air have been at it for a very long time.

Discussing the options of how long it will take to get from the first funding phase of your music business plan to payback and then to profit is a big part of the plan, and claiming it will happen once the public hears the music is the wrong way to go.

The advanced planning mixed with addressing the issues that may arise allows your career to move that much further and that much faster and helps to avoid many problems down the line since you already addressed them right out of the gate.

Your music business career plan as well as the creation of your music business plans for both present and future projects, recordings, and tours put together correctly, offer you a much greater chance of not only achieving the funding needed, but help to make your success in both the short and long term by having a road map for the present that can be used, edited, and easily adjusted for the future.

Your music business plan doesn't need to be fully funded for you to activate the plan and the actions. By having a fully formatted, budgeted, and organized music business plan, you can start working on the steps and elements that don't require funding. For example, you can begin to work on the initial phases of preproduction and recording as well as design graphics, and start your marketing before receiving the full amount. This also shows potential funders and investors your efforts even before funding.

You don't have to be the one to write your music business plan. There are music business consultants, entertainment lawyers, and others who have years of experience and can help you. But, if you are able to do the advanced research, address a number of the line items and costs mentioned in the chapter, as well as lay out some estimates with reasoning, you can save thousands of dollars and a great deal of time when it comes to getting someone to help format and finalize your plan.

Your time frame to success will run through these five steps:

1. Be realistic. Take a pragmatic approach to all the expenses as well as how long it takes to get the business off the ground.

2. Add the time for the sales of the product, the revenue from the shows, the profits from other merchandise items as well as licensing, insertions, and other opportunities for the artist and the music.

3. Make sure everyone is being paid and money is still being reinvested into additional marketing, promotion, and advertising.

4. Repay (with interest, if necessary) those who invested in the plan and who are currently owed money.

5. Last, but not least, pay yourself.

It can be — and usually is — a long road before you see a profit. Honestly, some businesses never do.

The best way to project the time frames of your music business plan and the success of it is to take a very conservative look at how you will sell, market, and advertise across the widest array of places to get the most attention and convert to sales, return on investment, and interest for the investors and profit for you.

Realize it may cost a great deal more than you may think. To make money in the music business and from a music business plan, that plan has to reflect the best marketing, promotion, advertising, and publicity to make the sales projections possible.

The bulk of any successful business plan budget is allotted to the marketing, promotion, publicity, and advertising. The product itself isn't where the most money should be spent. You need the marketing budget to be able to announce, launch, and maintain the best marketing to reach the most people for as long as possible.

The more organized, the more conservative in your projections, and the longer you have to both pay back investors as well as maintain the marketing momentum, the happier your investors will be and the sooner you will be able to profit.

Reviewing the Requirements and Costs of Success

One of the first places an investor, potential funder, or the owners of a label will look at in a music business plan is the expenses and costs section. Having the best-planned and most-detailed expense budget is where most music business plans fail. Even if you don't have a current budget or access to the money, add all costs and expenses to your plan. That way, when money comes in, you know where to place it. Here are 76 basic costs that show up in any professional music business plan.

Copyright fees	Publishing fees	Trademark fees	Attorney fees
Bookkeeping setup	Accounting costs	Music consultant	Music producer
Recording studio	Recording engineer	Mixing engineer	Mastering
Session players	Graphic designer	Web designer	SEO expert
Photographer	Videographer	Distribution	Marketing/ publicist

Apparel	Insurance (gear)	Healthcare	Grant writer
Web hosting	Miscellaneous Products	Press kits	Banners
Business cards	Postcards	Merchandise displays	Printing fees
Postage fees	Memberships	Instruments	Cases
Computer	Phone	Online backups	Website support
Music conferences	Gas/tolls	Vehicle maintenance	Radio promotion
Magazine ads	Postering	CDs/Vinyl	Download cards
Rent/mortgage	Hotels	Food	Salaries
Internet	Clothing	Flights	Hotels
T-Shirts	Cups and glasses	Merchant setup	Taxes
Towels	Stickers	Facebook ads	Twitter ads
YouTube ads	Promoted posts	Internet radio ads	Press releases
Website ads	Print ads	Laundry	Instrument repair
Local promoters	Personal insurance	Hair	Make Up

This overview shows that it comes down to much more than just recording and putting out the music. There are many other facets that have to be addressed, covered, and funded. Although you might be able to save money on certain requirements, you always need to have a great deal budgeted for the cost of marketing. In turn, you will see the returns of success. Marketing is one area where you don't want to skimp on spending. Learn more about marketing in Chapter 11.

Investing other people's money

People invest in your idea, dream, and plan. Paying back those loans should be your first priority when you start seeing a profit from your business.

Whether you find a private investor, a venture capitalist, a record label, angel investor, or take out a loan, understand that they aren't just giving you money. In most cases, you have to deal not only with the principal amount, but also with interest at possibly a high rate.

Your investors are taking a very big risk on you, so if all goes well, they deserve part of the reward. Whether your agreement with your investors reflects high interest, or a long-term percentage of the profits — or both — go into any meeting with an investor, label, or interested lending party knowing that they need to be paid back with interest.

Set up regular meetings to keep them in the loop about their investment as well as updates to instill additional confidence in their investment in you.

Create a bank account for the investment and expenses, and make it available to your investors. Show that the money is being spent according to the plan and as discussed. Also adding them to the account with login access to be able to only view the transactions helps keep them in the loop and feel that much safer about where their money is going.

Investing your own money

In most cases, you probably don't have the type of money that many of these larger-scale investors have at their disposal. Investing your own money in your plan will not only help the plan move forward but also show others down the line that you have equity in the game.

Don't be foolish when using your own money (or anyone else's, for that matter). Know the best places in your business plan to put your cash.

Bad choices

You can waste great deal of money on radio promotion and other public relations campaigns that are meaningless if there's no conversion to sales or real exposure.

I have heard dozens of artists talk about how they put this amount or that amount into a radio campaign that got all these plays and got them some chart ranking. Yet, when I ask them how many new fans showed up on their website or social media, as well as how many downloads or sales they got, they always look dumbfound. Their real results? Zip.

Doing these type of promotional pushes before your branding, marketing, and basic promotional structure is in place doesn't help and wastes money.

Major labels can spend upwards of $75,000 a week (sometimes more) to promote a single. So that $1,000 campaign you have budgeted for a month is not going to bring you to the ears of others. There are smarter ways to promote for real results and conversions than taking the radio approach.

A lot of examples of the power of radio date back to when there were a lot fewer radio stations. With all the terrestrial, satellite, and Internet radio stations, podcasts, and the ability to sync your music player to your car or stereo, the impact of radio is becoming less and less while the conversion of radio to sales is mostly working for those who have much more to spend.

Other bad choices

Hiring a producer who is way out of your budget is not going to guarantee a hit either. Also spending on number builders to add 100,000 followers on Twitter doesn't grow your fan base. These services charge you to build up views, adds, likes, and only showcase to potential labels, investors, and the industry. You waste money on ego-type things that look good on the surface but don't create results.

Better choices

Put your money in preproduction sessions, the graphic designers who help you build your brand, and the music business consultants who can get you organized and build out that music business plan to get funded. Put your money and personal investment into buying domain names, web hosting, and fundamentals you need, such as your branding, your graphics, getting contracts in order, and publishing set up correctly. Invest in your equipment. Create internal band agreements with lawyers and all the things that help the foundation of your success be that much stronger.

Lastly, track every dollar you spend or invest. All of it! Be able to show what you personally have invested and where it's gone. Keep every receipt, and track every dollar.

Investing time and resources

There are connections you can make that that don't offer financial assistance, but can provide numerous resources, services, and other needs that are part of your plan. Each person and band has different connections, networking resources, and ways to connect and engage with people that may be able to help and either invest their services or potentially barter and trade without money changing hands.

Some of these can include donations from friends who know how to do graphics or web work. Others might own a restaurant and would be able to sponsor or feed you during recording sessions. When you look through the expense list of your music business plan, think of the potential resources, people, and companies that you could contact for services, time, or assistance without asking directly for money.

Certain investments can come in the form of discounted or free musical equipment, along with assistance with touring or even media and promotion support. Again, make sure these are clearly defined as to whether you are going to pay for this down the line in cash, in percentages, or in some form of both. The devil is in the details; the last thing you want is for things to start heading in a great direction, but then have the devil show up and mess with what you didn't have in writing.

The more resources you can tap from friends, family, contacts, and companies, the easier it is to check off certain items in your expense budget. It may also be easier for some to supply services, products, or support by investing their resources or time, not their money, and it may be easier to gain sponsorship from some through cross marketing.

Time and resources should be treated the same as cash investments, and should be paid back with interest. This respect could lead to sponsorships, endorsements, or physical equipment down the line.

Looking at the Keys to Planning Success

To have that successful and fun trip where everyone has a great time and gets back alive, you make a solid plan and prepare for the best- and worst-case scenarios so that everything goes off without a problem — and if by chance something becomes problematic, you can take care of it right away and keep sailing on.

This is why your music business plan is so important, in the same way you need to plan for a sailing trip — food, clothing, toothbrush, suntan lotion, towels, first aid kits, flares, rain gear, life preservers , all the basic stuff that you need for a great trip as well as stuff in case the trip becomes not-so-great.

Planning to make it the best trip possible, while planning to prevent all the problems and then planning for how to handle the surprises that could possibly arise, makes the best plan for a trip and makes for the most secure chance that everything will go as you want it. The same goes for the music business.

Writing plans backwards

Hindsight is always 20/20, but try thinking forward and looking backward. In a sense, you begin at the finish line and plan your way back to the starting gate. By organizing your plan with the numbers, the success, and the end result written down, it can be easier to take it backward and see exactly what you need to do to get to where you want to go.

Planning backward can be exciting but also humbling and even a little painful. This becomes an exercise in understanding exactly what it takes to achieve what you want.

For example, say your plan consists of a $500,000 investment with return on investment and interest, and you plan to return a high interest rate of 25 percent with no additional percentages or royalties to come back to the investor due to the high interest. In 24 months, you owe $750,000, so the baseline of all revenue projects can be no less than $750,000 after you add what you want to make and have a final number. For this example, go with $250,000. Your plan should reflect an income of $1,000,000 from month 24 back to month one.

Think awkward and think backward

Every dollar spent on the front side has to be made back on the back side with the right percentages. Offering a higher percentage on the investment over long-term percentages gets your investors taken care of sooner and allows you to take more profits in the longer term sooner as well.

By planning and writing your numbers and starting with your plan backward, you can get a much better sense of not only the costs but an understanding of how to figure estimations to pay for those costs.

You can't cut corners on the marketing and promotion when it comes to justifying the revenues and the profits. Every time you cut somewhere in marketing, promotion, or publicity, you have to cut or reduce revenues, exposure, or profits.

Your 15-, 10-, and 5-year plans

Just as you can approach planning and writing a music business plan backward, it can be effective to write your success plan or your personal 15-, 10-, and 5-year plan backward as well. This goes for your personal as well as your business plan goals. For example, determine what kind of lifestyle you want (homebody or out on the road most of the year), where you want to live (very expensive LA or a small Midwestern town), and what kind of things you want in your life (a new Range Rover SVA or a used Kia Sorento). Using that information, you can figure out how much money you need to make and how much you need to work.

Do you see yourself spending years and years on the road, or do you want to tour for only so long? This is a very personalized approach and should be treated very specifically to you. Don't let others alter the vision you have for your life. You may find that some ideas or influences can change your direction, but still it's up to you, if you want to change it or not.

Covering expenses

Figuring out the priciest costs and then dialing it back with the exact details can help you hone in your expense numbers and at the same time enable you to know that you've listed every cost you need. Revisit a couple pages back with the 76 key expenses as a guide to build from. Then look to the order and amounts of expenses.

Cutting an expense to make a plan a little cheaper means you have to cut back on estimated profits as well. For example, if you set up a short tour, your profits won't be as large as a longer tour because less work equals less revenue.

Instead of touring, it can be better to put more money into online marketing, promotion, and advertising. Think about how much it costs for a single day on the road with your band. The food, hotel, gas, tolls, and time away from a day job can add up. Then think about investing that money into a single campaign for a single day to reach a much larger audience. Covering the expenses in the best way to reach the most fans for the most conversions brings you the most profit.

Spreading out the coverage

When you look over all your expenses, break them down by month or by quarter to see what you need. For example, in the first two months you may include several hours of studio time as you record, mix, and master all the music used as part of this particular music business plan. That cost is now covered and for the remaining months of expenses in a plan, it isn't a cost any longer.

Things like publicity, marketing, promotion, and advertising are costs that run through the whole plan. Again, by breaking down each element and covering what you spend each month and on what, the detail gives reassurance and a reduced sense of risk.

Covering the expenses doesn't mean listing just them. It means you cover

- ✔ The cost for the whole budget
- ✔ The breakdown of the cost each month
- ✔ The justification for the cost

The details of why this is in the budget, how it helps return the investment and interest to a potential investor, and what it does to make the project successful need to be in every line item of your expenses. Certain items that cause red flags or concerns in either the vague title of the expense or the high price tag can be covered and made much more comforting by the explanation, justification, and reason why that expense is key to the success of the project and why that expense needs to be covered.

Don't go it alone when it comes to covering the expenses. But get started on the outline by yourself. If you take the list of core expenses and cover them as best you can, then you can bring your expense budget to a music business consultant, producer, or music industry professional who is able to help you finalize the numbers, expenses, and justifications that much quicker. Not to mention, with all the work you do on the front side, you save money with the professional on the back side, because you have all the information prepared.

The expenses and costs section of a music business plan is one of the first items that potential investors look at. They want to see a smart budget that outlines the attention to detail and justifies each expense.

Covering your expenses with the right details and the right costs to ensure the best chance of success for the project connects you with the best people to help your project and plan succeed.

Setting a marketing budget

As I mentioned earlier in this chapter, the biggest part of your business plan is the marketing. It's one of the first lines on your expense sheet that investors look at to see if you budget enough to get the word out about . . . you. And if enough music fans learn about you and like your music, the quicker and easier those investors get paid back.

You may want the success, fame, and riches, but the first step is to pay back, with interest, those who paid for this project. It's a music business plan, you're being funded like a business, so you need to act like a business and realize that the business side enables dreams, goals, and creativity to flourish.

It's easier to get a loan for $100,000 than it is to get a loan for $10,000 in most cases. Why? If you have a project or product that you want to sell, it costs $10,000, and that's all you go after (which is something many bands did in approaching crowdfunding campaigns on Kickstarter or other smaller investors), you have the money to only create the product. But then how does it get sold? You need to budget for marketing and advertising to get your product noticed by those who want to buy it.

The majority of the money goes to marketing

Planning the bulk of your budget to go toward marketing is the smartest choice you can make. Some models show a 90/10 or 80/20 split offers a higher level of success at a faster rate. This means that 90 percent of the budget goes toward marketing. It's all about the marketing to get the word out about you, your music, and your shows. That's also why it's easier to get $100,000 over $10,000 if you're able to showcase that the bulk of the budget is spent on the marketing in order to make all that money back . . . plus some.

Get out of the mindset that you need to record in the most expensive studio with the most famous producers if you want to stay on a better budget. Ask any of your friends who are not musicians, and you just might find that they don't really care where Nirvana recorded or that your producer worked with Counting Crows. It might impress a few people, but it's not enough to bet that much of your recording budget.

In covering all your other expenses, realize one of the biggest keys to a successfully funded and profitable music business plan is one that puts the focus on the marketing and budgets the least amount to get the best product built and market it the best way possible. That doesn't mean to cut corners in the studio with producers, musicians, and the recording process as a whole. It means you carefully and precisely budget as best you can and save where you can to allow as much as you can to go to marketing.

Marketing to get heard

No matter how amazing your music, your musicality, and your other musicians are, or how great you look, perform, or record, if the marketing isn't in place, you're not going to get noticed and move forward.

The music business is an oversaturated world, and without a marketing, publicity, promotion, and advertising presence to get the word out about you, your music, your project, your shows, and your merchandise, you might find yourself spinning in circles and not going anywhere.

Covering and estimating revenues

Many think that revenues come only from CDs, downloads, and concert gigs. But revenues can come from nearly countless different sources. Take, for example, the following list of different revenue sources:

- ✔ T-shirts and other wearables such as hats, sweatshirts, tank tops, and so on
- ✔ Posters

- Backstage pass product
- Items with your logo such as key chains, coffee cups, tote bags, and more
- Custom merchandise items, such as wine, clocks, jackets, and other special orders
- TV licensing
- Samples
- Sponsored and nonprofit gigs
- Publishing
- Private/ house gigs
- Composing for and selling songs to other artists
- Foreign translations
- Corporate video licensing

When creating the best music business plan possible, it's crucial that you build as many avenues to revenue as possible. It's hard to expect all monies to come in from touring or music sales. The more you diversify your revenue options, the better chances you have to make the money.

Buy in bulk! When it comes to the CDs, consider buying a CD burner and printer to create CDs or DVDs yourself. When it comes to ordering T-shirts, add as much as you can to your budget so you can purchase bulk amounts that enable you to make more in revenues on every sale.

In the music business plan, the revenue sources section is often the second section looked at because an investor or backer is going to want to clearly see how they are going to get their investment and money back.

Showcase as many different revenue-generating methods as possible as well as estimate with an extra conservative approach. Your chances of being funded are much better than if you claim you plan to sell a million CDs overnight.

Certain revenues take time to grow and as a whole it takes a while to shift from money spending to money making. It's crucial to make sure you have the expense budget to market all these different revenues to as many people as possible.

Three levels of estimated revenues

Building three levels of revenue projects can help instill confidence in your investors. Model 1, the most conservative of the three models, shows investment payback plus the agreed-upon interest. It also reflects enough to pay the all taxes and shows a modest profit. Model 2 showcases a high revenue estimate in between Models 1 and 3, whereas Model 3 is the most liberal estimate of them all.

For example, Model 1 shows an investment of $1,000,000 at a high interest return of 25 percent and no future percentages. In this scenario, a basic estimation of revenue is around $1.5 million — you can pay back the $1,000,000 investment plus the $250,000 interest as well as have 20 percent extra for taxes and a small profit left over.

So for Model 2, with $1,000,000 invested and $2,000,000 brought in, the initial investment sees double on the return.

And Model 3, the most aggressive of the three different models, shows $1,000,000 invested and $3,000,000 in revenue. Everyone is happy, and everyone did very well.

Spread the love and the revenues

When you think about how to reach a fan, you want to think about a better engagement with an existing fan as you reach out to a new one. Then when you add in all the social media marketing, spam, and pressure from many bands, the old-school approach of sell, brag, and pressure is dead and broken.

Putting constant pressure on existing fans while chasing new fans with the same old product has become ineffective. Instead, give your audience — both the existing fans and the new ones — something fresh more often.

Instead of going into the studio and pushing out a 20-song album and releasing merchandise items all at once, imagine if you went the route of rolling out new and exciting merchandise items over the course of several months. Think of the anticipation this would conjure up as you spread out swag for your fans and revenues for you and your investors.

By releasing a music product in the first week of each month and a merchandise product in the third week of each month, every 14 days you introduce something new. At the same time, you market the previous items that have already come out. This allows for the announcement of new items and music to run every two weeks.

Your new model calendar

Imagine that you have 20 songs in the can, the hat, T-shirt, sticker, bracelet, phone cover, computer skin, shot glass, coffee cup, poster, sweatshirt, vinyl pressing, and a tote bag.

Then you take 10 of the 20 songs and put them on two EPs (extended plays) with 5 songs on each. The first EP launches in month 1 of the project the second in month 7. Then the remaining ten tracks are launched one each month in between the two EPs. For the merchandise, you have 12 items that can be launched once a month, two weeks after the music at the top of the month and two weeks before the music coming the following month. Figure 4-1 shows what your calendar looks like.

	January	February	March
Week 1	EP 1 - Five Sing Release	Digital Single 1 Release	Digital Single 2 Release
Week 3	Poster Release	Computer Skin Release	Coffee Cup Release
	April	**May**	**June**
Week 1	Digital Single 3 Release	Digital Single 4 Release	Digital Single 5 Release
Week 3	Bracelet Release	Hat Release	Totebag Release
	July	**August**	**September**
Week 1	EP 2 - Five Song Release	Digital Single 6 Release	Digital Single 7 Release
Week 3	T-shirt Release	Phone Cover Release	Shot Glass Release
	October	**November**	**December**
Week 1	Digital Single 8 Release	Digital Single 9 Release	Digital Single 10 Release
Week 3	Sticker Release	Sweatshirt Release	Vinyl Release

Figure 4-1:
A calendar that shows when music and merchandise are released to fans.

This format allows for 24 different times when you get to talk about music and items being new. Then, with each new release, as you send fans to the stores where you have the items for sale, your first pitch is something new, followed by a mention of other merchandise items previously available.

Cross-market your items with exclusivity. For example, one of the songs from your EP, CD, or vinyl small pressing should not be available for digital download. Give the exclusivity that fans need to buy the disc or they won't be able to get the song. The same can go the other way around that one track is only available for digital download and is not available on any physical formats.

You don't have to record everything at once. You can set up the budget to allow for an extended releasing format and offer more revenue options that give a sense of constant newness.

The more you spread your revenue sources across a longer period of time, the better the chance you have to make that much more from each product as you continue to gain more and more exposure for what was just released, what's coming next, and what's come out in the past. This also helps to estimate more revenue from each of these sources for your music business plan.

Reducing risk for your investors — Failure analysis

The failure analysis comes together to support your list of expenses and explains what you're doing, why you're doing it, and justifies how it keeps your plan from going wrong.

The failure analysis is a long list of all the things that could go wrong and how it would be impossible for the investors to get back their money.

Whereas some keep this out of a business plan because they think it's too negative, this shines a much more positive light on you and your plan because you're being realistic. You address every possible worst-case scenario and then add how you plan to avoid it. Just like Winston Churchill said, "Let our advance worrying become advanced thinking and planning."

Numerous failure analysis templates are available online from which you can grab different elements. You can also ask friends, family, and those you know in business to help you with this part. Be the negative Nancy. Come up with every negative you can and how you and your budget can address them.

You can't cover every single scenario that could possibly go wrong, but plan as much as you can and you take the upper hand in keeping things going right.

Most elements that make a plan fail usually tie to lack of marketing and promotion. Most of your justifications are reinforced with a strong marketing and promotion budget.

As hard as it can be to showcase just how much a project and plan can fail, your failure analysis can be one of the root elements that helps define exactly how you can succeed.

Covering the marketing plan

As you finalize the budget for marketing and add in the reasons, justifications, costs, and failure analysis, you have the outline of your marketing plan. The budget you built for your marketing, promotion, publicity, and advertising is your marketing plan numbers. Now, just add the time frames and the exact details of how that money will be spent, and you have a simplified marketing plan.

For example, say you have $4000 listed for press releases to go out to all the newswires:

Press releases: $4,000

In the marketing plan, you list:

The press release service: Send2Press

Then you show the breakdown of each release:

Release 1 ($1,500): Press release for EP1 and announce touring information

Release 2 ($500): Three months later, smaller release focusing on one of the singles released or some kind of special event announcement

Release 3 ($1,500): Press release for EP2 and announce touring information.

Release 4 ($500): Three months later, smaller release focusing on one of the singles released or some kind of special event announcement

And finally, you have the justification. Using one of the most popular, professional, and affordable services to get this information out, the press releases give an online presence with four releases continuing to promote the band and the products while assisting the publicist and existing marketing online and off.

Each line item in your expenses for marketing can be summarized to explain why it's being allocated. At the same time, each item can help reinforce how that marketing prevents something bad from happening in the failure analysis.

With these elements organized in the simplest presentation, it showcases the organization, planning, and preventative maintenance that you have in place. Again, these plans can go on for pages and pages to compare previous sales charts, information on the music industry, and all kinds of forecasts and projections as well as facts about the business, but a lot of that ends up being fluff.

No one can truly create a long-term plan for the music business to forecast a five-year model. It's impossible and those who claim to know the future are guessing. Fancy charts come more from opinion than fact. A short-term consolidated plan with the best data for right now — and the best estimations that have to do specifically and personally with you — makes for better information and a more personalized plan to give to investors.

Funding Your Music Business Plan

You figured out the budget and considered all the costs; then you figured out all the different revenues and estimations of how you will make the money back. You've done the failure analysis and put the marketing plan in place, so now it's time to go fund your music business plan.

But first take two steps back and double-check what an investor see when he looks at your plan. Before you search for funding, make sure the presentation of your music business plan is strong, detailed, uniform, and professional. Also, check your website, your basic branding, and your initial marketing to make sure they all look clean, clear, and professional.

Your website doesn't need to be perfect, but it should be as close as possible. Make sure the content is spelled and punctuated correctly and that the site is easy to navigate.

The better you can showcase the whole package of you, your business plan, your present marketing, the online posts, and the efforts you're making on the most grassroots level without the funding, the more confidence you build in those who are considering funding you.

Avoiding the after/thens

Try to be the best turnkey type of operation you can. Get out of the mindset of the after/then failure scenarios:

- After I can stop working, then . . .
- After I have a little more free time, then . . .
- After I get some money, then . . .
- After I get management, then . . .
- After I get signed, then . . .
- After I have a social media team, then . . .
- After I get a little more sleep, then . . .

And this failure list goes on and on and on, lining up the excuses that never allow for the results to be created.

Soliciting for funds

Asking for money is the hardest part of the music business plan, and you better be prepared for a lot of nos. Still, learning how to ask for money and presenting your needs and requests to other professionals isn't just a great exercise in humility, it's something you have to learn for the long term, because this won't be your last music business plan. Even if it's not asking for money, you are soliciting to media, reviewers, talent buyers, booking agents, managers, venue owners, tour managers, music supervisors, and a wide array of others over and over again throughout your career.

Personalize your pitch

Every person is different, so every pitch has to be different. Stay away from the one-size-fits-all approach because one size does not fit all, and when someone feels like they're being given a sterile and template-style approach, they get turned off and they tune out very quickly. If you have a contact that you get a chance to meet, or a company has agreed to hear you out, then do your research and due diligence. Find out what they invest in, what they're about, and what they do and don't like or appreciate.

With the Internet and social media, you can visit their pages and get a sense of them from their information and their posts. Find out what you can about who you are talking with to get them to really give you a listen.

From the introduction email to planning a sit-down meeting, keep in mind a few key points:

- The investor has heard it all before.
- The investor sees music and entertainment as one of the biggest risks.
- The investor is looking to make money on the deal.

It's a strange thing that sometimes gets forgotten by those making music, but investors invest in projects and businesses to make money. They care about talent to an extent, but they invest to make a profit. They don't care how long you've been playing, how great this song is, what a reviewer said. They care about the investment being made back and then making money from that investment in the form of interest, percentages of sales, a piece of publishing, all of the above, or other opportunities with the artist.

In some cases, ego goes into investment, which can be used in your pitch. Impress upon an investor how she can be listed as the executive producer or even as a producer. Run the investment through a legitimate company/business entity to give her the sense of that much more of a direct involvement with the music, the band, and the success of it. There are a great deal of people who want to get into entertainment for that reason and it can be an angle to use, but still, go back to and remember the core: These investors are investing to make money.

Study and watch other people pitch

As crazy as it might seem, shows like Shark Tank can help you with your solicitation. The contestants on these business-type shows have a very short window to begin a pitch about their product and then discuss what they want and what they are prepared to give for it. It's entertainment, but it's also a great show to get a sense of what works and what doesn't work in a pitch and what you're prepared to offer in return.

As you solicit for funds, you're not asking for a certain amount. You're asking for the risk of that amount of money as well as support, which balances out to be a lot greater than just that amount in cash. Those who invest in you are taking a chance on you, your plan, and are risking a total loss if it doesn't work out. That's crucial to remember when you solicit and agree on what should be given back in return.

Avoid the big promises and the overused words. Talk assertively not dominantly; promise realistically not theoretically; delivery confidently not weakly.

The solicitation for funding comes down to the presentation of yourself, your plan, your work on the plan to date, and your preparation and organization leading up to the solicitation or pitch to an investor, sponsor, or company. Some of the best ideas have been passed on, stolen, or funded to someone else when the elements of both organization and protection are missing. It sounds awful, but think about it — would you put your own money into a project that you felt great about, but didn't feel great about the person who was presenting it?

Pay attention to your tone of voice, posture, inflections, and presence. Be aware of the uhs and ums in your speech. Watch for and control any stuttering, and do all you can to avoid fidgeting. You are the focus point of the solicitation, and that focus point has to be spot on for anyone to "show you the money."

Venture capitalists and angel investors

Venture capitalists (VC) provide startup money to many high-potential startup companies and projects. These investors tend to grab a piece of the equity (so they have a longer-term piece of bigger profits) and can be a little more challenging for musicians to get; however, some venture capitalists and VC firms have branched into entertainment.

Look online and search for entertainment venture capital or music business venture capitalist as a starting point when searching out these funders to see if they have an interest in you.

Angel investors work in a similar way. They're commonly referred to as business angels, informal investors, or angel funders. They can also provide seed funding for businesses. Angel investors want to see a business plan in motion and moving before being involved. So, again, having those elements of your business plan, branding, and marketing is viewed as a much more positive thing by everyone, but especially angel investors.

Venture capitalists and VC firms are more often than not investing money for a group of people, whereas angel investors tend to be individuals who invest privately, but still expect their money back, plus interest — and many times, a piece of the pie for the long term.

Personal and family loans

Personal and family loans come from people who know and have direct contact with you. Be careful here. Discuss very honestly and openly about what you're doing, and don't pressure.

Be generous when figuring terms. Just because they're family or friends doesn't mean their loan should include a simple payback. Give them consideration for a return on investment just like you would for a stranger.

As much as families and friends may want to help, make sure they aren't helping to a point that could hurt them in the short and long term. Be honorable and as you pitch and solicit to family or friends, make sure you ask if they can handle a financial loss if things go wrong or take longer than expected. Make sure they're loaning only what they can potentially afford to lose or risk not seeing back for some time.

Some family members and friends will do anything for you and not even consider the risk to themselves. Be that good family member or friend, and don't approach those who can't handle an all-around loss if the worst-case scenario were to occur. It can destroy friendships and ruin family relationships.

Friend and family referrals

You may have family members with friends or connections to people who might be able to invest or loan money for your project. Offering a referral percentage can also entice friends to connect you with others who might be able to help.

This can be one of the best ways to solicit with some of the people who you know best or have relationships with people you know. These people are being referred to you by someone else they already know. The ice has been broken, they have a basic idea of what you're looking for, and if they're ready to meet, set the appointment. You have a great chance to showcase your plan and professionalism with someone who feels comfortable with you and your venture, because you both have a mutual friend or family member in the mix.

Collateral items and second mortgages

If you really believe in your project and your career, then showcase that with putting up the collateral to help fund it or go after the second mortgage to finance your project on your own.

If the answer is yes, then you are many steps beyond that old mentality many artists get into where they believe all the funding should come from elsewhere. Put your money where your mouth is, walk the walk, and talk the talk.

Take a look at what kind of options can bring additional funding to the table, and track this progress as you solicit for more money. By activating the early stages of your music business plan with whatever equity you can get from a mortgage, second mortgage, some kind of collateral loan, or even selling certain item, you help the project as well as show investors you're all in as well.

When you show others you're willing to take a risk with your own assets, equity, vehicle, and savings, you say that you're all in and have full confidence, which raises the confidence of others.

Crowdfunding and its many issues

Crowdfunding and crowdfund investing have been hot topics ever since Kickstarter came on the scene some years back. They've gotten so popular that people have written entire books on the concept of crowdfunding, such as *Crowdfund Investing for Dummies* by Sherwood Neiss, Jason W. Best, and Zak Cassady-Dorion (John Wiley and Sons).

The plus side of crowdfunding is that you can reach out to your existing audience and see how they can help. That said, if your existing audience is small and not all that engaged with you, crowdfunding will be a struggle. It's also a struggle in the sense that so many people have overused it to the point of oversaturation. You also have to deal with the fact that many people have been burned by many projects where they didn't get what was promised to them or see the product come to fruition, even if it was fully funded.

Many crowdfunding projects have been heavily under-or incorrectly budgeted, which has caused issues for both artists and donors. Stay away from thinking all you need is X or making too many promises.

Use crowdfunding for a specified line item, such as food for an entire recording session or a piece of a marketing campaign like a month's worth of social media advertising. You could ask for crowdfunding funds to pay a publicist for one month, a graphic designer for a special piece of art, or build another page or two on your website. These are good ways to get a larger number of people to help through smaller donations.

Fans are asked to donate every day to this album or that project. Even though crowdfunding has dialed back a little, fans are still being asked to give all too often. Keep your asks to a minimum, and don't spam. Many have lost fans from bad crowdfunding campaigns.

Be careful with the crowdfunding approach, and when you read the success stories, make sure you dig a little deeper. Many of those who did so well already had an expansive and strong fan base. Using crowdfunding in a supplemental and small fashion gives you a greater chance to hit a goal and even potentially begin another campaign for another item.

Other options to find funding

Get creative, look online, talk to different people about referrals. If your plan has a nonprofit element to your music, set up a 501(c)3 and look to grant writers and other types of fundraisers. The money is out there; the people are out there to invest in you, but they are not waving neon signs. (Which, now that I think of it, would be heavy and somewhat dangerous.)

So, do your research, solicit to different companies, and reach out to fundraisers and grant writers to find the cash. Use creative angles. Funding is out there for those who really want to find it, and if you have the plan, the brand, and the organization together in a professional package, it makes it that much easier for you to fully fund your plan.

Handling the Organization and Legal Parts

In the middle of all the music, branding, and music business plan are the legal and organizational elements that make the business and any investments legitimate. This includes the internal contracts between each member in a band, the contracts with independent contractors you work with or have worked with, who wrote what, who is getting what, and the organization of the group into an actual business venture that has accounting and accountability.

These are the first pieces that make the puzzle that much easier to put together. These are also the first business-related questions that are posed by many larger funding groups in their applications. If you don't have the business elements in place, get them before you begin your pitch.

Lawyers and copyright laws

You need a lawyer to review your plan, assist with your internal agreements, and help set up an actual corporation as well as the bank accounts. This is a preliminary step that many musicians think is covered when the money comes, but those who organize this first have a place and a real business to actually deposit money in to. Chapter 9 digs deeper into copyrights, publishing, lawyering up, and protecting yourself.

The incorporation of your company with basic bylaws and fundamentals can be done online these days, but it's a good idea to get a lawyer to assist you with the process for the exact details.

Your copyrights and publishing need to be in order, as well. Who wrote what, who gets what from the writing, and who is included internally and externally in the compositions should be set down in writing. Again, Chapter 9 looks at the copyright and publishing elements in more detail.

Accounting, accountants, and auditing

An accountant can help review your music business plan and put together some of the basic structure for monies coming in and going out as well how they can be tracked and reported. Preparing a system for how you track the expenses and keep the receipts also builds additional confidence with investors and keeps you prepared for any kind of audits or tax reviews that could come your way.

Save and track every receipt. Think like you could be audited, because at some point you most likely will be. If not by the government, some investors will want to double-check to make sure the money is going where it's supposed to be going.

From the internal agreements to incorporating to copyrighting, accounting, and finalizing all the independent contracts, the best music business plan is held together by the glue of its legal and business organization. Your plan can state how it does all these wonderful things and exactly how it works, but without the organizational and legal elements to make it binding, your business is just a concept.

Promises, Percentages, Ownership, and Durations

With the interest or involvement of an investor, a number of investors, or an investment group, the last step is what they want and what they get out of the investment. Every situation and every investor is different. From the desired timeframes of the initial return on investment to in the amount of interest or other percentages, every situation is different.

You have only so much you can promise and so much you can give away. Be careful not to hand off too much in percentages and end up leaving you with next to nothing. Many larger-scale artists signed so many different deals with so many different people that when it's actually time for them to see a piece of the pie, they get a slice so small whereas others end up making so much.

Penalty interest needs to be a part of the conversation as well to discuss if things take longer on the payback end. The number of investors and the order of who gets paid back first or how profits are split among investors is also something to add to a checklist of discussions with your investors.

These elements all put down in writing along with every promise, percentage, level of ownership, and duration of the investment keep everyone on the same page of the same music business plan, so they can all expect and have a clear understanding of what needs to happen and how it happens.

Part II
Making Music and Creating Your Brand

SET LIST FOR KITTY LIKES AVOCADO

Orchid Island Brewery	2855 Ocean Drive C-1	Vero Beach Florida, 32963
Scheduled Start - 8:00PM	Actual Start: 8:45PM	End Time: 9:35
	CONTACT POINT:	Alden
	Phone/Email	772-555-5555 Alden@oib.com

1 Litter Box Funk
2 Spaded and Confused
3 Kitty Kitty Bang Bang
4 Growling at the Moon
5 Cantelope Tantrum
6 Allergic to Humans
7 Ode to Jackson Galaxy
8 Schrodingers Poison
9 Dancing on a Hot Tin Roof
10 Tongue Bath
11 9 Lives
12 You're So Basic
13 No Moe Baths
14 Grumpy Cat on Catnip
15 Cat Cat Goose

No changes in the set

Attendance	45 People	
Sales	10 CDs 4 Shirts	$200 in Merch
Best Reaction	You're So Basic	Loudest reactions of the night
Worst Reaction	Cantelope Tantrum	Seemed to bore people
Mailing List Sign Ups	19	
Pay for the night	400	
Capacity	60	
Other Acts	Opened for Bill The Cat	

Visit www.dummies.com/extras/musicbusiness for more great Dummies content online.

In This Part . . .

✔ Write, arrange, and produce your songs and your sounds.

✔ Learn how to stay on time and within your budget from pre-production through post-production.

✔ Understand the importance of your brand, and learn how to optimize your logo, font, and other images.

✔ Become familiar with keywords, your bio, and a call to action, and learn their importance when getting the word out about your music.

✔ Protect your music through the help of an attorney, an accountant, and more industry professionals.

Chapter 5

Writing, Rehearsing, Recording, and Performing

One way to become a better and more well-rounded musician is to learn the different aspects of your craft — from composing, writing, and arranging, to understanding the specifics of the room where you perform, and everything in between.

In this chapter, I take you through the different elements that have to work in harmony to enable you to create your music. Different rehearsing techniques can help you explain your sound to other musicians. And different recording techniques can help you produce the music you hear in your head. So by the time you're performing on stage, your music has the energy and arrangement you envisioned.

There are many different tips, opinions, and ideas on how to create music, write a song, or build an arrangement. Similar to art, however, they're all just opinions. Studying different writing techniques can help, but it's your song and you are the artist. Let your creativity flow and don't get locked in to the idea of what a song has to be.

Creating and Writing Music with Others

It would be so much easier if the people you worked with could just read your mind, wouldn't it? Or if you were able to simply get your ideas automatically out of your head and on to paper. Or if you could make your fingers, your voice, or your instruments do what you have in mind to the level you imagine it to be.

For many musicians, it's a major struggle to explain the magical music they hear in their imagination. The more you can hone in and grow your abilities as a writer, player, communicator, and performer, the easier it is to make that magic happen.

Learn the piano and the theory that goes with it. Whether you're a drummer, DJ, singer, guitarist, or sax player, take some piano lessons and music theory classes so you can communicate clearly with other musicians.

Collecting and creating ideas

If you're in the middle of creating a song and a section doesn't seem to fit, save that melody, hook, bridge, or whatever for another song instead of just tossing it away. You never know where it could end up, or how it could inspire you later down the line. This is why it's important to collect and save ideas.

With technology and simple recording programs like Garage Band, it's easy to track, save, and keep your inspirations. Or if creativity strikes and you don't know the notes, just hum the tune into your microphone, or you can even save it as a voice memo on your smartphone.

Collect ideas, riffs, melodies, rhythms, or whatever, and name the files accordingly. Don't just save these bits of inspiration as "track 094." Think about what you did, name them with clear filenames, and keep a spreadsheet to use like a palette of colors you can visit when you're writing a song. For example, Figure 5-1 reflects the track name, the track length, and other pertinent info.

Figure 5-1:
A spreadsheet can help organize your collection of ideas.

Track Name	Key	Tempo (BPM/beats per minute)	Time/length	Instrumentation Ideas	Riff/melody/chorus/hook/verse	Miscellaneous notes
Bentley's Growl	G	90-110 BPM	:07	Guitar, bass, banjo, accordion, drums, voice	Hook	Could work as a hook or a pre-chorus in to something with a punch or growl to it.
Auggie's Attitude	C	80-100 BPM	:20	Keys, Guitar, Drums, Voice, Harmonnies	Chorus	Use for a brighter song with dynamics
Sue's Dog Rescue	E	70-90 BPM	:15	Samples, Electric Drums, Keys	Melody	Main melody for a hip hop tune that could be used with a Snoop Dogg type rapping style on top of it.

You can go further into detail, if you like. Make the info in the spreadsheet easy to reference so you can find what you're looking for when you need it.

For example, say you have 15 hooks that don't have homes or songs, and you're working on a piece that has everything except for the hook. You can access your spreadsheet, check out your options, listen to the most appropriate in your collection, and see if there's a sound you like.

Sometimes just composing pieces can help build up your database of ideas when you are working on full songs. Consider some writing sessions where you're only coming up with a single section or one idea, instead of trying to create a whole song.

For every formula that this person or that person touts to make hit songs, there are millions of songs that followed that same formula and failed, just as there are many songs that have followed completely different formulas and became hits. Don't get yourself caught up in the "I must pen a hit" mentality. It will strip you of your creativity.

Writing alone or with others

Do you feel better about writing alone, or do you prefer to have a writing partner, lyricist, arranger, or producer to write with? There are pros and cons to both; it comes down to your personal style, taste, and preference, as much as knowing your strengths and weaknesses.

For example, imagine you have written an amazing song that showcases your composition, arranging, and production abilities, but you have terrible lyrics. If you bring in a lyricist to pen your ideas, however, you showcase the quality of the song across the board.

The main pro and con to writing with others

The main advantage to working with one or more writers is that you have a second set of ears, ideas, reassurances, criticisms, and a second creative force for composing, arranging, and producing.

The main disadvantage is that sometimes too many chefs can spoil the soup. Some people just don't work that well together, and it can cause miscommunication, hard feelings between two writers, and can show up in the music as well.

The main pro and con to writing alone

On the pro side of working by yourself, you get to be you, write what you want, and have total control of the song. Some writers and personalities find this easier to do. They might bring their songs to others for critique or criticism, but all choices, changes, and edits are for them to make.

On the con side, good or bad, it's all on you if you write alone. Your songs, your way. Just be aware that your song might be improved with another set of ears.

Writing with and without others: The best of both worlds

Instead of focusing on whether or not you should be a solo writer, have a writing partner, or even writing team, try it all. Write by yourself; write with another person; and maybe try to find a couple different people to write a couple different songs with you. Then try getting together a group of people and writing something as a band or as a writing group.

Explore your creativity and your communication style. Brainstorm and let others expand on your ideas while you expand on theirs. Try different avenues to writing and find out what works best for you when it comes to the composition side of music.

When it comes to songwriting and composition, it's a very personal thing. Learn how others have approached it, but make sure you're writing in a way that works for you. The more you learn, the more styles and approaches you bring to writing and composition, the easier it is to find your voice, writing style, and the best writing approach for you.

Protect yourself and your work as soon as it is created. Whether you write alone, with a writing partner, or as part of a writing team, make sure that it's very clear how the writing is divided and get that both in writing and copyrighted immediately. When decisions about song spilt agreements (who wrote what and what percentage they get), producer rights agreements (how little or how much the producer receives in royalties or payments), musician releases (either a percentage or the clarification that all they receive is what they were paid to play on the song), and copyrights are taken care of right at the start, pay-outs become worlds easier in the long run. In Chapter 9, all these elements — including copyrights, publishing, and agreements — are discussed in depth. A lot of artists have gotten into horrible situations because the clarification of who wrote what, who owned what, and who got what wasn't clear. Treat every song you write or write with someone else like it is going to make a million dollars for you. That way regardless if it does or not, you have everything in order, clear, concise, and legal.

Performing your material

After a song is written exactly as you want it, you can test the waters and explore your performance options. Think not only as the writer, but also as the arranger, producer, and even musical director. These are discussed in Chapter 3, where you can learn more about these and other music business careers.

How do you envision your piece being performed? Do you hear specific instrumentation? Does this song lend itself to a male or female voice? What kind of dynamics do you hear in your head? There are plenty of questions you can ask whether you or another musician is performing your work.

Remember that if you have someone else perform your song, they are going to put their touch on it. It's very rare that you find an artist who will do exactly as you ask them to.

By now, you've probably played your song faster, slower, in different keys, with different accents and dynamics, and whatever other ideas you've had. The more you explore your music, the better idea you'll have when you bring that song onto a live stage or in to the recording studio.

Always have a good idea of how you want your music to sound before you go into the studio. A great deal of studio time and money is wasted because the artist hasn't explored different ways of playing their music. The early stages of performing a song should be considered as part of the writing process. At this point, it leans more toward the arrangement, production, and performance aspects, but it's still writing and composition. Give your songs a couple of good test drives on a couple of different tracks and in a couple of different races to decide where you want the finish line. This can save you time and money when you get into the studio.

When you record it, you can record it again in a different genre, style, tempo, or feel. Sting's "Every Little Thing She Does is Magic" was written and initially recorded as a very slow and soft guitar ballad, before it turned into the Police hit that had a wild, up-tempo pop-reggae feel.

Using others peoples' music

Tread carefully when choosing to perform and record other peoples' songs. It's key to get all the permissions in place before you record or add other peoples' music to yours.

Many have the mindset that it's simply covering a song, or it won't sell all that much, but if you get caught using other peoples' copyrighted music without their permission, you go directly to jail, don't pass go, and don't collect $200. Ok, it's not Monopoly, but the fines can be severe, and it's not unusual to get caught. More about copyrights and permissions are covered more in depth in Chapter 9.

When covering a song, it's crucial to find out who holds the publishing for that song so you receive a mechanical license (a license that gives you the right to cover and sell that cover). This enables you to play, interpret, or create an alternative version of the song while still paying a percentage to the copyright holder.

You may also come across publishing companies and estates that are kind and give you permission to use older music for little to no cost. Still, never assume, never second-guess, and never try to pull one over and think someone won't find out you've used others peoples' music without getting permission.

Always double-check to see if a song is in public domain. Some older songs that are listed as public domain allow artists to play, record, and distribute, but some of those songs now have owners. Also, just because you have verbal permission from an artist to use their material, make sure you run it through both the copyright holder of the song and the person or company that owns the publishing for that song. More about this in Chapter 9. There are artists who think they can give you permission for songs that they don't have control over, even though they wrote them.

Covering someone else's music

A great deal of artists cover songs on YouTube and other video channels. Although there's a bit of a gray area in the legalities of it, if you're not profiting from the performance and have no kind of ad revenue on the uploaded video, it can be a great way to cross-market your version of a cover and use the name of the song, the name of the artist, and the fact it's your version to market online. As an extra precaution, tell people where they can find your website for more music and for more information, rather than saying that your music is for sale. Technically, that's selling — and that can get you into trouble.

Do your due diligence and research before you cover another songwriter's song. The best option is to avoid covers or having to spend extra time and money to use others peoples music.

The less complex you can make your career, the more revenues you can maintain. Leave the covers and other peoples' music off the products that have your music on them, and you never have to share or offer up additional profits that should be yours.

Breakin' the law with "Happy Birthday"

Many think "Happy Birthday" is public domain and can be freely used, but the song is owned by Summy-Birchard Company, a subsidiary of Warner Chappell Music, Inc. The song collects over two million dollars in licensing fees a year and is considered one of the most pirated songs because many places of business where it's sung are technically supposed to pay for it. Pretty crazy!

Don't dirty the profit waters. From an EP to an album to a digital release, make it your music or the music of people you are working with. It makes all the numbers cleaner and allows for more profits.

If you're not a songwriter and working with other peoples' music, try to connect with a single writer or writing team to reduce too many percentages going to too many people and leaving you with very little or next to nothing.

Rehearsing For Production and Performance

Many musicians see rehearsing as starting at the top of a song and rehearsing it all the way through every time. This can make the beginning of a song very strong but still leave the possibility that potential issues can appear further along in the song and at the end of the song as well.

Other issues with the performance of a song can arise from misunderstandings on sections, changes, chords, dynamics, and overall communication. This is why it's a crucial step prior to recording in the studio and performing live to rehearse your songs with your band or other musicians.

If you're hiring session musicians or working with other band members or musicians who are friends, work to get on the same page or chart so the songs sound the best they can.

You have a little more room to move for the imperfections during a live performance, but the problems are put under a microscope when you record. It's also the reason why recording costs can mount up. Your efforts to rehearse your songs the right way make all performances that much better as well as help you to get a tighter, more professional-sounding recording that saves you a whole lot of money.

Rehearsing for results

The following is a list of techniques for rehearsing your songs for arrangement, production, and performance to achieve the best sounds in the fastest ways. There's no right or wrong way to rehearse; find the method that works best for you.

- **Metronome rehearsing:** Practice your music with a metronome. Can you stay in time, or do certain sections fluctuate too much? It's not about being a robot; it's about defining the time, tempo, and groove that's going to work best for the song.

- **Heavy dynamics:** Try playing across the spectrum of loud! Sometimes the loudest parts can mask and cover issues that need to be addressed to make your music sound that much better.

- **A little faster and a little slower tempos:** If you have a locked-in tempo for your song, rehearse it a little slower and a little faster than the tempo you have set for it. By practicing on each side of the tempo, you're able to have a better sense of when something is rushing or when it's dragging. It also gives you a better sense of the pocket of the song and exactly where you want it to be played.

- **Much faster tempos:** Whether you know the exact tempo of a song, or you're just dialing what feels right, rehearse your songs at considerably faster tempos. By rehearsing at a much faster tempo, you can check the technical ability of the band to run through the melody, rhythmic hits, chord changes, and transitions of a song.

- **Much slower tempos:** By slowing down the song and rehearsing it as slow as possible (with a metronome to keep you in check), you can identify a variety of problems that might come from skipping over an issue that isn't being caught because of its normal speed. Think about the lick that you know how to play when you play it at a normal tempo, but when it's slowed down, you trip all over it because there's more space for things to go wrong.

- **Different keys or modulations:** Test the waters of different keys or modulating inside of the key to bring a different flavor, but also to see how the song sounds and how you can perform it with another set of notes. Trying different keys can also introduce creative ideas on soloing, or show where you might choose to add a modulation to the key you have for the song. Again, it builds up the strength of the performance and the musicality, too.

- **Different time signatures:** This is a great one to get your rhythmic and melodic phrasing in check but also to create new approaches and options to a song. Add a beat or subtract a beat from the time signature of a song and see how you phrase ideas with a beat missing or an extra beat added.

- **Switch genres:** If you have a song with more of a grunge feel, try it as a jazz piece. If you have something that's more hard rock and punchy, try it with a reggae touch. Experiment with a genre change to reinforce the feel or genre the song is in and give you additional ideas on small nuances and embellishments that you can bring in from one genre to another.

- **Minus-one rehearsing:** Make the vocals go away, or take out the drums, bass, or even guitar in a song and see how it feels to rehearse it that way. Sometimes certain instruments become a crutch for other player's ears, and those players might not have their specific parts down solid.

- **Invisible or blind rehearsing:** I like this one for musicians who are going into the studio as well as rehearsing for live shows. Turn around so you can't see each other or literally put on the blindfolds. (Bandanas, ties, and T-shirts work fine, too.) Think Luke Skywalker and Star Wars. You may not feel the force, but can you feel the tune, the changes, and the transitions without eye contact from the other musicians?

   In the studio, eye contact might be blocked and you may even be recording a part at a completely different time than the musician you need to lock into. On stage, if the lights are in your eyes, or if the stage is large, you might not have visibility there as well.

- **Backward order of the song:** Do you know your song front to back? How about back to front? I'm not saying you should practice the song in complete reverse, but by playing each section from the end back to the beginning, you can get a different perspective on transitions and changes that can help when you record or perform the song from the beginning to end in the right order. Even if the song is a simple verse/chorus–verse/chorus type of format, practicing backwards for the dynamics and singing the last verses first can help you see if energy or endurance might be an issue that should be worked on by the singer.

- **Looping sections:** An offspring from the play-it-backward idea is to loop sections, and play just those sections over and over and over to tighten them up and lock them in. For example, play the bridge — just the bridge and only the bridge — section of a song from start to finish. As you get to the end, start over again at the top of the bridge. (Rinse and repeat!)

- **Playing it front to back:** And last but not least, practice the song the way you want to record it or perform it.

From slowing down your songs to slowing down the different exercises that you work on when practicing your instrument alone, get out of the mindset of trying to do everything as fast as you can and get into the mindset to play it as well in the faster tempos as you can in the slower. The better the understanding of a song, part, solo, exercise, or rudimentary phrase at the slowest tempo, the better you understand the space, mechanics, and motions that are missed when you try to speed through it.

The extra attention to detail and efforts you put into rehearsing, the better your proficiency, musicianship, technique, and overall ability is in your songs and your performances. It also saves so much time and money in the production process from tracking to improvising elements, to making additions, changes, and embellishments.

Rehearsing to arrange

You have your songs where you want them from a foundational and basic arrangement standpoint, but how do you want to arrange additional over-dubs, horn lines, backing vocals, and other layering that builds in to the arrangement? Using many of the ideas from the previous list can help you figure out arrangements as well as who you might want to bring into the rehearsal room and potentially include in your recording.

After you find something you like, test it out with everyone playing together. By playing around with arrangement ideas and embellishments in rehearsals, you have more time to explore different sounds without incurring studio-time costs.

As you finalize arrangements and lock in the parts you want for a live band or the studio, make sure to make charts. Having charts for the song (the road-map for your songs; charts are covered in Chapter 6) and the arrangement can help session players knock it out instantly in the studio. This also makes it easier when you have to hire a backup or sub player to play these parts live. Get all of your songs charted and have them converted to simple PDFs that you can email to anyone who needs them. It's that much easier to get that track recorded when everyone is on the same page.

Rehearsing to record

Using the previously mentioned techniques while rehearsing for recording helps make the studio experience go that much better and take much less time.

If you have a producer, talk to him or her about the production plan (discussed in more detail in Chapter 6) and the tracking order to get an idea of what's going to be recorded when. The more prepared and in the zone you can be for the recording sessions, the better.

See if you can book a rehearsal session in the recording studio where you plan to track. Ask if the studio has any open dates or if you can wrangle a deal to have the final rehearsal in the studio.

The best rehearsing in preparation to record boils down to communication and planning. The more you know about what to expect when you enter the studio, the less surprised and the more effective you'll be.

If you hire top-notch session players, you won't have to rehearse as much. Still, adding a little to a rehearsal budget, or booking the studio for a possible rehearsal prior to getting everything set up and going, can get you that much more dialed in with your musicians.

Rehearsing to perform

How do you play on little sleep, little energy, and little drive? Probably not as well as you would if you were well rested, had plenty of energy, and had a full night's sleep. Still, many bands lose the endurance and energy toward the end of a show and the performance can become weaker.

When performers are tired, a live performance can lose energy. From the heat of the lights to a little too much alcohol, the volume on the stage and everything else, can begin to have an effect on the songs later in the performance.

People talk about how much you have to rehearse to have the best live show. One great way to build up your endurance is to rehearse full sets of full shows when everyone lacks sleep and energy. If you're in a place where you can rehearse at any hour, try getting everyone in to play and record at two o'clock the morning.

Practice your song transitions, and track them with different set lists. How do you end one song and go into the next? During certain rehearsals, focus on the end of songs and how they segue into the next. There can be magic in a moment of silence or transition. Rehearse the moves between the songs to help the motion of the songs and the sets as a whole.

To see how you look while playing, take video recordings of rehearsals and shows to review later. Take a look at you and your band. Seeing yourself on video can help you determine if you like how you look while performing. Maybe you need to make better eye contact with the audience; maybe you need to move around the stage more. Or maybe you need to move less. A video tells the truth about your appearance while you perform.

From working on projecting your energy when you have none, to how one songs flows into the next, to how you present yourself while playing live, rehearsals that focus on performances can help your live show become more memorable.

Rehearsing communication

Outside of the music, communication is the biggest element that ties everyone together. Good communication is rare in all businesses and artistic forms. Musicians who can connect, resonate, react, supplement, complement, and have a fundamental awareness of the person, the sound, the song, the dynamic, and the motion trumps the best technician or virtuoso type player tenfold.

Intended information and the agreed upon visual cues to the melodic, harmonic, and rhythmic hints and messages that can be shared are great, but also that internal connection is important. Understanding the personalities, the confusion, and the clarity among musicians is key.

Some are dominant communicators; others are submissive communicators. 'Sound weird? I'm not talking about "Fifty Shade of Gray" type of stuff. It's simple — different people have different personalities that affect how they communicate, how they perform, and how they react to others. It's about how you feel most comfortable communicating, engaging, reacting, and resonating with different people.

From more dominant personalities both in communication and in technique to the technical and softer styles of others that might musically enjoy someone else to take the lead, it's all about communicating in a way that works for different people with different needs that present different styles of communication.

It's not about getting everyone on the same page in a way where musically and creatively everyone agrees. It's about getting different people, like different notes, to resonate and create harmonies. If everyone agrees on the same points and communicates the same way, then all you have is unison and uniformity. When people are able to work with their differences, similarities, and dissonance of how they play and communicate, that communication, performance, and connection can be so amazing.

Most of the elements of communication and rehearsing come from the foundation of connecting with others when not playing. The better you can connect with other musicians the more practical, creative, and inspirational your connection and communication can be.

Preparing For Performance

All the smallest pieces put together the right way allow for the best results. Just like a chef in the kitchen who knows how to add the smallest splash of this or the lightest touch of that to completely transform a dish, the same can be said for the preparation that goes into a performance.

A great deal of performance prep comes down to preventative maintenance and advanced problem solving. Make sure your musical instrument is ready to for a performance. If you're a drummer, make certain you have backup drum heads. And if you're a guitarist, don't forget those backup strings — and maybe a backup guitar.

Have extras, backups, and the tools to repair the small and large issues that can occur. Invest in the right cases to allow for the safest transport of your equipment because taking care of the gear that enables you to perform your best is some of the best preparation possible.

Your body needs preparation, too. From simple stretching before and after a show from the drummers hands to the vocalists vocal chords, to the exercising and making sure the muscles you use the most often are in shape and able to support you. It might seem obvious, but enough sleep and even a nap before shows can help you stay energized. It's also important to eat the right types of foods to keep you energized and not weigh you down or tire you out while you're on stage.

Take care of your main instrument, which is you! Do everything you can to keep your energy up and keep you on top of your game and performance.

Your sound on stage and the sound check

What your music sounds like on stage and what it sounds like in the audience are two very different things. Every room, every stage, every sound person, and sound system is different. You might know exactly what you want to hear, and you think you know what's being heard out front; however, in most cases, you don't have a clue And generally speaking, the distance between what you think is being heard and what is actually being heard are worlds apart.

Ask the soundperson what they need from you, and tell them the basics of what are important to your sound. Put together a basic stage plot and input list that outlines the location of the instruments and the usual microphone setups for that configuration. (Stage plot and input list examples are available online.)

The more advanced notice a venue or sound person can have with your setup, the better the sound they can give to the front of the house and on stage.

The sound person works for the venue and is paid for by the venue. They don't work for you. Being rude to the soundperson that is working to get the best sound for you and helping with your monitors is a bad way to go. Ask nicely instead of telling them what you need. Don't bark orders or come off as rude. More than likely, you'd rather not go that extra mile to help someone who's yelling at you. Your sound person is no different.

Even if you're dealing with an incompetent or inexperienced sound person, work with and talk to them about your ideas with which you've had success, or that you've seen others do successfully.

Getting the best sound on stage and in the room comes from keeping everything you can in check and running smoothly. In the following sections, I tell you seven things to keep in mind to get the best sound on stage as well as out in the audience.

Keep communication between you and the sound person strong

Ask your sound person if they have any preferred signals to increase or decrease the volume. Get his name, and give him a list of names or the stage plot so he knows your names as well. Also, avoid asking the audience for sound feedback. It's rude to the sound person. You have someone at the front of house that is working to give you the best sound. Asking people what they want to hear or what they think can come off as rude and unprofessional on your part, while disrespecting the pro.

This also falls under listening to the sound person as he sound checks and giving him what he asks for. If he wants to hear the bass player, don't start adding guitar lines. If he's asking for you to play just the bass drum, don't add some insane drum solo. The quicker he can get the isolated microphones checked and addressed individually, the faster he can get to giving the band the best sound as a whole. The more he has to ask for something again, the longer it takes to complete your sound check.

Keep the tempers and egos in check

It's a fact of life; things are going to go wrong, and requests you have might not be heard or addressed in a timely fashion. Throwing a fit, yelling at the sound person, throwing a microphone stand, or any other childish, immature action is only going to make you look like the fool and keep the sound person from wanting to help.

Keep the volumes where requested

This goes back to the idea that what you hear on stage is not what's heard in the room. The volumes are set to help get the best sound for the audience out front. Don't assume you know what's going on out front and then make changes that hurt your overall sound. Three universal points are as follows:

- ✔ If you are asked to turn an amp down, turn it down.

- ✔ If you aren't sure if it's being heard in the front of house, ask.

- ✔ If you are having trouble hearing it on stage, ask for it to be turned up in the monitors.

Keep aware of changes and problems on stage

Don't assume that your sound person can see that you have a problem or that he knows your set and your songs. The more you can keep the sound person aware of the dramatic dynamic changes, the issues and the problems, the easier it is to hide those problems or keep problems from happening. The following are five common messages you need to tell the sound person:

- ✔ If you break a string, tell the sound person.

- ✔ If you are switching guitars, tell the sound person.

- ✔ If you are switching from brushes to using drumsticks, tell the sound person.

- ✔ If you have a song with major dynamic changes, tell the sound person.

- ✔ If anything is happening on stage that has a dramatic effect on the front of house sound, tell the sound person!

Give the sound person a set list as well. Include basic song times and key changes for songs both dynamically and instrumentally.

Keep hands off the sound equipment

Don't adjust a microphone on the drums or on the guitar amp without asking first the sound person. Again, every room is different, and most solid sound people know how to capture the best for that room. You can discuss options that worked well in other venues, but remember, this isn't other venues.

Keep the liquids away from the electronics

Look at where you're putting your water, beer, or drinks. Make sure you're not setting cans and glasses in a place that could cause a spill that shorts or destroys equipment. Liquids and electronics don't mix well.

Keep your feet off the cords (and don't swing them like Roger Daltrey)

Keep an eye on where you're stepping and standing. Sometimes there are a lot of cords and occasionally you might step on one, but get off of it as soon as you realize you did. Respect the gear of others like you would want them to respect your gear. On that same note, don't swing a microphone around by the cord like Roger Daltrey from the Who or toss it on the stage as part of your "vibe" or "intensity." Find other ways to showcase those elements without damaging other people's gear.

 Drummers, practice playing your drums with microphones on the kit. The main goal is to learn how to move around your drums without hitting the microphones. This is a major complaint both in the studio and in venues. Drummers who don't have the best technical prowess and ability can end up smacking the hell out of microphones and damaging them. Be aware of where you hit and where you aim. This makes sound people much happier and allows some to put up better microphones to get better sounds because they know you won't damage their stuff.

Getting your sound on stage sounding its best is a combination of your professionalism, your equipment being in top shape and ready for the stage, and how you work with the sound people. When those three elements are in harmony, your harmonies, melodies, and music sound that much better.

Setting up and breaking down

As crazy at it might sound, practicing and rehearsing your gear setup and breakdown can actually help your career. Setting up and breaking down is more than just the pain-in-the-butt part of any show; it's something that can help you stand out with producers, venues, managers, other bands, and music business professionals.

Your ability to expedite the fastest setup and get going as well as your proficiency to break down, get off the stage, and out of the way, all while protecting and securing your gear showcases a professionalism to the venue and other bands that is more and more rare these days.

Of course you want everything set just right to allow you to have the best performance and that at-home feel vibe of just sitting down to everything in perfect order, but the reality is that with every recording session and every show you have to break it down from wherever the gear is, load it into wherever you're playing, set it up so that's exactly as you like it, break it down again, load it out, and then load it back into your house or rehearsal space to be set up yet again.

I always used to tell people, I work from the same desk; I just switch offices every day.

Still, the key issue breaks down to these core elements:

- ✔ The fastest load-in and load-out
- ✔ The fastest setup
- ✔ The fastest breakdown
- ✔ All while being prompt, professional, and courteous

Load in, load out

Being able to load in quickly and in an organized way has its advantages. Aside from making short work of a hard job, you can likely get your car or truck parked easier. You can even take the extra time to explore the venue and stage, as well as learn the order of the evening. And when you get everything carted in and stored quickly and securely, you can take a big, deep breath. From the venue's standpoint, you're giving the impression that you can move and get things done.

Loading out involves accounting for your gear and getting it back to your vehicles safely and securely. Pay attention and make sure there's no chance of a mix-up where someone takes your gear and you end up with theirs.

The best load-ins and load-outs come from knowing how the puzzle of your gear fits best as it is being loaded into and out of vehicles, and as it's brought into the venue and up to the stage. Always remember to pack first what you don't need to unload until last.

Usually the drummer has the most stuff to set up. Packing her items to load out first, especially if you're loading up onto the stage, allows her to get set up faster and for sound check to get moving sooner.

Number your cases. If you have others that can help you load in or out, color by numbers! Make it easier to know what should go first and what should go last. It can also help with the inventory of cases to be sure that every single one was packed up. If you are like most bands, not every case looks the same; but if you have them all numbered as 2 of 14 and add a sticker with your website, email, phone number, and name, you're taking fewer chances and making it that much easier to track your equipment back to you.

Setting up

The quicker you can get everything set up, the quicker sound check can start and the more time you have to dial things in. When you have the setup down pat, you get more time to focus on microphone placement, the mix, and the monitors. Certain places allot a specific amount of time for the setup and sound check. If you're like me, you'd rather spend the bulk of that time in check, instead of getting ready for sound check.

Best practices for your gear in motion

Put in that extra effort and practice the way you load in and out, set up and tear down so you can complete each task faster, more efficiently, and make things easier on yourself at every step.

Practice the load

When it comes to loading in and loading out, it's a good idea to actually practice this a few times outside of a show. Load-in and load-out from your rehearsal space. And bring a stop watch and time it, too! See what makes it go faster and what makes it drag. Have a loading rehearsal where it's all about loading in and loading out. As crazy as it may sound, it saves you so much time, effort, and energy.

Saving time on the setup can come from practicing setting up your gear from everything being in cases or boxes to the point that you are plugged in and ready to go. But don't forget to add two things to the mix to help you set up that much quicker: an emergency case for the stage, and to mark you gear.

Your emergency case has all the extra backup gear and also that extra extension cord or power supply in case the venue doesn't have it. Never assume a venue has everything. Bring the backups you might need and make sure they are clearly marked as yours. Include extra batteries, duct tape, screw drivers, Alan wrenches, and everything you would personally need in an emergency kit.

And then mark up your gear. Whether you scratch a notch in to a cymbal stand or add a dab of paint or magic marker to that V point on your keyboard stand, mark up your gear so you know exactly where you want to have it be.

Musicians are fickle and they like things a certain way. I know. I had to have my toms at just the right angle, the cymbals perfectly where I wanted them and my stand just in the right locations. Even with my finicky, OCD approach to how I wanted to have my drum kit set up, I could have my large drum set; the one bass drum, four toms, two snare, drums, seven cymbals, and additional percussion up and right where I liked it, in under five minutes. Because everything was marked.

I had a drum rug that had taped markings of where every single stand was supposed to be. Every stand was numbered and marked from where the tripod should be extended to all the way to the angle of the cymbal or the top was supposed to be. That way I could set up and immediately work from the numbers and the markings. I got the exact positioning I wanted and was set up that much faster.

When you make those markings, I recommend using magic marker. It's easier to clean off and as you adjust your setup as your abilities or styles change, it makes it easy to alter the placement. By marking up your gear, you're able to achieve that perfect setup with everything in the perfect location that much faster and in turn, you get more time to focus on the sound check.

A picture is worth a thousand words and it could save you a thousand seconds from your setup time (that's only 16 minutes). Take a picture of your setups, where the knobs are set, or how you like your settings. Whether you need to slightly adjust them for a session or for the sound of one room to another, a simple picture can help to reduce and simplify your setup.

Breaking down and clearing the stage

In situations where there's an act waiting to go on after you, or if it's the end of the night and the sound crew is waiting to go home, get off the stage as fast as you can so that the next band can get going or your gear can be loaded out for the night.

You just finished a great set in the middle of a night that has three bands on the bill. Your part of the show is over, and now you're clearing the stage in respect for the next band that's coming up.

Breaking down on stage is one of the most disrespectful things you can do, especially when another band and the sound person are waiting for you to clear that stage.

Clear the stage as quickly as you can. As you go back to get something, see if the other band wants help bringing up their stuff. The more aware you are of the night as a whole, the more opportunities and better reputation you achieve.

Find out before the show where you should clear your gear. Take as much as you can in each trip, and take your trash off the stage, too. Broken sticks, strings, set lists, drink cups and water bottles, or whatever else. Leave the stage as you would like to receive it, even if the act before didn't do it for you. Be the better person and show some class.

Move your cases to the clearing area if you are storing them elsewhere and finish loading out. Leave one person talk to people or run the merchandise table, but get that gear moved and stored. When you leave gear at the side of a stage, you create the opportunity for theft.

Make life easier on yourself and your bandmates by determining the best load-in/load-out order to streamlining your setup to ensure everything is where you want it on stage, and knowing the fastest ways to clear a stage. You appear more professional and respectful and make hard work that much easier all around.

Set lists, set times, getting set!

Focusing on the format and the reactions of a set list can give a whole new and positive edge and effect of a show.

When noticing that certain songs seem to keep the energy of the audience going that much stronger while those same songs in a different order don't seem to have the same impact, take note and consideration for the order of the set.

Pay attention to how opening with a certain number of songs in one order, bring the people closer to the stage sooner, as opposed to those same songs in a different order. Keeping that awareness of what draws people in and what makes people seem dull can help you lock in much more effective, energetic, and engaging set lists and order.

Set lists can be tricky, and if you don't track your different set lists and the audience reactions to them, you're losing out on priceless information that can help you develop the best sets to create the most audience engagement.

Keep every set list you create and break it out into a spreadsheet with specific pieces of information, as shown in Figure 5-2.

Keeping track of a couple simple pieces of information can help the formation of your set list as well as enable you to know when to make a change or adjustment.

Print out the set lists well before your performance and make sure everyone is on the same page (no pun intended) when playing. You'll look that much more professional when you're not calling out song titles throughout the night.

You can add extra notes as helpful reminders between songs. Because sometimes musicians get carried away in the moment, many forget to say the name of their band or promote the latest album or product. Have prompts scattered across the set list to mention the name, the website URL and the social media pages, as well as point out the merchandise table. This helps you market yourself while the spotlight is on.

SET LIST FOR KITTY LIKES AVOCADO

Orchid Island Brewery	2855 Ocean Drive C-1	Vero Beach Florida, 32963
Scheduled Start - 8:00PM	Actual Start: 8:45PM	End Time: 9:35
	CONTACT POINT:	Alden
	Phone/Email	772-555-5555 Alden@oib.com

1 Litter Box Funk
2 Spaded and Confused
3 Kitty Kitty Bang Bang
4 Growling at the Moon
5 Cantelope Tantrum
6 Allergic to Humans
7 Ode to Jackson Galaxy
8 Schrodingers Poison
9 Dancing on a Hot Tin Roof
10 Tongue Bath
11 9 Lives
12 You're So Basic
13 No Moe Baths
14 Grumpy Cat on Catnip
15 Cat Cat Goose

		No changes in the set
Attendance	45 People	
Sales	10 CDs 4 Shirts	$200 in Merch
Best Reaction	You're So Basic	Loudest reactions of the night
Worst Reaction	Cantelope Tantrum	Seemed to bore people
Mailing List Sign Ups	19	
Pay for the night	400	
Capacity	60	
Other Acts	Opened for Bill The Cat	

Figure 5-2:
Your set list spreadsheet should contain pertinent information.

Organizing and changing up the set lists as you track the reactions helps you create better shows with a better order of songs in them. By adding notes regarding marketing plugs to saying something about the venue, the city, or the place that you are in, you connect that much more with the audience. Let your set list be like a map to a successful night as it leads you through a great show.

Chapter 6

Creating and Following a Production Plan

· ·

In This Chapter

▶ Setting up the production plan that works best for your plan and your production

▶ Decision making for pre-production through post production

▶ Staying on time, budget, and plan even when it takes more time and more money

▶ Preparing all the post-production for pre-release

· ·

*T*he information and details in your production plan can have multiple uses for multiple people. You can use it as a guide to stay on track with time and budget. You can also add it in to your music business plan and as well as a detail and justification tool for how you are creating and recording your product. It can also be used after the fact to look at what worked, what took more time or more money, and how you may need to alter future plans.

The organization, time- and money-saving advantages that comes from flowing a solid and detailed production plan enable you to create the best product with the least stress, hassle, and issues. Think of your production plan as a blueprint to help you stay focused and on task by building a strategy that covers

✔ Your budget from pre-production to post-production

✔ Your schedule

✔ Where you're recording and mastering

✔ Who is producing, mixing, and playing

✔ How you justify specific costs and how they're covered

✔ When you will release your work

Pre-Producing Your Production

Your production plan, in a sense, is the pre-production strategy for your pre-production plan to lead you in to your production phase, post-production phase, and release. Peter picked a peck of pickled what?

Recording as a whole can be incredibly intimidating, not to mention incredibly expensive at any stage in your career. The unexpected costs that can sneak up and bite you on the rear can end up costing you more than you planned to spend on the whole project. When you're deep in the thick of a recording, and you find out that this needs more time, you start to go over budget, you forgot that a certain person needs to be paid, or all these surprising and unexpected expenses begin to pop up, you can find yourself overwhelmed.

Your plan can be created by you or with the help of a producer (if you've already chosen one for the recording), consultant, management, or label. The pre-production plan covers and outlines everything prior to production or getting into the studio — from the rehearsals to the choices for producer, the budget for the recording itself through the mixing and mastering of the product and the release.

Setting up a timeline for the recording, a budget, and a basic outline of how the entire process goes allows for a great amount of savings in money, headaches, and stress.

Preparation for problem prevention

The preparation, due diligence, and double-checking prior to working in the studio, with a producer, and with other musicians, help to reduce the chances of problems and issues that can delay and even kill a recording altogether.

Part of the preparation includes the research on the right people to work with who can work the right way within your budget and your individual situation. This type of solid planning enables the whole process to run smoother with a better team of people on the same page.

Building, researching, and creating the right plan, with the right budget and the right people, helps to keep the scammers at bay and protect you, your music, and your plan that much better.

The amount of scammers claiming to be professional music producers, engineers, arrangers, beat makers, session players, top-notch studio executives, and so on is at an all-time high. If you don't have a production plan together and do your research, you're setting yourself up for failure.

Tracking yourself and your plan

The pre-production part of your production plan is the foundation that every-thing else is built on, including the budget, schedule, team members, and tracking. Not song tracking, but the tracking of the following:

- How to stay on track
- Where and why you might be off track
- How to get back on track
- Where you may be getting ahead of your plan
- Where to use extra time and money
- How to grab time or money from elsewhere if you fall behind

Your production plan becomes your primary budget- and time-tracking sheet for everything and anything have to do with creating your product from the inception to the pre-release. It's your personal business plan for just your music and can be added into your music business plan to show the exact details of where every dollar is being spent for making that music.

Budgeting and scheduling the time

When you build your time frames, you build the outline that keeps you on schedule, in budget, and on point. The biggest problem that makes a produc-tion plan go over budget is the lack of scheduling and the assumptions that everything will go ten times faster than it actually does.

Schedule time for preproduction, the recording sessions, the mixing, the mastering, and the release with extra buffers. This keep you from being so rigidly locked into a schedule that might see delays you can't control. Adding a couple extra hours for vocals, an extra day for mixing, or a little more time for rehearsals can give you the buffer you need.

If you don't need that extra time for one place, it can be used later if something else crops up and takes a little longer. You can also add that time to your mar-keting and the release budget to promote your recording that much more.

Planning for extra time helps to keep you and your schedule on track. If things go a little longer, you already have the time and budget built in; if you're able to stay under the allotted time, you can save that time and money and use it later for mixing or marketing.

By adding some room in your schedule for extra time here and there, it not only gives you a buffer, but it also shows those investing in you that you're on track, staying to task, and keeping on budget. When a certain element takes a little longer, like an extra four hours that are needed for vocals that you were able to take from saving two hours in basic tracking and a couple hours in overdubs, then you stay on point and show that you are budgeting and spending with an attention to detail. This also shows that you can problem solve using the existing budget and schedule you have and don't need to ask for additional funds.

The following sections show the core time costs that need to be budgeted in and scheduled for. Although each of these costs can tie into some of the team and people working on the recording, these encompass the time that's included in your budget and the scheduled amount of hours and days for each element.

Put aside time for preproduction

By answering the questions about how much preparation time you need, you save a great deal in the production phase. This can range from vocal lessons to working with your producer to review basic tasks before the clock starts ticking in the studio.

Plan and budget for preproduction time, and make the most of it. You can save a great deal of hours and cash down the line by going over and planning for all kinds of possibilities in advance before they end up costing you down the line.

Schedule demo sessions

Especially if you are still new to the whole recording experience, demo sessions in the studio can give you a solid idea of what happens when you go to track for the main sessions. You get an idea of the process as a whole — where the microphones are placed and how things work in a more relaxed environment. By understanding the process, you can save a great deal of time when the real sessions get underway. These demo sessions can also give you some time to experiment a little more and for a little longer because you're not on such a defined schedule inside of the actual production. Adding these sessions to the budget can save you money and time later in the actual production and, on occasion, certain rough tracks from the demo sessions can be used later.

Sometimes you can capture tracks and parts that are usable for the full sessions, too, which in turn can allow for more time to mix and play during the sessions.

Book rehearsals

Whether laying out a rehearsal schedule for the band leading up to the sessions or working to schedule rehearsals with some of the session players that you are bringing, having that plan for rehearsals makes the takes and tracking go that much better. One more step in the plan can outline what you want to cover and work on in each rehearsal.

In most cases you have to pay your session players to rehearse. Some do add a rehearsal into their fees, but be prepared to pay for rehearsals if you want them. Also note that many of the better session players won't need that rehearsal time. The good ones can sound like they've been working with you forever. Still, if that preliminary connection is something you need, book them and schedule those rehearsals with them.

Make time for arrangers and arrangements

If you need vocal, horn, or string arrangements, orchestration, or sample or electronic parts arranged for your songs, schedule the time with an arranger or the time to focus just on arrangements. Planning for this before the sessions can enable you to save time in the studio and with musicians to get those arrangements that much faster. You can find out more about arrangers and their job descriptions in Chapter 3.

Book gear rentals

It's not just about renting gear (such as drums sets, pianos, amps, guitars, keyboards, and other musical instruments); it's figuring out how long you need that gear. This is another reason why your production plan is so crucial. Imagine you have four songs with piano to record, and you want to get a very specific piano sound with the basic tracking. By planning to rent the piano for the first day or two and also planning for the piano tuner, you can knock out the piano tracks first and get that piano returned. Many studios do not have a piano, so planning the rental time, the piano tuner, and the time spent recording can save you a lot.

The same goes for drums. If you're tracking basics and drums for three days, schedule for four (just in case) and then get those drums returned so you don't have to deal with any additional costs.

Track hours and days

Estimating the days for basic tracking of the foundational instruments as well as a little buffer for a little extra time is a great idea. This is where you lay the drums or drum loops, the rhythm guitars, bass, keyboards, scratch vocals, and everything else to build from. If you're scheduling for a live band, the whole recording might be basic tracking. This is a customized task. Vocals, solos, embellishments, and enhancements come in overdubs (see "Overdubs and vocal sessions" later in this chapter"). Figuring out how much time is needed and scheduling for that depends on the amount of overdubs and tracks necessary.

There's no template or model of tracking that works for everyone. Take into consideration how much has to be done, how long everyone needs to get it done right, and then base numbers off these estimations.

Not everyone needs to be there for basic tracking. There are a number of artists I drummed for in the studio that I never even met. I was just in the studio with other session players and the producer. Again, it's a personal thing in how involved you want to be with your project.

Overdubs and vocals sessions

Overdubs are the extra tracks that are added after the basic tracks are completed. These include solos, samples, additions, and extra touches from vocal harmonies to percussion, strings to horns, extra guitars to miscellaneous instruments and sounds that are not recorded with the basic tracks. Schedule this time carefully to save the most money.

Keep in mind your vocalist may need to rest for a while and take breaks. Instead of having nothing going on as the clock is running in the studio, work on some of the overdubs to allow keep the production moving along.

Ask for some help in the vocal session scheduling to know just how long you need. This is one of the biggest areas where many singers think they can just knock it out of the park in a take or two, but then find themselves hours and even days later, over budget because of poor planning.

An artist I produced thought she could do all vocals in two days and fought me on the idea of scheduling six days over a two-week period. It ended up taking nine days over four weeks and going way over budget. By asking a producer or a vocal coach who has had many experiences to help you with a reasonable time allotment, you can plan more effectively.

Don't get too carried away in the overdub phase! There are many people who add more and more and more ideas along with more and more and more possible takes. This makes the mixing process longer and longer and — you guessed it — more expensive.

Every take you keep and move to mixing has to be budgeted and scheduled to be listened to, reviewed, and then compared to the others.

Every overdub or additional vocal track you add has to be budgeted and scheduled for additional mixing time of both that extra track or tracks and the mixing into the rest of the song.

Technical mixing

This is your first mix, the cleaning up. This is the kind of mix that can be done even at the end of the early phases of basic tracking. Make sure things are cut off where they need to be, properly named and titled so they can be referenced to in the main mix, and begin to give each track a basic scratch mix to make it easier to work with down the line.

If you find that you're losing steam in an overdub session, or the vocalist runs out of gas and you still have two hours left on the clock of the schedule that day, have the engineer spend the rest of that day and that budget with the technical mix and clean ups to be as productive as possible.

Main mixing

Think of mixing like putting the colors you want to use in a picture on your palette. Rather than painting a picture, you're "painting the song." In your mind, you already know the song. You have the idea of the tune, and you know the basics of what you want to hear. So now painting the exact picture is like the mix, from the amount of each color you use to how it's drawn across the canvas. In the same way, your song is a sound canvas, and a great mix can make or break a song.

Give the engineer some! (time alone)

In the early stages of mixing, I usually recommend that an artist is not in the studio at first. This allows the engineer, producer, or both to pull together a basic mix with everything set at a decent level before the extra nuances, fades, volumes, equalization (EQ), effects, and all the embellishments are added.

More than likely, you don't want to listen to an engineer spend all that time mixing the bass drum against the rest of the drum kit and then match it to the bass, vocals, and other instruments. My guess is that you'd rather come in when everything technical and basic is already taken care of so you can add your thoughts and creative touches.

Mix requests versus time realities

As you listen, ask for changes and work with your engineer or producer on the mix, or if someone else has mixed it alone, the end result should be a final version for you to take home, listen to numerous ways, and then make any last notes before wrapping it up and call it the final mix.

In preproduction, talk to your producer and engineer about what's happening with all the songs and how many overdubs you're initially thinking of.

Plan also for how many takes you want to go after and keep. All of these elements factor into exactly how long you should plan for a mix.

For example: If you are an acoustic guitar player and singer, looking to only record songs live with no harmonies or other instruments, your mix time will be days and hours shorter than a group with 11 members, a horn section, loops, vocal harmonies, effects, and quadrupling guitar parts.

Final mix time allowances

You brought the mix home and listened to it on a number of devices. That means reviewing it on: headphones, ear buds, car stereo, computer speakers, home speakers, crappy speakers, and while you were in the studio.

You won't be happy across the board, but if you address the elements you do hear, you can get the best mix possible. Although it might sound outstanding on the $10,000 speakers in the studio, the bulk of your audience doesn't have those speakers.

Making a clear budget and cutoff point for your final mix is a good idea. If you decide to go back and forth on many different changes and many different small tweaks, it will cost you a fortune and it will never be done.

It will never be just perfect, 'cause you're never going to be perfect. None of us are. There is an intelligent humility and acceptance that needs to happen when creating a song in the studio and it can be a challenge to look at any piece of art and say, "ok, its done!" But, by changing the thinking of "it's done" to "this is where I'm stopping for now," you can save a lot more time, money, and stress. Remember, you can always go back and record it again for another album or even as a single. Still, allow that closure for each song.

By setting clear time frames and budgets for your final mix and even the different parts of a mix as a whole, you can police yourself in a way to make sure you're staying on track. If you need more time, think of where in your plan you can pull it from. This is responsible time and budget management for the studio.

Also, final mix is not what the track is supposed to sound like in the end. It's how the mix and the levels sound; your final sound of the final song comes in mastering.

The master plan: Mastering

The mastering is the last step after the final mix where your music gets its final adjustments in volume, equalization, and overall tone along with fade in and fade outs. Remember — the mastering engineer is working with only two tracks. Changes made in mastering affect the entire track as a whole.

A mastering engineer can't pull up the drums or take down the vocal. Any effect, volume adjustment, or EQ is heard across everything. Mastering is covered in the "Mastering Your Music" section later in this chapter.

Allow a new set of ears on the mix to master the final product. Reach out to different mastering engineers and ask for before-and-after samples to get a sense of how each one approaches mastering.

Ask around and look for a price that works for your budget. It's the last step that's often forgotten early on, so in turn, there's not much money left for it. A well-mastered recording has that much more of a pop, punch, and warmth to it.

When you budget and schedule your time your costs in the most effective manner, you save the money, get the most accomplished, and are at your most productive. This type of budgeting and scheduling not only helps keep you on track, it can also make you less of a risk to investors that may be covering the budget. The more you show the detail, care, and considerations of every cost, especially when it is someone else's money, the easier it is to get those costs covered.

Setting your tracking order and plan

It's almost like creating a route or the navigation for the map of your recording. You would be surprised how many bands go in to the studio that are very well rehearsed with their music, but completely and totally unprepared when it comes down to how to track, what to track first, what to do last, and how to get the most out of every session.

Again, this is a very personalized thing based on the artist, your attention span, endurance, frustration levels, and overall energy. Everyone is different, so following a template might work for one person but not have the same effect for you. This is part of the post-production plan and needs to have some time allotted for you to choose the order of the product that you're releasing. This should take place before mastering because the mastering engineer creates this order, the fade in and fade outs, as well as the breaks between each song.

A good starting point is to think about how certain songs have felt in rehearsals or in shows. Maybe order seems to make everything easier, while another order makes things a little more difficult. Take stock and see what you can recall in your rehearsals, at your shows, and even when you practice alone. Be the detective and the compass for starting out with the best path through the best order for the sessions.

The following are other approaches to finding your best tracking order:

✔ **Be flexible:** The tracking order doesn't need to be locked down. Leave enough flexibility to let things change in the studio, especially with basic tracking. If everyone is feeling a certain song next, then go for it!

✔ **Get loud first:** Begin with a song that has louder dynamics. You know the song — something where you can really test out the volumes and help the engineer or producer dial in your sound that much better and quicker for the other songs. This can also help to stretch you out for some of the songs that might record better if you are all warmed up, dialed in, and have the blood flowing.

✔ **Prepare for the long run or long day:** Realize it's gonna be a long day and you may have to do a song over and over again to get it right. Some musicians think of the tracking order like a set list, which is one way to do it, but in a set list, you're playing each song only once.

✔ **Don't leave the hardest for last:** Between two easier songs, pop in that real challenging one. Coming off of a track that was easier and tracked faster can give you that extra boost of confidence to go into a more challenging tune, just as coming out of that into an easier track can almost be like a break from the time or effort needed in that harder track.

✔ **Think excitement, exhaustion, patience, and endurance:** Having a basic idea of when each member hits their exhaustion point or how you feel at different times in the day can let you know when it's time to stop and go home. Stay aware of those around you, and sense when they might be losing their steam or getting close to blowing their top. Always budget for breaks; they help endurance in the long run.

Charts for everyone before the session

Just like a map for the sessions as a whole, you need charts for each musician for the recording sessions. Whether adding into the production plan budget for someone to create these charts or if you create the charts yourself, giving everyone charts saves time and confusion.

Having charts for a session, even if you have the songs down pat, can help every song that much more. From having a chart for the engineer to charts for sessions players you might hire, or for musicians who might come in to do overdubs later, providing basic charts help create a simple road map for every song to keep everyone going in the same direction and staying on the same page.

You can adjust the amount of detail, simplicity, or complexity for each song. The three most common charts include the lyric chart, the chord/arrangement chart or melody charts, and the production notes chart.

Lyric chart

The Lyric chart is used as a guide for those musicians who might not know how to read music, but want to follow along. It's also helpful to have this chart during vocals to enable the producer or engineer to know what they're tracking.

Chord/arrangement chart

The basic chord chart simply covers the chord progression of the tune, even with simple scratched lines and the chord names. This is useful for musicians and for the engineer while in production and overdubs as well as mixing.

Where the chord chart shows the chords, the arrangement (or melody) chart reflects the melodic lines so a session player can easily read it. For more complex tunes with challenging and more advanced changes, stops, and difficult parts, this type of chart makes life easier and allows you to get the takes you want much faster and with everyone on the same page . . . literally!

Production notes chart

This an extra chart that many skip; however, come recording time, a great deal of the stops, reviews, and discussions are part of this document. Use it to avoid, among other things, bad takes. This chart is more descriptive than it is technical or musical in a theory sense.

Table 6-1 shows what a production notes chart might include.

Table 6-1	Production Notes Chart
Description	*Example*
Key	F major
Tempo	140BPM or beats per minute
Instrumentation	Drums, bass, vocals, backing vocals, guitar, keyboards, lots of horns, shaker, tambourine, cowbell and congas
How the song starts	Drums for two bars, then everybody
How the song ends	Fade out, so keep playing for a while
Watch points	Dynamic drop after the guitar solo Lots of harmonies in third verse, don't get too busy
Similar type songs	Kind of a Maroon 5 feel (Like their "Payphone" song)
Additional notes/vision of the tune	I want this really soft in the beginning and end, but punchy and raw in the verses. Horns will punch hard in the choruses, no need to overly accent in the choruses because the horns will have it covered later.

Again, the idea is to deliver the best road map possible for all the musicians involved in the song, so they can give you the best performance. The more information you can share and the more information that your producer, engineer, and other session musicians have, the better the track can be for you as a whole.

If you need help with charts or arrangements, add that into your production plan. Having someone help you clearly define the parts as well as work with you to develop the best ideas helps take your songs to a higher level.

A production plan isn't about having everything planned out down to the exact note; it's about making a plan so that every note, song, and idea you create in the studio is done in the most productive environment at the most reduced cost to create the best recording with the least amount of stress.

By creating all the parts of your production plan in advance of your production and hammering out all the details and intricacies that you want, you can make the sessions run smoother and allow for that much more time to create, embellish, and improvise.

Your Recording Process —Picking Your Producer, Mixer, and Musicians

Everyone has different abilities, needs, and requirements. Connecting and working with the right team, studio, and players can make or break a recording. In all cases, when finding the right studio, producer, engineer, and musicians, it always comes back to your due diligence.

Always double-check and find the reviews, follow up with past clients, and put in the time to research the people who are about to become part of your recording. Doing so helps you avoid potential issues with those who might not share your vision or work ethic.

Don't worry about a big name producer

It is not about the big name anymore or trying to get this musician or that musician to play with or produce you. The same goes for the studio where you're recording. Don't focus all your energy and too much of your budget on time in the same studio where a major name recorded. Just because you both use the same studio doesn't mean you'll see the same results and same profits.

Think of it this way — you don't have the same team, the same producer, the same budget, the same record deal, the marketing money and the tour support to allow that recording to become successful on the same level. Every situation is different, and if you don't take those differences into consideration, you get a terrible product from an amazing studio that ends up going nowhere.

Comparing your situation with their results

Keep the following thought in your mind regardless of where you choose to record or whom you choose to work with, from producers to engineers to arrangers and session musicians: *Make sure they have the ability to give you what you need with your budget, your ability, your team, and your time frame in mind.*

Imagine if you hired a chef that required specific ingredients, a set amount of time to prepare and cook those ingredients, and needed specific cookware to do it. You then tried to get him to work with ingredients he doesn't love, rushed his time frame, and gave him different tools than what he likes or knows how to work with. Your end result might not be what you want. Yes, he is that amazing chef, but the end results aren't all that amazing nor are they very tasty.

It's the same when it comes to a producer. If you try to hire a top name, but then don't allow him the time he needs to mix or produce to the best of his abilities, you're left with a celebrity name on a sub-par product.

On the other side of the coin, there are amazing studios that can fit all budgets with producers, engineers, and players you may have never heard of, but have stellar skill sets, great reputations, and excellent abilities. There are also the producers, studios, engineers, and musicians who might be the perfect match for your sound, style, and approach.

This recording is your baby. It's your project and regardless of how good someone may be or how great some studio may be, if it doesn't feel right to you, it's not the right person or place. Trust your instincts. Music is art, creating music is emotional, and working with the right team makes everything sound that much better.

Mixing up home studio and pro studio tracks

Do you have recording skills? Do you have recording gear? Do you know how to record? Do you feel more comfortable recording at home? A mixture of recording at home and in a studio can work well for you as well as save you a great deal of money.

This again comes down to finding the right producer, studio or engineer that can work with you and tracks that you might bring in from home. Very large scale bands like Aerosmith have been known to go in to a larger studio early on to cut basic tracks and get a drum set well miced up, then get the solid basics down to allow for vocals, guitars and other parts to be done in home studios. There is no rule that all the music has to be done all at once and all under one roof.

Other options include having a producer work with you at home instead of a studio to gather as many tracks as possible and then allowing him or her to mix at their studio. The better you can be captured and the more comfortable you are while recording, the better the music will be.

Talk to your producer or the studio about what you have for equipment as well as what they have. Discuss the options of what you might be able to capture at home and how it can be easily transferred to the studio. From renting certain microphones to having the producer or engineer come to your home and check over your set up for the best sound, mixing together home studio recordings with pro studio recordings can sound as if you recorded everything in a top-notch studio.

Picking the right studio, engineer, and producer

Eenie, Meenie, Minie, Moe. Book a studio by the toe . . . okay, not funny. But the choices and options for finding the right producer and right studio can be overwhelming. Still, remember this is your project, your music, and just as art is opinion and very personal, so is choosing a producer and a studio.

A studio is much more than a room, microphones, and gear. Is the vibe of the place comfortable? There are many different formats from the Pro-Tools to Reason, Ableton Live to Apple Logic Pro and Audacity and many others. These are some of the top and most-recognized software programs used in the music business today. I personally produced with Pro-Tools and it was my favorite, but I have heard amazing albums cut on Reason and Abelton too. When it comes down to the studio, a lot of it has to do with the engineer and how he knows the tools around him.

So how do you dial it in and find the studio that's right for you? Start by following the same due diligence that was covered a couple pages back. Ask for references, examples, and check out the reviews. Call people who've worked in a specific studio, and follow up to find out what others say.

Then, look at the rooms and the gear, talk about the budget, the time frames, and what you need to have done. Ask for project averages to get a sense of how long it will take from setting up to the average mix down times. Ask if they have session musicians who might work well with your project if your project requires it. And make sure you compare all this information and what's being offered with other studios.

Using session musicians recommended by the studio can oftentimes save you that much more time and money. Because these musicians have either worked with the studio or the producer before, you get the best performances out of them, that much faster. In turn, this saves you the headache and trouble of trying to bring someone new into the fold.

Listen, don't look

Don't get caught up in the size of the room, or the size of the mixing console, or the number of different isolation rooms. If a studio can capture an amazing drum sound in a smaller room because it has great microphones and an excellent engineer, a small room can be just as powerful as a humongous room. Some engineers work on computer keyboards and a track pad whereas others work on a 64-channel console. The size doesn't matter, and one is not better than the other, especially if they are both delivering the same quality result.

Digital versus tape

Time management in recording is crucial. Getting the most out of your time in the studio while staying in budget is key. Some studios still offer tape, but understand that with cutting on tape, doing overdubs, mixing, and everything else, tape is going to take a lot longer. There's something cool about the old-school element of tape, but it's an expensive way to go that can make a session take months longer than what you can do digitally.

Go digital with your recording. There are many audiophiles who will tell you how much of a difference that tape makes, but it's really hype. A great engineer who knows how to place microphones and mix well can give you that thick, rich, warm sound that most associate with something being recorded on two-inch tape. I've seen more and more people go to digital and find the right studio and producer to deliver a sound that even the most discerning ear can't tell the difference.

Choosing the producer, co-producer, or producer/engineer

If you choose a producer first, they often have their own studio or a studio they favor. Some producers can also work as engineers, and some producers like to have an engineer with them. You may want to cover some of the producing yourself and might need a producer only in a secondary fashion. Still, having that extra set of ears can be that much better to help you and help the project as a whole.

Again, ask the questions, listen to examples of their work, and follow up with those who have worked with them. The due diligence part is the most crucial part in finding that studio that's the best as well as working with that producer who can help to deliver the best results. It's a personal choice and should be based on the music, your needs, your budget, and your project.

Finding the right backup musicians or hired guns

Your friend might be a great guitar player, but is your friend someone who can handle recording at the level of a studio guitarist? This isn't something you want to find out in the studio with the clock running, watching time waste away as issues begin to compound . . .

After you lock in your producer, ask them if they have a great call list of players who they know well, have worked with a number of times, and can get it done right, quickly, and on time. Look to your producer or studio to help you find those players for the best results. Even with those references, make sure you get a sense of what these musicians have done and examples you can listen to.

Members can learn parts and there are ghost session players out there who can come in and fix a part and not even take credit. I know, because I was one of them. Still, if something isn't happening and is an issue or worry from the get-go, it's either a song that should be shelved for a later date or the consideration of a back up player should be brought up early on to keep things on schedule and on budget without feelings getting hurt and more stress being brought to the process.

Finding musicians outside of studio or producer recommendations

If you're looking for a musician who the studio or producer doesn't have a recommendation for, again, go back to your due diligence. Ask for the references, examples, and the reviews, and

- ✔ Don't get caught up in a pretty website or social media.

- ✔ Do look to see what others have posted about them.

- ✔ Don't be overly impressed about amazing videos that show blazing chops.

- ✔ Do look for references from people who say they can play what's needed for the song.

- ✔ Don't get sold on how good they look or how good their gear is.

- ✔ Do get more comfortable when other producers or studios say they act professional.

After the due diligence and double checking, go with your gut. It's got to feel good to you. The best keyboard player in the world might not be a fit for you or for your music. It isn't on them. It isn't on you, it is about a connection and a resonance outside of the music that can make the music that much better and get captured in the recording. Don't let anyone's résumé or references make you feel like you have to work with someone that you don't work well with.

Mastering Your Music

That final step after the final mix that brings the songs and the recording as a whole all together is *mastering*. Often confused for mixing, mastering is really a different beast all together. In mastering the technical stuff, such as placing the track numbers as well as the track sequence, arrangement takes place. Those song fade-ins and fade-outs take place in mastering too. This also includes the spacing between each of the tracks and adding the codes for the replication process. You might have picked the order in mix, but the technical elements are added by your mastering engineer.

Mastering engineers work with two tracks. They can't go in and lift a snare drum to be louder; if they raise the volume, everything in the song goes up. On the same note, however, a mastering engineer might lift a certain frequency that can make a snare drum or another instrument pop that much more. Make sure your mix is ready to be mastered, and stay out of the mindset that specific issues can get fixed in mastering . . . because they can't.

Understanding the importance of mastering

Mastering's main function or more of what can be heard is the dialing in of the average volumes by defining the peaks and the lows for all the songs as a complete body of work. The compression and equalization (EQ) are also worked in mastering across the whole mix. That final punch, warmth, continuity, and crack comes from mastering.

Ask a mastering engineer if you can listen to samples of a final mix and the final master of a song or of an album. It is the best way to hear those nuances that can be hard to explain. Just a simple listen between a strong final mix and a great mastering can help you understand just how important the mastering process is.

Prepare for your mastering and don't try to master while you mix. If you add too much compression to a final mix to give it that final sound you are looking for, you're actually tying your mastering engineer's hands and making their job harder to give you the best mastering possible.

On that same note, many studios and producers have the mastering equipment and the ability to master, but bringing your final mix to a mastering engineer is a better choice. Give it to someone who can listen with a fresh set of ears and take it to the finish line.

Researching different mastering engineers with that same due diligence you used for the studio, the producer, and the players is a good idea, too. You also may be able to get a higher echelon mastering engineer because the process as a whole tends to be a lot faster. Prices can range from $40 a track to hourly rates of $120 and up from there. The average for the past decade put a song at about an hour, but again, it really comes down to the complexity of the song and the elements, instrumentation, and tones in the song itself. Also grabbing some extra fades and sections for other use during mastering can add a little more time but pay in great ways down the long run.

Creating all your different products

After the product is mastered and complete, make sure you ask for a couple extra pieces from that final product to use for marketing, promotion, and booking. Every single product you create from a single song to an EP to a full album can have all sorts of subsidiary and secondary products to help sell that product more as well as open up more avenues for more revenues and more opportunities.

Mastering for samples, loops, and no vocals

As the final product is completed, and even before when you're in the studio, think about a series of samples, loops, and versions that you can use online and send to others. This includes a mixture of elements from the final mix tracks and the mastered tracks.

Loops and potential samples for others

Sections of songs that could be used by others can create more revenues from the songs you are trying to promote.

No-vocal/backing-vocal versions

As final mix is wrapping up, make sure to get a version of a no-vocal and a version with just backing vocals. The mastering engineer can use the basic mastering approach, compression, and EQ to these secondary versions that others might want to buy and potentially record for themselves. They need the original tracks, but by showing a master, you are highlighting just how good the song sounds. With the backing vocal version, you allow yourself to sing along to the track for performances at places that might not accommodate a full band.

Samples of each of the songs

The mastering engineer adds fade ins and fade outs so they can to be used for the online promotion of your music. These samples can also be used for booking as well. The rules for fades are:

- 10 to 15 second fade in and out of each song from the start of the song
- 10 to 15 second fade in and out of each song going to the end of the song
- 10 to 15 second fade in and out of each song at the hook/bridge
- 10 to 15 second fade in and out of each song at the chorus

Of course you aren't going to put them all up online together, but this gives you simple samples that you can mix and play around with from booking demos to other solicitations.

Most people aren't going to listen to your album in one sitting, but if you give them a mixture of samples you have from your mastering engineer, you create a fast demo that draws them in and makes them want more.

For example, if you have a recording with 12 songs that are all 3 minutes, 30 seconds long, and you send a link to all the songs, in a way you are asking for someone to listen to 84 minutes of music. If, however, you send a mixture of one track with the first 10 seconds of one song, with the second track fading in to the chorus, the third track being the last 10 seconds of the song, and so on, you just delivered 12 bite-size samples of your music, and you request only 2 minutes from the listener. This is way more respectful, professional, and has the potential to draw in way more interest from music industry mavens.

These samples can also be uploaded to social media pages and other sites to give examples yet not give away full songs that could be stolen if you uploaded the full track.

The extra time you take to create these extras can pay off in the long run. It's also a lot more affordable to do this while you master your main product and have that time booked in your production plan.

Your Pre-Release and Post-Recording Part

After you get the masters back, it's time to just release it, right? Wrong! The biggest mistake that happens after musicians get the final master back is that they rush to release the music and go to that mindset of "as soon as they hear it, it will sell." Unfortunately with no preparation between the post recording part and the pre-release, the bulk of these recordings fizzle and die out before they have a chance to shine.

After you put all the time and effort into making the music, give it the attention it deserves by being patient and preparing the launch for the most effective release to give it the best chances at creating as many sales and opportunities as possible.

Setting up your release plan options

Depending on your budget and your plan, the marketing of your release needs to begin before the release date, not after. Regardless of having a major budget or a grassroots budget, working on building the momentum, optimization, information, and promotional materials before a release date helps the release date, the release, and your marketing as a whole have a longer life. You're delivering more than a product — you're releasing a marketing campaign with all sorts of online and physical attributes that draw people to the main product and the promotion of your shows.

Releasing materials in order

Spread out the release and the subsidiary products over a span of time. Don't just launch a recording and then give a link to a site that can create a dozen one-off products. That leaves you with a lot more work to do in order to continually draw the interest of a new fan, while maintaining the interest of an existing one.

By breaking up a large recording into a couple EPs as well as adding some songs only for download, then releasing different products like T-shirts, cups, hats, and posters at different points in time, you're able to keep interest up in both new fans and old ones as they are offered new elements while advertising the main product or products.

Understanding exclusivity in song sharing

Stay with the idea of sharing and posting snippets and samples of songs, instead of putting up full songs that can be stolen. At the same time, be careful what you put out for free. Although free songs can be a way to market, you most likely won't be able to charge for them later. If you found out about a product that was given away for free for a long time, and all of a sudden had a price tag on it, would that turn you off or make you want to buy it? Think of how your marketing ideas will affect your products. On the same side of the coin, imagine you have a song that's on the Internet for free and someone wants to license it exclusively. If they found out it was out there for free, they might lose interest.

Providing music samples, freebies, and teasers

The best route to go with marketing your product and release is with the samples of the songs from the release. If you choose to have a song that's available for free, that can be used too. Sometimes releasing a live version without the best mix for free can draw in people to buy the fully produced and mixed version. Adding samples that are spread out over time is the way to go. Once a week, add a new sample track, instead of releasing them all at once. Use samples of the outtakes, flubs, mistakes, and bloopers, too.

The more you can share over more time with samples, freebies, and teasers, the more interest you can gain and maintain in your primary product.

Make sure those samples leave them wanting more. Fade out on unresolved chords or places where big changes are taking place. Tease their ears and make them want more!

Take every production element into consideration as you create and execute your production plan with every detail addressed, the patience required, and due diligence to ensure you're working with the right people. This ensures that your plan turns out a product that represents you in the best way as it creates the best opportunities for profit and exposure.

Chapter 7

Creating Your Brand

- -

- -

*W*ith the advent of social media along with the importance of branding and the oversaturation of bands, it's a very bad idea for musicians to launch online or even into a local scene without dialing in the band name, font, logo, and tagline. These are the roots of your brand for building any type of exposure, marketing presence, or engagement.

TIP

Define, align, and commit to the basics of your branding to make them work for you right from the start.

Understanding the Importance of Your Name

It's only a name! Right? No, it's all about *your* name! It's the first step of connecting people to you and your music. Your name is what people Google to find your website, band bios, and tour dates. Finding the right name makes this decision-making process more important than just scratching out names on a yellow legal pad and narrowing it down to the one that everyone settles for.

For your band name — or your name if you are the artist — the ease of spelling that name is key. If your name is Nerol Namsie or Thurston Sedgewick Beauchamp III, you may want to consider a simpler name adjustment or even stage name. This helps people who might end up misspelling it. On the opposite end of the spectrum, common names such as John Smith or Delta can get lost in an online search. And finding a domain name could be problematic.

For example, if your band name is Delta, you are not only competing with one of the biggest airline companies around but you are also dealing with one of the biggest faucet companies, which is something that will get you heavily lost in the mix, especially in searches online.

Coming up with a name

Create a mixture of a name you like with what you are able to grab for a domain name. Compare that against what looks good on a poster, banner, or a pen. Then add in how it can be spelled or misspelled, and you've got a little more work on your hands than you may have thought.

It's a good idea to do an online search to see if any other bands already have your potential name. Even more so, however, it's important to see what companies share the name and who might have a trademark, copyright, or some level of marketing that tie into the name or phrase.

Just because someone else may not have the copyright, trademark, or ownership of a name, it isn't worth trying to take over if that artist or band has a serious presence with that name. When you fight an artist who already has a great deal of search engine optimization (SEO) in place, or you see potential confusion that might lead a fan of yours to another musician, ask yourself if it's really worth the fight. Pick your battles wisely and watch out for names, phrases, and ideas that are already immensely popular.

Avoid niches that might be too close to other bands or brands or nicknames that might confuse fans. When building the foundation for your brand, let it be yours and not tied to something or someone else that could take the spotlight away from you.

Your name is going to be with you for a long time. It will be on your album covers, website, social media, merchandise, and whatever else you can get it on. Make it something that you're proud of and do not see it as a placeholder till something better comes along.

It's fine to read up on the way that your favorite bands came up with names and be inspired by the process; just remember that the Internet has changed the music business drastically. Your considerations for creating a band or artist name in 2015 may not have same creative freedoms of an artist in 1975 or even as recently as 2005.

Draw from the creativity of creating a name but consider the business, optimization, ability to be found, and ability to draw the most people online as well as off with that name. Do your due diligence and research to make sure there's no trademark or legal ownership of that name, too. Keep all those considerations in the forefront to help you find the best name possible.

Making your name memorable, easy to spell, and not too long

Thurston Sedgewick Beauchamp III, which is a whopper and easy to misspell, would also be a challenging domain name to use as well as making the branding process with that name a whole lot more challenging.

Can you imagine www.thurstonedgewickbeauchampthethird.com as a domain name, or a social media page like www.twitter.com/thurston sedgewickbeauchampthethird/? Then think about how that would look if someone were trying to put that on a business card, flyer, letterhead, or even as a link in a post on a social media page. Way too long and offering way too many chances for someone to misspell it, misread it, or just miss it all together.

Do what you can to abbreviate and simplify. Think of this name on a stage banner behind you, or on a bass drum, business card, letterhead, or swag promo pen that you might have for people who leave their names for an email list.

Also, consider the domain name when you create email addresses. Thurstonedgewickbeauchampthethird@thurstonedgewick beauchampthethird.com is a tad lengthy. Make that name a little shorter for every possible use in your branding in order for more people to connect with you.

Searching for availability beyond the domain name

It's more than just capturing a domain name after you have a name that you think might be *the one*. Make sure it works across social media pages, and then go for it.

Imagine you have a domain name — go with www.kittylikesavocado. com — but it's already taken on Facebook or Instagram. So you come up with some obscure name that has nothing to do with Kitty Likes Avocado, but has some meaning to you . . . maybe something like Fluffy Fruity Cat. What you've just done is create a greater challenge for someone who wants to find you on that network. The more difficult you make it, the less chance for follow-through. So make it that much easier for fans to find you anywhere and everywhere with your name and brand.

If you can't find the name, look to other names that might add music to the end of a band name or simple adaptions. Don't just go after a .net extension. It is better to grab all the extensions you can to secure that brand for you.

Grabbing more than just the dotcom

Don't forget the other extensions that are available. Grabbing the .com may not be enough of a deterrent for other musicians, or others not even in music to buy the same name but with a different domain extension. The top seven most recognized extensions for domains are .com, .co, .org, .net, .us, .info, and .biz.

It's a great idea to lock them all up, and it's great branding if all are available. If you don't find a .com available and jump to grab the .net, you're already making your online branding a little more challenging if that .com is already well optimized. In other words, if fans search for the name, the search results come up with a page of information about someone else and not you.

Hundreds more domain extensions have been added, including .club, .name, .music, .photography, .singles, and even .xxx. As some will gain steam in the coming years, right now, the top seven in the United States are all worth reserving for your band name. If you want to go a step further, reserve some of the international domain name extensions like .uk. The reservation of these extensions won't only lock in and reinforce your brand and your name, it also keeps others from trying to use that name because you locked it down and have taken control of it online.

With the reservation of other domain extensions or even misspelled domains, you can create individual landing pages that point to your main website to build up additional search engine optimization. Check with your website designer or check out *Search Engine Optimization For Dummies* by Peter Kent (Wiley) to make sure that you follow the right White Hat methods so that you're not penalized by Google for Black Hat methods. White Hat methods are preferred by Google; Black Hat methods are frowned upon and can get your website flagged, making it even harder to be found.

Simply put, White Hat methods are the type of SEO practices that you want to use, whereas Black Hat methods are frowned upon and can get your site blocked and lowered in its ranking. For more information about White Hat and Black Hat methods of SEO, look at www.warriroforum.com, which shares some of the most up-to-date SEO tactics.

Even if you're unsure of how to create landing pages, reserve those domain names and extensions, and point them at your main website or even at some of your social media pages. Reserve the domain names and own them so someone else doesn't have the option to buy and use them.

Securing free emails for your name and brand

The following list shows the top eight free email sites. If your band name is Kitty Likes Avocado, then sign up for or secure these eight email addresses as well your domain name emails.

- ✔ **Gmail:** kittylikesavocado@gmail.com
- ✔ **Outlook.com:** kittylikesavocado@outlook.com
- ✔ **Yahoo! Mail:** kittylikesavocado@yahoo.com
- ✔ **Inbox.com:** kittylikesavocado@inbox.com
- ✔ **Yandex:** kittylikesavocado@yandex.com
- ✔ **AOL Mail:** kittylikesavocado@aol.com
- ✔ **Mail.com:** kittylikesavocado@mail.com
- ✔ **My Way Mail:** kittylikesavocado@myway.com

This doesn't mean you have to manage these eight emails! Just set them up with the basic information and check to see where you can forward each of these emails to your main email. This also means that they won't be available to others who might like the name or might want to set up an account that people think is you.

Keep a simple spreadsheet for all the emails, blog sites, social media pages, and everything else online with the six elements shown in Figure 7-1. It keeps confusion to a minimum and allows you easy access when you log in to sites you haven't been to in a while.

MASTER INFORMATION LIST - Kitty Likes Avocado

EMAILS

NAME	ADDRESS	WEBSITE	LOGIN EMAIL	PASSWORD	NAME (LOGIN)	UPDATED
DOMAIN MAIL	info@kittylikesavocado.com	http://hostmonster.com/	info@kittylikesavocado.com	Jenny6675309	kittylikesavocado	1/1/2015
GMAIL	kittylikesavocado@gmail.com	https://mail.google.com/	kittylikesavocado@gmail.com	Jenny6675309	kittylikesavocado	1/1/2015
ZOHO	kittylikesavocado@zoho.com	https://zoho.com/	kittylikesavocado@gmail.com	Jenny6675309	kittylikesavocado	1/1/2015
YANDEX	kittylikesavocado@yandex.com	https://mail.yandex.com/	kittylikesavocado@yandex.com	Jenny6675309	kittylikesavocado	1/1/2015
OUTLOOK.COM	kittylikesavocado@outlook.com	https://login.live.com/	kittylikesavocado@outlook.com	Jenny6675309	kittylikesavocado	1/1/2015
AIM MAIL	kittylikesavocado@aol.com	https://mail.aol.com/	kittylikesavocado@aol.com	Jenny6675309	kittylikesavocado	1/1/2015
YAHOO MAIL	kittylikesavocado@yahoo.com	https://mail.yahoo.com/	kittylikesavocado@yahoo.com	Jenny6675309	kittylikesavocado	1/1/2015
MAIL.COM	kittylikesavocado@mail.com	https://mail.com/	kittylikesavocado@mail.com	Jenny6675309	kittylikesavocado	1/1/2015
INBOX.COM	kittylikesavocado@inbox.com	https://inbox.com/	kittylikesavocado@inbox.com	Jenny6675309	kittylikesavocado	1/1/2015
MY WAY MAIL	kittylikesavocado@myway.com	http://myway.com/	kittylikesavocado@myway.com	Jenny6675309	kittylikesavocado	1/1/2015

BLOG SITES

NAME	ADDRESS	WEBSITE	LOGIN EMAIL	PASSWORD	NAME (LOGIN)	UPDATED
WORDPRESS	https://wordpress.com/	https://kittylikesavocado.wordpress.com/	kittylikesavocado@gmail.com	Jenny6675309	kittylikesavocado	1/10/2015
BLOGGER	https://www.blogger.com/	https://kittylikesavocado.blogspot.com/	kittylikesavocado@gmail.com	Jenny6675309	kittylikesavocado	1/10/2015
WEBS	http://webs.com/	http://kittylikesavocado.webs.com	kittylikesavocado@gmail.com	Jenny6675309	kittylikesavocado	1/10/2015
WEEBLY	http://weebly.com/	https://kittylikesavocado.weebly.com/	kittylikesavocado@gmail.com	Jenny6675309	kittylikesavocado	1/10/2015
WIX	https://wix.com/	http://kittylikesavocado.wix.com/kittylikesavocado/	kittylikesavocado@gmail.com	Jenny6675309	kittylikesavocado	1/10/2015
BLOG	http://blog.com/	http://kittylikesavocado.blog.com/	kittylikesavocado@gmail.com	Jenny6675309	kittylikesavocado	1/10/2015

NAME	ADDRESS	WEBSITE	LOGIN EMAIL	PASSWORD	NAME (LOGIN)	UPDATED
FACEBOOK	https://facebook.com/	https://facebook.com/kittylikesavocado	kittylikesavocado@gmail.com	Jenny6675309	kittylikesavocado	1/10/2015
TWITTER	https://twitter.com/	https://twitter.com/kittylikesavoca/	kittylikesavocado@gmail.com	Jenny6675309	kittylikesavoca	1/10/2015

Figure 7-1:
Keeping a simple spreadsheet can help organize your online presence.

With each of the email addresses you set up, you have one more place where you put your name, one more place someone else can't use that name, and one more place where you're able to fill in a profile or information that leads people back to you.

Locking up the free blogs for your name and brand

Just like securing free emails, lock up the six free blog sites with your name and your brand. Again, this doesn't mean that you have to blog on each of these sites, but you can connect them and share from your main site.

- ✔ **Wordpress.com:** `https://kittylikesavocado.wordpress.com/`
- ✔ **Webs.com:** `http://kittylikesavocado.webs.com`
- ✔ **Wix.com:** `https://kittylikesavocado.wix.com/kittylikesavocado/`
- ✔ **Blogger.com (BlogSpot):** `https://kittylikesavocado.blogspot.com/`
- ✔ **Weebly.com:** `https://kittylikesavocado.weebly.com/`
- ✔ **Blog.com:** `http://kittylikesavocado.blog.com/`

I use WordPress, and I find that with all the plugins, the SEO functions, and the ease of use that it's the best site to blog from and be able to share information with all your other social media or blog sites. As you sign up for each site, make sure to track it in a spreadsheet to make it easy to log back in and fill in the profiles completely. Every page on your website and signature on a blog should point people back to where you want them to go or where they can connect in other places.

The more basic information you have on each page, whether it's a social media page, blog page, or email profile, the more you are getting your brand out in more places.

Signing up for all the social media pages

Some musicians talk about how they focus on a specific page or pages, and whereas that's not the most productive way to connect with the largest audience, the more places and more sites where fans can find you, the more you can connect with a larger audience. Regardless of the time spent on certain social media sites, it's still key to reserve your name and your brand so everyone can find you.

Signing up for the following 28 sites for musicians as well as making it a regular habit and part of the schedule to continue to sign up for new pages is the best way to spread your name and brand across the Internet.

Google+	YouTube	Facebook	Live Journal
Twitter	Instagram	Tumblr	Last.FM
About Me	Ello	MySpace	Skyrock
Spreaker	Pinterest	LinkedIn	VK
Flickr	Vine	Reverbnation	Meet Up
Deviant Art	Reddit	Tagged	Friendster
Snapchat	Vimeo	Ask.FM	Music Xray

Like the blogs and emails, fill out the profiles in full. Add everything you are allowed to. From linking your other social media pages to uploading videos, audio samples, your bio, and your pictures, it allows you to create one more place that potential fans may come upon that will lead them back to you.

Just as with the blogs, many of these sites have sharing functions where you can post links or automatically have the content you create shared to them. So after you have a post, it can be as simple as sharing a link from your blog or from one social media page to all the others in minutes.

Don't copy the same content into every post. And if you share a link and put a headline on it, change that headline a little so that Google and the other search engines don't see it as copied content being cut and pasted on different pages.

Certain sites need you to put up a certain amount of content over time or achieve a certain number of followers to be able to choose the vanity URL you want.

As you find out about different sites, get on board, sign up, and see what happens down the road. If a site is a bust, at least you secured your name. If that site develops over time, you already have a page into which you can begin to put more energy or time. Plus, those who look to see if a name's available and find that every search result comes back with you will most likely be kept from taking or using that name.

Getting your name out there

Get your profiles set up on TripAdvisor, Yelp, and Amazon. Musicians are always looking for reviews for their music but often times don't think about leaving reviews for other people. If your Amazon account or a band Amazon account reviews books, other people's music, and products while leaving reviews about hotels you stayed at or restaurants you ate at on the road, you have a few more sites that are connecting you with that many more people.

It's not only securing your band name on some more sites, but again, by filling out the profile in detail and putting some efforts in to your reviews, you may attract people to your profile page and get them to click through to find out more about you and your music.

Connecting through these other pages can connect you with a large group of people who may not be looking for you at all, but then be drawn to you from a review you leave for a musician, product, hotel, or restaurant — and all while cementing your band name and brand on one more site online.

Securing your name on other sites

Create a music publishing company with the name of your band. Even if you have your songs published elsewhere, secure that name as a publishing entity. Set up an Amazon account with your band name, travel review sites, and even your business legal entity. Secure the Skype chat name, KIK name, Yahoo! Messenger, and anywhere else. Take control of your name to the point that no one else has the option to use it.

Adjusting a name for a site when unavailable

If you find a solid name and in certain places it is unavailable or you are not quite able to get it across all domain extensions, social media pages, review sites, emails and blog sites, but you are set on it, then work to stay as close to that name as possible to have the best branding of that name as possible. For example, if you are able to secure /kittylikesavocado in most places but there are a couple where the name is unavailable or by a small chance taken, stay close to the name.

Some sites like Twitter have character limits, so you might need to make alterations when your band name is too long. Instead of going for something completely different, however, try to stay with the brand and at least the first part of the name. For example, Kitty Likes Avocado can have that as the name in the title, but the web link is `https://twitter.com/kittylikesavoca`. It still leads people to the name and maintains the first part of the brand: kitty likes. If the name is not available at all, try URL names like /kittylikesmusic or /kittylikesband. Always try to have the beginning of that URL the same as the others.

If you are able to keep your name and then add the word *music* at the end, that is one way to make a slight variation while maintaining your name and brand. Switching up to all sorts of different names or using words like *official* come off unprofessional and cheesy. That continuity of your name and your brand gives it that much more of a chance to continue to reach more people who are both searching directly for it or stumble upon it by accident.

Capitalizing on misspellings

Don't assume that people will spell your name right, even if you have an easy name. Think about the easiest ways that someone could misspell your name or band name, and consider buying those misspelled domains.

Now, this isn't like your correctly spelled name; you don't need to buy up nine different misspelling extensions or sign up for social media sites with that misspelling. That would be an excessive and ineffective waste of money. Still, grabbing a couple misspellings and simply redirecting them to your correct spelling or creating a couple landing pages that can send people to the right website is effective.

 Try adding some misspellings of your name into your social media and blog posts. It can create some optimization for your content that allows for someone who misspelled your name to find content that is about you. Also between the domain and some misspelled content, search engines may start to correct the misspellings and point them right to you.

Protecting that name

With the work you do in reserving, purchasing, owning, and controlling the domain name, different domain extensions, emails, blogs, social media pages, reviewing pages, business name, and the misspellings, you have the best chance that no one will use that name or phrase. They would have a very hard time trying to market it, when it is all pointed at, coming to, and belonging to you.

Copyrighting a name is not allowed. You can't copyright a domain name, either. These are pretty big misconceptions. This also includes your tagline. You can copyright elements of what is put on a website, but you can't copyright a website. That all falls under U.S. patents and trademarks, which is an option, but a very expensive one. The best steps to take for the protection of your name and brand initially is to lock it up so that no one else would want it or be able to use it and then look into the trademark options. If you're able to lock up and have all those different elements in place with that name, then it's worth going after the trademark.

Just because a name doesn't show up online, doesn't mean that someone else might not have the trademark on it. As mentioned earlier, do your due diligence, and make sure that name isn't trademarked before you put all that work into it.

Getting Your Logo and Font Working for You

Think about how many logos and fonts you see every single day. Then think about how you are able to recognize them from great distances . . . such as McDonald's signs, Subway signs, Shell Gasoline signs, and logos on top of Boston Red Sox or New York Yankees baseball caps. Think of the way the font or typeset is used on those teams' jerseys. Imagine the Honey Bee on Honey Nut Cheerios or even the logos and fonts of Facebook, Instagram, and Google. They all have familiar, uniform, and easily recognizable fonts and logos. Look at the cover of this book; then look at the fonts and the covers of any other For Dummies book.

Those similarities mixed with the uniformity and consistencies of recognition when it comes to logos and fonts allow for brands to be effective and have that impact. A great deal of your fan base comes from people who want to feel a sense of comfort because you and your brand have been around a while.

Consistency and uniformity in your design

Regardless of your logo or font, stick with it and stick it everywhere. Your font needs to stay the same so more people will recognize it as your font that goes with your logo. Imagine if you saw the Disney name in the cursive Coca Cola font. It wouldn't make sense.

Consistency and continuity in your branding date back to well before Internet and online marketing. The recognition of a brand becomes psychological. That comfort in consistency can bring in a potential fan with the ongoing recognition that much more over continuing to try your name in a series of different fonts with different logos all over the spectrum.

Make sure your logo and font are legible on the smallest item (such as a pen) to the largest item (such as stage banner). As much as you might want to go into amazing detail in the logo or a wild cursive and thin typeset for your font, the lack of clarity and legibility will hurt the productivity of your marketing and promotion.

Making your designs shine to increase visibility

As you begin to explore what you want your logo and font to look like, think about all the places they will go. The logo and font, in many cases, are the very first things that most people will see. They might see it on a T-shirt, poster, sticker, bass drum at a show where you might be opening for another act . . . your logo/font should be seen everywhere.

The more places you can imagine where you need your logo/font, the easier it is to make the final decision about what it should look like. Give a thought to how your logo/font might look on the following:

Letterhead	CD	Website header	Social media header
Posters	Clothing	Coffee cup	Water bottle
Online avatar	Bass drum	Towels	Bracelets
Shot glasses	Car decal	Buttons	Hats
Dog tags	Stage banners	Phone covers	Pens
Business card	Promo folder	Stickers	Merchandise table banner

Some of these items will only have the logo on them like the online avatars, those little graphics that are associated with each of your social media posts, but most of these items should have your logo, your font, your tagline, and your URL.

Keep the different products and placements in mind as you design your graphics or work with a designer in the early stages and you will have a logo and font that is able to work well across the spectrum of your branding for a long time to come.

After you're close to zeroing in the logo and font you like the most, upload them into the Google search function for photos. This helps you see what Google might bring up for comparisons. Although you might feel really strongly about a given design, if it's uploaded to Google and comes back with a large brand that you might be aware of or looks too much like another artist, it can be a good idea to make some alterations at that point to make it a little bit more yours and look a little less like it is someone else's.

Designing before you begin with the designer

There is a lot you can do before you hire a graphics designer. By taking the extra steps early on, you save money and time because you already have some ideas dialed in and sketched out.

A logo and font is a personal thing beyond just the business elements and you can mix business and personal together. Think of it like a combination of the two so they can work together and let your personality shine. If you think only business, you chance something being too boring; if you think only personal, you chance it not being business-like.

Make sure the designer you choose has these business and branding elements in mind. Some designers take a more artistic route. Align with and hire a designer who is going to brand you for the best level of visibility across the board, the web, and all products. By discussing with your designer the uses of the logo and font and how it needs to work, you give them a better outline and starting point to work from to give you the look you want.

Think about the things you like in fonts and logos as well as the things you don't like too. Begin to write up a list about what you like, what you don't like, and examples that you can show a potential designer from the Internet to get them going in the best direction possible.

For example, if you like the green in the Starbucks logo, mention that you would like Starbucks Green to be considered or used in some way. You don't have to find the exact color that Starbucks uses; the graphics person can do that.

If you like the four-leaf design in the Hilton Garden Inn logo, mention you like the four leaves and go into a little more description about why. Do you like the idea of four small emblems? Do you like the square that the leaves are in? What is it that draws your eye to that design?

Sharing the same concepts around fonts can help, too. Copy and paste links or pictures of five fonts you like as well as five fonts you hate. Note what you like and don't like to give your designer some direction.

Writing your band or artist name in a Word document and then formatting it using your favorite fonts can be a helpful tool. Find something you really like, then hand it off to a designer to edit and alter so it's yours. This can make the whole process easier and faster.

The more basic information you can give your designer about what you like and what you don't like, the easier it is to get your logo and font done. The logos that can cost the most come from the need for too many back and forth ideas mixed with poor planning and communication.

By almost pre-producing your logo and font before going to a designer, you get the same effect of pre-producing a song before you go in to the studio. Everyone is on the same page early on.

Finding the right designer for you

Just because a designer has a great résumé and has done great work, doesn't mean they are going to be a great fit for you. In the same way that you want to find the right recording studio or the right producer, you want to find the right designer to work on the image and font that you want for the front and center visual for everything.

Own your logo

The designer is working as an independent contractor and has no ownership and no way to receive percentages after the work is done. Buy your logo, buy your font, and don't allow for a situation down the line where they look for a cut in merchandise or items that have your logo or font on them. Make sure a very simple independent contractor agreement is signed and in place so that you have full ownership of what's been created for you.

Make sure the designer designed it

Make sure the logo and/or font the artist designs are actually designed by them! There are some designers who may use stock images or images that they stole from some one else to apply to your designs. Although there is no way to completely safeguard this from happening, adding a no-liability clause to your agreement with your designer should state that if someone comes back to you claiming the work your designer did for you came from somewhere else, it is on the artist to remedy the situation and pay what is owed. If it's found that the artist is at fault, and you need to rebrand the logo and the font, the designer is responsible for all fees connected with hiring another designer and making the adjustments to all your materials.

Get that logo in all formats

Make sure the designer gives you the logo and font in all file formats — from PDF to JPEG and the actual design files in Photoshop or whatever program they use. Again, you want to own these designs and have access to them to easily be able to adapt them for posters, social media headers, your website, your merchandise, and anything and everything else. From high-resolution printable files to low-resolution images that can be shared on social media, you want to have the array of files to be able to have the array of options as things come up.

Look at the work done they've for others

Make sure you like what they've created for others, and make sure that what you like was created within the budget you have available for design. Looking at what someone was able to design for $5,000, when you only have $500 to work with can be an issue. Find examples of logos the artist created and how they worked for both online presentation and physical products.

Get a statement of work with the invoice

Find out their costs, and get a statement of work from the designer. This way you know exactly what's being done, how many times you can go back and forth for edits or alterations, and when costs go up to meet expectations and deliverables.

Give the same attention to detail when looking for the best designer that you would give to anyone involved in the business side of your career. Along with looking at examples, be sure to contact references and former clients to ask about their experiences.

Designers competing for your logo

There are websites like 99 designs.com that first ask a series of questions about what you are looking for, then a number of designers get a chance to create their interpretation from the info you've given to them. You get to pick and choose from many options.

The cost of creating a logo can go from a virtually nothing to breaking-the-bank pricy. There are artists out there who can design a basic logo for as little as $5 through websites like Fiverr.com; however, you could go all the way up to a $12,000 design. Make sure you get all the information about the job and the costs before you start. I can't stress enough how important it is to hammer out a mutually agreeable contract so there are no big surprises at the end of the project.

For some of the less-expensive options, you get less edits and alterations and less formats. A safe, basic cost for budgeting a solid logo and font in all the formats can sit between $400 to $1,200. On the higher side, some designers create logos for upwards of $10,000.

Looking at different formats, sizes, and options

You need more than just the design and the logo. In some cases, a designer can help you create different formats of your logo for use across both physical and digital media; in other cases, you have to settle for fundamental files and basics from the designer and then find someone to help create a series of different sizes, formats, and layouts for your logo and font. Be sure to add to your statement of work that you will receive the graphics in .jpg, .png, and .eps formats to allow edits, adjustments, and changes to go much smoother and much cheaper.

At the foundation of it all, you want files that you can edit and adjust. You need the highest resolution possible for creating a gigantic stage banner, whereas you can use a lower resolution for your website. Your middle-of-the-road resolution is high enough to look strong online and on your promotional documents, but low enough to load a page fast.

From the front page of your website to your Facebook, YouTube, Google+, and Twitter headers, the consistency and continuity needs to be uniform. From your letterhead to business card, promo package to merchandise items, each of these has different size requirements and needs to be designed a little differently while still keeping the brand looking like it is coming from the same place.

Allowing for a page on your website or a link to a Dropbox file for promoters, booking agents, media, and others to be able to download the files in the formats that they need for posters, online ads, or to put in to local papers about your gig will help keep that professional and uniform look that much stronger.

The following is a list of the different ways to make your logo available for industry professionals (as well as to yourself) either online or accessible through the click of a link:

- ✔ The logo alone
- ✔ The font alone
- ✔ The logo and font together
- ✔ The logo, font, and the web address
- ✔ The logo, font, web address, and the tagline

These are the images that are used the most to promote you, your image, and your brand. This set is also used to create all of your merchandise, posters, business cards, letterhead, and anything else that you can put your logo on.

Have these five variations available in three levels of resolution. The first set in high, medium, and low resolution, should be available as links for anyone to access, while the higher resolution versions can be used by professionals for posters to be made and other merchandise materials to be created.

 When people request graphics, always send them a link unless they specifically request the file sent attached to an email. Large files can take a while to download and can tie up someone's email account, which is why a link is preferable.

The second set is created for your online presence. This includes the formats of the front page or the first things people view when they come to your website and what they see on the top of all your social media sites.

- ✔ Website main design or front page template
- ✔ Facebook header and avatar
- ✔ YouTube header
- ✔ Google+ header and avatar
- ✔ Twitter header and avatar

Across all social media sites, your brand should be consistent and in plain view. In other words, the logo you use on Facebook should be the same as the one you use on your website, or on YouTube. This makes it easier for fans to know they've found "the real deal" when they find your sites and pages.

Don't take one design and try to resize it to fit each of the size requirements for graphics on your website, Facebook header, Twitter header, and so on. It'll look messy, stretched, blurry, and unprofessional. Each of these has different requirements.

Pay careful attention to the requirements of each header as you upload as well. Follow the instructions as you click the image upload, format the designs per those requirements, and you will have the best-looking images on every page and on every device where your page is pulled up. Look at *Facebook For Dummies* by Carolyn Abram and *Twitter For Dummies* by Laura Fitton and Anum Hussain (both published by John Wiley and Sons, Inc.) for the exact sizing requirements for each of these social media sites and the graphics they allow.

The fundamentals of your branding, especially in the imagery, is the recognition of that brand. Make sure your fans know it's you! Stay uniform, stay consistent, keep true to the different file requirements for the different sites, and stay strong in how your logo and font show up across all mediums.

Using your logo and font on everything, everywhere

Now that your logo and your font are locked in and you have the files you need for all your different advertising options, you're in good shape and look professional to fans and potential investors.

Stay with your logo and font together on everything where you can. Make sure that you place your logo everywhere a graphic can be used. From the bass drum head to the poster, on the CD to the coffee cup, the car decal to the sticker, the letterhead to everywhere and on everything, make sure that logo is on it.

You can adjust the color of it, the way it's angled, and the basics of what's added around it, but make sure the logo remains the same. Your logo should always be consistent.

The same goes for your band name and the font. Except for your when your band name is used in printed articles and interviews, make sure your font is also consistent. Keep it uniform, and make it instantly recognizable.

Sometimes a promoter or marketer will use a different font. Going all diva won't help relationships, and it's not the end of the world. Always offer the links to your logo and font in various formats, but play nice if they don't use it. When it comes to you and the materials you create, however, always have it clear, consistent, and uniform.

Your logo and font help your branding base as they bring recognition to your music and your content. Take the time to get the best logo and font that you can as well as making it one you can stand by and continually use for a good time to come. As your popularity grows, the font can be removed, leaving just your logo, allowing people to know it's you with out any words at all.

Think the Rolling Stones tongue. Talk about an easily recognizable logo. And think, also, of Metallica. This is a great example of the font mixing with the logo to identify the brand.

Lastly, by creating, paying for, and owning it, regardless of who becomes involved with you or your band, you still have full ownership of the base of your brand, which allows you more profit on many more products on which you put your logo.

Branding Yourself

The art of branding includes the consistent use of your logo and font. When fans and consumers see your logo, you want them to picture you and your music in their minds . . . maybe also conjure up an image of what a great time they had at your last concert, or how much one of your songs means to them. Combining your logo and font with good marketing options is what branding is all about.

The application of your brand draws people to connect with you. They are going to see you in most cases first, so make sure what they see is clear and uniform; that's where your brand comes in. The uniformity, clarity, and consistency of your presentation from the logo and font to the tagline and other content can make all the difference in someone taking the time to click through or even recall your name after seeing it for some time to know what to look up.

Think about your brand as not just being memorable, but something you want people to memorize and relate to other things that will draw them back to you. From your name to the font you use for your name, the logo to the website and the ease of being able to find you regardless of what social network site or web page you are appearing on, how you remind your potential fans to look you up and how they relate to things outside of you or your music is all part of branding yourself.

The final step is taking all the visual and written parts of your foundation and marketing that brand to the widest audience possible through as many different avenues as possible with as many different topics as possible.

Optimizing your imagery on the web

Just uploading your logo and your graphics to your website can become one of the biggest missed opportunities in optimization of your logos, your graphics, and your pictures. The common mistake is that some one has an image or a photo and it is automatically named 64735264894.jpg or logo3.jpg. Some sites automatically change the name of the file as it is uploaded, but sites like Google love and optimize well-named photos. For more information about SEO, look at *SEO For Dummies* by Peter Kent (John Wiley and Sons, Inc.).

Name your pictures accordingly. Imagine you have a picture of your band with your logo in the middle. Going back to the Kitty Likes Avocado name, try renaming the photo:

kitty likes avocado, Funk rock, band picture, promo shot.jpg

You capture your name, the style you play, which is a little more vague and more likely to be searched on. This helps optimize that shot for the Internet and helps with the SEO for it.

Just because it's a picture of you — or even a video with you in it — doesn't mean it will optimize because you are visible in it. Your extra steps to name photos the correct way help yours photos be seen by that many more people who are searching directly for you. And others might come across you because of the key words you added to the photos.

Keeping consistency and uniformity in your branding and your close

You can create all kinds of different online content, from pictures and videos to some seriously good writing . . . even links to your website or related sites. When you create content for the web, always close with a call to action. This means that you send your reader off to do something specific; in this case you send them to your web page. Figure 7-2 shows a personal call to action from me, directing readers to my online presence. As part of this content, be sure that you maintain consistency and uniformity in your logo. As already stated, you want your fans (or potential fans) to see your logo and instantly know who you are.

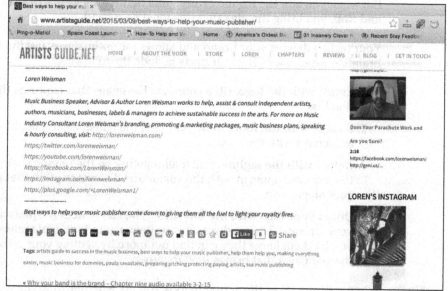

Figure 7-2:
This call to action gives readers several options for finding me.

Crafting Your Tagline and its Viability

The first words that define your brand to most people are your tagline. This is the information that gives the initial short definition or elevator pitch about exactly who you are. The elevator pitch is that 3 second no more than four or five word description that summarizes you. Everything you want to tell people isn't covered in a tagline, of course, but it creates the connection from your logo to your name to your sound and what you are about.

Your logo might not translate to someone thinking you're a musician. Your name might not, either. Let's say your band name is Kitty Likes Avocado, and the logo has a cat with an avocado. Your font clearly spells out Kitty Likes Avocado, and while it's perfectly clear to you that it's a band, others could think it is

✔ A cat product

✔ A fruit fly preventative

✔ A wellness and health blog or magazine

✔ A site that puts up random cat videos

✔ An avocado advocacy group

✔ Whole foods for cats

But when you add the tagline **Fruity Funk Scratching at the Drapes of Rock and Roll,** you bring the idea that this must be a band.

Your tagline defines your brand and allows for optimal use and the best branding experience. The four parts include the following:

1. **Entice with the logo.** Give your fans the image that captures their attention first.

2. **Engage with the font.** Show your fans the name, clearly legible as it associates with the logo.

3. **Define with the tagline.** Pull it all together so the person seeing it ties the logo and name in with the summarized elevator pitch that serves as your slogan too.

4. **Direct your fans with the link/URL.** The call to action equals a trip to your website. The reader saw your logo, name/font, and tagline. Now, you let them know they can find out more by visiting your website. It's the last piece that brings it all together.

When your fan takes the action to look you up, whether from the website they see associated with your logo, font, and tagline, or they remember your name and do a web search, they're looking specifically for you. Not someone with a name similar to yours; they want more info about you. By maintaining consistency and uniformity with your logo, however, your web traveler will have little doubt that they've found the correct page when they arrive at your site.

By maintaining the uniformity and having that same logo, tagline, and font showing up everywhere you are online, it brings a better sense of security and showcases a higher level of professionalism.

Just because you might not know, recognize, or see a tagline with an artist you like, doesn't mean they don't have one as part of their branding plan.

Creating a tagline to entice

With all the other elements in place, your tagline has to define, encapsulate, summarize, and draw interest so people want to know more. Here are a few examples of taglines that make the reader want to know more:

- Fruity Funk Scratching at the Drapes of Rock and Roll
- Heart-Driven Happy Pop
- Indie Retro Folk-Pop Duo
- A Gentleman of Soul
- A Rocktress Sculpted in Blues and Soul

Memorable taglines: Everyone has had one

Most recognizable brands have a great tagline. And you can bet that lots of time and money went into creating, testing, and marketing the words and phrases you know well.

Still, as memorable as they are, they also come from long-established companies that allow the phrases to be a little more vague, but they still show up with the logos, the fonts, and the websites, just like yours. Make sure that tagline is memorable, but also make sure it has the elements in place to entice, describe, and define a little more than some listed here.

I'm loving it

Live in your world, play in ours

Melts in your mouth, not in your hand

Don't leave home without it

They're grrrrrr-eat!

The best a man can get

These short taglines can only hint at the full description of what the artist or band may sound like, but that's exactly what you want. Think a quick one-two punch to draw everyone in. In a sense, tease them with the basic elevator pitch to make them want to stay on for a couple more floors to hear more about you.

Too many artists feel like they need to encapsulate the spectrum of who they are, where they came from, how they are doing something unlike anyone else, and just how amazing they are. On the opposite end of the spectrum, as an example of bad taglines, other artists with a little less confidence almost dance around long-tailed descriptions that can turn a potential listener or fan away like, "well, we have this sound that's kind of like someone else . . ."

The lack of confidence in the delivery of the tagline, as well as excessive arrogance, can turn away potential fans quicker than you can imagine.

When a tagline is clear, assertive, short, and can fit on a business card, it can help you move forward and invite people to want to know more.

An enticing tagline is a converting tagline. It makes people want to know what you're about!

If you were to go with

Rock and Roll

as your tagline, it's not very descriptive or memorable. It doesn't give the potential fan any reason to learn more about you.

On the opposite end of the spectrum, however,

> **Rock and roll that takes you on a journey through time and space as it makes you yearn for more as the groove feeds your soul**

is incredibly long and ineffective. Being way too vague isn't going to help draw in more people, just as being way too obvious or going with oversaturated terms that don't give enough detail won't spark any interest either.

Avoid telling people how they will feel, react, or respond to your music. Let them experience that for themselves. People are more sensitive to that than you might realize and even if only subliminally, you telling them what they will feel can become a challenge and a turn-off.

Asking others for help

Asking for fans to help with descriptors of your sound and your band can help you to take a step back and hear the words of how others would describe you and your songs. That fresh perspective can help to narrow down as well as find new word combinations you might not have thought about before.

Don't try for perfection

Avoid trying to come up with the perfect elevator pitch to describe your band or sound because it's next to impossible. Whatever you find will not hit the nail directly on the head, but a solid tagline will

- ✔ Encapsulate the overall basics of you and your sound
- ✔ Consolidate a few words to peak the widest array of engagement
- ✔ Create the interest for people to learn more about you

Location, location, location

Read it out loud. Think about how it fits on a business card, sticker, letterhead, and how it works with your font and logo. Does it look good across the online spectrum as well as on T-shirts, coffee cups, buttons, posters, and so on?

Keep your tagline font different and smaller than your name font. Worry less about the font of the tagline than the font of your name. It should be legible and clean but noticeably smaller as well as clear that it is serving as the tagline and not an extension of your name. Don't use the same font as your name. Because the tagline will be smaller, keep it a simple and very readable font. Never let a potential fan confuse your tagline with your name or think it's part of your name.

Applying Your Logo, Font, and Tagline

At this point, its not back to the drawing board, but it is time to go back to either your designer or someone who can set you up with the final formats for all graphic applications both online and off. Designs for web work, social media headers, products, and promotional materials should occur after the branding is in place.

All too often, musicians rush to get going on a website design or begin work on products without having the branding basics in place. There are also way too many web designers who will waste way too much time as they begin certain designs that need to be changed after the branding is finalized.

The branding is the foundation. The logo and its colors, the font of your name, and the tagline make up the roots of your brand that stretch out through your website, social media, promotional materials, products, and more. So start with the branding designs before you go to website design, graphic header designs, and product designs. You'll save a great deal of time and money.

Creating branded letterhead and press packs

For your promotional materials, apply the logo, font, tagline, and URL on every page. The easiest way to remind yourself of the importance of the branding on your letterhead and promotional packages is to think that every single piece of paper and part of that packet might get lost or mixed up with hundreds of others. The consistency and uniformity of your core branding and information on every page means that regardless of what happens, everyone looking at your materials, together or separated, will know it's you.

Keeping consistency everywhere

Across the board — from car decals and coffee mugs to the stage banner social media headers — keep your branding uniform and consistent. The familiarity in the designs and colors will prompt instant recognition!

Make sure your tagline is as much a part of your products (coffee cups, T-shirts, and so on) as your logo and name. Every time someone wears the T-shirt or takes a cuppa in your mug, you're getting free advertising.

Allowing the base of your branding to be rooted in the strongest uniformity that shows up everywhere and on everything brings that many more people to you, your music, and your products. Bring them in with solid branding from the business side and then keep them hooked with the creative side that was your main focus in the first place — your music.

Chapter 8

Getting Noticed: Your Keywords, Bio, and Call to Action

The root of your online presence is based in your content, not your music. Surprising statement, huh? Well, it's true. That content is often what people see first, usually before your music is ever heard. With correctly formatted keywords and keyword phrases, a well-optimized bio with closing signature, and the call to action that sends people where you want them to go, you're allowing yourself to be seen by that many more people, that much faster. With all these pieces in place, everything from publicity to posting online is worlds easier, takes less time, and has a greater impact.

With a cheat sheet template of all your keywords, keyword phrases, bio, and call to action in place, you have the materials for your own posting, promotion, and marketing. This enables you to send solid material to industry professionals, publicists, promoters, and reviewers in an instant.

Creating Keywords and Phrases for Your Bio

Before you paint a picture, you first need colors on the palette to work with. It's hard, frustrating, and ineffective to write a bio from start to finish without some type of "paints." Create a couple different lists of words and phrases, and you create a palette of different colors to paint the best bio for you right onto the canvas.

Although hiring a great writer to pen your bio can leave you with a work of art, all too often you're left with a bio that is much too long and can't be used effectively for its full online marketing potential.

To create your palette of phrases to use when crafting your bio, start with filling in each of the following eight lists with two- to four-word phrases that best describe your responses. Some phrases and words may overlap, but don't worry about it. Those could end up being some of the strongest descriptors for you to use.

List 1 – You or the band: Write 10 to 20 phrases that describe you as an artist or your band as individuals. Use words that best describe the personality or personalities, what you stand for, stand by, and believe in. List what you'd want to share with a new friend or potential lover. This list can include things like *history buffs, video gamers,* and *sushi lover.*

List 2 – Your music: Write 10 to 20 phrases that describe your music, approach to music, and your sound. Add the descriptors of your sound, your approach to music, your genre or genres. Have fun with this list. Avoid phrases like *Rock-n-Roll* because they're too vague and overused. Instead, try adding a word or words on the front or back to give it a more individualized punch, like *Melodic-n-Methodic Rock-n-Roll.*

List 3 – Your influences: List ten of your biggest musical influences and why. Include a short bullet point or sentence as to why and how you were influenced.

Your influences don't have to sound like you! If you're influenced by a classic Swedish progressive metal band, but you sound like modern dance pop, keep that one on the list. You are relating and connecting to more people that might enjoy or be influenced by the same thing but who also like different styles.

List 4 – Your comparisons: Write ten of the best comparisons to your sound and style. List who you think you sound like, and ask friends who they think you sound similar to. You can also add aspects of certain artists without claiming to be compared to the whole band. For example, "The crazy drums of the Who with the reggae feel of the Police." (Now that I think of it, I'd kind of like to hear what that sounds like!)

List 5 – Non-music influences: List the influences outside of music in your life. Maybe you're influenced by chefs, painters, racecar drivers, poets, writers, entrepreneurs, religious figures, politicians, or astronauts. Add them in this list.

List 6 – Comparisons outside of music: Write then comparisons outside of music. Imagine who you might be compared to if you were in another field. I was once called the *Gordon Ramsey of the Music Industry*. It brought an element of a persona outside of music to relate to someone in music. I liked that. The musician biz guy to the cook. Often comedians, celebrities that are not musicians, and even fictional characters can help fill this list out well.

List 7 – Five reasons why you think someone should listen to you: Write five things that you think makes you stand out in the music business. This list can be challenging as you determine five key points that make you stand out in the sea of musicians and bands today. Think hard here and don't shortcut. This can to go into your bio, and it can be used to explain who you are to investors, labels, managers, and others in the industry.

List 8 – Five elements you have going against you: Write down five elements or issues you have going against you. This is the humble list and the hardest one for many people. Write down what could make your career fail. As crazy as it sounds, this list is just as important as the others for finding the keywords that will help prevent this from happening. From medical concerns to criminal records, prior contractual obligations to debts, this is where you reveal the issues that are usually kept internally, but need to be considered and addressed. This is information that investors, labels, and managers are going to want to know as well.

These eight lists with over 90 phrases lay the foundation of your palette, to build your keyword phrases, bio, and call to action. Now it's time to pick up the brush, mix a few of these together, get rid of some other colors, and start to hone in on what best describes you.

Avoiding certain keywords and phrases

As you look over your lists of words and phrases, remove certain phrases that are too common and familiar. The following covers words that are over-used, oversaturated, or could deliver a message that's going to hurt more than help. Even if one of these exactly describes what you're looking for, use different words or phrases and avoid these at all costs. For example, saying "A different type of band with a unique and innovative sound" to describe yourself doesn't tell anyone anything about you or your sound.

- ✔ Innovative (Way overused.)
- ✔ Unique (Once again, way overused.)
- ✔ New (Everything is new, it's not helping.)

✔ Different (As soon as someone decides you sound like someone else, then you're no longer different to them, and this can kill interest.)

✔ Never been done before (The industry sees it as all been done before.)

✔ Hard-working and driven (Shouldn't that be everybody? Why say it?)

✔ Thought-provoking lyrics (One of my favorites; not to pick on anyone, but could you imagine an artist describing their lyrics as stale and boring?)

✔ Team players (Again, something you need to be in this business, no need to state it.)

✔ As soon as you hear it, you'll know! (Another overused phrase that also brings out a cockiness you don't need.)

✔ Music with a message (All music has a message, so avoid this phrase.)

✔ Showing up the rest (Don't talk bad or down about others when you look for the best words to represent you.)

There are many bands and artists that want to reach the exact same people, fans, industry professionals, and media contacts that you do, which is why the bio and the keyword phrases are so important. Take the time to build your keyword phrases and bio so you're seen by the most people possible. When creating the best keywords, phrases, bio, and call to action, think about how these phrases influence:

✔ A new fan

✔ An existing fan

✔ A friend

✔ A reviewer or interviewer

✔ A music industry professional

✔ An investor, sponsor, or potential endorsee

Create phrases that enable you to connect with a diverse group of people. When you send out promotional packages, each package will be personalized, but the basic content and keywords should be uniform in all of them.

Reviewing your keywords and phrases for discoverability

When reviewing your main phrases, look at those bands that can be or have been compared to you. Do a little research to find out what their phrases are so you can find the best ways to describe you while not using too many phrases that result in other bands and artists coming up that aren't you.

For example, when you search "fruity funk scratching at the drapes of rock and roll," it results with Kitty Likes Avocado. But if a band uses a less-descriptive term or phrase, such as "classic rock and roll," too many different artists show up. This less-descriptive term doesn't help the band that wants to be found.

Try searching Google and YouTube to see which keywords phrases conjure up. Does your search bring up similar artists and bands that may have fans you want to attract? Those are some keepers then! Although you want to point people directly to you, a great number of phrases are already taken. Still, it's better to be found as part of a search with another band that's close to your sound and style than to not be found at all.

Most people searching online for music like yours aren't searching for you directly. They haven't heard of you yet! They're searching for the words that describe your sound or bands that you might sound like, so keep that in mind as you create the phrases that best describe you.

Think of it as drawing people to new a restaurant. You don't want to go too broad or too unique. Think of phrases that give people

- An idea of what you're about
- A sense of familiarity with something they already know
- A comparison to things they trust and like
- A chance to explore, yet still feel safe
- Ideas and concepts that they can relate to, outside of music

Your keywords, phrases, and bio can have a positive or negative psychological effect on a potential fan, industry professional, or media contact right from the start, so make it a good one by using descriptors to draw people in and avoiding the overused statements that push them away.

When building the keywords and phrases, stay confident, but be humble. Can you use those words to describe yourself to a new, young fan and use those same words to describe yourself to one of your biggest inspirations, heroes, or idols? Uniformity is key! Make sure you find the words that express confidence but also humility.

You can use many of the analytics sites to get a sense of the exact ratings, position, and use of keywords and phrases, but this is something you can get lost in and can be a major waste of time. Google Adwords can help you know the exact rankings. www.ubersuggest.org can help with different phrasings, almost like an online thesaurus. These additional tools can help in refining your word choices.

Making a Keyword-Rich Descriptive Bio

Your keyword-phrase-rich bio should include a tagline, which often is used as the last sentence of the short bio. Keyword-phrase rich means that you've used phrases that can be searched on to lead back to you in Google, YouTube, Yahoo!, and Bing. This tagline is the content that should be seen everywhere and on everything, from the album to T-shirt, the pens to the stickers. This is that elevator pitch descriptor that will often draw fans in first when they come to your written content after they may have already seen your logo or tagline. For more about taglines, refer to Chapter 7, "Creating Your Brand."

Starting with a short bio

Creating a clear and informative bio (around 100 words) is a crucial aspect of your marketing. Many bios are long, drawn out, and don't immediately describe anything about the artist, music, style, or sound. To craft your short bio, follow these steps:

1. **Start with your one-liner, the first sentence of your bio.** This is a little longer than the tagline and unlike the tagline; this has your name in it. By mixing together and combining some of the keywords, build a sentence that includes three keyword phrases. These phrases combine to make a short first-introduction sentence. Here's an example of the phrases used for Kitty Likes Avocado:

   • Rock and blues

   • Alternative funk

   • Pop-infused sound

   Then add inviting words that showcase humility with confidence or humor to connect them. For this example, how about "serves up" and (for the humor element), a lead-in with "clawing at."

   You can also play with words like:

   • Deliver (s)

   • Perform (s)

   • Share (s)

   • Explore (s)

   • Combine (s)

These words connect the descriptors in an inviting and humble way (to see some words to avoid, check out "Avoiding certain keywords and phrases" earlier in this chapter). Then add an element of humor, something tied in to your name or sound while still focusing on the root of the music.

And here's an example of the complete one-liner for Kitty Likes Avocado:

> Clawing at the alternative funk genre woven in to a scratching post of rock and blues, Kitty Likes Avocado serves up a smooth and fruity pop-infused sound with the attitude of a kitten on catnip.

For your one-liner or any type of content, invite, share, and ask, instead of tell, order, or force. Don't tell people how they're going to feel, what they're going to think, or what they need to know. Share instead of shout! Allow them to choose how to react.

Comparisons outside of music can work. For instance, "like a kitten on catnip" gives an example that people can relate to and be interested in learning more about. On the opposite end of the spectrum, telling someone your sound is going to hit them like a train running off the tracks insinuates a certain arrogance as well as an image that might be more mocked than draw curiosity or interest.

2. **Bring in the tagline you designed with your logo.** The tagline should serve as the closing sentence of your short bio, and there should be content in between your one-liner and your tagline. Make sure your content flows from one sentence to another. Here's the tagline from Kitty Likes Avocado from last chapter.

> Fruity Funk Scratching at the Drapes of Rock and Roll

And here's the one-liner going straight into the tagline for use later on.

> Clawing at the alternative funk genre woven in to a scratching post of rock and blues, Kitty Likes Avocado serves up a smooth pop infused sound with the attitude of a kitten on catnip. Kitty Likes Avocado is fruity funk scratching at the drapes of rock and roll.

3. **Fill in the rest of the details for your short bio to create both the short bio and extended elevator pitch.** Learn more about an elevator pitch in Chapter 7. Think of your tagline as your speedy three-second catch phrase. Think of your one- liner as the six-second introduction, and of your short bio as the elevator pitch lasting no more than 25 seconds. They're all fast, and they're all to the point and deliver that first impr ession message you want to get across.

Read it out loud, with all the content you create. See what it sounds like and not just what it reads like. This makes all your content read and sound that much better across the board.

Now add a comparison sentence that captures readers' attention. Add the details or descriptors of a comparison to an artist like this:

- The genre combinations of Sinatra or Sid Vicious

- The energetic vibe of Phish

- The similarities of Little River Band

- The combination of Nirvana and Grateful Dead

- The element of Drake and Moby

These bring a connection and comparison to that artist in a way that entices the reader to want to know more about you. Using two to four comparisons in the second sentence while using these different descriptors takes your bio up to a whole different level, reaching more people. In the following sentence, use keyword phrases to expand on the one-liner and tagline. Apply that idea of expanding and contrasting here. Many times, some of the one-liners and taglines you might have thrown away can be used as this third sentence.

Have fun with it. Use a play on words or create a combination that would pique curiosity, such as:

> If Nirvana had Michael Buble on vocals and a horn section; or imagine The Police and Chicago playing Billy Joel songs. This touches the tip of how Kitty Likes Avocado's sound and songs can be described.

Then wrap it up. Find a closing sentence before attaching the tagline at the end that pulls it all together.

Here's an example of a full short bio with a one-liner opening, body, and tagline at the end that includes comparisons, influences, and basic details:

> Clawing at the alternative funk genre woven in to a scratching post of rock and blues, Kitty Likes Avocado serves up a smooth pop-infused sound with the attitude of a kitten on catnip. Mixing an array of inspirations like Steely Dan, Red Hot Chili Peppers, Buddy Guy, and Justin Timberlake with each member's diverse musical background creates their large musical litter box of soul. If Nirvana had Michael Buble on vocals and a horn section, or imagine The Police and Chicago playing Billy Joel songs, that touches the tip of how

their sound and songs could be described. Taking nothing all that seriously, enjoying their catnaps and daily smoothies with different fruits, avocado, garlic, and ginger, their playful music comes from an array of influences, attitudes, humor, and arguments. Kitty Likes Avocado is fruity funk scratching at the drapes of rock and roll.

To add the tagline at the end of the bio, reiterate the name of the band and go back to adding one of the connection words, such as is, delivers, shares, performs, brings.

It's that simple and it should be that brief. Explore deeper versions of longer bios, but always start with your short bio to pull in new fans and make them want more. Your elevator pitch written at a series of different lengths allows you to capture attention instead of sending it running for the hills. Stay away from three-page bios that go on and on; they only serve to turn off reader interest.

"So and so started playing at the age of 4" and "this artist has had the music in them since they can remember" are some of the worst opening lines you can use. Think fast; think catch and capture the imagination of your reader. You have seconds to draw in or lose a new fan. Make those seconds count with the best phrasings.

Creating a medium- and longer-length bio

The longer bios give you a little more room to add thoughts and fuller sentences that are not so much about the keyword phrases, search engine optimization the elevator pitch. You capture them in the short bio and keep them reading on. This is where you can go into more detail.

Your medium bio adds a second paragraph to the short bio (see the previous section) to make it twice as long. Your long bio then adds one more paragraph that makes the bio three paragraphs in length. Keep the continuity by always keeping the short bio as one paragraph (about 100 words); the medium bio (about 200 words) should include the short bio paragraph as well as a second paragraph; and then the long bio (not over 500 words) should combine the short and medium bio with a new third paragraph.

Do not use more than 500 words for your long bio. Use those extra details you want to put in the end of the bio into content, blogs, and videos about the band on your website and social media.

In the medium bio, expand on the keyword phrase lists you came up with.

✔ Things about the artist or band outside of music, such as

- The bassist is a terrible driver.
- The guitar player can't go two days without pizza.
- The singer has five cats.
- The drummer is still a garbage man.

Take the approach of gaining interest through headline-like sentences as you build the medium and long bio. Use the words and phrases that you came up with before to expand on fun, interesting, and even heartwarming tidbits about you or your group.

That vicarious relationship with a fan or potential fan can draw them in that much more. Relate, share, and connect with your audience. Stay away from using the medium and long bio sentences to talk about how much you rock; how you're taking over the business; how you show up all the rest; and how the reader has never experienced anything like you before.

Instead, focus on sharing your hobbies, stories, beliefs, and experiences. Here are some examples:

> Kitty Likes Avocado takes a nerdy and technical approach to the lyrics while still keeps a funk-based dirty sound in the music.

A little silly, but puts a better and more relatable idea across rather than stating

> Eloquent, deviant, and thought-provoking lyrics that sear the ethereal soul over a bed of the best distortion you have ever known.

or

> An avid runner, the vocalist views certain shows like marathons and trains his voice like he's heading out on a two-hour jog.

Again, relate to your audience. Show confidence in the words, but stay away from the excessive hype.

The medium and long bio give you room to play, but don't go playing too long. You can expand some; don't go on and on. Shorter and more compact bios get greater attention than four-page diatribes. You grabbed them with the short; now expand, extend, and embellish just a bit, but don't get too carried away.

Understanding the importance of your influences and comparisons

The comparisons and influences section of the bio helps catch the attention of readers who might like those artists, plain and simple. Including a couple comparisons in the short and medium bio gives you a line to those that are fans of the ones you choose. With influences, add those in the longer bio. A fan might be inspired by the same person, band, artist, or thing as you.

Don't worry about being compared to others. It's a good thing and enables people to relate to you and opens a door to you that otherwise wouldn't be there. Comparisons and influences in your bio extend your net and your visibility. These influences and comparisons can also make for great social media posts, videos, and content down the line. Talk about, write about, and share what another artist does that influences you and your music, or offer your thoughts on how you are compared to them.

Keyword phrases for filling in the blanks

Filling in the blanks is a good way to showcase where you came from, but also adds a sense of humor that can be fun. This is specifically for coming up with additional keywords and content to add to sites like Google+, Facebook, and others that allow for longer bios or additional information on the artist. You have plenty of room on many different sites to add information that can include influences, sounds comparisons, other names, bragging rights, or other content like occupation, employer, and so on. These websites serve as places for references and optimization.

For example, with the influences for Kitty Likes Avocado, they went with a joke around the ideas of cats:

> Top Cat, Bill The Cat, Bentley, Heathcliff, Scratchy, Stimpy, Grumpy Cat, Henri le Chat Noir, Angry Cat, Tom, Garfield, Cheshire Cat, Cat in the Hat, Sylvester, Black Cat, Catwoman, Hello Kitty, Puss in Boots, My Cat from Hell, Cat on a Hot Tin Roof, Colonel Meow, Hellcat, Felix the Cat, Morris, Arlene, Schrodinger, Music Business Cat, and Jackson Galaxy

The theme here is humor, but it also ties into the kitty vibe. It doesn't always have to be a joke, but what different words, character, or phrases can you use around the idea of your name that a web search might bring to you? In this case, you used the cat theme of famous comic cats to sexy fictional cat characters to that dude who trains cats.

Comparisons are easier than you think

Comparisons don't have to perfectly compare with you. Similarities, comparisons that might pertain to a single instrument, a vocal styling, a production element, or a songwriting element can be included. Don't worry about an exact comparison, and think about the wider range and the array of similarities. Figure out elements of your sound that can be compared to other artists, and you can compare vocal styles, guitar sounds, piano riffs, and more. The versatility of different aspects allows you to expand on different names and reach a much wider audience.

Kitty Likes Avocado's comparison list includes: Toad the Wet Sprocket, PFunk, James Taylor, Jason Mraz, Earth Wind and Fire, Chicago, Nirvana, Soundgarden, Red Hot Chili Peppers, Michael Buble, The Police, Snoop Dog, Garth Brooks, Pharrell Williams, Mumford and Sons, Stevie Wonder, Michael Jackson, Tribe Called Quest, Cat Stevens, Daft Punk, Pearl Jam, and Steely Dan.

That's a diverse list, but if you step back and think about the smallest aspects of each artist, it's completely possible to compare each of them to the band.

All your keywords, phrases, influences, and comparisons make for additional reinforcing marketing content down the line. Your inspirations do not have to sound like your music. If you're a death metal band that's inspired by Barry Manilow, add that sentence. Discuss what you like about Barry. While you sound nothing like him, you might connect with others who have similar tastes to yours.

If a social media site asks where you are based, add that city or town. With the room you are given to add elements of comparisons, similarities, or any type of additional information, add it! The more you fill in, the more you expand and extend where you are allowed, the more you are reaching out to those that could be searching. Fill in any and every blank space on any and every social media site you sign up for to build up that many more ways to be found.

Adding a Call to Action: Give Fans Direction

The *call to action* is your signature for blogs, videos, and other content that serves as a direction for where fans should go to find out more. It should get your audience to do something — usually in the form of clicking links, calling a number, or performing another activity to get more information. In most cases, the best calls to action come from the one-liners and taglines in your bio, and they close with a few of your key social media sites and your website. As you market yourself with strong content, you want to close with the places where people can get to you.

If you create the coolest piece of content, something that goes crazy viral and is shared by other people, how are they going to find their way to its creator if you don't give them direction? Always close with the call-to-action signature in videos, blogs, and longer-form content.

Building the best signature for your content

Your signature is your calling card, the set of directions, and marching orders to allow people to know, at a glance, who you are, what you do, when you're playing, where fans can find out more about you, and how to get in touch with you or your management.

You gave them the content to spark their interest; now give them the information, location, and branding to set that interest on fire. Using the examples from earlier in this chapter, take the one-liner and then add the tagline:

> Clawing at the alternative funk genre woven in to a scratching post of rock and blues, Kitty Likes Avocado serves up a smooth and fruity pop-infused sound with the attitude of a kitten on catnip. Kitty Likes Avocado is fruity funk scratching at the drapes of rock and roll.

This creates the one liner and the tagline as well as capturing a number of keyword phrases that help build the bio, including alternative funk, rock, and blues and pop-infused. After you add your one-liner and tagline, add the elevator pitch for what they can get and where they can get it:

> For more info about Kitty Likes Avocado, their shows, music, merchandise, videos, news and updates, visit: [Your Website Here]

The band name is repeated for a third time, and part one of the keyword phrases from the tagline is used again. Without the web links, the example call to action looks like this now:

> Clawing at the Alternative funk genre woven in to a scratching post of rock and blues, Kitty Likes Avocado serves up a smooth and fruity pop-infused sound with the attitude of a kitten on catnip. Kitty Likes Avocado is fruity funk scratching at the drapes of rock and roll. For more info about Kitty Likes Avocado, their shows, music, merchandise, videos, news, and updates, visit: [Your Website Here]

Close with the name of who's delivering the content to get the conversion of people who want to learn, see, and connect more. This is more effective than constantly asking people to like, follow, and share all the time without giving them a reason.

Leading your fans

When picking your domain and social media names, think easy, consistent, and uniform. The easier it is for a fan, industry professional, or reviewer to know your online name, the easier it is to lead them to where you want them to go.

When searching for domain names for your website, search at the same time for what is available for use on social media sites. As an example, the following list shows my name on 16 major networking sites. I was able to capture them all except Google+. The uniformity and consistency make it easier for people to find you and go where you want them to go.

http://lorenweisman.com/

https://twitter.com/lorenweisman/

https://myspace.com/lorenweisman/

https://spreaker.com/lorenweisman/

https://instagram.com/lorenweisman

https://linkedin.com/in/lorenweisman/

https://reverbnation.com/lorenweisman/

https://vine.co/lorenweisman/

https://plus.google.com/+LorenWeisman1/

http://loren-weisman.tumblr.com/

https://youtube.com/lorenweisman/

https://facebook.com/lorenweisman/

https://pinterest.com/lorenweisman/

https://soundcloud.com/loren-weisman/

https://about.me/lorenweisman/

https://vk.com/lorenweisman

You may have to make certain adjustments due to a specific character limit, but stay with the beginning of your branded name. For instance, https://twitter.com/kittylikesavocado is not allowed because it has too many characters; for this site, you use https://twitter.com/kittylikesavoca.

When you use your call to action, keep it simple. Give your website, twitter, a video channel, and Facebook addresses. (As social networking sites change and evolve, you can change the networks in the call to action.) For example:

http://kittylikesavocado.com/

https://twitter.com/kittylikesavoca/

```
https://youtube.com/kittylikesavocado/

https://facebook.com/kittylikesavocado/
```

Keeping the call to action the same is a good idea, but if you find a boost of popularity on your Instagram site, subtract one link and add that link instead.

Always remove the *www* in a website address. Start with http:// and if the page you're sending them to has a security certificate, add the s to make it https:// — search engines read that faster because it's a secure site. Also, double-check to make sure you're adding the link correctly. Some secure sites require the www, so whereas `https://barnesandnoble.com/` won't connect you, `https://www.barnesandnoble.com/` takes you to the book site. The same goes for the forward slash at the end of a domain name.

Make sure to also add a forward slash at the end of a page. Adding a link like http://kittylikesavocado.com with no forward slash only allows the search engines to look at that page, whatever is on your landing page for your website. When the spiders crawl through, (those parts of search engines that dig deep into the pages) and all you give them is a page, adding the forward slash and creating `http://kittylikesavocado.com/` tells the spiders that there are other pages. Instead of stopping on the front page, you give the spiders a green light to look at other options like: kittylikesavocado.com/about, kittylikesavocado.com /music, kittylikesavocado.com/contact, kittylikesavocado.com/store, and so on. Some pages send you to a dead page with the forward slash, so always double-check. Look into building a website for dummies as a reference for secure and nonsecure websites.

When you bring all of these tips together, you get your full call to action with explanation, description, and direction like the one from Kitty Likes Avocado:

Clawing at the alternative funk genre woven in to a scratching post of rock and blues, Kitty Likes Avocado serves up a smooth pop-infused sound with the attitude of a kitten on catnip. Kitty Likes Avocado is fruity funk scratching at the drapes of rock and roll. For more info about Kitty Likes Avocado, their shows, music, merchandise, videos, news, and updates, visit:

```
http://kittylikesavocado.com/

https://facebook.com/kittylikesavocado/

https://instagram.com/kittylikesavocado/

https://twitter.com/kittylikesavoca/
```

With the full call to action, direction to your website or three other social media sites, you have signed, sealed, and delivered the best directions for people to find you as well as given them the best directions on where you want them to go.

Content . . . Then call to action

Always present the content before the call to action. You're engaging with fans and reaching out to new ones at the same time. If all you do is constantly list gigs, ask for people to buy music and merchandise, or like this page and share that link, you exhaust and lose your audience. Sharing is caring and connecting brings the conversions. Try these:

- ✔ Share that photo and then close it with a call to action that tells viewers where they can see more photos of you with your call to action.
- ✔ Post that video and then tell people where your other videos can be seen with your call to action.
- ✔ Add lyrics and tell fans where they can hear the music with your call to action.
- ✔ Write a blog that talks about experiences, influences, or stories to engage your existing audience while you entice the potential new fans as you sign it with the call to action.
- ✔ Review, highlight, or share about another artist where you cross-market but still end with your call to action.

Watch for spamming. Your call to action is a closer and not the lead-in. Direct market yourself, your products, or music — once to twice a week (at most) is best. If you do it every day, you end up spamming and potentially losing the audience. Avoid spamming by always sharing content that leads to your call to action.

Your action of content keeps your existing audience engaged as you work to connect with more and more people. The more you post the right way, create and share content that is yours (and even other people's content), followed by a call to action, you're entertaining, networking, and engaging first, then directing them to the store where you want them to buy music and merchandise, the links where they can find out where you're playing, and the links including your website and other social media pages where they can connect with you next.

Optimizing Your Message

With a strong one-liner, tagline, short bio, and keyword phrases in your bio, it's time to optimize your message, words, and brand everywhere you can. Organizing and creating a Word document or spreadsheet cheat sheet makes this task easier and faster. Set up a simple list in a file folder on your desktop for yourself that includes the tagline, one-liner, short bio, call to action, and your main keyword phrases from your bio.

Keep the photo images of your logo, font, main photos, and headers that you have designed in that same online folder. Use Word or spreadsheet docs so it's easy for you to access, copy, and paste any of the content. This makes optimizing your message, content, information, and images as easy as click, copy, and paste. It also streamlines all your branding content, so that when a new social media site is added or a reviewer, industry professional, or booking agent requests those materials, you have them organized and readily available.

In the file, include all the sites, emails, passwords, and any other pertinent information for the places where you placed this content. This also serves as a reminder to check these sites and make sure they are still live; if a format has changed, you can make the small adjustments.

Placement and uniformity of your tagline, bio, call to action, and keywords

Now that you've organized your content, it's time to optimize across the web. From your own website to social media sites to your physical and digital promotional materials, you have the pieces of the foundation together. Now to lay the blueprint. Your logo, band name font, and tagline should be everywhere, from digital content to physical products.

Your tagline

The uniformity of your tagline is almost as crucial as your name. Think of the tagline as the descriptor for your name and your logo. The average person walking down the street will see that band name, artist name, or logo, but will they know it's a musician? Even if you have a website on that hat, T-shirt, sticker, or whatever — what makes them take that next step to look you up? It's that tagline, and it's the first element that should be placed on everything from products to graphics to the top of your website and social media header graphics. Own your tag line and get it everywhere. For more information about taglines, check out Chapter 7.

Your bio, keywords, and call to action

This is where placement is as key and crucial as it is simple. For every social media site you have, add as much of the information as you can. The content length on different sites will differ. For example, on Twitter you only have 200 characters on the front page, so if you use some of that space on your band name, you might only be able to use your tagline or squeeze in that one-liner. (Learn more about one-liners earlier in this chapter in the "Starting out with a short bio" section.)

As different sites only give you so many words or characters, take stock in what's available. For instance, on Twitter, don't worry about filling in your website, because Twitter gives you a free field to add your URL without taking away from the 200 characters. The same goes for your location; you can add that in a separate field. Make the most of the small spaces you have on sites like Twitter to get as much information out there as you can.

On other sites, such as Facebook and Google+, you have ample room to add your full bio and even close it off with the call to action. If there is the room allotted, then add your content. Other websites will offer forms for you to fill out with content such as influences or comparisons; fill those in from your keywords sheet with as much space as they allow. The same goes for keywords. If a site asks you for keywords or keyword phrases or a post on YouTube, Tumblr, or any other site, then add them. Don't go crazy, but get those keyword phrases you want to be searched for on the sites where people are searching.

Different keywords to collect

Think about ways to use words and descriptors that tie into the phrases that you planned as well as the content that can be engaged and enjoyed in the moment. If you're posting something around the baseball playoffs, make baseball analogies. It doesn't matter if you're into baseball, football, hockey, soccer, or any other sport. It's about how you can tie a word, phrase, or idea to the media of the moment and the phrases that everyone's using. From the relative events happening in the moment to the long-term words that can grab people looking for similar elements but being drawn to you, always take that extra second to check and be aware of what is happening on any given date or time.

Keeping it all uniform

Uniformity and continuity is important because the more places online where the same information is posted the same way, the optimization drives higher and higher online. Spend time on each site that you sign up for to find out how much you can post of your bio, where you can place your call to action, how many links you can add, and if you can upload other media as well. As mentioned earlier in this chapter, it's imperative to keep the information the same everywhere.

Keep the keyword phrases tied to you and your list. You can add keyword phrases that are related to the content or post you are putting up, but as a whole avoid adding keywords that have nothing to do with you, the content, or your music. It's a practice that can get you in trouble with the search engines and comes off like you're spamming.

Using hashtags with keyword phrases

Hashtags — those links proceeded by the pound sign (#) — create a searchable link for users with an interest in certain words or phrases. Your keyword phrases can be helpful to add some extra punch to your bio, call to action, and specific keyword phrases when allowed on certain sites. Make sure if you are using a hashtag in a bio that it works as a hashtag. It looks unprofessional if you're overusing hashtags; they end up being words with a number sign in front of them. Most hashtags should be used in your content and posts.

Hashtagging your name or song names are not usually items people are searching on. For example, #KittyLikesAvocado is a waste of a hashtag, though adding #Fruityfunk, #smoothpop, #alternativefunk, or #popinfused has a chance to capture an array of people looking for those specific topics and descriptions.

Check in with www.hashtag.org when creating certain content and posts to see what's popular and being clicked. While #rockandroll may be too big of a search, #rockandrollballetsounds turns up nothing. The key is finding a happy medium of your words, what people are searching on, and how you can be seen with all the millions of people out there trying to grab attention with hashtags.

Hashtag keyword phrases can slowly be added to your materials. While no one might be searching #fruityfunkscratchingatthedrapesofrockandroll, which is the tagline for Kitty Likes Avocado and a bit long for a hashtag, adding that hashtag to posts every few weeks as well as the hashtag of your band name can help to slowly build up your brand recognition over time. The organization of your content, keywords, bio, and call to action makes picking, choosing, and switching out hashtags easier and faster for each post you have up. It also makes tracking what's working and what isn't a whole lot more simple, too. When you see engagements and sales going up after certain posts, you can figure out which words, phrases, and hashtags are working best for you.

Be careful with hashtags and go a little more sparingly on sites like Facebook with three to four hashtags, and two to three maximum on sites like Twitter. Other sites like Instagram are practically fueled by hashtags and hashtag searching, so go to town. (Instagram allows for up to 30 hashtags. Add them all.) But also, try to build some content around it for a potential reader.

Switching them up also gives you a better chance at reaching a wider audience. Whereas you might use a specific keyword phrase or hashtag that ties directly to you, if the post is about a football game, another musician, food, or anything else, add that hashtag as well. But, always make sure you are hashtagging relating items and not just grabbing a hashtag to try to grab a fan. Some sites penalize for that if you are caught. For instance, if you put up a post about a new song called "Roger's Foot Funk" and you add the hashtag #HappyFourth because it's a hot tag due to it being July 4th, it's really not helping. What you use for hashtags should directly relate to what you're posting. If you want to use #Happyfourth as a hashtag, then write a post about the holiday.

Using hashtags on Twitter

Twitter allows for hashtags right in the bio, so applying them can add that much better of a chance of being found. For example, here is the Twitter bio for Kitty Likes Avocado.

> Clawing at the #alternativefunk genre woven into a scratching post of #rock & #blues, #KittyLikesAvocado is #Fruity #Funk #scratching at the drapes of Rock&Roll

This is the first part of their one-liner, tied to their tagline. Because you only have 160 characters to use for your Twitter bio, you have to mix elements of your bio. Still, keep it as uniform as possible. In this case, the first half of the one-liner sentence goes right into the tagline.

Now, the band has seven hashtags in its bio, including its name:

> #Alternativefunk #rock #blues #kittylikesavocado #fruity #funk #scratching

Although *rock*, *funk*, and *blues* are more widely used and vague terms, they still show up as you put up an Instagram post. They're still helpful more in the moment, while more personalized terms like your name or even #musicbusinesscat result in people finding content that's mostly yours.

Using hashtags on Instagram

Instagram, a social network designed for sharing pictures from mobile devices, allows 30 hashtags and 2,200 characters. Pushing beyond these limits means only the photo will be posted, and you lose the promotional elements of your content and hashtags.

Think beyond just a picture or a selfie. Consider how to market and connect to people who see you on Instagram and convert them to fans, followers, and customers ready to buy your music, merchandise, and concert tickets.

The easiest answer is by not getting lost in the sea of people who are just posting pictures for fun and popularity. There's a great business aspect to Instagram; just remember that before you push to upload a shot with a funny phrase and make it a post that's nowhere near as effective as it could be.

Focus on a YouTube, an Instagram, or a Google+ post and then share that link to other pages to expand your reach by keeping it simple and saving time. Just make sure to add a solid headline to tell people where they're being sent and the gist of what they're going to see.

Putting it all together for best results

The combination of using your keyword phrases, bio, and call to action to create uniformity on your website, social media sites, and promotional materials takes you miles beyond many others.

When the industry sees the application of content branding early on with artists, it shows professionalism and an attention to detail that many lack.

Having your primary keyword phrases as well as your call to action, short, medium, and long bios ready to copy and paste will save you time, make it easier to add content to new sites, all while optimizing your brand, band, and content everywhere. The compounding, consistency, and uniformity of your bio, keywords, call to action, and well-designed posts online as well as well-produced promotional materials offline allow for the best chances to get your message and music out.

Chapter 9

Securing Your Music and Brand

In This Chapter

▶ Clarifying your work and play relationships

▶ Dealing with contracts, lawyers, and expectations

▶ Handling publishing, copyrights, and who gets what

▶ Protecting your music and your sanity

- -

The security of your art, music, brand, and well-being in the music business should absolutely be a priority. All too often, though, it ends up being addressed way down the line, usually when problems arise from issues that weren't understood, agreed upon, and put in to writing early on. Security for your music, brand, content, graphics, and business is easier, more affordable, less stressful, and more productive when you address it in the early stages. If you've ever asked yourself the question "should I get this in writing?" the answer is a resounding yes. Always!

Finding the Best Types of People to Work With

Securing your art and career takes more than you alone. Even in the most independent do-it-yourself (DIY) models, lawyers, accountants, consultants, and advisors can offer the best approaches for contracts, bookkeeping, copyrights, and publishing. Many who claim to have self-produced all their music often have a co-producer in the background or in the wings. The job description of a music producer is covered in Chapter 3. Basically a producer helps to organize the music, the musicians, and the recording process. On the opposite side of the fence, those who claim they just downloaded a template contract or started a company online without consulting a lawyer have only an entity that is nowhere near as secure as they think.

Find the right lawyer for you and for your situation, someone who comes with credentials and recommendations. Odds have it the guy who represents a famous person in the music business or handles a major artist isn't the professional you need. Find someone you can work with on your budget with your goals in mind and the ability to deliver for your needs.

Finding the right fit comes down to what people can deliver for your given situation and not what they have delivered to others in situations that are very different than yours. It's also about making sure that you research each person. Email or call references, and do your due diligence that these lawyers, publishers, accountants, and other business professionals have done for others what they claim they can do for you. Always check to make sure they have done it recently.

A great lawyer who hasn't had any real independent clients in ten years most likely is not a good fit if you are an independent artist. Times have changed in the music business. There are way too many people, companies, and services that haven't done anything of substance or been able to help clients in years. They use their reputation from the past to lure in clients who they end up hurting more than helping. Choose carefully and do some solid research of those you want involved with your career.

Locking in the foundation of your business

It's important to secure a solid business foundation when you're first starting out. By having trustworthy business professionals (such as lawyers, accountants, and so on) on your side, you can address questions and potential problems at the jump. You need expert advice about how to set up your business, how to incorporate (if that's the route you need to go), how to handle money and property, and how to keep your taxes paid. In the (unlikely, I hope) event that your business or partnerships aren't successful, you'll already have a plan in place to handle details such as cash and property disbursement as well as intellectual property rights.

Best friends and band members can become bitter enemies. That record deal you thought would lead you to worldwide stardom and fame can end in disaster. The idea you have on how money and items are supposed to be split up might not be the same idea that others have. The security and clarity comes from working with the right people who are on the same page as you. Good lawyers and accountants are worth their weight in gold and can help you avoid music-business problems when things go both right and wrong.

Imagine every person involved with you in your music business venture as if you were bitter enemies, and you completely detested the sight of each other. Then imagine everything that could possibly go right goes right as well as everything that could possibly go wrong goes wrong. From there, begin the lay out a plan, from the contracts and agreements to the percentages and promises, while everyone still likes each other and everyone is feeling good about the new venture.

Assessing the personalities to work and play with

Beyond the skillsets come the different personas when choosing whom you want to work with and who will work with you. Everyone has different styles of communication, and everyone has different ways that they like to work together. Just as certain artists are better off as solo artists, others are better as band members. Learning about the personalities and communication styles as well as following up with references can help you make strong, informed decisions.

You may find yourself smitten with another in the early stages of a relationship or dating, but maybe that little alarm in the back of your mind goes off. You wonder how an argument might play out, or how compromises are made when two people want two entirely different outcomes. Always listen to that little alarm.

Think about the best, worst, and middle-of-the-road scenarios in regard to your working relationships and find solutions for any problems. You can save yourself thousands in billable attorney hours if you have much of your contracts and agreements planned out before you meet with your lawyer. From who gets ownership of publishing or copyrights to what the band might owe a member, knock out those details early on.

Defining your limits of compromise

As you work to get everyone on the same page, realize early on that how that page looks to you and how it looks to someone else could be very different. Dissimilar people from diverse backgrounds usually have different beliefs. Whether in a business, romantic, or even a creative or musical relationship, compromises have to be made to make the relationship work. Still, there are areas where you may not want to compromise at all. This is where the waters can get a little rough.

As you begin any relationship, discuss your views and beliefs, as well as where you're willing to compromise and where you won't in order to build the right foundation with the right types of people that will work the right way for you.

Crediting and copyrighting your music with others

A common example is in the writing phases if you are a band. Some people believe that the drummer playing a part over a song that another member has written makes the drummer a co-writer that deserves both copyright and publishing. Others believe that the drummer should not get writing credit because it's drums being added on to a song that has already been created with lyrics, chords, and a basic arrangement. This can slide over into those that have added a single lyric and want credit for writing to someone adding a horn arrangement and looking to get additional credit or a form of ownership.

From writing, producing, and recording issues to the person designing your logo, website, and your merchandise . . . are they expecting a piece of the pie? If so, what size? Or are they expecting payment as an independent contractor? Addressing these types of questions, which can be different for everyone, helps you avoid differences when the money begins to come in.

The best relationships come from each person understanding the other's point of view, even if they might not agree with it. Apply a little give and take with compromise as well as an acceptance of where another stands firm and won't budge.

Solving problems before they arise

Nip it all in the bud before the flower grows, and you can create beautiful business bouquets. Before a note is written, before a song is recorded, before a logo is sketched, before a domain name is purchased, before a website starts getting coded, and before a dollar is spent on anything, begin addressing problems to prevent problems by putting it all down in writing among everyone involved.

This doesn't mean going to a lawyer before you make every move or every decision; it means clarifying in writing what you expect and what others expect from you. This enables you to all get on the same page, find compromise, or realize that working together might not be the best fit. Get your problem-solving hat on before problems arise. This can prevent many unpleasant issues down the line.

Big red flags should pop up when someone says, "Just come in to the studio; we'll deal with fees later." Always have a simple agreement or a statement of work with an invoice; otherwise, you could end up with legal hassles later.

Think of this worst-case scenario that has happened to so many musicians, both famous and independent. A producer can take claim of writing, publishing, and recording, because they recorded and produced a track for free. The track becomes popular, and the producer can claim that they need compensation and a percentage as well as co-writing and production credit.

Handling internal and external agreements

As you lock in the understanding, get on the same page, make your compromises as you stand your ground, and clarify the expectations all around, it's time to get a lawyer involved. Many musicians think they can't afford a lawyer or budgeting money for contract reviews is money that could be better spent elsewhere. Well, if you think a lawyer is too expensive now, just wait to see how much a lawyer will end up costing you if you wait too long and issues rear their ugly heads.

These agreements and contracts are not only for long-term projects and the day-to-day people involved; they're also for anyone who's working for just a short period of time. The more clarity and understanding everyone has, the easier the outcomes will be.

Getting it down on paper

You decided what you're willing to compromise on and where you're standing firm, and maybe you clarified who owns and gets what. Now it's time to take those last steps to identify how specific situations should be handled. The following sections look at a few possibilities that you and your attorney should anticipate.

Death

What happens if a band member dies? Designate who gets their profits or their percentages; make a plan if they owe money to the band and decide how that will be handled. Decide how that person will be replaced and how they will be paid.

Theft

Theft is a terrible thing, and having a no-liability contract certainly protects you from big problems. For example, imagine the producer you're working with steals a loop, sample, beat, or part from someone else, puts it in your song, and then you get contacted for copyright infringement. The liability is on that producer and not on you. Having a contract with a no-liability clause in place can keep you out of harm's way to a point, especially when the copyright owner comes calling for remedy or payment.

You're the weakest link; goodbye

What happens if you want to fire a band or team member, or a manager? Set in place clear elements that enable someone to be fired along with what they receive upon separation. Getting this in writing can sidestep massive drama.

Left behind

Have a clear understanding of what happens if the lead singer or anyone in the band gets a deal and wants to move on without the other members. Make sure the details for a left-behind scenario are in place to allow others to profit or at least be paid for what they've previously invested in. These are issues to ask and address early on from sharing a percentage with the other members that are left out of the deal to having a flat fee paid to them.

Every artist, band, and scenario is different, so there are no simple answers. You can go to a third party, a consultant, or even a lawyer a little early to discuss options, but the best plan is to discuss these among band members first.

After you have all the basics on paper and everyone is in agreement, it's almost time to bring in an attorney. With so much prep work out of the way, you'll be miles ahead and that much more protected.

Last step before going to the lawyer

Before starting the clock with a lawyer, talk to members of other bands — maybe even hire a music business advisor — to review the documentation and see what might be missing. Looking at agreements online as well as asking to see the contracts other bands, studios, producers, and graphic designers use or have used in the past can help you zero in on the most information possible to present to a lawyer.

The more you can have done, agreed upon, and prepared on paper, the easier you make it for your lawyer, and the less it costs to prepare all the needed documents.

Lawyering up

Make the most out of the time you can before going to the lawyer. Hiring a lawyer where you sit around a table and try to hash out basic elements is a waste of time and money. You don't need to discuss the publishing percentages in a lawyer's office. This should be done before you get in there.

With all those ducks in a row, now its time to bring in the lawyer and get all these agreements formatted, signed, and executed. The foundation of this type of organization makes things much easier for you and also makes you look much more professional. From an investor standpoint, since you removed a great deal of risk and potential problems very early on, you appear much more like a safe investment.

Learning some legalese

Read over everything with your lawyer. By now, you may begin to have a basic understanding of some legal terms. Also, see if any of the contracts you just drew up can be used as templates for future contracts. This would cut down on cost and confusion later down the line.

Accounting for legal and business documentation

Even in the magical world of music, your taxes still have to be paid. And whereas some artists have ducked taxes and proper accounting, others like Lauryn Hill have gone to jail for it. Financial accounting has to be a priority. You don't have to know every tax law or be a certified public accountant (CPA), but you need someone who's up to date on those laws and can help organize your receipts, records, and revenues correctly and legally.

On the same side of the coin, your accounting structure has to be formatted legally if you expect to find investors to support you. The better the accounting you have in place, the easier it is to pay taxes, and also gives you the ability to write off deductions.

Contact a CPA or accountant to go over a simple plan and help you set up bank accounts so that you track and pay taxes on every dollar that comes in. You also need to track where every dollar is spent; this enables you to keep track of your outgo, what's tax deductible, what isn't, and maybe where you can cut back on costs.

 Organize to be audited. Ask an accountant to help you set up a financial tracking plan as if you were audited by the IRS or potential investor. Simplified accounting software like QuickBooks can help with this, too. Pick up "*QuickBooks For Dummies 2015*" by Stephen L. Nelson (John Wiley and Sons) to learn more.

The key elements of your accounting consist of tracking the following:

- ✔ Product inventory and sales
- ✔ Costs to create inventory

- ✔ Paid bills
- ✔ Taxes owed
- ✔ Receipts for purchases

Again, your well-formatted accounting documentation serves to keep you in check with Uncle Sam while at the same time helps potential investors or backers see that you are financially organized and able to handle an investment. This is something that most musicians skip on and then find themselves in deep water with the IRS. Organize the documentation and bookkeeping when there's very little coming in. This makes it easier on all fronts when both costs and profits begin to pick up.

This also means you need to save every receipt having to do with you, your music, and your business. That Starbucks coffee you got after you loaded your gear should be saved. Save receipts from gas stations to the tolls and everything in between. Accountants can help you with taxes if they have the information that you enter in to QuickBooks, or another financial program, along with actual receipts for money you paid out.

Use small, dated envelopes to store your receipts each week and then shove those envelopes into a larger letterhead-size envelope marked with the month. This makes finding those receipts easy-peasy.

QuickBooks and other financial software are great tools, but you need copies of those receipts. Whether you scan every receipt into your computer or maintain the physical receipts:

- ✔ **Keep every receipt.** You never know how it might be used as a potential write off; or, if you are audited, you need to prove a purchase.

- ✔ **Always ask for a receipt.** From drinks to food, to laundry to gear, ask for those receipts. Any time you spend money, as for a receipt, save it, enter it, and maintain it.

- ✔ **Print out every receipt.** Print out receipts for purchases from online vendors such as iTunes and Amazon, or take a screen shot and add it to a file of online receipts. It's easier to have physical copies stored in case of an audit, and it also becomes a lot easier than trying to dig through old emails to find online proofs of purchase.

Although you can't write off every single receipt that you save for every single penny spent, changes in tax laws may allow for opportunities when you're filing at the end of the year that weren't available at the beginning of that year.

At the same time, entertainment ventures can put up a great deal of red flags. With all the expenses you can write off, if you were to be audited, you wouldn't want to be caught without a receipt to back up your purchase.

Copyrights, Publishing, and Ownership

Copyrighting your music is the only way you're going to get paid. It's the first line of defense for control and ownership over your songs as well as to prove legally that the music is yours. Copyright can be explained in lots of heavy terms, and it can be good to take a look at www.copyright.gov to learn more about the process and how it works. In the simplest definition, however, a copyright *protects* your work, *proves* it's yours, and that you're the legal owner. This enables you to have that work published so you can get paid through different types of publishing licenses.

Your rights as the copyright holder allow you to perform, reproduce, and distribute your work, as well as allow others to cover or copy your work — with you getting paid, of course.

Copyrights, publishing, and ownership can seem like a confusing maze to get through as a musician. There are books upon books about the distribution of ownership, percentages, and the tricky balance of who owns what, who should get what based on what they put in early, or how much they risked or took a chance.

Many artists forget those who came in the early stages to help finance recordings and develop careers. Later on, they cry foul because of how much they still have to pay to those people. Remember that those who get involved early on, especially those who were a part of getting your business off the ground, will likely stay involved as time passes.

The same applies to those who record the music, produce the graphics, create and manage the website and merchandise, and finance the tours. The best way to navigate through this maze is to build a foundation that's as much yours as possible before going to others for money and help. The more you invest with both your time and money, the less you need from others.

Understanding music copyright basics

Copyrights can be tricky and the definitions even trickier. It's true that the minute music and lyrics have been written down, recorded, or stored, a copyright is created. The poor man's copyright, as it was commonly called, is where people mail a copy of the work to themselves, the postmark serving as proof of origin. But just like writing something down, you're not providing all that much proof of when a song was written or copyrighted.

The first copyrights allowed exclusive control for only 14 years; that was it. Now, when you copyright a work, you own it for the rest of your life and then it can be transferred to another, whether it be an heir or someone in your will. That individual will own it for 70 more years.

When you apply for a copyright, there are two basic forms you use (both of which can be found at http://copyright.gov/forms) — the Performing Arts or Form PA, and the Sound Recordings or Form SR. Doing your due diligence and filling out both can be the most prudent way to go because when registering a new song, you want to protect the copyright in the composition separately from the copyright for the sound recording.

You use the Performing Arts (Form PA) to copyright and protect the composition, lyrics, or anything that's been written. The government description is "Use Form PA for registration of published or unpublished works of the performing arts. This class includes works prepared for the purpose of being "performed" directly before an audience or indirectly "by means of any device or process." Works of the performing arts include: (1) musical works, including any accompanying words; (2) dramatic works, including any accompanying music; (3) pantomimes and choreographic works; and (4) motion pictures and other audiovisual works."

You can find Form PA at http://copyright.gov/forms/formpa.pdf.

The other form, (Form SR) is for the copyright on the actual recording of your copyrighted song (or your recording of another's copyrighted song). The U.S government states to use Form SR " . . . for registration of published or unpublished sound recordings. Form SR should be used when the copyright claim is limited to the sound recording itself, and it may also be used where the same copyright claimant is seeking simultaneous registration of the underlying musical, dramatic, or literary work embodied in the phonorecord."

You can find Form SR at http://copyright.gov/forms/formsr.pdf.

File Form PA before the sound recording to protect the composition first.

With your works copyrighted, you can now publish them with either your own publishing company or with an established music publisher and begin to make money on those songs. If someone uses your music without permission and you have the copyrights in place, you can remedy the situation under the premise of copyright infringement. And here's another good reason to keep your attorney's number handy.

Understanding music publishing basics

A music publisher helps organize and prepare your music with all the different types of agreements, such as song split agreements (who gets paid what on the writing side), producer rights agreements (what share if any the producer receives), and copyrights and registrations with performing rights organizations such as ASCAP, BMI, and SESAC (see www.ascap.com, www.bmi.com, and www.sesac.com, respectively, for more information on these organizations and what they do).

Music publishers are then responsible for pitching and placing the music by researching options, tracking trends with music, and connecting with music supervisors, film, and TV producers, video game creators, advertising executives, and even other artist managers and reps to find placement for your music.

Then they are responsible for securing the licenses that allow for songs to be used as well as tracking copyright infringement if someone's using your music illegally. Finally, and what artists find most important about music publishers, is the tracking, collecting, and distributing of the profits from songs being placed in movies or TV, music played live, and other licensing options discussed later in the chapter.

A publisher is also responsible for negotiating the rates and deals as well as collecting the money and enforcing your copyright. Most publishers take 50 percent of the money that they bring in as their fee. If you sign with a music publisher, legally you assign your copyrights in exchange for one half of the profits made from these licensing deals.

Do your due diligence with music publishers. If you sign a deal with someone who isn't at the top of the publishing game or is a bit shady, he has control of those copyrights for as long as you signed the agreement. This means that if you find an opportunity for one of those songs, you still have to pay the music publisher even though he didn't do any of the work. If the interest comes from publishing company other than the company you have that song with, they have to get a sub-publishing deal through your original publisher, which may interfere with a deal because everyone will be making less.

You do have the option to form your own music publishing company, as well as the option to assign certain songs to music publishers but not your entire body of work. Think about what options work best for you, and consider starting your own music publishing company, regardless if you're actively looking for licensing opportunities or not. If an opportunity comes your way, you can work out a deal for that song, through your own publishing company, and make the most off of the song. If you're an American, information about starting your own publishing company can be found online at www.ascap.com, www.bmi.com, or www.sesac.com. If you're another nationality, do a Google search for *starting a music publishing company in (country)* to get the right links to get started.

Some record labels and investors may add to their contracts that they receive all publishing revenues until they've recouped their investment as well as made the interest they want. Others take a percentage of publishing revenues. Keep this in mind as you move forward and look at agreements, potential record deals, and investments early on.

The advantage of using an established publishing company or music publisher is that their contacts could allow for many opportunities. Now, however, with the ability to get music out there easier (via the Internet), it can be beneficial to have your own music publishing company in addition to working with a more established publisher.

Figuring out licensing options

Whether you go the route of an established music publishing company or you start your own, you want to get as many licenses for your music to create profit. Licensing your music means just that — you or the music publisher allow someone to use a product that you own (your licensed music) but you don't transfer the ownership. The deals created from licensing your music, ironically enough, is called publishing.

There are seven key types of rights and licensing options you can have for your music. The following sections take a look at each.

Public performance royalties

Public performance royalties are tied in to your songs being played in public places such as venues during live concerts or even played by a DJ, on the radio (Internet radio included), television, and public events. With your ownership of the copyright, you have the exclusive rights to perform your song in public. Technically, no one can play your song in public unless you allow it and you get paid for it.

Performing rights organizations like American Society of Composers, Authors and Publishers (ASCAP), Society of European Stage Authors and Composers (SESAC), and Broadcast Music, Incorporated (BMI) track and collect these royalties. These are only three in the United States, and they can help you as the copyright holder as well as your music publisher track what's being played, how often and where, and help to get you paid for it.

Mechanical rights and licenses

Mechanical royalties, as they are often called, come from the reproduction of your music — in other words, someone else covering your song. The Harry Fox Agency in the United States is the most recognized organization that helps you or your music publisher in mechanical collections as well as connecting people that want to cover your material with your publisher or you to strike the deal to allow for it. The Harry Fox Agency has released an online mechanical tool called Songfile to help artists connect with copyright owners so they can strike mechanical licensing agreements for covers. With already 2 million songs in the database, this is a great option.

Digital rights and licenses

The digital area is a mess. This is where copyright holders and publishers are supposed to receive money from the plays in digital formats including limited-use or protected downloads and streaming, as well as subscription sites. But Spotify, Pandora, and many other streaming apps and sites aren't paying, and musicians and labels are waving red flags. Don't expect much profit here until things get straightened out. And I'm not talking any time soon.

Print rights and licenses

Print rights and licenses cover music that you compose or own the copyright that's made into sheet music. The sales or the agreed terms of an amount of money for a specific number of prints can be made here. This isn't a very common revenue stream for an independent artist, because most musicians are finding the music online and perhaps transcribed by others, but with growing recognition, it can become one more avenue of revenue.

Synchronization rights and licenses

Using the more hip lingo — "Sync Licensing" — synchronization is where your music is synched up with images and visuals such as television shows, movies, commercials, and even corporate videos. Payment amounts for this type of use can vary widely. Some people have seen royalty checks as low as four dollars for music being inserted in to a lower-level cable show, whereas others have been paid $40,000 or more for theme music. These types of deals come through connecting with music supervisors for shows, movies, and ad execs for commercials.

 Allowing certain music for free can open doors to different connections as well as music supervisors that can become aware of you. Whether it's you running your own music publishing company or through a music publisher, don't get greedy. There are a lot of shows, commercials, movies, and programs that need music; the more you get heard, connected, and inserted into shows, the more people you can reach, and the more money you can ask for.

Sampling rights and licenses

To properly and legally use a sample, you need to go through the person who owns the sound recording as well as the copyright owner. Most larger labels take ownership of the sound recording, so getting clearance through the copyright owner or the person who wrote the song is not enough if you're thinking of using a *sample*, or a snippet of your song.

When it comes to profits from samples, the amount varies widely. Some give away samples for free and use the marketing to point back to the original song; others work off a flat fee or a cut of the mechanical royalties.

As far as using other people's samples, try to avoid it. With 50 percent of your publishing already going to the music publisher, you have to deal with percentages from investors as well as whatever is owed to others involved in your song, so make the most off every song. Don't use samples. Make the music 100 percent yours, so you don't have to slice off one more piece of the pie to one more person when money starts to come in.

And don't steal samples; don't try to hide them and hope to get away with it. Yes, some musicians rip off samples every day, but those who get caught — usually those on their way up as their music is getting more and more recognition — can be sued for over $100,000 in copyright infringements, not to mention cuts of what product has already been created and sold.

Foreign rights and licenses

Foreign rights and licenses pertain to using your music in another country. Publishers from both yours and the foreign country enter into a sub-publishing agreement to license your music outside of the United States. Whether an artist in another country is covering your song in public, using a sample, or using your music for a movie or TV show, you need to sub-publish with the publisher in that country to make it legal and get paid.

Regardless of starting your own publishing company or signing with a music publishing company, make sure you're doing your due diligence and clearly understand what's happening. As mentioned earlier in this chapter, you're assigning your copyright of a song or songs to a publisher, usually for an extended amount of time. Find out what they have done and whom they have worked for, then contact those people to find out how they have liked working with them.

See if there are any complaints against them or unhappy artists. You are assigning ownership to another when you publish and while a great deal of money can be made, a great deal of both money and opportunities can be lost if you are with the wrong person or team. Those extra steps and double-checking will allow you to keep your forward motion in check for the present and far into the future.

Graphic, web, recording, product, and investment stakes

Getting something for free early on can seem like a great thing; however, you could end up paying down the line, and it can cost you ten-fold or even more. Remember the old adage: There's no such thing as a free lunch.

From getting free graphics to help with creating a website, there can be costs associated with that branding down the line. For example, a graphic designer can claim that because she did your logo on speculation, she should get a piece of everything that logo goes on from stickers to T-shirts to albums and other products. As another example, your website designer may claim the website he built should allow him a percentage of profits for an extended period of time. Others who might offer something for free early on but want some sort of payment later include studios, producers, musicians playing on your songs, and even investors who come on board early on.

Security and control of your career can be lost due to the freebies or lack of clarity early on. Not fully understanding what a business partner or contractor expects down the line can leave you with the smallest piece of the profit pie, if you even see any profit at all. There are stories of groups that made millions of dollars in a year and ended up barely making enough to cover their business and personal expenses.

A good rule of thumb is that free is never free; make it very clear what you will give for work performed and that all parties understand your terms. To learn more about contracts, see the "Handling internal and external agreements" section earlier in this chapter. Get it all in writing and you will get yourself in the safest place to keep everyone on the same page.

Determining the terms

You first need to determine the terms of your deal. If you know what your net income will be, you can find a reasonable percentage to pay your contractor. If the income amount is undetermined at the time of making a deal, you can offer and compromise on best guesses and estimations. Be sure that everyone involved in this percentage deal understands the terms and the timeline. (This might be a good place to bring in that attorney; check out "Handling internal and external agreements" earlier in this chapter.) The clearer this is made, the cleaner things will be across the board for those who are receiving a piece of the pie.

Net or gross cuts

Be clear about how much money is coming in at what point. If someone thinks more is being made but they're not getting enough of the cut, it can cause tension. If someone is receiving a percentage off the gross, they are receiving a great deal more because it is cut off of everything. If you're offering net, which is recommended, your contractor receives his cut after costs, fees, and expenses are taken out.

Deciding what percentages go where and to whom

In any deal, you can determine what's included as well as what's not. For example, if you're paying a musician a small cut from royalties of the song, you might not want to give him anything from T-shirt sales; however, someone who helped with your logo might get a cut of the items that have that logo on them, but nothing from the music.

The investor risk is usually the highest and they will look for the most in return for taking the biggest chance. Keep that in mind as you negotiate. Many will end up losing very lucrative and potentially profitable deals by turning down offers that fairly consider all parties. It's important to understand that as much as the music is yours and the focus is on you, those investing in you to market and promote that music need to be considered for much more than just getting their money back.

Investors invest to make money. The riskier the investment, the higher the return they deserve due to the risk they took.

Music is one of the highest risks when it comes to investing. When you negotiate fairly with that in mind, you open the doors to many more opportunities for investment.

The more you are able to pay out in interest, the less the amount people look for in longer-term percentages. Many musicians balk at a high percentage and look to offer a lower percentage for longer, but getting an investor out earlier or offering a higher interest rate and a smaller percentage if they are looking for both means more for you in the end.

Working with Publishing Companies, Labels, Managers, and Investors

As you cut your deals, set your percentages, and secure both your rights and profits, the decisions you make early on in your career can have long-term effects. The biggest percentages of profits that you share are with your publisher, your label, your manager, investors, or whatever mix you have involved.

Working to communicate, create, and comprehend the best working relationships gives you the sense of security in the best relationships while clearly knowing what is going where, who is making what, and what the expectations are of everyone involved with you, your brand, and your music.

Deciding on self-publishing versus finding a publishing company

Most publishing deals that you get into with a music publisher or music publishing company require 50 percent of the royalties. As unfair as that might seem, this is an industry standard. By maintaining your own publishing company, you get to keep 100 percent of the publishing. The trade-off, however, is that you have to handle and execute the job of a music publisher.

An effective music publisher is constantly researching and finding opportunities for placements, as well as tracking where your music is being used and how collection and payment is made for you. With this in mind, it can be a good idea to work with a music publisher.

However, you don't have to assign your whole catalogue to a single publisher. If they ask for that, move on and look for another publisher. Just as the music industry has changed, all the jobs inside the industry have changed as well. Where publishers early on would ask for long terms and exclusivity as well a larger body of work, these days you can find music publishers who will negotiate numbers of songs and time frames.

Having your own publishing company can become a full-time job as you work to find placements, track where music is being used, and follow the changes with all the streaming and digital insanity. More about self-publishing was covered earlier in this chapter in the section "Understanding music publishing basics."

Your best role in music

If you choose a path as a songwriter with little interest in touring or promoting, and you prefer the idea of getting your songs licensed, covered, and placed everywhere they can, handling your own publishing is easier than being in a band that wants to go on the road and has to work to promote themselves. In a sense, by being in a band, you're doubling and tripling the workload.

Get your own publishing company set up either way. Even if you have no songs in it, you have the organization in place. If an opportunity arises, you have the ability to publish that song yourself. Working with a professional music publisher or publishing company that has a good track record in the last couple years with no complaints from artists or others can be a great outlet for your music, too. Easy instructions and directions to form a music publishing company can be found online at www.ascap.com, www.bmi.com, and www.sesac.com, the performing rights organizations in the United States.

A single publishing company can publish a single song. You do not need to give them your full catalog, and you can put different songs with different publishers as well as publishing your own, too.

Soliciting to a record label versus going independent

One of the most frequently asked questions is whether to solicit to a record label or go independent. Many people see these as two different options, when in a sense they're similar in what needs to be done for either direction you choose.

Some think it's as simple as sending music to every record label you can find; then getting signed; then magically everything takes off. There's a very dangerous misconception and delusion from a great deal of musicians who think, "Once they hear it, I'm a shoe-in for a deal."

Over 95 percent of people signed to a record label from the smallest independent labels to the largest and most financed labels fail.

The same exact problems can occur from the independent side of things. Many people think signing to a label allows an artist to focus on recording and on touring while the artist who wants to go independent has to handle money, booking, branding, and other costs and considerations.

Think less from the standpoint as to whether you want to go the independent route or solicit to record labels, and first think about how you will present yourself for solicitation for all your needs. Whether you choose to go after a label or do it yourself, the presentation for getting a solid consideration from a label is the same as the presentation for finding the money to get into the studio, build up the branding, and execute the marketing and promotion budgets.

The same steps need to happen whether you're looking at the requirements needed from an independent standpoint or wanting to sign with a label. If you take the steps to stay as independent as possible with investors to support the costs you need, larger profits can come your way. This, over the bands that sign away their lives as others do all the work and then of course, see a lot less in revenues and profits in the long run.

I advise all musicians to take the independent route. In many ways it's still like going to a major label. You have to work on building and funding your music business plan as well as execute it (see Chapter 4), but your involvement, efforts, and attention to detail allow for better profits for yourself and those funding you. This also increases your ownership and works a great deal better in your favor over signing with a label; you end up with greater control of you and your career.

Breaking down a "deal"

A great deal — and I'm talking about the majority — of record label owners and employees out there don't know what they are doing. That deal you think you're getting when you sign on the dotted line is a bad hand. (Playing card pun, okay?) Again, keep thinking due diligence and research. The majority of those record label owners, employees, and executives can't help you or your career. They're not funded correctly or with enough. They are not organized professionally or with the right team and even though they are nowhere near what they claim to be, they use templates of contracts that can take complete control of you, your career, and opportunities you won't be allowed to have with others.

Signing an exclusive agreement that contracts you to a record label that gives the executives, employees, or owner of that label control of you, your music, publishing, and rights — where they leave it vague about exactly what they have to do for you — can legally prevent you from working with others and leave you locked up for years to come.

Look at a worst-case scenario as an example: If a record label gives you a deal to record in the studio and puts ten grand into you and your project as they take your publishing and look for a high return on investment, how will you get money for the branding, marketing, promotion, and touring? What are you able to offer those potential investors? You have tied yourself up in a record deal that isn't a deal at all with a record label that isn't really a label at all due to the lack of cash flow, experience, knowledge, and artist's support, and you end up losing out.

The good, the bad, and the greedy

The best way to protect yourself from the scammers, snake-oil salesmen, and hype artists and the bad deals they bring is to keep that due diligence and research going before signing on any dotted line. Find out who these people have worked with, how much was invested, how much was returned, and how much time it took. Call up the bands and artists on those labels. Check into state and county websites to make sure these companies are legitimate and are filing and paying taxes.

The more you look into a deal, the better deal you can get . . . and the easier it is to say no to the bad deals and the bad companies out there. Don't make decisions in desperation. That album you think has to be recorded right now and this label that will get you into the studio tomorrow could be a scam to steal your music, sound recordings, and publishing.

There are good deals out there with a small amount of honorable, professional, and profitable labels that invest wisely. There are also good deals that you can broker with investors that garner the right amount of money to handle all the different elements required to see a return on investment.

Your chances for landing a good deal increase if you have solid music business plans that show how the business is organized, where money is spent, and how you expect to keep the business on track. For more about music business plans, check out Chapter 4.

Understanding your responsibilities to investors

In any situation when it comes to labels and investors, you lose ownership and control for a period of time. This is why you have lawyers reviewing contracts and best- and worst-case scenarios. Your attorney can clarify any confusion and allow the process of more ownership or the majority of ownership to eventually come back to you.

Anyone that gets involved financially with you is looking for a piece of the pie, whether in higher interest and no percentage, lower percentage on their return on investment and a higher percentage of ownership and profits, or a much higher stake in ownership for the long term and getting back only their initial investment. Because your investors expect something in return, the moment money comes to you, you create a business partnership complete with responsibilities and loss of some ownership.

For example, if your four-person group makes $1,000,000 in a year, but you owe 90 percent of that to investors, each member of your group is only making $25,000 piece for the year. But if you can get the bulk paid back to investors as well as some larger interest so you could maintain more of the profits, after all the costs and a little higher payback, you can make 40 percent on that million, and each of you make a very comfortable $100,000 for that year.

In any situation when it comes to labels and investors, you lose ownership and control for a period while you pay back your investors. Still, if you have clearly laid out in publishing deals, record label deals, or investor agreements how your business works from the financials to the percentages, the ownership stakes to the security, you can maintain that much more control of your career, music, and brand. That's why creating your music business plan discussed in Chapter 4 is so essential for the success and security of you and your music.

Part III
Marketing and Promoting For the Long Haul

The Top Six elements in your editorial calendar include:

- **Type of posts:** Blogs, pictures, audios, videos, quotes, reviews, and so on
- **Scheduled posting plan:** What is tentatively going up and when
- **Titles and primary keywords of blog and video posts:** To see what's being captured
- **Back-up post list:** For use at any time
- **Advanced post planning:** For events, holidays, and anniversaries
- **Recurring themes:** Or pattern posts

Part III

Marketing and Promoting
For the Long Haul

In This Part . . .

✔ Learn how uniformity, consistency, colors, logo, font, and content make it easier for fans to find and recognize you.

✔ Check out how an editorial calendar can help keep you organized and ensure that you're including key elements when posting to social media.

✔ Discover how to mix physical (offline) promotion with online (posts, blogs, and more) marketing to keep you in front of fans.

✔ Create well-planned promotions and releases to make your events stand out.

Chapter 10

Building Your Website and Social Media Presence

*Y*our online presence makes every aspect of your networking easy peasy. There's a reason why they're called social networks, you know. But for you, they're both social and professional networks. Whereas most people use social networks to share with a group of friends, or to connect with people they've been out of touch with, you're reaching as many people as possible, building and maintaining your audience.

The more places you are, such as your website, social media sites, review sites, and other listing sites, and the more consistent your information, graphics, links, content, and call to action, the more interest and engagement you draw. Building up your website presence is much more than just building your website. Think of your website as the anchor or home plate where all the other sites, pages, and places point back to.

By building a professional-looking and accessible website that enables every visitor to connect to other sites you're on, you make a better link with fans to draw them in and take them to your music, website, store, and you.

Graphics Designed For Everything Online

After you decide on the logo, font, and graphics for your band, think about how all of those branding elements will appear on your website. Your first task is to make sure your graphics are formatted and designed to be used for everything and every place you are online. (Check out Chapter 7 to learn more about graphics creation.)

Your uniformity, consistency, colors, logo, font, and content make it easier for fans to find and recognize you. From your website to your Twitter account and everything in between, let your audience know that it's you without a doubt.

Generally speaking, people have very short attention spans. A brand-new fan clicking through a link that might look confusing to them, such as only having a Click Here icon or an undefined or non-descriptive link, can click away or move on. Giving them comfort in consistency allows for better new fan engagement. Clarify where someone is directed if they click a link for a better conversion of click-throughs.

Logos, colors, and uniform designs

After you have your band's logo and font, you get to choose your colors. Using a consistent color scheme for your website as well as every social media page you have gives you the most uniform impression and promotes fan recognition.

Recognition is everything. The similarity in look, design, and feel on your website and everywhere else you have your band name font, logo, colors and information allows for people to recognize you that much more and that much faster.

Remember, many people need to see and hear about you before they click through and spend the time looking into you. The more uniform your online appearance, the better the chance that potential new fans will become band supporters in no time.

Aligning primary images across all sites

As your audience grows and gets to know and recognize you, be sure to have the same images running across all your online sites. If you choose a primary band picture or artist picture, make it the avatar across every site.

An avatar is the photo you see next to each of your online posts. From Facebook to Twitter, LinkedIn to YouTube, that little photo is a key part of your marketing. It shows up for every post and comment you make. Better yet, it shows up when you make comments or posts on pages other than yours. Keep your avatar uniform across all social media sites; and when you change the avatar on one site be sure to change them all to stay consistent.

This consistency allows for a better online familiarity. This also enables people to feel that much more confident when they click through to another page to download a song, buy a product, or connect with you elsewhere. When they recognize that image, it reinforces to the visitor that they're in the right place.

Showcasing your font and color the same way

Keep that font the same for every graphic and page. Just as you share the logo and the color scheme across all sites, make sure that your font stays exactly the same, too. Think of fonts and typesets like Coca Cola. You recognize that familiar cursive even from a distance. Same goes for McDonald's, Subway, Ford, Starbucks, and hundreds of others that can have the same effect for you online.

Think about the last time you were driving down a dark highway looking for a sub sandwich and you saw a sign for Subway far off in the distance. You knew that there was a Subway shop there before you could even make out the words. That's the effectiveness of a uniform font and color scheme.

Approaching header graphics

On many social media sites you have the option to upload a header graphic. Facebook, Twitter, Google+, and YouTube are four of the primary sites where headers are used. They also have different requirements for what can be uploaded, the type of content allowed on those headers, and the sizes that best fit each page.

Visit each social media website and search on the size requirements for the headers. Then when you or your graphic designer create your website, create the headers for Facebook, YouTube, Google+ and Twitter at the same time. Keep the same idea, theme, and color of your website header, but adjust it to each of the required specs so your images don't look stretched, pulled, or cut off. Here are the size requirements for each:

- ✔ **Twitter:** 1500 x 500 pixels
- ✔ **Google+:** 2120 x 1192 maximum size or 480 x 270 minimum size

✔ **Facebook:** 851 x 315 pixels

When designing for Facebook, your header will be blocked on the lower left side for the Facebook photo, which displays at 160 x 160 pixels.

✔ **YouTube** – 2650 x 1440 pixels

This one is very important to get right. It's not just about the desktop display on a computer. When you upload the right-sized image for YouTube, it look professional on a tablet, a mobile, and TV display.

Aligning your header graphics with your main website graphic and including your font, logo, tagline, website address, and color scheme helps to connect and draw in that many more people who recognize and want to connect with you.

Promotional graphic download page

You want to be able to get your logo and other promotional materials to your fans as well as to promoters and venue owners as quickly and easily as possible. One way to do this is to add a promotional graphic download page to your website, or have a page that links to a Dropbox account or place where visitors can easily download key images. The following list shows what materials you should freely make available:

✔ Logo

✔ Font

✔ Logo and font

✔ Logo, font, tagline

✔ Logo, font, tagline, web address

✔ Blank booking poster

✔ Album poster

✔ Promotional 8 x 10 photo

Have each of these items in a high-quality format for printing as well as a low-quality format for web use. Having versions in JPG, PDF, and Photoshop formats enables easy access to those who may be promoting a show, doing a story on you, or helping to market you.

The easier you make it for others to promote you, the better the marketing you receive.

Uniformity across the social media universe

The more you keep your colors, graphics, logos, and content aligned, the more recognizable you become. The foundation of your graphics and images in your website and social media crossing over to your products enables your brand to be that much more effective and reach that much wider an audience.

Some sites don't allow you to have headers like those on LinkedIn, but that photo for the page or avatar can still be the same as all your other sites. The same goes for the content. Your bio, your call to action, and tagline all help your cross-promotion in pictures, graphics, and words.

Using your content in a uniform manner

Just as you keep the consistency with your graphics, the same goes for your content. Different sites allow for different amounts of content but add all you can everywhere you can; just keep it uniform. While Twitter offers a shorter amount of characters in a bio than Facebook does, make sure to add the key information first and then the extras where allowed.

For example, on Twitter, you may only be able to add your tagline and some of your one liner as well as a single website and location. While on your Google+ Profile, you can add a bio as long as you like, location and previous locations, work info, skill sets, influences, bragging rights (yes, that is an option on Google+), other names and as many links as you want to your website, your social media sites, sales sites, and anywhere else.

 Fill in every space you can with every piece of information allowed. Don't leave any stone unturned or any field blank. The more information you have, the more you can optimize. To make it easier, have a template spreadsheet for all your content, so you can copy and paste the information to any site as well as new sites that pop up.

Using your call to action

After you have set up all the graphics, headers and content across all your sites, don't forget to add the call to action in your posts — that short summary that covers who you are and where people can find more information out about you; that fast summary that starts with your one liner, then your tagline, and then is followed by a few other social media sites and the main site where they can find you. Here is the call to action for Kitty Likes Avocado:

Clawing at the alternative funk genre woven in to a scratching post of rock and blues, Kitty Likes Avocado serves up a smooth pop infused sound with the attitude of a kitten on catnip. Kitty Likes Avocado is Fruity Funk Scratching at the Drapes of Rock and Roll. For more info about Kitty Likes Avocado, their shows, music, merchandise, videos, news and updates, visit:

```
http://kittylikesavocado.com/
```

```
https://facebook.com/kittylikesavocado/
```

```
https://instagram.com/kitylikesavocado/
```

```
https://twitter.com/kittylikesavoca
```

Using this as the signature and sign off for a blog on WordPress, for a video on YouTube, for an audio on SoundCloud or a picture on Instagram identifies who delivered the content that came before it and tells the reader, listener, or viewer exactly where to go to get more.

Cross-marketing each social media site

As you sign up for each social media site, market the other sites as you draw everyone back to your primary website or your stores. Think of social media sites like different items on a menu. The more you have, the more chances you get to draw someone into you, your music, and your shows.

Signing up for a lot of different sites doesn't mean you have to post individually on each one. It is more about spreading your graphics, your message and your content in a consistent and uniform way to more and more places to draw in more and more people.

 The more sites you cross-reference with your graphics, your information, and your call to action, the more you are cross-marketing and reaching across that many more markets to come across that many more people. Keep the message, the image, and the look uniform and it will allow you to form a much bigger reach.

Home Base for Everything: Your Website

Many ask if a website is even needed these days with so much focus, engagement, and conversion to sales happening on social media. Yeh, a website is still a requirement. Think of your website as your home base, where everything out there links back to you. On the opposite side, this is where you can link everything to send people out to all your different social media sites like Facebook and Twitter, stores like iTunes and Amazon, audio sites, streaming sites, video sites, picture sites, blog sites, and everywhere else.

Directing people where to go

Think of a map, all its roads and points of interest. Your website becomes the same type of legend for everywhere you are online. Similar to a map, your website is a map to lead people to social media sites, video sites, store pages, and other links about you. And like a well-organized and helpful map, your website should present the basic details and directions for where your fans can go to find out more about you as well as have the right information for industry professionals, reviewers, and booking agents.

The website also enables people to come back from one social media site and be able to find all the other social media sites you are on. This way they can choose where they prefer to connect with you.

Whereas you might think Facebook is where you want everyone to be, a fan that primarily uses Tumblr could click through on a Facebook post they came across to your website and find your Tumblr link clearly accessible and visible on the home page of your website, which they could then choose to click on and stay connected with you there by subscribing to updates or following you.

Don't force fans to follow you on one specific site. Give them the opportunity and the option to connect where they want.

Populating your website

There are books and more books about website layout and requirements with a great deal of different ideas and options. In fact, many people make their living at designing and populating websites. To get started, though, a good rule of thumb is to make sure the fundamentals are in place. This enables the easiest website to build and delivers the best results. The following lists the basics that are required for an easy-to-use website. (To learn how to create an efficient and eye-catching website, check out *Building Websites All-in-One For Dummies*, by David Karlins and Doug Sahlin [John Wiley and Sons, Inc.])

Home	Equipment/ endorsement links
Bio	Promotional/ booking info/downloads
Pictures	Copyright notice
Videos	Privacy policy
Music	Contact information
Blog	Email list signup
Schedule	Subscribe/unsubscribe
Products	Store links
Reviews and testimonials	Social media

Many artists are moving to the scrolling one-page format, as you can see at http://kittylikesavocado.com/. This is where the main information is placed on one scrolling page with links to other subsidiary pages while still sharing the core information. This format also looks clean on mobile phones and tablet devices.

Many of these requirements are able to come from your social media pages and updated automatically in to your website. For example, the YouTube plug-in called TubePress (if you're using WordPress for your website . . . and you should as it gives you the easiest options to update, edit, and alter your website) automatically updates your video page on your website with the videos you post on YouTube. More about WordPress plugins can be found in *WordPress Web Design For Dummies* by Lisa Sabin-Wilson (John Wiley and Sons, Inc.).

The same plug-ins pull pictures from Instagram, audio samples from SoundCloud, and blogs from your blogging page. This gives you the ability to consistently update your website without needing to even visit your site. Still, it's important to create new content on a weekly basis that's put directly on your website to help with your SEO.

The top of your website or the first page (called a home page) that shows up on computers or mobile devices should immediately give everyone a strong sense of who you are. Your logo, font, color scheme, and tagline should be present.

Have links visible and immediately available to direct visitors to Facebook, Twitter, YouTube, and Instagram for social media. Also provide clear tabs for people to get to your music, bio, and your contact info.

Attention spans are short these days. By presenting your core elements you're able to engage people and make them stay longer to learn and hear more of you.

Don't make people sign up to see your website or force them to like a page to enable them to get more information. Many up-and-coming artists follow this method from more established artists, and it turns people away. You can have exclusive content that people have to sign up for, but don't make your first appearance be met with forcing a website visitor to sign up for an email list or like a page before they get a chance to decide if they like you.

Letting professionals do it right

Although you can easily build a free website, I recommend using a professional web designer to design your site the right way. A well-designed site coupled with a content management system ends up saving you thousands along with giving you the ability to change the site yourself without having to pay someone every time your content needs to be updated. Although WordPress is a free blog and website option, have a professional designer create a WordPress site so that you have lots of options for visitors.

Hiring the right web designer to layout your website and then give you instructions to update each section is a much better option than building a site on Wix or some other free website platforms. It's worth the investment, and the results are so much better. You don't need to spend tens of thousands on a website, but you may find yourself in a range of a few thousand.

Subscribing to email lists more from your website

Email lists and enabling someone to subscribe to your website allows people to get the updates they want. Keep in mind that many of these people already are connected with you on social media sites, so as you might recap and share some previous social media posts as part of your email to fans, make sure to deliver something exclusive to this list that can be seen only if they're part of the list.

Easy access to subscribe and unsubscribe

Make it easy for someone to sign up for update, but at the same time make it easy for people to unsubscribe. Some fans don't want the extra emails, or they may find they get updates and information from social media or other places. That little Unsubscribe button at the bottom of email lists shows a great level of respect as well as helps people realize they can easily unsubscribe.

Updates: How many updates and how often

Some artists send out emails every single day and oversaturate their audience. Once a week is the most you should send out updates with once a month being the best choice. This monthly time frame enables you to create exclusive content for the email list and give people a great update as well as a recap of the previous month.

Ezines, newsletters, and online newspapers

Sites such as paper.li (`http://paper.li`) help you create a simple newspaper and newsletter-type format where you can create headlines from URL links. You can also share other people's content that you might like to add to the newspaper. Because the link goes directly to someone's content based on their sites, there's no copyright infringement; however, don't share links to subscription or private unsecured pages without asking. It's best to share content from public social media sites like Twitter, YouTube, Instagram, and blogs.

A newsletter or online newspaper might seem like a good link to share through your social media pages; however, it takes away the exclusivity and the connection with your audience. If your audience can get everything they need and everything you are posting from your social media pages, your fans have no reason to sign up for your mailing list. The aspects of exclusivity you offer in different places with different mediums make people want to be that much more connected in that many more places.

Keeping a Website and Social Media Template Form

Maintain a social media template form file as well as a spreadsheet or a Word document that includes website and social media logins, passwords, and other information. The template makes it easy to stay consistent with your web content, and the spreadsheet can include links to all your key graphics, headers, avatars, photos, video, and music. Having all of this in one place makes easy work of updating and changing your online content.

Your content cheat sheet

All your branding information placed in a simple content sheet allows you to copy and paste everything you need onto every new site you have. As you make changes, that sheet allows you to know where you need to update too.

In this sheet have the following elements listed out in a Word document or Excel spreadsheet to allow you to make sure that every keyword, phrase, sentence, and paragraph is being used the same way across all pages. You don't need to rewrite all your information over and over. Work from the sheet that includes the elements shown in Figure 10-1.

This long list makes your life easier. It also makes it easier for those who help market and promote you. Having these all in one place as well as knowing what links go where showcases a higher level of professionalism.

KITTY LIKES AVOCADO

TAGLINE	Fruity Funk Scratching at the Drapes of Rock and Roll
ONE LINER/ MISSION STATEMENT SHORT	Clawing at the alternative funk genre woven in to a scratching post of rock and blues, Kitty Likes Avocado serves up a smooth pop infused sound with the attitude of a kitten on catnip.
SHORT BIO	Clawing at the alternative funk genre woven in to a scratching post of rock and blues, Kitty Likes Avocado serves up a smooth pop infused sound with the attitude of a kitten on catnip. Mixing an array of inspirations like Steely Dan, Red Hot Chili Peppers, Buddy Guy and Justin Timberlake with each members diverse musical background has created their large musical litter box of soul. Kitty Likes Avocado is Fruity Funk Scratching at the Drapes of Rock and Roll.
LONG BIO	Clawing at the alternative funk genre woven in to a scratching post of rock and blues, Kitty Likes Avocado serves up a smooth pop infused sound with the attitude of a kitten on catnip. Mixing an array of inspirations like Steely Dan, Red Hot Chili Peppers, Buddy Guy and Justin Timberlake with each members diverse musical background has created their large musical litter box of soul. If Nirvana had Michael Buble on vocals with a horn section, or consider a combination of The Police and Chicago playing Billy Joel songs, that might just touch on the tip of how their sound and songs could be described. Taking nothing all that seriously, enjoying their catnaps and daily smoothies with different fruits, avocado, garlic and ginger, their playful music comes from an array of influences, attitudes, humor and arguments. Kitty Likes Avocado is Fruity Funk Scratching at the Drapes of Rock and Roll.
CALL TO ACTION	Clawing at the alternative funk genre woven in to a scratching post of rock and blues, Kitty Likes Avocado serves up a smooth pop infused sound with the attitude of a kitten on catnip. Kitty Likes Avocado is Fruity Funk Scratching at the Drapes of Rock and Roll. For more info about Kitty Likes Avocado, their shows, music, merchandise, videos, news and updates, visit: http://kittylikesavocado.com/ https://facebook.com/kittylikesavocado/ https://instagram.com/kittylikesavocado/ https://twitter.com/kittylikesavoca/
LOCATION	VERO BEACH, FLORIDA
COPYRIGHT	© 2015 Kitty Likes Avocado
PUBLISHING	Kitty Likes Avocado Music
BOOKING CONTACT	Booking Contact: Barbara Brown Booking and Management Group Barbara Brown - http://bbbamg.com/ Email: Barbara (at) bbbamg.com Phone: 424-645-7683
BRAGGING RIGHTS	Coughing up the largest sonic hairball ever heard.
OTHER NAMES	Kitty hates grapefruit, Kitty loves cashews, Kitty hates bathtime, Here Kitty Kitty and Kitty Kitty Bang Bang
PRIMARY KEYWORDS	Alternative funk, rock and blues, pop infused sound, attitude of a kitten, array of inspirations, diverse musical background musical litter box of soul, playful music, array of influences, humor and arguments. Kitty Likes Avocado, Fruity Funk, Scratching at the Drapes of Rock and Roll.
SKILLS KEYWORDS	singing, writing, playing, performing, scratching, clawing, meowing, recording, mixing, mastering, marketing, promoting, advertising, networking, engaging, shedding, growling, biting, drumming, rocking, rolling, funking, serving, infusing, laughing and napping.
COMPARISONS KEYWORDS	Toad the Wet Sprocket, PFunk, James Taylor, Jason Mraz, Earth Wind and Fire, Chicago, Nirvana, Soundgarden, Red hot chili Peppers, Michael Buble, The Police, Snoop Dog, Garth Brooks, Pharrell Williams, Mumford and Sons, Stevie Wonder, Michael Jackson, Tribe called Quest, Cat Stevens, Daft Punk, Pearl Jam, Steely Dan, Cat Power, Cat Deeley, Cat Cora, Cat Anderson, Cat Osterman, Cats on Fire, Polecats, Cat on a Smooth Surface, Cat Party
INFLUENCES KEYWORDS	Top Cat, Bill The Cat, Bentley, Heathcliff, Scratchy, Stimpy, Grumpy Cat, Angry Cat, Tom, Garfield, Cheshire Cat, Cat in the Hat, Sylvester, Black Cat, Catwoman, Hello Kitty, Puss in Boots, My Cat from hell, Cat on a hot tin roof, Colonel Meow, Helicat, Felix the cat, Morris, Arlene, Schrodinger, Music Business Cat & Jackson Galaxy
Promotional Graphic Download Link List	http://kittylikesavocado.com/promotionals
Links List to testimonials or reviews	http://kittylikesavocado.com/testimonials
Video Links list	http://kittylikesavocado.com/videolinks
Stage Plot, Input List and Tech Links List	http://kittylikesavocado.com/stageplot
Link List to Social Media	http://kittylikesavocado.com/socialmediasites
Song Sample/ Audio Links List	http://kittylikesavocado.com/songsamples
Store Links List	http://kittylikesavocado.com/stores
Graphic Download Links List	http://kittylikesavocado.com/GraphicDownloads
Photo Links List	http://kittylikesavocado.com/Photolinks
Affiliate Links List	http://kittylikesavocado.com/Affiliates

Figure 10-1: From the tagline to keywords, all pertinent website information is kept in a single file for easy access.

Linking your promotionals with Dropbox

Whether you have your template form and all the graphic images hosted on your website or not, also add them to your Dropbox. Dropbox is a file hosting service that has cloud storage and file synchronization. It enables you to store your content list as well as all the items shown in Figure 10-1 and share them as links.

Dropbox can be set up where anyone can access your files, you can set time limits for access, and you can even set up passwords for people to access only certain links. Visit www.dropbox.com and sign up for 5GB for free; larger accounts are available for nominal costs.

Sending links to people for download is faster and easier than sending files. Don't choke other people's emails with large attachments; simply send a link and description of the link. This way, you save megabytes and bring up your level of professionalism.

Put that photo in Dropbox and name it correctly: KittyLikesAvocado8x10Promo.JPG

Add it to Dropbox, which gives it an address like this one:

https://www.dropbox.com/s/7uuga7o64m0a3z9/
KittyLikesAvocado8x10Promo.JPG

Ask your webmaster to set up a redirect so you can give it a vanity name such as: http://kittylikesavocado.com/8x10promo/

This enables you to send a simple link in an email that looks like this:

Kitty Likes Avocado 8x10 Band Promo Photo – For Download at Dropbox at http://kittylikesavocado.com/8x10promo/

You now have a streamlined and professional look. And you have clear links as well as a description of what they contain.

You can easily access and share links directly from Dropbox on your phone or have the links to all the different files in Dropbox saved in your content cheat sheet to easily remember them. Think of it like an online promotional kit that is at your fingertips at all times.

With the cheat sheet, the links to all your key materials, graphics, all information for and from your website and social media pages are that much more accessible and make it that much easier to update, change, and share.

Links, All the Links, and Nothing but the Links

Linking, adding links, creating links, and sharing links in the most professional manner helps to get the most people to click through those links and send your audience, potential fans, and industry professionals where you want them to go.

Keep in mind it's more than just adding a link and assuming someone will click it. Too many get spammed with emails containing links that send them everywhere from virus-infected sites to downloads to pop ups and everything else they don't want to see. The more you can define a link as well as clarify where that link is taking someone, the better chance you have to get viewers to click it. The less music, video, and photos that are sent as attachments and replaced with clear links to where the music, videos, or photos are hosted means you're not choking a server or cluttering someone's mailbox.

I think it was the Meghan Trainor song that said, "It's all about the links, 'bout the links, no attachments". Maybe I got that confused with something else.

Links for fans

The links you share with fans online in posts and email newsletters as well as on your website should be clear and descriptive.

"Click here:" is not descriptive. Instead of directing a fan to click on a link, give them a description of the link and where you are sending them.

For example, instead of posting:

Click here for new video - <u>Video Link</u>

post this:

Click this link to see our new video for "Kitty Kitty Bang Bang" on YouTube at `https://youtube.com/watch?v=quetdyr1324r3`

or with a redirect of a vanity URL:

Click this link to see our new video for "Kitty Kitty Bang Bang" on YouTube at `http://kittylikesavocado.com/kittykittybangbangyoutube`

In the first example, you tell someone to click for a new video and give them a hyperlink. They don't know where they're going, what they're going to see, or if they can tell if they land on the right page or not. Some viruses can automatically affect links on someone's computer and send them to spam or worse . . . a virus.

In the second example, you cover all the issues. Your readers know what the video is titled — Kitty Kitty Bang Bang — and they know where it's hosted — on YouTube. They can see the link clearly listed and hyperlinked to know that they are heading to the right place.

In the third example, the vanity URL makes things look a little nicer and cleaner. That redirect sends them to YouTube and just like the second example, it's clear where they're going.

This also means if something weird pops up on their screen, they know they're in the wrong place.

Always look at the lower corner of your screen when clicking on a hyperlink, vanity link, — actually on any link, now that I think of it. A small address should display and tell you where you're going. Some links are affiliate links (you learn more about them a little later in this chapter in the "Affiliated links" section), and they either track where the click through is coming from or send you to the exact country's page for that link like GeoRiot (which I also touch on in the "Country translating links and GeoRiot" later in this chapter).

With any type of link, give people a clear description of what the link is, where you're sending them, and what they'll see, hear, read, or watch when they get there. Your clarity builds security and trust with friends and fans alike.

Before you send an email with a link, post an online update with the link, or add the link to a web page, double-check that the link actually goes where you want it to go. It's easy to accidently mess up a link or copy it wrong. Make sure that link's directing people in the intended direction.

Affiliate links

Affiliate links lead people to the pages where you want them to go but can also become a small revenue stream as people click on them for you. For example, if someone clicks an affiliate link from a post or one of your web pages and is sent to Amazon, you can make a small affiliate referral percentage from that click-through and purchase if you have an Amazon Affiliate account.

You can also ask fans to help by spreading the word on their pages about your affiliate links, which you can spin to help fund a recording or tour. On the other side of the coin, you can entice fans to set up their own affiliate accounts to help promote you while they take a small percentage for themselves. Both options can help spread the word that much better.

Country translating links and GeoRiot

If you have a link on your website or on a post that sends someone to Amazon or iTunes, you're actually sending them to one specific country out of the massive worldwide storefronts each has. Amazon has 14 different stores around the world, and iTunes has a whopping 155. The problem lies in if someone in India clicks your Amazon.com link, they end up in the U.S. storefront instead of their own, which means they're much less likely to be able to listen to (and purchase) your music. This is because links that aren't globalized provide a poor user experience since fans can't purchase in a foreign storefront due to language, currency, shipping, and distribution problems. End result, the possible loss of a sale or download.

With GeoRiot (which I recommend everyone to have), your links are automatically globalized and can make your Amazon and iTunes links go directly to the store from which each listener is most likely to purchase. So for a single GeoRiot affiliate link for a download or product, every fan from around the world is able to quickly and effortlessly download or purchase your music. For example, if you go to http://geni.us/fordummies. it takes you directly to "Music Business For Dummies" on Amazon for whatever country you're in.

On top of all this, GeoRiot also acts as an affiliate link where you can connect an Amazon or iTunes affiliate account and make money from those clicks and purchases.

Any link that goes to Amazon or iTunes should have a GeoRiot link. You can find GeoRiot at http://georiot.com/ and set up your affiliate accounts for Amazon and iTunes through their respective sites.

By setting up affiliate accounts for free on other Amazon sites, aside from the country you are in, you can also see those affiliate percentages come in from around the world. It's a small amount, but it still creates an additional revenue stream.

As an additional bonus, if someone clicks through your GeoRiot link to Amazon and then ends up buying other items, such as a TV, a couch, or a larger-scale and more-expensive item, you get an affiliate percentage of that, too. Pretty cool!

Links for industry

Use vanity URLs, whether leading music-industry people to your website, your Dropbox, or directly to videos, audios, and other pages. The clean description makes it easier for industry professionals to reference and also lets them know to where they are being pointed. To learn more about vanity URLs, check out the "Links for fans" section earlier in this chapter.

The easier you make it for industry professionals to be able to access everything from downloadable poster files to audio samples to stage plots and input lists, the better chances you have of those professionals wanting to work with you again and again.

Streamlining all your information, downloads, contracts, and everything else showcases a professionalism many lack. Even if you don't know how to create a redirect or vanity URL, ask your webmaster or a web professional to set these up for you. You want these in place.

Dropbox links over file-sharing sites

Set up that Dropbox account and share simple Dropbox links for fans, industry professionals, and media folks to download. Some of the other free file sharing sites can force a user to go through a number of sign-up requests and make downloading that much more of a challenge.

Send that simple link for easy download. Or if it's someone you're working with, ask them to sign up for a Dropbox account, too, so that you can share materials that can be easily accessed and edited.

Whereas some of the information you're sharing is fine to be out in the public and easily accessible online, other information such as contracts and some of the higher-resolution graphics should be a little more controlled. Set up password protection for these links on Dropbox, and add expiration dates of access to these items to keep things that much more secure.

Best Practices and Tips for Social Media Sites

Content is king and draws people back to your website, stores, products, and you. The constant sell and ask has become oversaturated and is viewed as spam by most people. Applying the most engaging content that draws a direct and indirect interest in you is a requirement to connect with new fans as you continue to maintain and keep interest brewing with your existing fan base.

Your conversion and engagement is more important than your like or fan counts. If you have 100,000 followers who aren't engaging with you, sharing your posts, buying your merchandise, or coming to your shows, then you don't have a fan base. Just as content is king, the conversion of the content also shares the throne.

Your fair sharing of content

Quality over quantity is going to win every time, and it's the best approach to take. Whereas it's key to produce regular content on a daily basis, an excess of too many posts every day will come off as spamming and annoying.

If someone who follows you on Twitter isn't following that many people, and you post 20 times a day, you're clogging up their feed because they see way too many posts from you.

Just because someone likes you, is friends with you, or is connected with you, doesn't mean they're following you. Many social media sites allow for the passive-aggressive un-follow. They are still connected with you as a number, but they don't see a single thing from you.

Posting for quality connects that much better than posting for quantity. Formatting a post to be effective as a whole, but then working for a number of different sites is the best approach to take. Posting a photo on Instagram that's shared to Twitter and then added to Facebook as well as Flickr and Tumblr is a great example of sharing content over numerous sites.

Dueling dualities of your posts and engagement

Every post has a three-fold purpose. If you keep that in mind before you post, it enables that much better conversion and engagement with each post you put on social media. Here are the three fundamental pieces and actions:

1. Engage and draw interest from new fans.

2. Maintain interest and engagement with existing fans.

3. Convert new and existing fans to purchases, shares, and promoting to others.

It really is that simple, and unfortunately it's forgotten all too often. If you're only building your new audience and ignoring the engagement with your current audience, you end up losing them. It becomes a vicious circle.

Pushing to connect only with more fans and new fans leaves the existing or older fans out of the loop and feeling as though you're only selling and marketing to reach others online. No fan wants to feel like they're forgotten.

Engaging directly with each fan

Although it's a challenge to connect with each and every single fan online, your sense of engagement can make a fan feel like you're talking directly to them. This is a powerful tool for your social media toolbox and why each post should be delivered in a way that makes the reader feel like it's connecting with both the existing and new fans simultaneously.

You do this by creating content that entices everyone and then ends with the call to action or directing where you want them to go to purchase music, merchandise, or share other links.

Posting content versus posting the sell

The content comes first and then the sell comes next in order to engage and maintain new and existing fans both. For example, if Kitty Likes Avocado posts on Facebook for people to go to iTunes to download an album that's been out for more than a year with a link to the iTunes store and nothing else, that's just a flat sell. It also falls flat with people who have been connected with the band for months and months. These folks have already either purchased the recording, or they haven't purchased it yet, but the incessant push comes off as redundant and spammy.

Imagine that you post about a new album some friends just released. You give the link and ask your fans to check out the new music and leave a short review. At the end of your post, you can add your call to action so they can find out more about you . . . and voilá. You've just offered something fun for new and existing fans, that being a new band and a place to go for new fans to find out more about you.

This creates a connection and a desire to engage from fans new and old. It allows someone to not feel spammed or pressured whereas it makes those existing fans search for your band in their feeds because you spend more time with fresh content over continually pushing the old sell.

It's okay to have certain posts that are just for the sell, too. Just make sure you're on a 1:9 ratio for that sell. One complete add for an item, download or product, and nine others that start with other content that sends viewers to you for more information on the sell. Content first, sales pitch second. Nine out of ten doctors recommend it!

Automating messages can be trouble

At one point, an automated message was sent when a fan starting following you. This feature had a great conversion rate . . . for a while, at least.

The bad side is that these autoreplies can come off as impersonal and turn off fans. Be careful if you add an automated message on Twitter. Give it a sense of personalization, but keep it professional and make it something that's giving and not asking for more. Go with something like "I'm so glad you're here!" rather than "Thanks for the follow, now go add us on Facebook at this address." You can see the difference between personal and impersonal, exciting rather than stale.

Also avoid having music start to play as soon as someone arrives at your website. Some might be at work, in a library, in class, or other quiet places, and not only will it be annoying, it can slow the connection and loading time for others. Allow people visiting to choose to play the music instead of forcing it on them.

Other options include adding a message about a free download, or inviting fans to check out a new song sample. You can also add a link to a video — or better yet, to a video that welcomes a fan and gives them an introduction that is not available as a public video.

Once a week, take a look at the people or companies that add you on different social media sites. If you send an automated message to someone that might be able to help you, whether it be through a service, booking, or media opportunity, your automated message might turn them away. Try sending personal messages when you can to acknowledge the individual and/or company that's connected with you. It can open up that many more doors.

Respecting the fan, not the fan number

Identifying that you just hit a milestone of 500, 5,000, or 50,000 fans is something for you or for industry professionals to know, not your fan base itself. By posting updates about how humbled, excited, or amazed you are to hit a certain number of fans, followers, views, likes, friends and so on, while cool for you, disrespects those who have been with you for a long time.

Maintaining the respect for every single fan from the oldest to the newest is crucial in keeping engagement and conversion strong. Respect your fan base for your fans, not for the number of fans. This is one of the biggest and best practices to implement online and off.

Marketing to fans outside of music

You might not be the biggest soccer fan and couldn't care less about the World Cup. Football season and the Super Bowl might be too rough for you, or the World Series and baseball is may be too boring for you. Still, these types of sporting events, along with big movies and other pop culture-style happenings, could be important to many of your fans.

You don't need to become a fan of sports, films, and cultural events, but respect what your fans are into. Adding posts on social media like "the last thing I will do is watch the stupid Super Bowl" could offend a fan who's a big football fan and turn them off to you.

Instead, try to tie into some of the larger events with a post about a song, a Super Bowl discount you're offering fans, or something that enables that much more engagement with those who are already engaged with the event.

Desi Serna, the author of *Music Theory For Dummies* (John Wiley and Sons), offered a Super Bowl discount for his book and added the hashtag #Superbowl. In this instance, Serna showcased respect for those who were into it, grabbed the trending hashtag to potentially be seen by those who may not already be connected with him, and offered a special/discount on his products.

Your effort to practice consideration for others' interests brings that much more interest to you in a vicarious manner.

Political or religious posting

There's an old saying that you shouldn't talk about politics, religion, or sex at the dinner table. While sex in many ways is much more common talk these days both online and off, still be careful when it comes to political and religious postings.

What goes for politics . . .

If you want to talk politics and that is part of your vibe, brand, or music, then go for it. That said, however, understand that fans might be turned off and turned away by your political beliefs. If you're able to keep your political beliefs for your personal life, you may find a much greater chance to reach a much wider audience. Too, keeping your politics to yourself also opens the door for you to be an escape, especially in times of elections or crazy political controversies or major news.

When everyone is yapping, posting, and screaming about the crisis of the day, many might find a greater connection and engagement in your social media postings and music if they can come to a page that isn't ridden with the headlines they are seeing everywhere else.

. . . . also goes for religion

If your music ties into your religious beliefs and it's part of you and marketing your music as a whole, then go for it. For example, if you're a Christian band or a Gospel singer, obviously religion is your thing. But if it's more of a personal viewpoint, then let it be just that. It's not about hiding who you are or what you believe; it's about connecting with as many people as possible first from as many different backgrounds as possible.

Overly personal and private posting

Engaging with your fans is a wonderful thing. Giving them pieces of you outside of music is also great for a vicarious connection to elements they might have in common with you. Still, leave some of the details private, and let your personal and private life be just that — personal for those you choose to directly share it with and private from those who don't need that much information.

Keeping your personal life private is for your safety, too. Artists need to be careful when they state where they're going along with talking about break-ups online or sharing too much romantic information. This can encourage stalkers or people who could become obsessed with you in an unhealthy fashion.

When shooting videos for social media, avoid having your bed or an excess of personal effects in the background. Shoot with flat backgrounds or backgrounds that don't identify your home, room, or location.

News jacking posts and comment jacking

While it's good to cross-market and tie into certain mainstream events, draw the line at *news jacking*. News jacking is where you take a news-related or trending post that has absolutely nothing to do with you and use it in an exploitive manner.

News jacking works two ways. You might share news about the death of a celebrity and then create a post that puts the focus on you or your music. Or someone posts about a topic that has nothing to do with you and your music; a topic-related thread goes on but then you post something about your new song or a concert date.

Think before you post or add your comments to something. There are times where it's not about you, not about marketing you, and just not the right time to promote. Keep that practice in mind when you're planning a post or commenting on someone else's.

Repeating posts over and over and over

With the lack of creativity or the desire to promote a certain song, video, link, or whatever, many musicians post the same exact thing over and over with the mindset that it'll be seen by more and more people.

In a sense, this breaks all the good-practice posting rules by being redundant and not considering the audience that's already seen the post.

I was on a Twitter page for a band that added me and saw that their last 20 posts were the exact same post. Same content, same hashtag, same link to their iTunes page to buy a song. This is a perfect example of what you don't want to do.

If you want to bring continued attention to a purchase link, video, social media site, and so on, reset the headline and revamp the content to reinforce the interest in fans both old and new.

New content can close with an older link, but always keep the headlines new and fresh. Think like a paperboy in one of those old black-and-white movies: "Extra, extra, read all about it!" Capture your fans and followers with fresh content and then draw them to where you want them to go!

Try to keep repetitive posts to a minimum, but when you are repeating, change the headline to maintain the overall interest from the person who has already read it before to the person seeing it for the first time.

Keeping an eye on the walls

If a new fan comes across one of your social media pages for the first time, do they get a sense of you, your music, and your brand or are they inundated with "@soandso thanks for the add" or "@soandso that's too funny" type messages along with way too many retweets that have nothing to do with you?

Keep those walls clean and remember that this is the first visit and first impression for a new fan. From your Facebook page to your Twitter feed, from the YouTube videos you share to your Google+ page, make sure that people know about you and don't have to dig in or scroll down too far to get that information.

Keep your walls clean and check them every few days to see how they look from the standpoint of a first-time visiting fan. Make sure you're presenting yourself in a way that draws people in immediately over making them have to search and scroll for information.

Download Google Chrome, and when opening a page to see how a website, social media page, or blog appears for a first-time viewer or for someone not already connected, click the three horizontal bars in the upper-right corner of a Google Chrome window. The third option down is the New Incognito window. By clicking that and then going to your different social media sites, you can get a good quick look at what an unconnected person sees.

When it comes to eyeing your walls, check the comments now and then. Certain social media sites may not alert you when someone leaves a comment. It's not a bad thing to leave negative comments up; however, certain comments can border and cross the line of disrespect and good taste and even be very creepy and just wrong. Check in once a week or once a month across your pages to make sure nothing is disrespectful or abusive. Blocking or preventing those posters from posting can ensure it doesn't occur again, at least not from them.

Another way to handle comments is to simply not enable commenting on certain pages. Some find it easier to deliver content on certain sites without engagement. If you find that too many people are posting disrespectful posts or spamming your walls, blocking all comments can work well to prevent that.

Engaging and tolerating the critics and the haters

Not everyone is going to like your music, and there are a lot of people on social media who are more than happy to share that fact with you. Take it all in stride and don't worry about trying to defend your music, look, show, or anything else. The more lit up and defensive you get, the more these people keep on keeping on and digging in deeper.

Think of that whole bully concept from grade school, and apply it to social media. Then think about how art is subjective, and you can't please everyone. No one is right; no one is wrong, It's all opinion, and everyone has a different one.

The cooler you can be, the better the long-term results. Engage, but play nice, even when they aren't. This works well for your appearance with other fans, but also with how you're seen by the industry.

It's not just good practice tips for your social media for your fans. Labels, managers, investors, and other industry professionals don't look only at what you post, but also at how you engage, react, and respond to the good and the bad. You're showcasing your content on social media, but you're also showcasing your professionalism.

Long-term effect of good posting

Every post should be something that's helpful for your branding, marketing, and promotion a week, month, or year down the line. When you start with fresh content and then close with your call to action, that content can serve to promote you, even if the call to action or close is announcing a single gig or an event.

Tracking your posting plan and maintaining an editorial calendar for how and when you post helps organize ideas, get ahead of schedule, and plan better. Plan your attack from blogs to photos to reviews to audios and everywhere in between.

Chapter 11

Planning for Content Marketing throughout the Year

• •

In This Chapter

▶ Creating your content plan and editorial calendar

▶ Formatting your posts, blogs, videos, and audios for the best results

▶ Adjusting your content for mainstream, trends, events, and holidays.

▶ Understanding and tracking the conversions and results of your content

• •

ontent marketing is an ongoing part of your marketing and promotions throughout your career. It never stops, but it can become easier in time. Starting with the right content plan and applying an editorial calendar can reduce the confusion as they help you to understand the conversion of your content.

Knowing what works best for you, what engages the most people, and in the end what converts to fans, sales, and attendance can only be found out by you. Some claim success by posting specific content at specific times, but in the end, every artist, product, and fan base is different. By planning, tracking, organizing, and scheduling your content, your marketing efforts will go that much further, faster, and easier.

Maintaining Best Website and Content Practices

Your approach to content that expands across your website blog and on to social media as well as the social media posts that can be automatically added to your website need to showcase the best professionalism and presentation with an aim to reach, engage, and connect with your existing fan base while enticing and drawing in new fans. Too, these pages and posts should showcase professionalism toward management, labels, investors, booking agents, reviewers, and other music industry mavens.

Showcasing the strongest and freshest content to engage those previously mentioned, while not giving off the sense of redundancy or coming off spamming, is not as challenging as you think. When you have a calendar in front of you to help guide, track, and choose your posts, this task gets easier.

Taking that extra time to properly name a photo, title a video, format a blog, and choose the right hashtags, links, and attachments allows your content to not only work for you for the day you post it, but also work effectively for years to come as it optimizes and compounds against all the other content you put out there.

Not every post needs to be about music, shows, and merchandise. Vicarious, relatable, funny, serious, romantic, and other topics can be used as strong content that draws people back to you and your music.

Editorial calendars

Planning out your posts in advance as well as setting up a tracking system to understand your engagement and conversion levels makes everything easier than attempting to create new content every day. By setting up your editorial calendar to cover these key elements, creating, posting, tracking, and understanding conversions for your social media takes a lot less time and causes a lot less stress.

An editorial calendar should include

- ✔ **Type of posts:** Blogs, pictures, audios, videos, quotes, reviews, and so on
- ✔ **Scheduled posting plan:** What is tentatively going up and when
- ✔ **Titles and primary keywords of blog and video posts:** To see what's being captured
- ✔ **Back-up post list:** For use at any time
- ✔ **Advanced post planning:** For events, holidays, and anniversaries
- ✔ **Recurring themes:** Or pattern posts

The following figures show a basic four-week calendar, listing a split of content from audios, blogs, videos, links, quotes, pictures, and reviews. Figure 11-1 shows them laid out repetitively where every day is the same in the month. Figure 11-2 shows them scattered. But both supply seven different styles of content that can cross over each other but still deliver consistent content to market you and your music.

People respond differently to different types of content as well as how it's presented. If you find that videos have a greater result than quotes, then lose the quotes or reduce them and add another video to the editorial calendar and the schedule.

SUNDAY	MONDAY	TUESDAY	WEDNESDAY	THURSDAY	FRIDAY	SATURDAY
1 Audio	2 Blog	3 Video	4 Picture	5 Quote	6 Review	7 Link
8 Audio	9 Blog	10 Video	11 Picture	12 Quote	13 Review	14 Link
15 Audio	16 Blog	17 Video	18 Picture	19 Quote	20 Review	21 Link
22 Audio	23 Blog	24 Video	25 Picture	26 Quote	27 Review	28 Link
29 Audio	30 Blog	31 Video				

Figure 11-1: Uniform version of a four-week calendar.

Courtesy of Loren Weisman

SUNDAY	MONDAY	TUESDAY	WEDNESDAY	THURSDAY	FRIDAY	SATURDAY
1 Audio	2 Blog	3 Video	4 Picture	5 Quote	6 Review	7 Link
8 Video	9 Audio	10 Blog	11 Link	12 Picture	13 Quote	14 Review
15 Link	16 Review	17 Audio	18 Blog	19 Video	20 Picture	21 Quote
22 Review	23 Link	24 Quote	25 Audio	26 Blog	27 Video	28 Picture
29 Audio	30 Blog	31 Video				

Figure 11-2: Scattered version of a four-week calendar.

Courtesy of Loren Weisman

Defining each piece of content

The idea of posting audio and video files, blogs, quotes, reviews, and links can be overwhelming. This is a big reason why many artists stick with pictures and either skip or shortcut other content forms.

The trick to making it less overwhelming and more inspiring is in the definition and options of what you can create with each type of media. The following sections look at definitions and descriptions of each type of content.

Audio

Audio files aren't limited to just songs. Yes, you can post songs, but this also can include podcasts, short audio snippets of songs, and short audio cuts from gigs, backstage, on the stage, in rehearsal, or anywhere else. You can also share samples of songs that will be recorded soon as well as bloopers from the studio and stage.

Blooper audios and mixes of a number of bloopers mashed together can make for excellent down-to-earth content. You may have been frustrated in the studio when you were trying to get a certain take just right, but a compilation of bloopers shows your humorous side and can attract listeners to the final version of the song. In a world where everyone is always trying to showcase perfection, show them that no one is perfect and give them a laugh.

All samples that you post should be copyrighted, and you should have your copyrights in order before you post any music online. It's true that as soon as you create it, it's technically copyrighted to you, but in the world of stealing and sampling, it makes it worlds harder to prove it's yours if you don't have your material correctly copyrighted.

Keep those audios short. Don't give away full songs, or if you post a full song for free, realize that it's hard to remove it and make money from it down the line. Audio shorts under three minutes, just like videos, get more listens and completed listens all the way through over longer audios. Mix up the audios, create themes, and have fun. These don't have to be perfectly mixed either. You can record audio right into Garage Band or any recording software on your computer, or even into a smartphone for use as solid content.

Upload that audio to SoundCloud, Spreaker, or another audio sharing site, and use that page as the link to all your other social media pages when you have an audio posting day.

Video

Short videos are amazing for engagement and optimization on your website and across social media. This is one time where quantity can trump quality. Don't get me wrong — you still want quality in each video you post with strong, engaging content. But having only one high-cost, heavily produced music video is nowhere near as effective as having ten short videos shot on iPhones. With ten short videos, you deliver lots of new content that markets you, your music, and your merchandise.

Add videos to YouTube that show how a song was written and include a short profile on each band member. You can also include a review for another band, talk about products or equipment you use, make pop culture references, tell who influences your band, show fan video profiles — use your imagination and you'll be amazed at how many other creative videos you can post for your fans.

Shorter videos, such as those under three minutes, have that much better a click-through rate. Videos four minutes and longer lose viewers much faster than videos under three minutes.

Videos also have a higher level of optimization. Correctly formatting a video can help it to jump up in all search engines that much faster. Later in this chapter, I explain the basic steps to video formatting.

Pictures

Pictures and images are great additions to social media. Unfortunately, too many artists upload only an image and do not even post a headline for it. Pictures, like videos, that are formatted correctly can help the image jump up in optimization and be found in more searches.

Audiences engage with relatable pictures. In other words, don't send just shots from the studio, rehearsals, band shots, or audience shots. Add fun pictures that have nothing to do with music but are helpful to market back to you. You audience would likely enjoy images or views that have a Flat Stanley addition to them, like a CD cover, piece of merchandise, or a picture of someone wearing your logo that can add that extra touch.

From landscapes to food to cars, old toys, animals, and more, your expansion of photos can draw a great deal of views and interest. Why not show your dog biting down on a CD cover and give it a headline that says "This one reviewer chewed us up and spit us out."

Not all pictures have to be humorous, but that little step outside of the box can make for better pictures and more available content. Add in fun headlines to gather even greater interest, especially on sites like Instagram, Flickr, and Pinterest. (For more info on social media sites, check out Chapter 10.)

Adding hashtags and a call to action on sites like Instagram can cross reference you, the picture, and the contents of the picture to a wider audience, helping to give you that much better a chance at a larger conversion to fans and sales.

Quotes or jokes

Quotes can be anything you like, pertaining to music or not. They can also be funny, shorter posts that aren't as expanded as a blog format. Add pictures sometimes; other times, don't add pictures. This allows for another form of content that can draw in and engage people looking for short tidbits.

The following is an example of a quote post I used a number of months back:

"Romeo & Juliet isn't a love story. It's a 3-day #relationship between a 13 & 17 year old that caused 6 deaths. Sincerely, those who read it." – Unknown

This was posted on Facebook, Twitter, Google+, LinkedIn, and a number of my other social media sites as a joke that engaged people, caused shares, and kept ongoing and consistent content to be posted.

It wasn't directly marketing me, my book, my speaking, or my services, but it continued to maintain engagement.

If the quote or joke isn't yours, do what you can to add the author of it. Give credit where credit is due. Adding a link to the person's Facebook or Twitter page is also a great way to give credit and connect with that many more people.

Again, it doesn't have to be all about music. Of course, your fans love music, but may want to know more about you. Allow for the connection outside of music in a vicarious or relatable way and you draw people to click-through to your pages.

Reviews

Reviews and testimonials are great cross-marketing draws and pieces of content that should be added on a weekly basis. Highlighting another band, a product, or instrument you use, a restaurant where your band ate, an attraction you checked out on the road, a hotel you stayed at, a place you played, or a service you used helps give you a wider reach to people who may like the other band, the restaurant, hotel, service, and so on.

Adding these reviews to sites like Yelp, TripAdvisor, and Google can further optimize your name, review, and you to others who are interested in that place or service.

You want reviews for your recordings, so look for people to add positive comments to your social media pages, iTunes store, Amazon listings, and everywhere else. Reviews and testimonials can put you in front of others who might never otherwise see you.

Make time each day (outside of a weekly review of a band, product, place, and so on) to add a simple review to a different site. Once a week, put a focus on a given person, place, or thing to review, and share through all your networks.

Blogs

A blog can be the most challenging to create, but it can also become the best long-term optimizer of content that gets picked up by the search engines and helps get you connected with more fans.

Blogs can and should contain pictures; if you're hosting your website with WordPress, you can share it through all your social media sites via your website.

With all the different topics that you can cover, think of your blog as a head-line or keyword that people search on to find your music and you; then, work off the title to draw in those fans not only for the day you post it, but also for the search engines to grab months and even years later.

Have fun with titles and the content in a blog. Talk about a variety of topics to get reads and wider-spread opportunities to reach a larger audience. Top ten lists, discussing your favorite things, asking why the sky is blue, and so on attracts more readers than:

Kitty Likes Avocado Band Blog 6-14-15 Entry

The following list is an example of five titles that can draw interest from people searching for music as well as searching for other topics:

✔ Top Ten Pick-Up Lines Our Drummer Has Used at Shows

✔ Why Mary Poppins is the Greatest Movie of All Time

✔ Favorite Restaurants on the West Coast We Visited on Tour

✔ How to Win a Free T-Shirt from Kitty Likes Avocado

✔ What Our Superhero Alter Egos Would be for Every Band Member

You can also add blogs that discuss why you use only a specific guitar, drumhead, or drumstick. These types of blogs have multiple benefits that can include optimizing the brand, which you can use to solicit sponsorships or endorsement assistance down the line.

All the content you post helps you more over time as your optimization and formatting compounds. The more content you have going up on a regular basis, the more it optimizes for that single post as well as all the other posts that came before and those that will come after.

By hosting the blog on your website and sharing the blog link on social media, you're directing people back to your content as it brings them to the website where they can find out where to buy your music, your products, or come to see you.

Link or pitch

Sharing links and having content that is an all-out sales pitch to one of your stores, one of your products or one of your other sites to connect or engage with is not a bad thing, but it should show up no more than once a week or even once every ten days.

With all the branding, content, and information in place, your call to action on your social media sites and in your videos help with a solid pitch and sell.

Inviting approaches to connect on social media

While you might not spam your fan base all that much, many other bands do and even your best intentions could be viewed and misconstrued as spammy and annoying, making your fans want to block you. Take that into consideration and create a headline pitch that brings someone to a link. This is crucial in the oversaturation of forced asks with no detail. These types include:

✔ **Go add us on Facebook at** `https://facebook.com/kittylikes avocado/`: Change this to *If you're addicted to Facebook and would rather connect with us there, you can find us at* `https://facebook.com/kittylikesavocado/`. *New post only on Facebook about last week's recording session!* In this ask, you aren't telling the audience to connect with you everywhere; you're giving them a choice.

✔ **Join our YouTube channel at** `https://youtube.com/channel/UCjxt99IgyGQkUGq14chOdZw/`: Change to *If you like YouTube updates when we post a video, consider subscribing to our YouTube channel at*

`https://youtube.com/channel/UCjxt99IgyGQkUGq14chOdZw/`. *for all your video needs without any of those pesky words from Kitty Likes Avocado. Search Studio Outtakes for a funny blooper video that's available only on YouTube.* Again, a softer ask. This also explains to the potential subscriber they receive notifications and makes a little joke about other social media sites.

✔ **Check out our new single that will knock your socks off at** `https://soundcloud.com/kitty-likes-avocado/`: Change to *A mix of Barry Manilow and Aaron Lewis were trying to tackle a Bruno Mars song is what we're told our new single sounds like. You be the judge. Find the song on SoundCloud at* `https://soundcloud.com/kitty-likes-avocado/`. Adding a picture of Barry Manilow and Aaron Lewis next to each other as the photo for the link post could add a little extra curiosity. There's humor and a couple recognizable names for comparison. By offering the fan to be the judge, you're letting them decide what they think or how they feel after hearing the song.

✔ **Buy our T-shirt at** `http://geni.us/fordummies`**:** Change to *In the market for an all-cotton tan-colored shirt that's super comfy, goes with everything, and has our logo all over it? Our new Kitty Likes*

Avocado shirts are available in S, M, L, XL, and XXL. We'd love to be added to your T-shirt collection. More info, sizes, and prices at: `http://geni.us/fordummies`*.* This gives a more inviting ask to purchase a product with information, color, and a connecting sense from the band about how they would love for you to have their shirt.

Your pitch for someone to click a link and then buy a song, connect on another social media site, subscribe to a blog, buy a hat, and so on has to contain something that draws them in and makes them want to find out more.

Don't tell your fans or audience how they'll feel after they hear a song, see you live, or experience something you deliver. Allow them to feel it for themselves. The overly dominant approach of telling people what they feel is assumptive and pushy. By giving them the chance and the offer to decide, you engage your fan base and potential new fans that much better.

Considering other content ideas

Maybe you have an idea for a regular content concept or a mixture of two or three. Go with it. Your creativity, continuity, and uniformity dramatically increase your views, networking, engagements, and conversions. As you create a theme or concept, go with it for a while. Test the waters, and keep an eye on the results and interactions.

Good content connects you with those looking for the content but not necessarily looking for you. Topics and posts about events outside of music that people are searching on can help draw them to your post on that topic and then, in turn, they can find out more about you.

Crafting content concepts

Inside all the different types of content — like blogs, videos, photos, and audios — that you post and plan out in your editorial calendar, add different concepts and pieces to further more interest in you and your music. Adding these supplementary elements to your content not only helps keep the content and your postings more engaging, it also mixes things up a bit and can make the viewer look a little deeper.

Easter eggs

An *Easter egg* is an intentional inside joke, hidden message, or feature in a work such as a computer program, video game, movie, book, or crossword puzzle. Whether in a video, blog, audio file, or any type of content, add those Easter eggs now and then. For example, in a blog, you can use different colors or different fonts for certain letters, and over a series of days or weeks, spell out a word. Let readers know that there's a secret word or phrase spread out across a series of blogs and if they figure it out, they get some kind of prize.

Using your editorial calendar to track what you put up and when, it's easy to create those hidden messages, images, or elements across a wider spread of time.

By offering the prize, you re-engage the fans who have already seen the content or skimmed through it to read that much closer and look that much deeper. They also spend that much more time on your site.

Then those who skipped certain content or didn't see those posts at all, will go through them with a fine-tooth comb. Although their main goal may be to win something, they get more engaged with you and the posted content. This can help with the conversions to purchases you're looking for.

Make sure the prize is something pretty good. In a sense, you're asking a fan, follower, or potential fan to dig through a whole bunch of material, so make it worth their while.

Prizes don't always have to tie in to you or your music or your products. While a CD, a T-shirt, a coffee cup, and a hat might entice some, offering something like a $50 gas card, a free oil change gift certificate, or another useful item may be that much more of an enticer to connect with you, join your mailing list, or whatever is required of them to be able to be entered in the contest.

Keeping sites and content public

Don't force fans to like you, your pages, or to sign up for a mailing list before they can decide if they actually *like* you, your music, and your content. Forcing them to do so is a bad idea and can make people move on very quickly to another artist or band.

Give each page the sense that it offers something exclusive to draw people in. Have a single video on YouTube that isn't shared on your other pages, photos on Instagram available only on Instagram, and certain posts just for Facebook.

Don't make your social media pages private. Give people the ability to see you as soon as they click through to you.

Personal pages versus band pages

Things can get confusing between personal and professional pages. The easiest solution is to make your personal page and the content private; then use a nickname or other name for Facebook, Twitter, and other sites you are on.

When people search on your name, they go directly to your fan or music pages in one step. On your personal pages, using images that aren't related to your music or images of you playing music can keep people from confusing the page with your band or artist page. Using pictures for avatars that aren't you, your logo, or anything to easily identify you is a good way to go, too.

If you state, "This is my personal page, go follow my fan page here," people can get put off. You may mean well and only want to send a potential fan to the places where you have the right type of content, but it can start things off on the wrong foot.

Whereas most of the time it's easier and faster to share content across social media sites, have a little bit of exclusivity here and there for people to look around. With your monthly email newsletter, be sure to offer more than just a recap of the posts and content of that month. There should be a couple articles that are shared only for those who signed up for your list; otherwise, they have no reason to be added to your mailing list.

Comments and commenting on other pages and posts

Just as you look for positive engagement, negative posts, critics, and flat out jerks can also comment on your walls. Anything too graphic or really mean should be deleted, but leave some of the negative posts on and engage with a thicker skin, being the better person and taking the high road. Being able to handle a few blows to the ego can be good for your marketing as well as life in the music business as a whole.

When you comment on other pages or posts, you're representing yourself to your fans and others in the industry when using your artist or band pages. Post accordingly, play nice, and project professionalism, even when the other person might not be acting all that mature.

Sharing other people's posts to promote you

Sharing other bands' posts or posts from those you're cross-promoting is a helpful way to connect with a different audience, and you may see the same actions reciprocated. Don't get caught up in quid pro quo, and expect because you share a post that they will share one of your posts.

If a post resonates with you and you want to share it, give the post a headline that leads your viewers to it and offer a basic reason why you're sharing it.

The potential for viral down the road

That post from a few months ago or a few years ago might just get a second wind stronger than the first. Realize that everything you post could serve as additional marketing and promotion far down the line or in some of those cases, even go viral when you least expect it.

Continuous consistent content

The continuity of your content planned out and posted on a regular basis gives you the highest visibility, best optimization, and best chance of engagement with people both looking for you and those looking for something else but finding you instead.

Use your editorial calendar and a file to store content that might be more suitable around a holiday, someone's birthday, or another type of event instead of creating content and posting it that day. It's so much better to have a solid piece of content going up once a day over posting five things in one day and then not posting for a week.

Even when posting show announcements, album or single releases, product releases, and so on, spin it for something that's helpful for that day but that can also help to draw people in the following week, month, or even year.

Think how it's read by someone who may have 1,000 other bands in their feed. Use a strong headline to grab people's attention, engage them with content, and then give them the easiest ways to find out more about you, a product you might have for sale, or a gig you might be playing. Post to be found with the strongest content over posting to be seen with excessive posts of substandard content. This uniformity and regularity helps to maintain your existing audience while it draws more and more people to you.

Formatting Your Content

Each piece of content you add to your editorial calendar needs to be formatted before it's posted. By formatted, I mean make sure you're choosing a primary keyword or phrase and adding a call to action.

The way you format the content is a crucial step prior to posting. Well-formatted content helps optimize it for that day but also gives your overall web presence that much more of a boost.

Take the time to format correctly before posting to get the most out of every day and every post.

The following sections look at tips and applications for each style of content to help organically boost visibility and optimization.

Blog formats

Blogs can be the most difficult to format and have the most details. There's no need to have others write content for you or pay teams to write blogs when half of those content writers are sending prewritten materials that are only slightly adjusted for you. These simple rules help boost your blogs to be seen that much more and reach higher page rankings that much faster as well.

Having a WordPress-hosted website and blog helps with your optimization. Adding the free plugin WordPress SEO by Yoast helps by showing you a checklist of items that should be applied to make a blog or a page optimization friendly. More about WordPress in Chapter 10.

Your primary keyword phrase

The primary keyword phrase is the main phrase your blog and content is built on. This is what you want to show up when people are searching for that specific phrase. The more you change up the phrase in different ways to get into as many different searches as possible, the more people will be able to find you. More about keyword choosing and keyword phrases in Chapter 8.

For example, your primary keyword phrase needs to show up in the URL for the page. So if your blog is titled:

Fruity Funk Scratching at the Drapes of Rock and Roll — Meet KLA

and your primary keyword phrase is Fruity Funk, this should show up in the URL like this: http:///kittylikesavocado.com/2015/01/01/fruity-funk/

Keep that phrase interesting as you tie it into the title of your blog. Think news story; think read all about it; think excitement and how you can best draw the interest for someone to click through. Combining a strong primary keyword phrase with a solid title under 70 characters gives you a headline that people want to click and read more about.

With blogs, make sure your primary keyword phrase is broken up by dashes between the words.

Besides the URL, your primary keyword phrase needs to be

- ✔ In your article heading.
- ✔ In your meta description.
- ✔ In at least one sub heading (an H1, H2, or H3 heading).
- ✔ In the first paragraph of your blog content.
- ✔ At least 1 percent of your total word count. For example: If you have a blog with 500 words, the keyword phrase needs to be inside the content at least five times.
- ✔ If you add photos or videos to the blog, the primary keyword phrase should be included in their filenames.

Again, never repeat primary keyword phrases for titles. Always change up the primary keyword phrase for each title. That phrase can be used again as a secondary phrase, but should not be used again for any other primary keyword phrases.

Outbound links or crosstown traffic

Adding outbound links to your blog to connect it to pertinent or relatable materials will also help build up the SEO and help to create links to other sites and pages. An outbound link is a link to another page, website, or social media that's not yours. Linking to products you use, other bands you play with, social media sites for venues where you're playing, and anything else helps to connect that post and content to other web and social media pages.

Minimum and maximum lengths

Make sure your blogs contain at least 300 words. This shows the search engines it's a real article and not something too short that could be over-looked. Stay under or top out at no more than 900 words, because you have to follow all those previously mentioned primary keyword phrase rules with more words in a blog, the more times you have to add that primary keyword over and over.

Each title should be at least 40 but under 70 characters, including spaces. And your meta description of the blog or blog summary should be over 100 characters but under 150.

Readability is key, too. Trying to construct a blog with the sole focus on building up SEO is a bad idea and can get your blog and website flagged by search engines like Google, Yahoo!, and Bing. Make your blogs readable, and don't overdo it with the use of keywords.

Don't forget the call to action

Sign off your blogs with that call to action. If you create a great piece of content that gets shared by numerous people who read it, but you don't give them the basics on you, your music, and your links, you could be losing a very large potential audience.

Even if the blog is hosted on your website, don't assume readers will scroll up and click through to read your bio, check out your other links, or connect with you. Make sure you close your blogs with a call-to-action signature that delivers your tagline, tells people where to find out more information, and offers them links to click right through to find out more and connect. Make it as easy as possible for people to connect over expecting them to dig that much deeper.

Using stacked blogs

A stacked blog includes a video, photo, audio, or any combination thereof, whereas a simple blog might contain only content and a couple images. Get creative and let your blog work for you. Stay in the mindset of how content or a blog can work on the day you put it up, but how months later that primary keyword phrase can show up in search engines and still be effective.

Video formats

The primary keyword phrase is king and should be repeated a good number of times. It's important to realize that videos aren't optimized by the content or quality of the actual video;, they're optimized by how the content is created around that video and how that video is uploaded.

Here are a series of tips to follow when you create your videos and format them for upload:

- ✔ **Keep your videos short.** Under three minutes is going to get more people to watch all the way through.

- ✔ **Keep your video title under 70 characters total.** This allows for better optimization as your video title is no more than the maximum length of what Google and other search engines see as a proper title.

- ✔ **Use the primary keyword phrase.** Make sure the title of your video contains your primary keyword phrase. Also, ensure that the title of your video is repeated four more times in the body of content of your video, as well as listed as one of the tags for your video. For example, if the title of your video is . . .

Fruity Funk Scratching at the Drapes of Rock and Roll – Meet KLA

. . .it's 63 characters with spaces, so it's under that 70 character mark. For this video, the primary keyword phrase is "Fruity Funk," so the file-name title of the uploaded video should be fruityfunk.MOV. By renaming the video as the primary keyword phrase, you upload a video with information directly relating to your keyword.

An effective YouTube video should have at least 300 words in the description. This formats it like a blog and also gives you room in the description to optimize more phrases and words. Back to your primary keyword phrase "fruity funk." Make sure that's the name of the actual video as well as placed into the title of the video, repeated at least four more times in the description of the video, and then is added in the tags section of the video.

Using at least two to three words in a keyword phrase that you want to capture is a good idea, but also realize Google is pushing phrases that are longer or called "long tail phrases," so make sure to add those into the mix, too. Adding a question or longer sentence can help with optimization as well. For example, a phrase such as "How do you scrape" is a great intro phrase for a video that could be titled: "How do you scrape at the drapes of rock and roll? KLA Video Blog."

At the top of the description for the video, add two links to your website and a social media page. The first thing most people see on their screens is the first couple lines of content below the video and the title. Give those viewers a chance to quickly and easily click through to get to more of you.

Embedding links into the videos is a great idea, too, but have those links at the top of the description for people to click through immediately.

When adding links to YouTube and many other social media sites, putting only www.kittylikesavocado.com doesn't always become a hyperlink. Add http:// and lose the www so it looks like http://kittylikesavocado.com. This format makes that address a hyperlink and easy to click through immediately.

Don't repeat a primary keyword phrase

Do not repeat a primary keyword phrase on YouTube, your blog, or anywhere else and avoid repeating them in your blog, too. Keep track of the primary keyword phrases you use and don't use them again as primary keyword phrases. They can be used as secondary keyword phrases in other videos and content. Overusing a phrase gets that phrase cancelled out for you when it comes to optimization and hurts the search results over time.

Body of the video content

After the two links, repeat the title of the video and give a description about the video. Close with your call to action and some more links at the bottom to create the most effective video upload possible. You can also add six to eight other tags besides your primary tag, and you're good to go.

Here's an example of it all put together for the best video content (description of the video adding fruity funk a few more times and then closing with your call to action):

> Primary keyword phrase: Fruity Funk
>
> Video name: fruityfunk.MOV
>
> Video title: Fruity Funk Scratching at the Drapes of Rock and Roll – Meet KLA
>
> Video tags or secondary keyword phrases: fruity funk, kitty likes avocado, rock and roll, alternative funk, pop infused, kitten on catnip, scratching post
>
> Video description:
>
> ```
> http://kittylikesavocado.com/
> ```
>
> ```
> https://facebook.com/kittylikesavocado/
> ```
>
> Fruity Funk Scratching at the Drapes of Rock and Roll – Meet KLA.

This video formatting helps to move you up higher in the rankings of YouTube as well as on other search engine sites. Take the time to set up your format, and keep a template that enables you to create the format that much easier.

You can create a number of video descriptions and formats first, then simply shoot the video and put it and the formatted description in a file with your editorial calendar. Sometimes, creating a number of videos in advance to be used over time can save you both time and hassle, making it easier to upload on those days when you're busy but still need top-notch content.

While there are issues with YouTube regarding payments and streaming for music for larger-scale artists, it doesn't mean you should avoid it all together. Using YouTube for content videos that cover you, the band, interviews, and other forms of content is the best for optimization. You don't need to post full videos of your music, but make those content videos on YouTube for your promotion, the promotion of your music, and for viewers to learn more about you.

Picture formats

Name those pictures! Just like videos, don't upload a photo to Google without renaming it. No one is searching for 8384765yrj.JPG, but if you have a promo band photo with a filename that's titled promo-shot,band-photo,kitty-likes-avocado.jpg, some of those terms may show up in the Google engines.

It's not just the pictures; it's also how they are formatted on the photo sites like Instagram, Flickr, and Pinterest. As mentioned in Chapter 10, Instagram gives you the best bang for the buck — being a photo-related site, many people see your picture and you have the ability to add up to 30 hashtags per photo.

Add the location and tag people in the photo to share it with a wider audience. Sharing an Instagram photo through Tumblr and Flickr can also be a great asset, but if you're taking advantage of the 30 hashtags, like you should, repost the picture to Facebook directly so that you're not sharing a really expanded post with way too many hashtags.

Don't tag people in photos who aren't in the photo or have nothing directly to do with the photo. That's spamming, and it's very unprofessional.

Put in the time to add a description of the photo, use the headline to introduce it and close with your call to action. This dramatically helps in the immediate and long-term visibility of a photo. Too many people waste a chance to make a photo really work to their benefit in the short term, but also in the long term.

Make every piece of content work as hard as it can for you. Describe those pictures, and take the time to get them up everywhere with all the information so they can reach as far as possible for as long as possible.

Keep taking pictures

Whether you're using the just pictures or you're adding pictures to blogs, keep taking pictures! The more pictures you use, the easier it is to avoid any type of copyright infringement or confusion with other pictures from other people. Your photos don't all have to be music-oriented, but having that file of different pictures you keep in a folder for online use gives you that much more to work with and keeps you from getting in potential copyright trouble.

And don't forget the memes, too! Sites like Meme Generator (www.memegenerator.com) enable you to upload pictures and create memes (those funny pictures with comments you see on Facebook and other social media sites). You can use already-existing images, but you can also upload your own photos and create your own memes.

Audio/podcast formats

Audios make for a great additional piece of content. Whether in a format of a short audio or a podcast, these pieces of content promotion can be downloaded or streamed by fans and played in the gym, car, on a bus on the way to work, and just about anywhere else.

Sites like Spreaker and SoundCloud can host your short audios and podcasts as well as help you with short audio pieces. Whether you record directly to SoundCloud or upload a track, the process is easier than ever and doesn't even have to cost you a penny.

Podcasts are basically audio blogs. They're downloadable files that people can listen to on their computer or any type of digital music playing device. These podcasts can also be distributed on sites like iTunes and iHeart Radio after they've logged a certain amount of listens. More information about the distribution options for podcasts can be found at `http://spreaker.com/`, one of the free sites where you can record or upload a podcast.

Audio lead-ins and lead-outs

Using Garage Band or another recording software can enable you to put a nice lead-in and lead-out to your audio blog or podcast. Keep it short and simple, and consider asking a friend to do that lead-in. Using a different voice can add an additional professional touch to it all.

Deliver that clear lead-in to what the audio or podcast is, and on the lead-out, make sure to reiterate your website, social media, and the rest of your call to action. Some may have access only to your audio, so make sure you give them the information to lead them to more.

Make sure all posts, whether audio, video, blog, and so on, have a clear beginning, middle, climax, and end. It helps to maintain, retain, and sustain your fans ongoing interest as you reach out to new people.

Avoid rambling on, laughing at private jokes, or jumping all over the place. It can be a major turn-off to listeners. See every audio or podcast as if it's the first time someone is hearing it or hearing about you, whereas at the same time keeping a certain consideration for those who might already be fans and have heard you before.

Keeping up with the content and filling in the blanks

On sites like SoundCloud you have the capability to use different hashtags as well as add a description. Take advantage of that space and fill in that content. Stay with the basic blog rules (see "Blog Formats" earlier in this chapter) as you repeat that primary keyword phrase a good number of times in that piece of content.

Just like video, audio doesn't automatically optimize; it's how the track is uploaded, named, hashtagged, and how content is added. Rename the URLs accordingly to make the topics, primary keyword phrase, and information crystal clear.

Overall lengths and times

Like videos, shorter audios have a better chance to be heard, and using more, shorter audios gives you more content, optimization, and share over long podcasts and audios.

Taking an audio and splitting it into a number of parts is a great idea and allows for that much more content. It also can entice someone that begins to listen to Part 3 of 3 to search for the other two parts and become that much more involved with you.

With the ability for people to download and collect podcasts, if the listener downloads a six-part episode that are ten minutes each, it still gives the listener the same content as if they had downloaded an hour podcast. All they are doing is listening through a few extra tracks. Breaking up those tracks can also build anticipation for those who are listening already while using each episode to capture that many more people and build up your online presence that much more.

Review formats

Reviews of your band or your own music can follow the form of a blog, video, audio, photo, or a mixture of all. In reviewing a band, a product, a place, or a location, the main goal is to cross-market with not only the fan base but also showcase your professionalism, appreciation, and respect that you present online.

In the simplest post with the least effort, add a short review that's a little more personalized and detailed than just "They rock" or "This place is good." Instead, aim for something closer to "Kitty Likes Avocado mixes up a number of genres while still staying grounded in rock and roll. These guys have a great energy on stage from start to finish."

Compose a review that you'd want to use if it was said about you in your review pages or testimonials. Take the time to construct something that is short, sweet, but detailed.

After you complete the review, add a link to the reviewed person, restaurant, band, or business's more popular social media pages and a link to their website. Another option is to review a song and add a link directly to it on iTunes.

When promoting someone else's link through GeoRiot, you you can earn an affiliate cut if the click turns into a sale. For more on GeoRiot, check out Chapter 10.

Sharing an audio, a YouTube video, or a picture can be an additional piece of short content for a review. The other option is to do an all-out blog, which can be a solid choice to do once a month for a band, place, product, or service.

Reviewing in full blog format

Give the same review as you would for that band, product, person, or service, but add that extra touch of optimization by following the blog formats. These reviews in blog format can be a great deal easier in many ways because you can gather most of the content from the band, product, or service you're reviewing.

Adding your personal review and then adding their photo, video, audio, or links can create an amazing piece of cross-marketing content that also more than likely gets the favor returned.

Link formats

For some of those simpler or smaller posts, sharing that simple link, but leading into it with a pitch that entices, as mentioned in "Maintaining best website and content practices" section of this chapter, is the best way to go. Sometimes after a longer content post like a blog, following up the next day with something short and sweet can work well. Draw your fans into the link to your song, product, site, or event, and if it's leading them to a purchase on Amazon or iTunes, add that Affiliate GeoRiot link for that much extra punch.

Deploying Prepared Content around the Calendar

Creating your plan of attack and adding that plan to your calendar makes for the final step before the content creation and posts begin. Think of creating the calendar as if you are putting paint on your pallet, then as the right day comes or a few days or even weeks before, create that painting that you post on the given day. Having the calendar also enables you to be able to track the trends, problems, and effectiveness of how your posts are working for you.

Beyond the content you come up with yourself, the following sections give additional content ideas to add to the calendar and format the various options mentioned in the chapter. Looking at your calendar from a farther-out glance enables you to prepare more content and fill in the blanks early on, making the whole content creation part go much faster and smoother.

Holiday and sporting events content

From Easter to Passover, the fourth of July to Labor Day, Super Bowl to the World Cup, try cross-marketing to holidays and sporting events. You might not celebrate a holiday or enjoy a specific sport, but it could tie you in with those who do and bring them back to you.

Birthday and anniversary content

Whether its musicians' birthdays, band members', the anniversary of Woodstock, or another person's birthday or anniversary that means something to you, tie into it and talk about it in your content. This is where you can also add in posts about "This Day in History" and why it's significant to you or your music.

Humorous content

Funny stuff, jokes, bloopers, or even silly facts about you make great content. If you're always serious, it can get old to your readers. Your sense of humor and putting humor in your content can capture that many more people.

Interview and news content

From band interviews to band news and anything in between, try to put a focus on what your audience hasn't seen before. Just reposting every interview can get stale, but by adding interviews and news from different sources that focus on specific elements or questions that haven't been asked, you can create that much more content that is much more engaging.

Chapter 12

Combining Online and Physical Marketing

In This Chapter

▶ Combining your online and physical marketing efforts effectively
▶ Building marketing materials for the future
▶ Creating marketing items that market and sell
▶ Using marketing methods for greater visibility

t's a balancing act; your online and physical marketing need to work in harmony. Your ability to work both the online and office sides of marketing expands your reach to more people. It's multitask marketing that gets you, your music, and your brand in front of as many people as possible to convert them to fans who buy your music, purchase your merchandise, come to your shows, and share you with others.

Cross-Marketing for Optimal Fan Reach and Sales

By mixing the right physical (offline; promotional items) marketing approaches, products, and promotions with the best posts, blogs, and online marketing angles, both aspects complement each other to allow you the farthest fan reach with the least effort and the most results.

You achieve this by having the root of your branding in place. From your color scheme to your logo, your font to your tagline, and so on, having these all consistent and aligned makes all your marketing efforts both off- and online that much simpler.

The keyword to remember is *recognition*. Your logo on a T-shirt needs to be the same as the logo on every piece of marketing merchandise and stage banner. The optimal connection for your cross-marketing comes from the continuity and uniformity of every item online and off.

Creating physical marketing results from online marketing

Create your online marketing first. It's more affordable and effective to create your online marketing, compared to the costs of physical marketing.

Designs that are initially created as online content can transition over to physical items such as posters, business cards, letterheads, and promotional items such as stickers, T-shirts, cups, and hats.

As you design online materials and graphics with your graphic or web designers, make sure to ask for high-resolution versions that can be used for the physical items. The resolution of those graphics has to be a great deal larger than what's needed for the web.

After your online branding is set up across your website and social media, look at how those designs would fit on merchandise — coffee cup, water bottle, sweatshirt, T-shirt, and any other items you can think of. Websites like Vistaprint enable you to upload graphics so you can see them directly on an array of different products.

The goal is to build familiarity from your online marketing and presence to reinforce the physical marketing and promotional items, including CDs, download cards, and vinyl.

People love familiarity, and that sense they get online helps draw them to the physical items, which fortunately can also be purchased online. Your continuity and familiarity coming from your solid online marketing is the key element in creating those sales. Let them see you online first to buy those physical items from you next.

Creating online marketing results from physical marketing

The same thing goes the other way around. For those who see your logo on a sticker or a T-shirt, or information about you on a poster, consistency is key, as mentioned in the previous section. The goal is for them to see you in the real world and then look you up in the virtual world.

Similarity from online to the physical spells success

The similarity and continuity of your physical products to what people see online makes a potential fan feel as though they're in the right place when this conversion happens. A fan who sees the same font, logo, or image as well as familiar colors and information from a piece of promotional merchandise as she connects online is reassured that she's looking at the right artist.

Guide potential fans from the physical to the digital

Don't expect people to automatically remember everything about you, and don't expect people to look all that hard for you when they do search. For that reason, make sure that the key elements of your brand — your logo, font, and so on — show up on physical products.

Just having a very cool logo and your name on a physical product doesn't give you the best chance of being found. Lead potential fans to your online presence where they can listen to and buy your music, find out more about your shows, connect with you, and purchase your merchandise.

The easier you make it for someone to find out more about you, the more people you are able to connect with. All merchandise and promo swag should not only serve its primary purpose — such as coffee in a coffee mug and a head in a hat — but should also lead people to your online presence.

Giving digital breadcrumbs

Your URL should be prevalent on all promotional items to make it easy for fans to go to your website. Showcase your tagline, logo, name in its font, and just as it needs to be legible online, keep it clean and clear on your promotional materials and marketing items.

A show poster can do more than just promote that show. Make sure you have your tagline, web address, logo, font, and a social media URL on that poster. The date might pass, or someone might not be able to make that show, but when you make it easy for them to find out more about you and connect with you, you increase the results of people being able to find you online.

Maintaining your online and physical marketing

This is the longest and most continuous part of your career. Marketing maintenance should take place at least five days a week online with numerous physical elements being put into place and into play weekly.

Spreading it out over time instead of all at once

Putting up ten twitter posts, a blog, and a video in two days and then not doing anything for weeks isn't going to help your marketing sustainability in either the short or long term. Postering or stickering a single area for a day isn't effective in getting the word out to other areas. It's all about spreading out your marketing to reach as far, wide, and often as possible.

Send stickers and posters to friends and fans in numerous cities so they can put them up over a specific period of time. By marketing to different areas at different times, you have consistency in your physical marketing while getting the chance to know what is working and what isn't.

Send posters or stickers along with some promotional items to a different city, town, or college campus once a week, and see how the reaction and conversion works. If you see more social media adds from a town you had stickers put across, then you can focus online marketing efforts on that location by looking up websites, social media sites, and physical media for reviews, interviews, and networking. Give yourself time to look at the conversions, and see what's working and what isn't to know the best places to concentrate on and the places to move away from.

Use an editorial calendar

The editorial calendar that helps you structure your online marketing posts can help you maintain your physical marketing plan, too. This includes a checklist of

- ✔ Postering and/or stickering
- ✔ Soliciting to a booking agent, talent buyer, management group, or venue owner
- ✔ Soliciting to a radio show, TV show, magazine, or newspaper
- ✔ Purchasing radio time and buying physical ads in different city magazines
- ✔ Sending free promo merchandise to bloggers, reviewers, and others in the industry

Taking the basic steps to mix in your physical marketing and physical reach helps to support your online marketing.

Online marketing can be worlds cheaper than physical. Although it's crucial to budget some money for physical marketing — such as radio ads and print ads in magazines and newspapers — the conversion rates to sales and profit are much higher and have much more potential in the digital world. Online marketing plus a budget for advertising that marketing, whether it be posts, graphics, social media sites, and so on, can't offer more attention for you than buying radio time all over the country.

Slow and steady builds the fan base

The more often people see you, whether on physical items being worn or used by others or through the posts you have online, the more you grow your fan base, create the conversions to sales, and keep the interest of the existing fan as you reach out to more people.

Creating Promotional Items

When you roll out your promotional and merchandise items, you create a win-win scenario for your marketing and sales. The T-shirt that was purchased by that girl at a show who wears it to her college classes the next day wasn't only a sale for you; she's now part of your physical marketing team.

For every item that's given away as a pure promotional/merchandise item, make sure your branded information is on it. From a T-shirt to a coffee mug or a hat to a sticker — well-formatted and branded promotional/merchandise items enable fans to spread the word to others who might never have heard of you. In a sense, people wearing or using your promotional items or merchandise are joining your physical marketing team without even knowing it.

Creating a physical items list

Start with building a list of items that includes both merchandise and promotional items. The difference is that whereas a merchandise item is still a promotional item, you want to make more profit in sales from a merchandise item than you would a promotional item.

The following is a list of promotional merchandise you can sell. Many smaller items have a high level of visibility that can draw people to you and your music online.

Bracelets	Napkins	Guitar picks
Posters	Coffee mugs	Can coozies
Postcards	Water bottles	Tote bags
Keychains	Thumb drives	Air fresheners
Hats	Wallets	Lighters
T-shirts	Match books	Pens
Shot glasses	Magnets	Bandanas
Patches	Pins/buttons	License-plate frames
Coasters	Stickers	Sweatshirts

Branding your promotional items

Make sure your logo, font, color scheme, tagline, and URL are on the bulk of your promotional merchandise. It's more difficult to get everything on a bracelet or a pen, but every item out there should deliver a clear direction on how to find out more about you online.

Don't expect people to remember your name, and don't expect people to spend a lot of time trying to find you. Make it easy for them to connect with you. Your promotional items need to promote! Give them the tagline, logo, and a name in a font that is easy to read. Get that website address on those items, too.

Picture perfect

Imagine a potential fan seeing any one of the listed items and taking a picture of it on his smartphone. The visibility, clarity, and readability of your name, logo, and branding makes it that much easier for people to find you and your music later.

Reaching more fans with promotional items

Don't look at every item as something that'll make a profit for you. By giving away various items, even the higher-cost items, at the right times to the right people, the profits come from the exposure this item gets for you.

From presenting certain items to media people when pushing a story to giving tank tops to cute bartenders who might wear them it's all about the physical marketing that draws them to your online marketing that connects them to the music, shows, and promotional merchandise you sell.

Look out for the super fan — the type of person who promotes like crazy, lives in your band T-shirt, and brags about getting something for free because he's your best fan ever. That super fan is a better marketer than the booking agent who probably has a million band shirts.

Plan on giving away a solid 20 percent of the items you create for promotional marketing. Items such as stickers should be given away for free unless someone is ordering them online; even then, charge only to ship them. Getting your name out there starts with giving away the items.

Creative exclusive interactive items

An interactive item can be a T-shirt with a quick response (QR) code to download an exclusive song that's not available anywhere else, or a pair of leggings that includes a gift card to Old Navy. This type of marketing brings up interest in and engagement of your products.

Different combinations that include a level of exclusivity sell and attract more attention for potential buyers than the same items without any extras. It's easy to add a QR code tag or download a password that leads a buyer to your website to not only get what you offer to them, but also encourage them to look around your site when they get there.

Releasing and promoting merchandise and promotional materials

Your promotional items and merchandise should roll out over time and not be available in one big store all at once. By expanding the release of different products and promotional items, you allow for things to stay new and interesting for an extended period. At the same time, it's more effective for the new fan to be drawn in when something is fresh and different.

Release and announce a new item every two weeks. It gives you the ability to promote a new item as well as market the existing items that are already available. Too, it gives you more time to monitor sales, and you don't have to create or choose all merchandise and promotion items at once.

Flat Stanley and contests for content and marketing

Put the different items out on a schedule and then take pictures of the items with people in different places like the Flat Stanley craze a while back. For instance, take pictures of your shot glass in a number of different famous bars around the country. (Rather than going from bar to bar, you can mail the shot glass to get the different pictures.) You can also ask fans to send in pictures of them wearing a T-shirt or holding a promotional item in front of landmarks, historical sites, and in different cities with different people.

Order in bulk and charge wisely

To get the best price, wait until you can order a bulk amount of items such as T-shirts, sweatshirts, and higher-cost merchandise. By ordering in bulk, the items cost less and, in turn, you see more of a profit. Too often artists rush to create the smallest orders and then end up charging more to make a profit, yet selling less because the items are priced too high.

Fans don't want to pay a fortune for merchandise. Justifying that the item costs you a lot so fans have to pay more is not a strong marketing point. Set your price points with a consideration of that fact, and you will make that many more sales.

It's better to make $150 from selling ten T-shirts at $15 each than to sell four shirts at $25 each. Keep in mind a key part of your promotional marketing is to be seen and promote your music. You want to recoup the money you put in to the products as well as make a little profit, but keep those prices reasonable and don't forget that you still need to give items for free at times. By ordering in bulk for higher-cost items, you save that much more and end up making more by keeping your prices reasonable.

Track the favorites and lose the low sellers

Order in bulk, and keep track of what's selling, but also keep an eye on the new trends in promotional items and merchandise. At the beginning of summer and the start of fall, in particular, see what's available, what other bands and organizations are creating, and consider adding those elements to your materials. Just like the marketing itself, your promotional items are ongoing and ever changing. Keep up with the trends and you can keep those sales numbers going up and up.

Setting up Promotional Graphics

Having a template of your core promotional graphics makes it easier to build online ads, layouts for physical products, promotional posters, CD covers, and everything in between. For quick access, keep graphics on your website or through a content hosting site like Dropbox or Cloud. This enables you to get the needed graphics to the right people for design, printing, or online use immediately and without sending crazy-sized files.

Online and print-ready graphic formats

When your designer is ready to hand over your logo, font, and core graphics, be sure you get them in a number of different file formats.

Having files available in file formats such as Photoshop can make it much easier for application of others that use Photoshop. Some media outlets request certain file types for different applications. The most common file types include the following:

- ✔ **JPEG (.jpg) Joint Photographic Experts Group:** These are good for web pages because the files are compressed and enable websites and online graphics to load quicker.

- ✔ **GIF (.gif) Graphic Interchange Format:** These files are used for smaller images that don't need high resolution or exceptional quality, such as buttons on websites and small header graphics.

- ✔ **PNG (.png) Portable Network Graphics:** These files have a transparency behind them, making it easier to load an image on top of a background of another color. Trying to do the same thing with a JPEG is not possible without using a design program like Photoshop because the JPEG is one solid image.

- ✔ **PDF (.pdf) Portable Document Format and TIFF (.tif) Tagged Image File Format:** These files tend to be larger and non-compressed images; they're generally used when printing on paper, on T-shirts, and other physical merchandise items.

Having these on file and available for use makes the whole design, production, and creation process go much easier. It also allows for promotional printing jobs to turn around that much faster as well as for less money. Spend the time and the money on the front side to not only get your designs the way you want them, but also to have access to the different file types that you need in the future.

Using premade advertising graphics

When creating the graphics for the website and social media, set up some simple banner ads that can fit on social media sites like Facebook as well as others. Having a sticker-style graphic for use on different websites goes a lot faster when you have some premade banners set up in advance.

The most common banners are 125 x 125, 200 x 80, 300 x 250, 160 x 600, 150 x 300, and 720 x 120. Design some basic ads using those formats to prepare for requests that commonly come in these sizes.

These premade ads should be just for the band. Having the logo, font, tagline, and either the website or a social media page to direct people to should be included in all advertisements. Detailed or adjusted ads for specific singles, albums or other products can be made down the line.

Buying and Running Advertisements

You have your ads, a post, or a video, and you're ready to advertise online or in print. The number one biggest point to keep in mind is to never carelessly throw money at advertising. You see greater benefits when you carefully place ads in different advertising venues and use different options. Then you can watch to see what's working and what isn't.

There's a major misconception that if you have a million-dollar marketing budget, you can make a lot happen. This isn't the case anymore, especially if that million is spent in the wrong way. Having a solid promotional budget doesn't mean you're going to get solid promotion, unless you're smart about what is being spent.

Heading to the presses — print ads

Print ads can be a scary investment. They can cost a great deal of money to get the exposure you need and are read less and less each day. Although online advertising has a much better chance at conversions, some print can work to your favor; however, choose wisely and realize that those most affordable print options usually mean that your advertisement will appear small on the page and bunched up with other ads, too.

Smaller, local, and read rags over big magazines

Instead of spending a fortune to buy an ad in *Rolling Stone*, diversify! Look at some key college papers, local entertainment magazines, and more centralized print that is likely far more affordable than even your area's major papers, and shows up that much bigger both in conversions and the actual size of the ad.

Running campaigns separately

Try one advertisement for a week in a San Diego college paper and then a week later in a Portland, Maine, entertainment magazine. Running the same ad in two totally different publications gives you a chance to see if you're being seen and what the conversion actually is. Switching up and not staying with comparable cities also helps make some weeks more affordable and allows you to test that many more markets to find trends that work for you. More about tracking your advertising in Chapter 17.

When you spread out your print campaigns as well as zero them into more direct areas when you go to print, you can get a much better sense of your growth and conversions. If you're contacted by clubs to perform, if you see a number of adds from your ads on social media, you get that much clearer a sense of how you are being seen, where and when.

Customize the print ad for the printed publication

Draw the attention by drawing from local interests and expanding those interests to wherever you are or to popular events in that area. Making a joke about coffee in the headline of an ad in Seattle could garner a lot more attention over another small ad that's promoting a band.

What to promote in a print ad

When designing an ad about a specific show, be sure to include information that's pertinent even to those who can't attend your concert. In other words, give people more information about you, your music, your tagline, and where they can connect with you online. Lead in with a headline that grabs the reader's attention. For example, if a school is in midterms (which is easy to find out by looking online at that school), create your ad geared to that event.

"Music To Study By! Take a Break With Kitty Likes Avocado!"

It applies and implies humors, consideration, and connection, which gets you seen that much more.

Using, exploring, and exploiting the options of online ads

Give your ads time to reach your audience, and create shorter campaigns to make tracking that much better. Too many rush to start a Twitter campaign thinking they are reaching the world, but then they find out they barely reached anyone at all.

Take advantage of options that sites such as Facebook, Twitter, and Google+ offer when you create your ad. You can specify the targeted age range, location, keywords, topic, and more so that your ad is geared toward the demographic you want. Like print ads, trying to do a massive international campaign on a small budget will not help to get you seen. The conversion to fans, sales, and engagement is in the focusing of your ads and tracking the effectiveness of them.

If you create an ad that's hitting people all over the country, you have no idea what responses and actions are coming from where. If you focus a campaign, however, and create small advertising runs that zero into key demographics such as age, location, sex, education, and a number of other different variables, you can learn the patterns of what works and what doesn't. There's a great deal of information online about how to create a campaign, but it considers only limited variables as well as elements that might not relate to you.

Start small with your ads

Try a given city, then target a limited age range and only women (or only men) and run the ad for only a week. Think about what's going on in that city that week . . . big sporting event? Summer celebration? Comic con? Hitting the really cold-winter cities like Green Bay and Buffalo in the middle of winter when more people are online can help draw people to your ad, just as hitting places like Orlando and Miami in the middle of summer, when people are inside avoiding the intense heat.

If you lean more toward an over-21 audience, stick in a tighter range of 21 to 25. If you're hitting a college town, go for 18 to 22 to hit the averages of the college ages. This all comes down to thinking a little more in depth and zeroing in on a target audience that sees your ads and connects with you.

Limit the time and the expense of an ad or campaign

Go shorter, go cheaper, and go sweeter until you know you have an audience and an ad that works for you. It's all about the conversion of an ad that connects you with fans and gets them to your website, social media pages, music, products, and shows. It can take time to grow campaigns and zero in on the best places, ages, and other details, but the more you track the results, the better each ad will work for you.

You may have an ad that targets a specific city, town, or location, or you may be targeting a limited group of people by age, likes, or education. But you're still marketing to the world on your website and social media. Keep that content coming and going strong. An ad is only as good as the content you have available as people click through to you. Ad campaigns to new and empty pages aren't going to give you the engagement you're looking for.

Move these small campaigns around the country — even around the world. Tie in short campaigns of five days to a week to cities where you're playing, places where you've been, and further away from where you previously had an ad to fully understand how people are connecting with you. For example, if you run a small campaign one week in Boston and then the next week in Worchester (which isn't all that far away), you might see overflow or not know exactly who connected with your ad where.

Tracking the details of the campaign

Track the money spent, the location, the age ranges, and all the other details, followed by the results. Look at how many people connected with you; your ability to garner any press, reviews or stories in that area; if you were able to book a gig there; and if sales or other contacts from bands for networking came about. These are all the key factors of a strong campaign.

The more information you get on what is and isn't working, the better every campaign that follows will be. Make sure you're switching up the ad and site formats. One week, try Facebook; the next Twitter; the following maybe both, but aim for different towns and cities entirely if you have the budget.

Switch up from advertising a post to advertising a page or a product. This allows for a consistent string of advertising that supports you, your music, your pages, and your content.

Following up on a direct ad

Soliciting to a club, a booking agent, other bands, local newspapers or entertainment magazines after a campaign is a great idea. With your more direct ad that's centrally located, you might have shown up in a feed that someone didn't click through, but you're now familiar and recognized when you reach out.

Getting Your Marketing Further Out There

You have your website up, your branding in place, your graphics in order, and a good deal of content on your pages. You also have music available for purchase and merchandise for sale, you started some ads, and are following your editorial calendar for blogs, videos, audios, and other content posting. Now comes the last and one of the most time-consuming steps — the constant push to promote that marketing you create.

The consistency and uniformity of the content you create as well as the marketing and promotional items all need to be supplemented with different ways to have them shared. It's not enough to just create the content; well-planned and executed content helps and is a tremendous part of it, but needs to be supplemented by fresh and different ways of enabling more and more people to find and connect with that content, you, and your music.

Email lists

Having that email list is a great way to maintain some of your fan base, but it's not the end-all be-all. Use your email list to keep fans and others up to date, but add some exclusive content that only people on the email list get. Your exclusivity offer will entice that many more people to join the list.

Although not completely exclusive, you can offer some content, offers, awards, and extras early to the email list before anyone else. Others eventually get to access these items and elements, but there's is an excitement about getting something first and exclusively.

Contests, Easter eggs, and content-digging games

Different ways to entice people to dig deeper into your content and music is a great way to interest and engage old and new fans. The result of contests, Easter eggs, and other content-digging games gets someone to look deeper for what they want while they learn more about you and your music.

Setting up a scavenger hunt

It's like creating a scavenger hunt for fans. You pull people in — through an announcement live onstage, a message going out in a mailing list update, or through your social media sites — to come to a specific place to win something. Everyone likes to win stuff, and when you make the prizes a little more interesting (not just your music and your merchandise, but also adding in gift cards or other prizes) you can capture more people who are looking at and listening to you.

Registering to win . . . plus some

Whereas building a mailing list is often a key element for many online contests, a great number of people will sign up only for that contest and then unsubscribe after they win or lose. Think of a potential entry for that contest as a fan with whom you want to share your band, music, and info. By keeping that in mind, it can be a little more personal than just collecting names and others just trying to win prizes.

Don't ask fans to just visit a specific page on your website and add their name and email; give them some direction to find out a few things about you as they sign up. For example, if you hold a contest to give away a free download of your last album along with a $50 gift card to Applebee's (not sure why I chose Applebee's, but still, mix up the rewards . . . food and music are a great duo) tell the potential winners that they need to:

- Name the type of car that's seen in your video on YouTube posted on this date
- Name the venue you played on that date
- Name the type of animal in a photo on Instagram on another date

✔ List the quote you used from the movie "Hunt for Red October" in a blog on another date

✔ Give the date of a tweet that talked about the Portland show.

Fans have to sign up to win, and they have to check out the entire video to find the car. Now while they're looking, they pay close attention to your content. The name of the venue is found on your schedule page, along with all the other dates and venues you have booked. As they search through your Instagram, they see other photos of you; and as they look for the quote in the blog, they read a couple of other blogs. Along these same lines, when they find the tweet on Twitter, they look at more tweets. While the potential contestant is digging deep to win something, they're exposed to a number of social media sites as well as your website as they learn more about you and hopefully become a fan.

The more they look around, the more they learn about and connecting with you.

Planting Easter eggs, hints, and patterns in your content

Contests help get you and your marketing out there with direct information that can be found pretty easily. Add Easter eggs and hints to have a little more fun with deep-digging fans.

An Easter egg is a fun diversion on a great deal of websites. They're a kind of link where you scroll over an area of a page and then see that you can click-through to somewhere secret. Your web designer can help add these, and they can be used for contests or rewards if people find them. More about Easter eggs in Chapter 11.

Hints and patterns in your content can run across your music, videos, photos, blogs, and anything else that you put out there. Think of spelling out a message over a series of ten blogs where different-colored letters spell out a word or phrase. Add a number or a letter to a photo, or even plant certain Flat Stanley or Where's Waldo-type things into band photos, and ask fans to find them. Overdub a message into an audio sample of one of your songs online and see if people can figure it out. Don't use "Paul is dead"; it's already been done!

The idea is to be creative and add an extra touch on the marketing you already created or are going to create to get you, your music, your content, and your information out there that much further. Using the contest angle attracts people who might not otherwise take the time to invest in your and your music, so take advantage of the time you have with them and get more than just an email address. Send them on a hunt to find out more about you.

Giveaways

It's a common theme and it's a smart one, giving away certain items on a regular basis. It's not about giving something away for free; it's about expanding your marketing by word of mouth. The winner of the giveaway tells his friends what he's won, and your name is out there in a social arena you might not have gotten otherwise.

Radio marketing is not the best approach

Be careful with radio. Just like any other kind of marketing and advertising, it's all about the conversions. The conversions for any type of marketing aren't based on the number of likes, listens, views, or plays; rather, they're based on the sales of music, product, and opportunities. This is where radio can be a major cost that delivers minor results and leaves you with a hefty amount of money lost.

The main element of advertising for radio comes in the form of radio promotion packages where a radio promotion company or promoter works to get airplay in numerous markets on numerous stations.

Unsold charted music

This is a common occurrence with radio where bands pay for a radio promotion campaign of a song that gets charted but never sell a single download. A vast majority of radio campaigns can get you charted and even register that plays occurred, but the problem is that no one really got to hear them and no sales resulted from them.

It's also important to know that radio campaigns on the upper echelon levels can range from $75,000 spent per week to promote a new single. Most artists can't afford 10 percent of that for a year.

With that in mind, if you consider radio marketing to get your music further out there, do your due diligence to find out what you can about the radio promotion firms you're working with and make sure that the results match conversions and not chart positions. Contact other clients directly and ask what they saw for jumps in sales, shows, and other opportunities from their radio campaigns.

Minimizing radio

In most cases, the cost to advertise on radio is too high a cost with the fewest results. Claiming you have a song at this position with this many plays or on this chart isn't something going to impress industry professionals. They see that stuff every day and want to know about your sales and conversions.

You get much more of a bang for your buck and further your music reach with money being spent online and on social media. It truly is better to spend the money promoting a new single on iTunes, Twitter, Facebook, Amazon, or other sites than taking the approach of radio.

Still, there are some smaller online radio promoters as well as radio packages that can add a little boost, but do your research. The bulk are scams and these are changing every day.

While payola and plugola have been illegal for decades, it still happens in many different forms every single day. It's just happening through the channels of radio promotion campaigns. You can pay to chart, and often that is exactly what happens. A song that was promoted is charted in a meaningless chart that got a limited number of plays and very few, if any, sales at all. All the more reason to minimize radio.

Social media advertising methods

Social media is where you see the most conversions and the most bang for your advertising buck. It's also the best way to get your message, marketing, and music out there online. There are hundreds of books and thousands of views on these methods, but it comes down to four simple types of promotions and advertisements. More about social media approaches in Chapter 10, and in *Social Media Marketing All-in-One For Dummies* by Jan Zimmerman and Deborah Ng (John Wiley and Sons, Inc.).

Page promotion

Page promotion is where you spend money to put up an ad that's pointing people to you through one of your pages online — your website, one of your social media sites, one of your sales sites, or any other site that's tied in to you.

Switching up the ad on different sites that point to the same site sometimes and different sites others times is a strong way to attract people. For example, at times, promoting your Twitter page with an ad on Twitter is useful, whereas during another week or short period promoting your website on Twitter works, too. The same goes for other social media sites.

Post promotion

Promoting a post, a blog, video, image, or audio as an advertisement is another method for social media advertising. This is where you promote a strong post that draws others in to read, view, or listen, which then prompts fans to find out more about you, your music, and your products.

Stick with posts that highlight you, your approach, and your vibe without selling. Let people see these promotions for posts as something that draws them in and not something that feels like an advertisement, even though technically it is.

For example, consider promoting a post on Facebook that has a picture of the band with a link to the website, and mentions a giveaway or album release with a couple of hashtags. This type of strong post can reach many more people.

Performance promotion

Promoting a performance that's a week in the future can draw strong engagement from people in that area. These localized, two- or three-day post promotions can be effective, but make sure you're promoting only those posts in very limited markets. No one in Buffalo needs to see an ad about a show in Birmingham, and you don't need to waste the money either.

Whereas a post is seen by anyone anywhere in the world on social media, running ads that promote to specific locations are seen by people in that area who might not already be connected with you.

Keep the radius of the town or city under 20 miles to the venue for the best effect and results. So if you are in Birmingham for a night and you promote a post about that show, keep it with in a 15-miles radius; in certain towns and cities that have a heavy college presence, you can specifically advertise to people that attend those schools.

Product promotion

A T-shirt, a download, a CD, or whatever product you want to share can be effectively advertised in a product promotion advertisement. These can be links directly to that product's Amazon page, iTunes page, PayPal product page, or wherever you want to send your readers.

All promotions need to be clear and should not run for an extended period of time. Short promotions and ads that run in different areas, such as specific towns or cities for a week at a time, can help with continuous exposure while reaching different markets. This also enables you to know which areas are responding and which areas are not as strong in followers, purchases, and connections.

Switch up the pages you promote just as you switch up the products, posts, and shows. Continue to work with shorter campaigns that are based in a regionalized area and then choose another area far away.

Don't oversaturate. Even if you have the financial means to run the four different types of advertisements at the same time, make sure they're all in different locations.

Search engine optimization marketing

When you apply SEO (search engine optimization) tactics to each post, you help make each blog, video, and photo that much more findable in the search engines. Check out Chapter 11 for a series of tips on how to format a post to achieve the best SEO results.

Even though a post goes up on that day you post it, if correctly formatted, that post can serve as an additional marketing push for a long time to come. Take the time to format the posts you create with the right formatting for both SEO and strong marketing to get the long-term results.

New phrases to attract and connect

Creating specific keyword phrases as enticing titles to your posts will lead more people to you. By thinking in terms of SEO, you can more easily come up with different ideas for posts, videos, audios, and photo titles. It's not always about a selling phrase but rather phrases that people are searching on that will lead them to you. Although "Buy Our New Album" might seem like a great phrase to start content with, "Funk Sounds with a Rock Feel" can be a better phrase to capture more interest.

Instead of something short like "rock music" for a keyword phrase (which a lot of people may search on), try for a long-tail phrase like "rock music for the pop fans." Long-tail phrases are just longer keyword phrases that are more than four words. Answers and statements are also great for SEO, like "how we approach rock and roll." For more information on putting together primary keyword phrases, check out Peter Kent's book *Search Engine Optimization For Dummies* (John Wiley and Sons).

Writing content around keyword phrases

When you work on your editorial calendar and plan out your posts and content, think about the keyword phrase you want to create first and then allow the content to flow. For example, instead of trying to come up with content ideas and then formulating the headline or primary keyword phrase you want to use, try thinking of a phrase for SEO like "recording studio tactics used on the new Kitty Live Avocado album." Here you have 65 characters, (which is a great number for titles on blogs or videos; always try for at least 50 characters, including spaces, and stay under 68 characters for the best SEO results) using the primary keyword phrase "recording studio tactics." From that title, the band can write a blog or shoot a video that talks about tactics used in the studio for their recording.

Keyword promotion advertising

With sites like Google Adwords, you can promote certain keyword phrases that people search on to highlight your posts, ad, or pages. It's better to focus on creating stronger posts that build up their SEO and show up in these searches rather than paying for certain words or phrases that help only for a short while.

Pay-per-click advertising

On Twitter as well as sites like Facebook there is an offer to pay a certain price for the people that click through when you sign up for certain advertisements. This means that when you create the ad, you are paying a certain fee for everyone that clicks through. This can be costly to get the click through and doesn't always mean it will convert to a sale.

For example, an ad on Facebook might lead you to an online shoe seller. The shoe seller pays Facebook for each click on its ad. Facebook makes money; the shoe seller gets traffic.

The artist buying the ad has to pay for each click from the social media site on which they're advertising. The plus side is that you can limit the amount of clicks or a certain amount that will not be exceeded.

Impression advertising

Impression advertising is a preferred method for marketing your ads. You can pay for the amount of impressions (or an advertisement) that show up on a given social media page. In some cases, they show up on normal web pages on other sites. Every time someone loads a page to a social media site or other website when your ad appears, that's an impression. Impressions allow you to be seen that many more times, which can help push your marketing toward consistent recognition.

Brand recognition and marketing come from consistency, which is a plus for impression ads. The other plus about impression ads with many of the services that sell them is that if they click through once, those ads continue to show up time and time again, which can help convert them to fans and sales over time.

Sometimes you can't tell the difference between an impression ad or a click-through if you're just the viewer. These ads show up in sections that are usually marked *ad* or *advertisement*.

Postering, stickering, and flyering

The use of posters, stickers, and flyers is part of old-school physical marketing that's been done for years, well before social media. As you design certain posters and stickers, make sure they can be effective as advertising even after a show date has passed.

Postering and stickering still have a place in marketing, but think before you stick and prepare before you poster. Many cities and communities fine you for posters and stickers in the wrong places — stickers can be especially problematic because they can be viewed as having defaced property. If your sticker has all the correct information on it (which you want, of course), it can be traced back to you.

Still, posters, stickers, and that physical marketing element can push you that much further to those who have not connected with you online yet. Consider making this a team effort, and have poster and sticker teams around the country (even around the world), helping you to connect with fans one flyer at a time.

Poster, sticker, or flyer info

Be sure to clearly and legibly include your logo, font, tagline, and website on your posters. Also take into consideration that your poster or sticker might be up in a location with many other posters and stickers (such as phone poles in college towns or bulletin boards in community centers). Make sure yours stands out with color and clarity. Make your posters those diamonds in the rough for your marketing that enable your information to shine. And make sure the basics of a poster can be clearly seen from a distance.

Posting with precision

When deciding where to place your advertising, think about high-traffic high-visibility areas, and ask the locals where posters and stickers are the most likely to be seen. Although you order posters and stickers in bulk, keep in mind the value of every poster to get the best marketing potential out of it and achieve the best results.

Look to locations that allow posters as well as places that have a good view for stickers. Taking that extra step to decide on a location will make that location of your poster or your sticker more effective. At the same time, be frugal. Postering the side of an abandoned building with ten posters side by side is too much these days. With many cities making this illegal and fining artists listed on the posters, it's not always the way to go. Spread out your message, and on a show day, add a few together in the same place to pack a little extra punch.

Posting with help to infinity and beyond

It would be impossible to travel everywhere you want to put up posters and stickers, but you can reach out to your fan base and find out what cities they're in, what schools they attend, and what places they're near. With that information, you can mail posters to them . . . or better yet, save a little money and send them the files to print. And voilá, you've created postering teams that'll get your name out into different communities.

Send a file to a local print shop and order a specific number of posters for your team to pick up. You can also add tape, staples, and other postering accessories to your print order to help your team get your posters placed. Add prizes, free merchandise, and other exclusive items as incentives for people to work harder for you.

From college campuses to clubs, to heavy traffic areas like coffee shops, bars, and shopping malls, get those stickers and posters out and up.

Posting legally

I probably should take a moment here and talk about posting legally. Each city has specific rules and laws about postering, and you want to follow them and stay within the law. If your stickers are branded right and clearly identify you, you make it that much easier for someone to find you and potentially fine you.

Yes, you can't control where others put your stickers or hang your posters, but hang in the right places, avoid illegal spots, and if you are sending posters or stickers to someone, do a quick check to see what's legal for that city or town by looking on the local town or city website. Stay out of trouble!

Posting with respect

Don't be the person covering someone else's poster or sticking a sticker over someone else's sticker. You can find great spots that have a lot of posters already there, but look for a space and only cover over other shows that have already happened. Just because someone else is doing it wrong doesn't mean you should, too.

Paying for postering

There are poster companies and people out there who hang posters and flyers for a fee. Do your due diligence and check their references to make sure they are legit and really do put up the materials. For larger shows in bigger cities, getting the assistance of these types of teams can help with the visibility for the show.

Paying for placement

A new theme that's showing up is paying a small amount to have a poster put in a window of a restaurant, bar, bookstore, coffee shop, or other business. Some of these businesses allow for posters to be put up in their windows for free depending on what the poster looks like and where the venue is, but another option is to approach certain key businesses and ask if you can have your poster in their window for 10 to 20 days out from a show. Offer them a dollar a day to start and a free download or CD.

Getting and Giving Reviews for Marketing

Reviews are a wonderful thing. A particularly well-trusted reviewer or source can immeasurably help get new fans to connect with you. At the same time, when you review other bands, venues, restaurants you've visited while on the road, products you use, and places where you've stopped (hotels to local attractions), you open up as a voice that people want to follow and then learn more about you and your music.

Negative reviews can be a good thing. Music is art. Art is opinion. Allow peoples' opinions to shine, even if those opinions aren't the most favorable. Not everyone is going to love you, so share some of those negative reviews and show a sense of humility.

Going after the reviewers and review sites

Whether you reach out to an editor, a blogger, or a celebrity for an endorsement-type review, be concise, sweet, and to the point. Email is always best in most cases and the solicitation with personalization helps get you considered for a review over the sea of bands and artists sending the same type of email.

Review and solicitation etiquette

Keep in mind that the email you send is being sent by thousands of others. Get right to the point, stay humble but confident, and personalize the note specifically to the reviewer or the publication. Check out the reviewer's, blogger's, magazine's, radio station's, or newspaper's website and add something to your email that shows you're aware of them on a personal level. Include a comment about how you liked one of their specific reviews to show your respect for the reviewer.

Summarize the album with a simple tagline, and always send links. Never send attachments unless they are requested. Tell the reviewer if you're going to be in the area in the near future; even if you aren't, give a compliment to that reviewer and state how you'd love to include their view positive or negative on your music.

Reaching out to celebrities

Getting that celebrity endorsement can be very cool to add to your website or promo package. Take the same respectful approach as you would to others, but add the reason why you want that review. If they were a major influence, inspiration, or had an effect on you, add it into that brief pitch email.

Search for their contact information through their website or through their agent. Don't send a public message on Facebook or a tweet that you want them to check you out and give you a review. It's unprofessional, overdone, and isn't going to get you anywhere.

Stay clear, simple, concise, and understand that just like the smaller reviewers, they may not respond. Don't hound them. If you don't hear back, let it go.

Going after radio and print

With radio and print, spread your search a little wider. As you research different reviewers and blogs on the Internet from people who aren't located near you, search for a music magazine site in Seattle on one day and then look for one in Miami the next. The day after that, try San Diego and then Bangor. Then go overseas.

The goal is to spread your reviews around the world and not just have them in a small radius of your backyard. Reach out and search for online reviewers. Today with the ability to easily send files, you can build up an impressive initial review package that includes reviews from all over the world.

Posting reviews

No more than once a week, post reviews as blogs. Note that it's okay to put a couple together. Make sure you're profiling the blogger, site, paper, but posting every single review as they come in will end up being too much and come off as arrogant.

Giving those reviews to others

Review other artists you have played with, musical equipment you use, hotels where you stayed, places where you ate, services you used and so on. Just as you search for those to review you, build the karma points and review others.

Reviewing bands

Whether it's other bands you played with or saw live, give them a review. Visit their website, their Facebook page, or their most popular social media network, and leave a review for them, their show, or their album. This is great marketing, and opens you up to the reviewed band's audience.

Reviewing brands

From the gear you use to the car you drive to gigs to the things you can't go without, go review them on Amazon or whatever sites they have online. This again can open you up to a larger audience and also helps down the line for endorsement discussions.

Reviewing restaurants, landmarks, and hotels

On sites like Trip Advisor, Yelp, and Google, review the places where you ate, the hotels where you stayed, and he landmarks you visited while on the road and in between gigs. This can up your exposure and connect your audience with you outside of your music to keep them that much more engaged.

Some of the smallest steps can help push and expand your marketing reach by miles each day. Give yourself a daily reminder and task list to reach out for reviews, provide reviews, and work to get those posters up both physically and virtually (online). All of this helps your presence grow.

Chapter 13

Planning Music, Merchandise, and Event Drops

. . . .

In This Chapter

▶ Creating the best foundations for your product release or event

▶ Promoting with the best tools and the best time frames for maximum results

▶ Organizing and implementing your release plan with media

▶ Spreading out releases and events for highest and maintained visibility

. . . .

***W**hether you're ready to release a single, an EP, an album, or even a new piece of merchandise, the right planning prior to an event gives the release support to make people aware of what you're putting out there. From the promotional campaign to the content, from the marketing online to publicity support, the planning and execution make all the difference.*

Creating Well-Planned Promotions and Releases

Tens of thousands of singles, albums, and products are released by musicians with the biggest and smallest promotional budgets every year. The ones that get heard aren't necessarily the best; they're heard because they had the marketing support to reach more ears.

Mixing individualized promotional plans with each product or event gives you the most fuel to drive your marketing to the most people. By planning for every item and event involved in a release — from how you market it, to how you get others to help you market it, to how you create the content around it to enable it to stand out in a sea of other releases — you can get your product in front of more people.

Release plans include the follow-ups and the tracking of what worked and what didn't. This enables you to refine and adjust for each event or product release, continue to expand the reach, and grow the conversions to sales and attendance.

Despite what the movie said, just because you build it doesn't mean the fans will come. This is one of the top misconceptions in the music business. It's just as important to put the same amount of detail into how you release a product or plan a show as it is to detail the product or show itself.

Planning release events

Differentiate every show, whether it's a release party or a gig. Every show should be more than just a gig and although you might put a little more promotional money into a release event, keep in mind that every gig should have something special about it. This helps it to stand out from all the other bands that have shows or events at that time.

Making it stand out from a normal gig

Give free release copies to the first few people through the door, or to those who help sell a certain number of tickets. This is one way to make this gig stand out from others. When doing a release event, see if you can dress up the venue or club with things like streamers or balloons.

Give those attending a sense that it's a special party for that night. Shop at a party store or a dollar store and buy some inexpensive party favors that make the event more festive and leave a positive impression on the audience.

For those who help poster or promote online, give free copies of the release or other merchandise items for their efforts. Take pictures and short videos of happy people with their new swag. Document what others missed by not being there. Some may have skipped the event because of disappointing "events" that were nothing more than shows. By posting images and sharing some short clips, you enable others to see what you mean when you say it's a _release party_.

Release parties don't always require a live venue

Just because you release an EP or an album doesn't mean you have to have a live show at a live venue. You can have an album release listening party that focuses on the album itself.

Finding a bar, restaurant, coffee shop, or live venue for the listening party enables you and other band members to talk to those attending as well as media that you invite. This type of event is the exact opposite of the louder environment of a live show where you're on stage most of the time.

Some who aren't fans of live shows more than likely will come out to these types of low-key events, and you can have the new album as well as other previous releases playing on the sound system.

Joining forces with others

Consider looking for another band or even a new product that could partner with you to make an even larger event. This can also tie into sponsorships from a restaurant that might supply some food, a liquor company that might pair up with you, or even a company that has nothing to do with entertainment or hospitality that helps with flyers, social media ads, or other types of promotion.

A great event can cost an arm and a leg, but you can get a helping hand and a leg up by tying in your event with another and looking for different types of sponsorships.

The more you personalize an event through sponsorships door prizes, specific themes, and unique giveaways, the more the event stands out. Another way to make the event even more special is to offer specialty food and snacks as well as drinks created just for that night.

Promoting time frames prior to release

Start sharing information about an event five weeks out from the actual date. This gives you the time to connect with the most media possible for the most exposure possible. Certain event calendars and news articles need to be received by magazines, newspapers, and TV/radio stations at least a month in advance for inclusion.

Planning your promotion start dates for an event or for a release helps to remind you of when everything should go out. From the first press release to last-minute flyering right before a show, your promotion plan will make easy work of getting your info out there.

Contacting the media

At the same time you send out a press release — the who, what, when, where, why, and how of your event or release — search for local reviews in the area where you're playing. Also, look for people outside of the immediate area to review your product.

Certain reviewers should receive an advance press release that "scoops" the other media outlets. This makes it more enticing for them to consider reviewing you. You can still push for reviews on a product that has already been released, but you get a great deal more attention when you have something new and unreleased.

Look at local media for potential interviews that you can do for the release or the show to be scheduled prior to your event locally. Just like soliciting for reviews, see what interviews you can get regarding the product release to continue to build up steam and gain additional marketing momentum for your release.

Directing your advertising directly to fans

Constantly posting about events and gigs in one location is a disconnect to those who are thousands of miles away.

As discussed in Chapter 11, you can ensure better engagement with fans near and far by creating relatable content first and then promoting the release or the event. For example, instead of first giving a date, time, and link to a release party at the Bitter End in New York City and then telling everyone to check you out there, you can upload a shot of the Bitter End and share the direct link to the website. Mention that this is the oldest rock club in New York, that it opened 1961, and has hosted countless stars. Then at the bottom of your post, add the date you'll be there.

This allows fans nearby to be that much more engaged and possibly come to the show, and fans far away learn something about a historic rock club. The same goes for the product releases. Create marketing content for a press release or online post about something that happened during the recording of a certain song. The relatable story draws engagement that much more while still enabling you to promote in a way that connects with new and old fans.

Posting event flyers

It takes more than one postering for an event, especially if you're just starting up. Postering at the six-week mark, although effective for larger-scale more-recognizable names, isn't as effective for less-established artists.

Put the focus on social media and reach out online as you begin to poster lightly three weeks out in key locations. Then plan to poster a little heavier two weeks out, with the most concentration one week out from a show over a couple days.

If the show isn't local and you're working with either a postering company or your own street team, keep the same tempo of postering. Putting everything out too soon could cause potential fans to forget about your event; putting everything out too late and close to the show could result in fewer people because they already had plans.

What goes up must come down, or possibly be covered over. Keep that in mind and spread out your postering over that three-week time frame leading up to your event. That way, if others cover your posters, or if posters get taken down from certain locations, you can always put up more.

Expand your horizons and time frames between shows

One of the best elements in promoting a show for attendance is making sure there's a solid distance between your shows both in days and miles. The more time that passes in a 25 to 50 miles radius, the better chance you have to engage the interest of a potential attendee over someone who just saw you perform a couple weeks ago.

When you play too often in a very small radius, an event's potential is diminished. The audience might have just seen you a week ago! By adding at least 9 weeks or more between playing in the same city or 12 weeks or more playing at the same venue, you can expand your audience and promote to people who need to see you over the bands that play in a very small radius every weekend.

Prior to your or any release shows, give your product time to get advance reviews. Don't put it out as soon as you can; give your music a chance to have some advance stories created about it to push the buzz that much further.

Running a Productive, Well-Promoted, and Profitable Event

It comes down to thinking of a show as more than just a show when having an event that's designed to make you money, help your promotion, and be as productive as possible. Too many artists and even managers have a linear mindset to shows and events. Instead, think of every show and every event as an opportunity for that night and all the people who attend, but also for all the people who may have seen or heard about the event, those who were told about the event, as well as local media with whom you now have a greater connection.

Preparing, promoting, producing, and performing to create the most profitable events come from seeing how the event is not only a great one for the moment but also how it can help to make every event and every gig that follows that much better.

Track it, study it, and learn it. From every contact you build for every venue to every media contact to every city, maintain the lists to make future bookings for events and shows that much more streamlined the next time you return.

Renting versus booking a venue

When you create a release party, an event, or even a gig, sometimes renting can be a better option than booking. Some venues allow you to rent the venue as a whole, which can allow for more profits in the long run. Whereas renting can create costs on the front side, working to build up sponsors and event supporters can allow for that much more profit after the show is over. When you book a venue, you work with a booking agent, venue manager, or someone directly involved with the venue. This individual usually handles the basic elements of sound, lights, door, merchandise sales, some promotion, and payment. When you rent a venue, however, you're responsible for all elements from lighting to payment, but as you take control of those extra elements, you have a better chance to make that much more money from a show.

Discuss with a venue the options of an event and showcase your willingness to promote and help make a show that much better instead of just showing up to play. In most cases a venue owner or manager who sees an artist taking interest in marketing and building up an event will work that much harder for you.

Advantages of renting a venue

When you rent a venue, it means that the door and ticket sales, in most cases, are all yours. This makes you an event producer, in a sense. This also possibly gives you the chance to bring in your own sound crew in certain venues and take a little extra time to prepare for an event over just being seen as another act coming through the door.

With venue rental, owners and management may also treat you that much better because they know their room is paid for and covered for that night. The other benefit is that it puts you into a producer mindset with no expectations of others helping, which can help you apply the best methods for producing, promoting, and marketing shows whether you rent the venue out or not.

Disadvantages of renting a venue

Understand that when you rent, you don't have a pay-to-play situation. You are completely responsible for the event and the room, which means you're also completely responsible for many marketing and promotion that'll drive ticket sales. You're also responsible for your staff. From a door person to someone selling merchandise, to someone selling drinks, these all become your responsibility as well.

Checking out other types of releases or events

Before you book a night, see what you can find out about other events in that particular city that night. Although you might not always be able to land the exact night you want, you can avoid being booked on a night where something big is happening that takes away the attention and attendance from you.

Local advantages of other events

If you're coming up the West Coast on February 7, 2016 and could book a show or a venue in Santa Clara 6 to 12 months in advance, you'll find it'll be one heck of a party. The 2016 Super Bowl is being played there and that would set you up for a pretty good chance of having a very large crowd.

Looking at areas that have events earlier in the day or events that can feed into nightlife or have people looking to go out to business conventions and nearby sports events (not at the same time as a proposed set though) can give you more possible booking options. Aligning with state fairs, county fairs, political events, city or town anniversaries, and a dozen other types of events that are already drawing a pre-established fan base can help your attendance as well.

As you look to various cities, towns, colleges, and other locations, look at their school schedules, event calendars, and anniversaries as well as other acts that might be booked nearby on the same night. This kind of advanced recon, if you want to seem a little military, can help you win the battle of filling a new venue in a new place.

Disadvantages of other events

Just as you want to look for opportunities that resonate and bring people out, also look at events that might keep people in or away. This goes for other big football towns regardless of whether they are in the Super Bowl or not. The week before finals in a big college town or a summer gig in a large college town might not have that many people there. And a gig on Thanksgiving isn't going to draw a big crowd, yet the night before Thanksgiving could be a winner.

This also goes for larger-scale artists coming to town. If a local theater or bigger venue is hosting a top-level artist in a smaller town, playing that night might not give you an opportunity to capture a crowd. This is different in bigger cities, but in some of the smaller cities and towns, a big artist or a few popular artists for that area can keep your room empty. By doing that recon and seeing if you can either open for or be a part of a bigger, more-established artist's bill or play on a night when less is happening in order to steer more people to you, it gives you a better chance of making your event or gig better.

Connect with local entertainment writers and bloggers as well as event calendar staff for media in that area. They can be a great help to know some key times when you should not be booking and other times when it is better. Also, see if you can find out any early announcements for other acts or events coming through town. By sending them a free copy of a recording or some merchandise, you're networking with one more media source that can be a continued resource for you down the line.

Hiring a publicity or event management team

Publicists, event planners, and promotion teams can bring an extra one-two punch to your larger-scale event, such as a release party.

This group of professionals can help build a greater media presence as well by designing an event that can be much more newsworthy. They can also help find sponsors for the event to assist in additional promotions, allowing the event to be seen on a larger scale.

Although you issue your press release five weeks prior to an event or show, connect with an event manager, publicist, or team a couple months earlier when you're ready to get a plan in motion.

That extra time allows for the most options to be put in place as well as to present and act on different opportunities available for you.

From location and venue ideas to bringing sponsors on board and creating a marketing plan, publicists and event planners have connections and contacts that not only help you for one night, but can change your promotion as a whole for that area. Hiring these professionals can be an investment that pays dividends down the line and helps you with ideas you can apply yourself.

Hang onto the information and contacts you make or receive through an event planner. The next time you do an event or show in that area, you have a database of information you can draw from and not have to hire someone else.

Avoiding the oversaturated hype game

When you promote to the world about an event that's never been seen before, a night like no one has never experienced before, and how it will be the best thing anyone has ever heard, you set a very tall bar, making it all that much easier to disappoint. And because so many make the same claim so often, you're going to get lost in the sea of noise as well as automatically start off on the wrong foot.

By avoiding the excessive hype about an event or show and putting more focus into assertive, well-branded and strong marketing, you can attract interest in a way that helps you stand out and gives you the biggest chance of playing to a huge audience.

Hyping with humility

Barnum and Bailey took the Greatest Show on Earth phrase to a whole new intensity. It was more than just the animals, acrobats, and the stunts; it was the ring master and his ability to take the show to a completely different level for every fan and every viewer.

In the early years, before television, a lot of that hype was true. Many had never seen anything like the Barnum and Bailey Circus before, and at the time, many believed they might never see it again. It was hype, drama, and promotion that worked back then. Now, fast-forward to the present where people are drowning in hype and drama every day. They're being told who's the best singer, what's the best movie, the best show, the best product, and so on. Yet, the majority isn't impressed by any of it at all and it tires them out.

That doesn't mean that you shouldn't be hyping, but it means you should be hyping with humility. Instead of using these large-scale and overused phrases, work on the descriptors and various comparisons to draw people in. The "Tightest funk sound to make you dance your butt off " can become something like "Bringing you a night of music with funk we'd love you to dance to," or "Dance like no one is watching to the sound of our funk and soul."

Make slight adjustments and pull back on the hype by adding humility while still being confident, assertive, and funny. This attracts that many more people.

Letting the feelings flow

Instead of telling people you're going to "rock them" or "make them dance" or "bring them to a whole new level," change your tone to allow people to feel what they will. A big negative part of the whole oversaturated thing in hype is when the band, a poster, or even a post online promotes the idea of what an audience member will feel, experience, or do when they see your show.

With the oversaturation of being told what to feel mixed with the subconscious combativeness of people saying, "well I won't be told what to do,", it's both consciously and subconsciously annoying, overdone, and arrogant. Instead of telling fans you're going to rock their socks off — which is old, kind of hokey and overdone — try creating a poster with a whole bunch of socks underneath a guitar or a drum set with your logo and font above them and a caption that reads, "the number of socks we hope to rock off."

The less saturated the hype with more of assertive, confident, and inviting marketing and promotional posters, posts, or advertisements, the more you connect, engage, and draw interest from both existing fans and those who are just learning about you for the first time.

Tie your promotion and hype into parts of your events. If you have a poster displaying the socks underneath a guitar or drum set with the pitch of hoping to rock this many socks off, add a giveaway element — people with the craziest socks win a six pack of socks from Hanes, or print your logo on a pair of socks as the prize. For every aspect of promotion, see what you can bring to the table to both further promote the show and draw additional interest.

Applying Your Branding for Announcements

When you make your announcements for your shows through press releases, advertising, online posts, and even invites, reinforce and reiterate your branding in every piece of material that goes out to the public. The announcement supplemented with your branding makes everything going out to media, reviewers, and fans clear, concise, and consistent. More about branding aspects are covered in Chapter 7, "Creating Your Brand."

Creating your press release

Keep your press release under 400 words and get right to the point, whether it's an announcement, product, or event. Make the release quickly cover the who, what, when, where, why, and how of the information you're putting out there.

Your release also should cover standout points about why your product or event draws people in and why media should be interested in either covering it or doing a story on it. Just saying it's a new album, or you're "dropping a single," "playing this night here," or whatever else doesn't garner interest unless you're already famous. Dig deeper to entice, attract, and excite those who read thousands of boring press releases and announcements every day.

Core elements for your release or announcement

The following are 11 key content or written elements to include in your press release template:

1. **Title:** The headline; the attention grabber
2. **Where:** Where the release is coming from, the date, and who is distributing the release
3. **Opening paragraph:** Highlight the exacts, the times, locations date, or product
4. **Body paragraph one:** What makes this event or product special; add extra incentive
5. **Body paragraph two:** A second element about the event or product to make it stand out for the media
6. **Quote:** Quote from the band or artist about the product or the event
7. **One-liner:** One line about your product or event
8. **Second quote:** A quote about the event or the product for more reinforcement
9. **Cost of the event, product, or items:** Even a general idea of cost
10. **Close:** Up and coming elements that might garner further interest
11. **Contact:** URL, contact point, and how to be in touch

Press release example

Figure 13-1 shows an example of a release that combined both a product and an event with the launch of my book tour in 2014. This covers each of the 11 elements previously listed and allows for the most interest from the most people to make the event itself successful.

276 **Part III: Marketing and Promoting For the Long Haul**

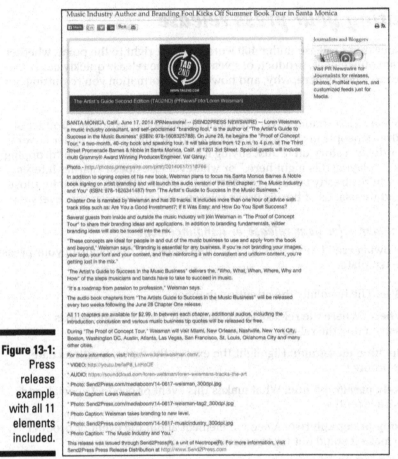

Figure 13-1:
Press
release
example
with all 11
elements
included.

Courtesy of Loren Weisman

There's no need to add "immediate release" to the top of your press release if you're sending it out yourself. This is commonly copied and a thing of the past when releases were faxed or mailed out to differentiate from other releases that were not set to go out that day. Lose the immediate release line; it doesn't need to be there, and it makes you look unprofessional.

The more info you add the more interest you create

It's not about writing a book; it's about using 400 words to draw as much interest in the event or product as well as serve to maintain and continue to grow interest in the future as your announcement or press release continues to build online optimization.

In the release shown in Figure 13-1, I list about guests coming, how I was releasing a series of audio chapters spread out over 11 months, and the kick-off location, as well some of the other cities for other events. I also cover the basics about the product I was selling, including the description and a couple quotes I had for it.

This helped make the event and the press release more than just a single piece of promotion. There was a focus on the discussion of branding at the signing, showcasing more than just a book signing.

These elements and this template applied to your event or product press releases give you better exposure, optimization, and engagement from both fans and media.

Focusing the direction of a release

If your release is about a product, be clear about the key locations where that product can be purchased. If your release is about an event, add a little more information or include the short bio of the location where you're playing.

Either way, keep it interesting and keep it full of sentences that could easily be grabbed and reorganized by someone who might write a story about you or your event.

If you make it easier for a reviewer, writer, or editor to do a story on you or your release (like using the 11 points mentioned earlier in this chapter), you have a better chance of getting promotion and publicity from it. Think from the standpoint of who you send your release to, and make it easy to get a story written about you and for you.

Press release distribution

The distribution of your release is just as important as the release itself. Use a mixture of a distribution service as well as a personalized list of contacts that you can build up for each city as well as national contacts.

Using Send2press.com, a news and press release distribution service, is one of the best things you can do for your releases. They offer a wide array of options and numerous pricing levels for everything from writing to editing as well as distribution and optimization of your releases. There's no better service and no better way to put out your press releases. I've used them for over a decade, and they're the best option available for any business putting out a press release.

Whether you use Send2Press or another distribution channel, use a reputable source to move your releases and announcements to dramatically extend the reach of the release. You also send out the release yourself, but by linking that release from a real newswire or a popular site where the release has been posted to, it brings up your credibility and professionalism and gets more reads and conversions.

Adding photos, video, and audio to release material

In certain packages you can add photos, videos, and even audios to help bring more interest to your release. By creating special audio samples of songs (short samples, not full tracks) as well as new pictures tying into the event, venue, and video, you build up and reinforce your press release and all the promotion behind it. If you're able to add a link, a picture, a video, do it, do it now! (Cue the Schwarzenegger voice.)

Sending to the right audience

While sending out a press release or announcement to music reviewers, event calendars, entertainment editors, and music critics is the primary audience to focus on, also approach genres and people outside of music and entertainment who still tie into and relate to you vicariously as well.

For example, if you're into fashion, make sure your distribution service sends that information to fashion magazines and fashion editors. If animal rescue is your thing, be sure to include a number of animal shelters and rescue groups in your press releases, as well.

If you have a song with a science fiction feel to it, send that release to some sci-fi blogs, magazines, or websites. By thinking on a wider level outside of the normal music channels, you build the visibility to make that release and its distribution hit a much wider audience.

Don't overdo it, though. Sending a release to a place that has nothing to do with you, your event, or your release, as well as distributing to places that specifically tell you not to send releases will get you blocked and hurt future opportunities.

Personalize your emails

After the distribution service sends out your release, use a link from them to send out direct releases to the people and contacts you have compiled in the industry. Personalize the release to the individual or company you're sending it to, and don't mass email every one.

For example, if you send a copy of the release to a local entertainment magazine about an event at a venue they covered before, start with a Subject line that shows the email is personalized — *For consideration of a live show review from Neato Music Mag at Mulligans on July 3rd, 2015.*

Don't just send an email to the first contact you find from a magazine or website. Dig deeper to find out who you should send those releases to. Many websites have specific contact email addresses or contact points for news, releases, and information. Discuss in the opener how you love an article about another band from an article they have previously, go on to tell them you are playing there and when, then add your short bio and call to action. Then give them a link to the press release for the event.

Offering drink tickets or merchandise items to an editor or a reporter is a good way to ensure a media presence. Offering a drink or a T-shirt to a reviewer might encourage them to show up and write a worthy review.

Always add the press release link in your personal emails as well as online. You can add the headline or a section, but always send a link. It showcases a higher level of professionalism and online it keeps you from creating duplicate content on numerous sites.

Not everyone is going to read it

Just because you send it doesn't mean anyone reads it. Services like Send2Press can send out thousands of releases to numerous media, networks, people, and companies, but that doesn't mean everyone sees them.

This goes back to making that headline and information really catchy to get someone to open that email and read your information. They can then follow up with you or advertise the release through their channels.

By understanding that not everyone reads it and working with a distribution company as well as a press release writer, you can hone each release that much more effectively and get it opened and read more often.

Press those releases every few months

Put out press releases every couple months on a smaller level. Not every release has to be a massive high-costing, sent-to-the-world-style release, though having at least one or two a year keeps your name out there and the optimization for your name and your information high.

Smaller or localized monthly releases about a certain gig — and again, not every gig — help to keep you moving across the newswires and punch up your presence and awareness.

Buying Advertising: Physical and Digital

Both digital and physical advertising reinforce the branding and marketing you have in place. Ad campaigns from Twitter to radio, from postering to purchasing promoted posts, and everywhere in between give you, your music, and your message the extra push to the audiences that aren't looking directly for you but may be looking for what you're about.

When buying advertising, it's beyond just the sell of the product, the show, and the merchandise. It's the involvement, the connection, and the engagement that drives up the interest and draws people to click through, find out more, and covert to fans and customers. Buying ads is about expanding your visibility off of the branding and marketing you have in place. If that branding and foundational marketing isn't there, it's worlds harder to convert those ad budgets to actual sales.

Brand first, market second, advertise third

Advertising a social media site that doesn't have anything posted on it doesn't help draw the interest of someone to follow you. Too, paying for radio ads to promote a song that isn't available for download or purchase doesn't get sales for that single.

By first organizing your branding and beginning a grassroots campaign of creating and posting content for you, your music and your products, you have the foundation for a much more effective advertising campaign. This not only promotes what you're advertising, but also enables the people seeing the ads to get a better of a sense of you with that much more to look at, read, listen to, and connect with.

Advertising is all about exposure to conversions

Regardless of whether you're advertising digitally or physically, the end result should be the conversions to fans, sales, and attendance. Avoid being caught up in the world of fake exposure, views, likes, friends, plays, or in the radio advertising, rankings and chart positions that don't mean anything.

If you pay for a radio advertising campaign that gives you a top-ten chart position but it doesn't amount to any sales, you essentially paid for a position that means nothing.

Every advertising choice should be made with exposure to the opportunities and conversions in mind. Your advertising should bring in those who don't know of you, draw in those who have heard of but haven't connected with you, and engage those who may be connected with you but need that additional interaction or information to purchase your music, merchandise, or come to see you.

Changing up the ads, the locations, and durations

Whether you run an online ad or an ad in a magazine, think on a smaller level about reaching a wider audience. For example, instead of purchasing an ad in a magazine for 12 issues/12 months, buy smaller ads in smaller and more local magazines around the country for single runs.

Reaching a wider range of potential viewers in various places for less money is much more effective than spending too much in one place and being seen by only one audience. The costs of running an ad in a single city entertainment magazine over running an ad in *Spin* or *Rolling Stone* is going to be worlds cheaper. And for the money, you can run much larger ads.

Also take into account that fewer people are engaging in print media these days. *Spin* and *Rolling Stone* are nowhere near as popular as they used to be, and the bulk of the fans you want to reach are not reading a lot of those publications. Yet, the local entertainment magazines that show up in coffee shops, venues, and other spots are still read by a regular audience.

By switching up your options for advertising with numerous locations for shorter durations, you expand your audience and reach exponentially. If you find one advertisement or area is doing that much better for you, then rinse and repeat — try another ad in that same place.

Don't get sucked into advertising campaigns that promise chart positions or likes, views, or friends. A chart position, like, and view mean nothing if they're not part of conversion to actual sales and engagement. Careers are destroyed from artists shortcutting and spending big money on hype that doesn't convert to profit.

Physical advertising: Posters, radio, magazines

Set a clear and concise budget for your physical advertising. Along with tracking the results, you have to know what is working, what isn't, and where ads work best for you. The bulk of your budget for advertising finds a greater conversion rate with online and social media advertising, but physical still plays a part. Keep in mind that the conversions, the key elements of postering, radio, and magazines still play a part in advertising and can help to expand your visibility and audience.

Radio advertising options

When looking into advertising for radio, do your research on who's listening in and when they are listening. Many questionable radio advertising and promotional packages deliver outdated information from years back. It's key to differentiate and do your own due diligence to find out what's up-to-date and what's outdated information. More information about radio promotion can be found in Chapter 12.

Many stations have not only a local audience, but thanks to the Internet, they have an international audience as well. And with streaming audio, listeners can take their favorite local station along with them on cross-country trips. When buying radio time, check if the station has an online presence. That way, you reach a much larger audience.

Different stations offer different types of promotional packages that range from song plays to short ads to promote songs, albums, and bands. Another type of advertising is through a paid-for interview that's edited and run like a regular radio commercial. In choosing the best route for you, look at your budget and the market in which you're advertising. Green Bay is going to be a great deal cheaper than Chicago, but Green Bay has a great deal fewer musicians in it.

Postering options

Applying a weekly budget to numerous postering companies for well-placed posters or stickers of your band is money well spent. It's not about painting the town red, just giving your brand a presence in a city or town where you're either playing soon or would like to get some exposure.

Collect information about postering and promotional companies in numerous markets around the country from colleges to larger cities and everywhere in between. Find out about prices to print and post in key locations to get that physical and visual introduction to people who may have never seen or heard of you.

Make sure your posters are clean, clear, legible, and showcase your brand, logo, information, and website URL. Make it easy for people to find out more about you as you make the postering budget work to its fullest potential. You can learn more about postering in Chapter 12.

Magazines

When it comes to magazines, think smaller for larger results. Smaller and local entertainment papers and magazines can offer great visibility to a market that's still reading them and help to bring some of those people to you.

Look at magazines in locations where you may be playing, and talk to other musicians about their experiences with different magazines and papers that allowed them better exposure. It's not about the name of a magazine; it's about reaching as many people for as little money for as much conversion as possible.

Look up different cities, towns, and schools to find the best places to advertise and the most-read magazines.

If you're on the fence about whether you should advertise your product or event in a physical magazine, or on radio, or if postering is questionable, but it's still a city, town, or location where you want to build a fan base, then trust your gut and go for the online advertising. The majority of effective, profitable, and converting advertising has moved online anyway. Many high-price-to-advertise magazines have less-expensive options to run ads in their online editions.

 Spend less for physical advertising in your hometown market. Put up your own stickers and post your own posters. It's much easier to find the direct contacts for print, radio, TV, and other media, make those personal emails, visits, and calls yourself, and you can spend the money for the advertising in other places to build your exposure that are farther away and not as accessible.

Online and social media advertising

The best conversions for your advertising budget occur online. The various options for online advertising range from banner ads to click-through ads; to promoted post, video, and audio ads; and promoted page ads. Even Google Adwords gives you extra punch and best chance to expand your reach online.

From promoting a single to a store where people can buy your single to the keywords or even the genre your single is in, online advertising gives you the best chance at conversions with the best information to be able to track who clicked what from where to the analytics of what is working and what isn't. When you pay attention to all the data, you can formulate a budget and a plan that's ever-changing, expanding, and converting. Advertise products on a wider scale, and promote events in areas close to the venue to punch up the engagement.

Content capturing from advertising

The graphics you create for your events, releases, EPs, and even singles can provide you with marketing materials.

From online ads to the graphics on the pages where your ads point to, the content, graphics, and information on each page has to capture the people that clicked through the advertisements if you want them to buy the product or consider attending the event. Keep the clarity and readability of your ads strong and able to jump off the page or screen. You learn more about organizing your graphics for ads in Chapter 7.

Make sure the branded content that describes you, your music, your brand, and your call to action is clear in your advertisement. If there isn't content capturing, containing, and converting the person clicking through, it's a missed opportunity. And if you're doing a pay-per-click ad, you're spending money on a zero conversion.

Engagement advertising for maintaining conversions

You want to create consistent, uniform, and strong marketing content on a regular basis. And when you have a new product or a new event, the same applies to your ads.

The advertisements need to be short, sweet, clear, and engaging to get that click-through from the potential buyer or audience member. Stay away from the following lead-ins for your ads:

- Check this out
- Must see show
- Showing up all the others
- If you don't buy this track now . . .
- Showing up the haters

There are dozens more oversaturated phrases with ego and arrogance that turn people off and away. Instead, work your descriptions, tagline, and humor in to the advertising pitches. Use a simple white background with your logo and a phrase like:

- Two and a half weeks in the studio and all I got was this lousy T-shirt. At least the songs sound good.
- Our latest effort for your audible enjoyment (Lead-in for a download)
- Single? Come meet other fun singles at this show! (Lead-in for a show)
- Everyone needs that extra T-shirt. . .right? (Lead in for a T-shirt promo)

Every element of humor, humility, and uniqueness coupled with simple graphics and short lines helps to bring that many more people to you, your events, and your products.

New and changing for sustaining

Don't think of an advertisement as having to be the template for all products and all events. Have fun with slight adjustments and edits to keep things fresh. When it comes to events, put that advertising focus in a linear way by aiming those ads to people within a given city or location radius. Although you change events, gigs, or locations, these can be similar to each other. That event promotion you do for Baltimore can be the same for Oklahoma City except for the change in date, time, and venue.

Still, make sure to add that extra touch for each event and show, especially for the people who pay attention to all the ads regardless of where you play. From ads that mention giveaways to the smallest differences, make each single, each merchandise item, and everything that you put out there something that entices fans in the moment and for that item, but also draws them to look at your other products and other items.

Switch up your advertisements. Try different areas and locations with different pitches and graphics. Track what drew the most and what drew the least engagement. The name of the game is trying, testing, and tracking new ideas for advertising. As long as you're tracking, you know what works for you and what needs to be adjusted.

With each item you market and put advertising behind, that light tweak and adjustment for each product enables you to be able to maintain the interest of the existing fans while enticing the interest of a new fan and potential sale.

Track the product sales per ad that goes up, and keep all this information. You don't have to be a mathematician to analyze it all, but if you have the data, use it to understand what type of advertising and style works to connect the most people and create the most conversions.

The exclusivity of your products and advertising

On top of the advertising and promotion you create and purchase for your products and events, look both forward and backward. By looking backward at what worked and what didn't for the conversions of any event or release, you can plan forward with a smarter, more educated approach to continue to grow sales and exposure.

Don't get trapped in the mindset of putting out an album and then spending a year and some promoting it. For a singular release or album, the promotion constantly centers on the same exact thing. By spreading out your releases into EPs, single downloads, different merchandise products, and events, you have more opportunities to present new ads and new items that market for the moment as well as highlight past products and pre-promote what's coming in the future.

As you plan the promotion, advertising, and marketing of any event in the present, by spreading out the products, the music, the releases, and the advertising for all these elements, you build interest across the board, from the existing fan to the new fan, and everyone in between.

Part IV
Maintaining Your Successful Career

Your tour data collection sheet includes:

- Name of the city or town
- Venues, websites, social media sites, contact points, emails, and phone numbers
- Local high-drawing bands that would work well with you
- Local radio information (websites, contact points, emails, phone numbers)
- Local TV stations and contact information
- Local newspapers/entertainment magazines and contact information
- Local entertainment websites and bloggers
- Local promoters, poster services, booking agents, and event promoters
- Friends, relatives, or personal contacts (a free night in a house will save on hotels)
- Local music shops/instrument repair/ rentals (never need it till you need it)

 Visit www.dummies.com/extras/musicbusiness for great Dummies content online.

In This Part . . .

✔ Learn how book and secure shows for an extended tour, and how to survive and thrive while on the road.

✔ Learn how to solicit and ask for sponsorships and endorsements.

✔ Discover how to tap into events, experts, and options, such as music conferences and music festivals.

✔ Find out how tracking your progress can help to keep you on the road to success — from completing your monthly paperwork to maintaining an exercise program.

Chapter 14

Touring and Performing

In This Chapter

▶ Booking and securing shows for extended tours and runs

▶ Networking and connecting with media, other bands, and venues for support

▶ Surviving and thriving on the road and on tour

▶ Responsibilities, preventative maintenance, and problem-solving on tour

*B*eing out on the road and up on the stage is some of the most fun a musician can have. Although it offers the chance to bring in a great deal of the profits for a band or artist, it can also be one of the most expensive parts of a music business plan and career. Costs, such as gas, food, and lodging mount up quickly. By planning a tour in advance from booking to marketing, budgeting to scheduling, and working with the venues, media, sponsors and fans, each tour can help make the next less expensive as each becomes more profitable.

Handling the issues that are specific to touring yourself for a while helps you learn the ins and outs of the road before finding a road manager. Tools and services like Remote Control Touring (you learn about them in this chapter) are also an option that can help with many of the organizational aspects.

The more detailed outline of expenses you can create, the easier it is to figure what you need in advance of touring and where you can save money while on the road.

Booking a Tour

It seems like a simple concept to many. You'll just call this venue or email that band and you can hook up a 30-city tour and take over the country while making all this money and gaining all this exposure. The reality is that touring without a plan and a budget can end a band.

Get your touring knowledge up by taking small steps as you extend your shows further and further from your home base. This gives you a better sense of what to expect along with learning what people are like to live with and work with out on the road.

Starting small

Instead of going across the country, try going across the state. Think of it as a Fisher Price My First Tour package. Budget a small seven-day run where you aren't traveling for too many hours between cities. For example, if you're an east coast band, you could plan for Boston, New York, and Washington, DC on the way south and then Philadelphia, Newark, Hartford, and Worchester on the way back north.

Plan the hotels, food, and gas for the whole run. Also, realize that early on in touring, you spend more than you make from playing. That amazing opening spot you got in NYC might only pay a couple hundred dollars, if that — and you still have to make sure everyone is eating, sleeping, and traveling to the next show.

Try planning a tour with vacation days from your existing day job or saving up a budget that allows you to cover your personal bills and expenses while the traveling expenses are covered in the band's budget. Don't plan to make a penny from this short run — definitely don't plan on big profits from merchandise sales, either.

Putting together the tour puzzle

When you begin to plan your tour, research the venues in a certain city where you want to play. You might be appropriate as an opening act for bands that are already booked into those venues. Working as an opening act can open doors to larger audiences in areas where you're not well known . . . yet.

As you reach out in the different locations, find out what's available for you and what options you have. Tours are not booked by calling a town and telling them you want to play on this day or that night. Rather, tours are built from researching all the cities you want to hit and looking at what's available and open. You then build travel plans around those openings so you're not traveling too far each day, and also have the space between each city or market to have the best impact. Playing in Miami on a Thursday and having booked Nashville the next night means almost a 14-hour drive.

At the same time, if you have a point A and point B booked, like Miami and Nashville spread out over seven days, you could fill in those dates by playing your way up through Orlando, Jacksonville, Savannah, Atlanta, Chattanooga, then finally Nashville.

When calling cities or venues that are in between stops, up your marketing and draw more interest by mentioning you're on a tour and want to fill certain dates. Talk about how you can market their city and venue, and how you bring a lot more to the table when you showcase that you're looking to help market a show rather than just asking for a gig.

Beginning your database — your tour data collection sheet

For every city you want to visit, for every college you want to play, whether in the closest radius to the farthest distance from home, begin your touring data collection sheet composed of the following information:

- ✔ Name of the city or town
- ✔ Venues, websites, social media sites, contact points, emails, and phone numbers
- ✔ Local high-drawing bands that would work well with you
- ✔ Local radio information (websites, contact points, emails, phone numbers)
- ✔ Local TV stations and contact information
- ✔ Local newspapers/entertainment magazines and contact information
- ✔ Local entertainment websites and bloggers
- ✔ Local promoters, poster services, booking agents, and event promoters
- ✔ Friends, relatives, or personal contacts (a free night in a house will save on hotels)
- ✔ Local music shops/instrument repair/ rentals (never need it till you need it)

The contacts on this list can help you market in every town or city you go to as well as connect with people essential to your tour. Just because you book a gig on a tour and you might play a whole bunch of other shows doesn't mean that you can't promote and market every date the right way. This becomes part of a massive database you access and use for years to help with your bookings and even help when you have managers and agents that take over booking for you.

Additionally, add to the list after you get to a show or a location. Track the interviews you do, the places you eat, or the hotels or fan homes where you crash. The more detailed you are, the easier it is to budget the next time around.

There are websites and books that can help a great deal with collecting this information, but many of them are old and outdated. Your follow-ups and double-checking ensure that you stay on top of what's what and who's still involved when it comes to contact points and having the best information.

Share your database with other bands that are collecting this information as well. Working with other groups that can update this shared database can help you access more up-to-date information about places you haven't been to as you're helping those other bands that haven't been to where you've gone.

Marking the best path

As mentioned earlier in this chapter, the best-case scenario touring path shows you traveling four to five hours a day at most between shows. On the East coast, this is easy to do; there are a great deal more cities, colleges, and markets a lot closer together than the West coast.

As you mark the path for your tour, work on building connections east of the Mississippi where there's a dense concentration of people, colleges, venues, and opportunities, especially when you're first starting out.

Travel versus opportunity versus pay

Apply to festivals and larger-scale shows as a supporting act that pay a little more money and can help you fill out additional dates on a tour. For example, if you're based in Boston and able to book a summer festival in Chicago, look for opportunities on the way such as Springfield, Albany, Rochester, Buffalo, Cleveland, and Detroit. Instead of driving 15 hours straight, see if you can leave four days early and hit Albany, Buffalo, and Detroit en route to the festival and then Cleveland, Rochester, and Springfield on the way back home to Boston.

Some days the money won't be there, at which point you may have to drive straight for hours on end. Wherever there's an opportunity to play one more place, however, and make one more connection with an audience, even if it's for a little less (or even nothing) en route to a bigger opportunity, take it when you can. Use it to make that next stop one that pays that much better.

Take a day here and there

As you begin to build up recognition, there are times where filling in every gap can exhaust you and even make you sick. In turn, this may force you to cancel gigs. Make sure to take some days off to rest. You can still get out there and promote in a city you just played, pre-promote in a city you're playing next, or stop in a city you don't have on the tour to do some research and make some connections, but make sure to take a down day to rest and recover. This way, you maintain the energy and endurance to be at your best on stage.

Stopping in cities you're not playing

Touring is all about promoting you, your music, and your shows. While you are en route in between cities, if the time allows (and if you get up early enough, it should), stop in a city, at a school, or visit a location where you're not playing and do some marketing.

Although it's not for this tour, the connections you make, a little postering, or grabbing some of the local entertainment magazines or newspapers can give you a leg-up when you plan your next tour.

Every stop, whether for a show, a bathroom break, a bite to eat, a hotel, or a day off, is somewhere that you can connect to new people and opportunities. From putting up a postcard in a coffee shop, to adding a sticker to a venue wall, to making some direct connections at a music store, make every stop an opportunity for the future.

The path of a tour is never the same — at least not until you achieve a high level of recognition. Your creativity mixed with an assertive effort to reach out helps build the tour you're planning in the moment, but also helps future tours and shows.

Just because a venue says no or the schedules just can't click, play nice, stay nice, and stay in touch. Your professionalism and respect helps keep you in the back of their minds as both an option for a gig and a possible backup.

Aligning with the best established acts

Connecting with bands that are well established with a strong fan base in cities where very few people know of you can help build awareness and a fan base for you.

Research the bands and artists that would be a good fit for you. Focus on the ones that have not only a great social media following, but have positive reviews about shows, articles written about them in local websites and magazines, and pictures of full shows.

Aligning is about offering, not just asking. Instead of finding out that Cantaloupe Temper Tantrum has this amazing following in Smithville and sending them an email saying that you want to open for them on a specific date, tell them about your local following. Talk about how you would cross-market a show and invite them to perform where you have a greater pull. Entice them in a way that shows they're getting something from helping you as you explain how you want to help them.

A band, a booking agent, or a venue gets calls for opening spots and requests for shows every day. Present yourself as someone who these bands, agents, and venues would want to work with by showcasing your professionalism and humility.

Touring as an opener is cooler than it sounds

If you can piggyback with a band as an opening act, you have hit the jackpot in many ways. A great deal of the responsibilities for booking, organizing, and solidifying dates, locations, and shows are taken care of. On top of that, by opening for a more established band, you get to play in front of larger audiences than if you were out there headlining.

Reach out to different management groups, record labels, and touring and talent booking agencies with a simple solicitation letter explaining who you are, what you sound like, information about your brand, and ask about future opportunities as a warm-up or opening act.

Solicit these organizations every day from labels to managers to booking agents to festivals and everyone in between. Get the word out that you're both professional enough to take on the road and humble enough to be a great supporting and opening act.

Back up that band

When band members get sick and have to cancel a show, who fills in? Well, it could be you. As you reach out for opportunities to open and support other acts, also solicit and ask to be considered as a backup. This helps more on a local level for places you're near, but sending requests to be a backup for an act that cancels may open doors to larger scale opportunities for shows, festivals, and additional gigs.

For example, if you're on the road and have a down day in between Ft. Lauderdale and Jacksonville, reach out to venues you want to connect with in Tampa, Melbourne, Orlando, and Gainesville, and explain you're available last minute and only a couple hours away.

The way you work on connecting and aligning with established acts, venues, booking agents, and management takes you worlds farther than just having a great show. Of course you want the music to be top notch, but the people on the booking side of things want work with professionals they can trust and the ones who can help their show or their venue every time.

Playing the cocky role, bragging, and telling booking agents and venues how you can show up every band and rock their socks off will only turn them away. They've heard it all before and if they get a sense that your attitude is going to hurt their venue or their headlining artists, they will pass on you in a second.

Booking the media as you book the shows

With the database you have begun to build with the research you have done in other cities for all the information, once you lock in a show, prepare to promote it. In chapters 12 and 13 the marketing ideas for promoting shows from online posts to press releases and postering to cross marketing for the venue are covered. Practice these marketing elements as you book your shows so that every show has the best marketing in place that reaches the most people.

Early contacts make for later promotion

Open more doors by sending press releases to the local media and making contact with others from your database.

Reach out to local businesses that may help sponsor your event. Ask a local restaurant to pay for flyers as you promote the restaurant or give them some free merchandise to give away. Ask a local radio station to do an interview as you give them music, merchandise, and swag. Stay creative and look for those early contacts that can lend a helping hand as you cross-promote each other.

Don't promote too soon and get your information lost and forgotten about, but don't wait till the last minute, either. Look to that five-week range for a press release to go out prior to the show, and share highlights as you get closer to the show in their city.

Creating the touring information database as you book

As you get a booking in a new town or city that you don't have information on, research as you solicit to that new venue. Also, reach out to other bands that have performed there as well as local bands, and ask for advice or tips on what helps to promote a successful show at that venue in that city.

Ideas can range from contacting a popular DJ to avoiding some hype guy that doesn't have the clout he claims to. Other ideas can include knowing where to poster and where it isn't worth the effort. Find out who sponsors shows or what type of companies or businesses like to be involved with bands. This can be great advanced information that can make that stop on the tour more productive and effective.

As you request information, offer up information about your home base or places where you have tips. The more you offer, the more you receive.

Be newsworthy. The more you market to your tour's strengths, the more you entice the local media to want to do more for you. Getting a booking on the momentum and promotion of what you are doing on the road is a lot more exciting than "Another band coming through town tonight. . .wee hee." Excite the media to exploit and promote you.

Tour Preparations

Whether you're going out on a 7-day run, for 17 days, or for 70 days, the preparations for touring are all the same. They just adjust in the frequency of time, expenses, revenues, and results. Follow the old Boy Scout model of being prepared mixed with

- ✔ Preparing for all the ins and outs of a tour and being on the road
- ✔ Preventative maintenance to keep some problems from arising
- ✔ Problem-solving measures in place for when problems occur.

This allows you to prevent bad things from happening and fix the things that do go wrong (and usually more quickly, easily, and — in most cases — less expensively).

It's not about being negative; it's playing the devil's advocate and having every duck in line and quacking in unison. The better prepared you are, the better profits can be made and the longer you can stay out on the road. This increases the chances for coming back out for a longer tour, with larger audiences and larger returns.

Regardless of how much you plan, prepare, and set aside for issues, new surprises always find a way to sneak up on you with every tour. By crossing the Ts, dotting the Is, and paying close attention to the details, those surprises will get fixed and be less damaging.

Financing and keeping to your touring budget

Touring costs a great deal and in many cases more than people realize. Build up a conservative but considerate budget that takes into account all the requirements to sustain a tour and get an artist or band everywhere they need to be. Look for ways to cut expenses, such as finding a coffee shop for Internet access or staying with friends, family members, or fans. Pack a cooler with bottled water and snacks to save a little cash (those things are pricy at gas stations and hotel minibars!). But there are still the core costs that add to a budget and have to be addressed and planned for before you ever hit the road so you won't get stuck on the side of the road in the middle of the night, in the middle of nowhere.

A great deal of profits from a tour is based on pure speculation. From a high-paying festival to a show that's cancelled and no one gets paid to a great night where you get a piece of the bar and sell a whole bunch of merchandise — all of this makes it challenging to give exact numbers for the revenue side of a tour. But as you build up your presence and supplement it with your marketing, new music, and branding, touring and shows will continue to grow in profits to your favor. Just realize that it takes time.

Laying out your costs

The first step is to look at all the costs and create some simple math that considers where you're going and what you can save on each trip. The following list shows the top 15 costs and issues that your budget needs to address:

Personal bills/debts	Hotels/lodging
Food	Gas
Laundry	Parking
Hygiene items/makeup	Hair cuts
Tolls	Car maintenance/oil changes
Marketing/promotion	Printing
Postage/shipping	Phones/Internet
Gear/repairs	

Note that this list doesn't take into account serious medical injuries occurring on the road, which are worsened if a band member doesn't have medical insurance. Theft or gear being broken beyond repair also needs to be taken into account, both situations big reasons to spend a little more on securing your vehicles or bringing gear into hotel rooms or homes as extra measures of security.

Calculate the higher side of the mileage your vehicle gets with average gas prices to get a ball-park figure on what you need for gas.

Life goes on, even when you're on the road. And that means you still have to pay your personal bills, such as rent, utilities, car payment, insurance, and so on. Create a total budget, figure out how long you'll be on the road, and that should tell you how much you need to make per week to maintain your home life.

Figure out how many loads of laundry need to be done each week. You can figure an average of two dollars for each wash and two dollars for each dry to get an idea of laundry expenses.

Figuring out your routes in advance for driving can tell you about tolls and bridge fees. This can also include ferries if they need to be taken to play on islands.

As you go over each cost and figure out each day first, you get a clear understanding of exactly what has to be made or what's required to get you on the road, performing and playing, while still sustaining and living.

By understanding and justifying the expenses first, you get a much clearer idea of what needs to happen for revenue and for sponsorship or investment support.

Sponsors for touring support

When you've set up the tour outline, with cities, venues, and other bands as well as a basic budget that considers all your costs, look to sponsors for touring support as a solid option and good approach to take.

From the larger sponsors of hotel chains and car manufacturers to the smaller ones like restaurant chains and even clothing lines, there are a ton of companies to pitch to. Many of these pitches for sponsorship that showcase an exclusivity of products or services that you already use in some way can help connect you that much easier. Finding simple ways of promoting these companies — such as on posters, stage banners, your website and social media — can become mutually beneficial.

Consider graphic wraps or large stickers around your vehicle or vehicles to promote your sponsors. You can also use postcards and promotional materials that showcase a given venue or event is being presented by or partially presented by a sponsor. Using sponsors like this can help build up your tour revenue that might not come in as quickly through your performances.

Sponsorships that range from vehicles to gas to places to eat can help reduce your costs while you get out there to reach that many more people.

Complex costs and simple savers

Figuring out in advance the cities and the distances can help you look for couches to crash on or places to stay. Offering prizes and rewards for cooking the band a meal, giving them a place to stay, or filling up a few tanks of gas can excite fans and help you dig into their network of people.

Visit coffee shops that offer free Wi-Fi to avoid adding that charge in a hotel room. Join a rewards program for gas or hotels to earn points toward fill ups and free rooms. And as mentioned earlier in this chapter, pack a cooler full of snacks and bottled water to save hundreds of dollars in food costs, which in turn helps implement simple savings into your budget and allows for more money to be made and eventually pocketed from touring.

Pre-Op for your tours and working from the road

While you're still at home, start building up an arsenal of items you need on the road — strings, drumsticks, extra hygiene items, merchandise, and so on. While you still have your day job and some income coming in, it's a good idea to stock up.

Save for back-up gear or put money aside in a separate bank account for devastating emergencies, such as gear being stolen. Also look into both medical insurance and instrument insurance to help make a horrible event become much more manageable.

Anderson Musical Instrument Insurance Solutions LLC is a great company to look into for insuring your instruments. Although it might seem like an extra cost, the sanity, security, and safety of having that coverage/policy, especially while you are on the road, can save you a fortune. More about Anderson at www.anderson-group.com.

You can prepack certain gear and clothes and have it sent to you while on the road. Too, you can send clothing and items home (such as a winter coat if the weather turns warm while you're out or souvenirs that you collect) to save space and help you travel light.

If you don't have the cash for pre-op items like insurance, or you haven't started a small savings account, you might consider postponing the idea of touring until you get more financially stable. You don't want to get out on the road and run out of money, or lose all your equipment and not be able to fulfill bookings.

The more you can prepare for touring, the less it costs you when you get out on the road. Buy items like makeup, Listerine, toothpaste, and other hygiene necessities in bulk. Stock up on drum heads, strings, batteries, cables, and other gear and items that will need to be replaced. Buying them in bulk saves you a fortune over needing to pick them up at a rest stop or music stores around the country.

Tour packing: What to bring, what to leave

As mentioned earlier in this chapter, you don't need to bring it all with you. Mailing things home or having certain boxes mailed out a few days in advance to a venue, hotel, family member, or fan that you can trust can save you a great deal of room and hassle, especially if you have a smaller vehicle.

Packing really comes down to the length of time you're out on the road as well as what you need and what you can leave behind. The lighter you travel, the easier touring will be for you.

Compress, compact, and consolidate

If you're out for a week, instead of bringing along a big bottle of shampoo, a large tube of toothpaste, and all those other space-taking hygiene items, pick up those travel-size bottles and compress your stuff into the most compacted form.

For those longer runs in bigger vehicles, have a hygiene box and a laundry box (sealed for your lack of smelling pleasure) so that it's less to carry in and out of a hotel or place where you're staying. The lighter and tighter you can pack your hygiene items, clothes, and everything else, the easier it is for transportation and for space.

It's okay to wear the same thing

Don't bring that much on the road. It's not like people see that you're wearing the same thing two days in a row or three times in one week. Budget to do laundry rather than carry different outfits and clothing all over the place.

Comfy clothes

Remember to pack your comfy clothing. When you're on tour, you spend the bulk of your time on the road and in between the gigs. Make sure to pack the comfy jeans if you're a guy, the leggings if you're a girl, and whatever makes you feel relaxed and happy. It makes much more sense to be comfortable when traveling than wearing adaptions of stage clothing that doesn't allow you to relax.

Left behind

Leave the bulky stuff when you can, and avoid bringing high-maintenance items — those that require dry cleaning only add more to your on-the-road expenses. Think about how you want to present yourself for tours with the clothing, makeup, and the accessories that are easiest to carry and clean.

Look up clothes-folding videos online to keep your suitcase compressed and tight. From underwear to T-shirts, pants to jackets, and everything in between, there are a series of clothes-folding videos that help you keep things looking that much better while you make a little more space for a couple extras.

Scheduling the drive times

The not-so-rock-star side of touring is that you have to wake up at a decent hour. Each day, you need to get to the next city a good number of hours before a sound check, and do additional marketing, promoting, and research on where you're playing. It's crucial to look at every show as the foundation of your networking, relationships, and connection with that given location.

By scheduling realistic drive times with the consideration for roadwork, rush hours, and weather, it's better to overestimate the time to get somewhere rather than underestimate and cut it too close. Even if you get somewhere early, it gives you the extra time to promote that much more or potentially visit an in-between city to open up that many more opportunities.

Sleeping is overrated. Skip a couple snoozes on the alarm clock and get a couple extra minutes or hours ahead of those that stay in bed. You're out on the road, make your mark and make those connections, instead of sleeping till the last minute possible to arrive just in time for sound check.

Google maps only deliver so much detail

With the Internet, just plugging in the drive time is not enough. At the same time with the Internet you have the ability to check local traffic and find out info that Google and Siri might not know yet.

Every morning, check the basics for time frames from Google or Siri, but take an extra second to find out about roadwork on your route. Reach out to the venue and ask if there are any issues in the area; also ask about short cuts, free parking options, and other tips as you come into a new town.

A rest stop or in-between city can be an opportunity

From rest stops to stopping at a couple coffee shops in a town that's between two destinations you can allow for extra promotion for future shows on future tours.

Grab a local entertainment magazine or a free paper, stop by the local music stores, and find a few places where you can put up a postcard, a sticker, or some flyers to get a little visual interest.

It's not always about instant conversion and someone taking a picture of a sticker or looking you up immediately on their iPhone. A great deal of conversions for interest in products, bands, services, and people come from that consistent recognition — that person who saw a sticker, saw you on a friend's social media page, remembers a passing ad on Twitter, or an array of other places. That consistent recognition over time can set up for them to see you in just one more place to finally get them to click through or look you up. Get those branded elements out everywhere to go after those who might need to see you in a number of different places before they convert to fans.

Tracking the numbers to stay on track

As you build up your database for each town and place you play, keep track of the numbers of each location from costs to expenses to help you understand what worked and what didn't. You have that much better information for planning when it comes to tours through that city down the line. (For more info, check out "Beginning your database — your tour data collection sheet" earlier in this chapter.)

Detailed tracking results

When you understand the sales of physical items likes CDs, T-shirts, and other merchandise in each location to how many people came to the show, signed up on your email list, and in turn connected with you online, you have a better sense of how to build an audience in a given town or city as well as know exactly who you can reach out to for a little extra help.

By engaging at and connecting with people at each show, as well as knowing what worked, what sold, and what didn't, you can get a better feel for a town or city. Talk to those who attended to find out if there were other events happening, what the best nights are in that area, and how they might be able to help bring people out to future shows.

Tour costs

Larger cities are more expensive all around than small towns. For example, some venues have free parking, whereas others don't and you're on your own. And parking fees are costs that you should track. Tracking the touring costs for each individual stop helps to deliver more accurate numbers and costs for each location.

By planning on the higher side for cities and locations you're unsure of, the details and tracking you collect allow much tighter numbers for locations. Everything from free parking to staying with a family member are costs that can be shaved off of this location and placed somewhere else or saved and not needed all together.

Track and take pictures of the places where you stay, the restaurants where you eat, the venues where you play, and the bands you perform with. Not only does this give you great material to use for social media, future content, and extra posts, it also enables you to build up images to include in proposals for future sponsorships.

Tour profits

Tracking what you are paid and what you make is only the first step in figuring out tour profits. Add to your database about how much you make and how each venue pays to better estimate profits for your next visit. Note if they pay a flat fee, a percentage of the door and bar, or if you're required to sell tickets; note also if they sell your merch and if they take a piece of your profit to help you make projections for coming tours. This also enables you to have a clearer understanding of payments like flat fees over varied payments such as percentages and attendance-based profits.

Even when a tour is exceeding expectations and profits are coming in strong, stick to the budget. Money that is re-invested into marketing delivers the best conversions. Don't turn into a diva overnight and start to book more expensive hotels or eat more expensive food. Keep on track to allow for profits to grow even more and have a cushion in case emergencies pop up.

On-the-Road Responsibilities

As you get started on the road, it's your responsibility to take care of promotion, marketing, interviews, hotels, sales, bills, and most of all sanity while on tour. The rock star party idea of touring is only for a very limited few who have heavy levels of support and sponsorship.

You can still have a blast and a great time, but partying every night until all hours in the morning and skipping out on the responsibilities that allow every show to be its absolute best as you work to make the next visit even better takes its toll. By approaching every day on the road as a mixture of having fun but also handling all the responsibilities of the tour, every show and every tour can continue to get better and better.

Time management

The hardest and trickiest aspect of touring is time management. There are enough hours in the day to get everything done. It just comes down to how you use and delegate those hours while you're on the road. There are four places where you spend the bulk of your time on any given day:

1. In your hotel or lodging situation (usually sleeping)

2. On the road driving to the next town

3. At the venue or a radio station, TV station, or marketing-related place

4. In a restaurant, coffee shop, or convenience store

By applying the best time management and best use of each location, you can get the most done and allow for that extra time for yourself.

With the great deal of marketing that needs to be done online, invest in a phone plan and a wireless card plan for at least one or two computers. For the hours spent on the road, if one or two people can still work while you're driving, you can save hours of precious time. It also makes it easier for you when venues don't have a good Wi-Fi signal — or Wi-Fi at all.

Time on your side in the hotels or lodging

Keep your hotel time to a minimum and use it for rest. Bands that sleep in till the last possible hour lose daylight marketing options that help the promotion of the show that night, the next one, and the one after that.

You can still have that weekend sleep-in on the road, but adjust it between members if you're in a band so that someone is always being effective. The more consistent marketing and promotion going on, the more results and conversions you can achieve.

On the road again time management

Having that wireless card so that work can be done on the road helps to keep you in touch while you're on the drive. This is also a great time to make calls and do band interviews as long as you're in a good reception area.

You can confirm arrival times for that night, research last-minute places to post or add that evening's show, research the following night's location — obviously, a great deal can be done on the road and while you are driving.

If you're a solo act, bring someone along to work the tour with you. Two is better than one. It makes driving easier, getting work done easier, and having an extra person to control the merch table while you're on stage can make all the difference. When you're touring even as a solo act, don't go it alone!

Sitting on the loading dock of a stage

Don't just bring in your gear and wait your turn. Make contact with the other bands and talk to their managers. Introduce yourself to the venue staff and exchange information while you see about upcoming events where you might be able to connect again. The before and after show period can be a great networking time. Just as you're out there during the show engaging with the audience, make sure you're engaging with the staff and the other bands, too.

Work to arrive at the venue a few hours early to give yourself the time to do a little additional postering around the venue and connect with local music stores or media outlets at the club before you do sound check.

Avoid being the antisocial band that's slowly dragging in their gear. Get that gear inside and after the show, get that gear packed up and out of the way so you have the most time for connecting, engaging, and networking. Learn more about loading in and out in Chapter 5.

Fueling up on gas, coffee, or food

Even at rest stops gas stations, or coffee shops, make the time to promote and market at least once every stop. Whether you hand a sticker to a wait-ress in a restaurant, put up a postcard on a bulletin board in a coffee shop, hand off a free CD to someone pumping gas next to you, or any other give-away or marketing stunt you can pull off, make the time to make every stop, every place, and every situation an opportunity for a few more people to know about you.

Limit the partying and the really late nights. Have your fun and enjoy the road for all it's worth, but allocate the time to allow every stop to be the most promoted, productive, and profitable.

By writing down or having a list in your phone of the tasks you want to accomplish each day, you can manage your time on the road to be as productive as possible with the time you have and the places you go.

For more time management hints and tips, check out *Successful Time Management For Dummies,* 2nd edition by Dirk Zeller (John Wiley and Sons, Inc.).

Hotel, lodging, and sleeping professionalism

Whether you're staying in a hotel, an Airbnb, or at a family, friend or fan's place for a night on tour, be respectful and professional so you're welcomed back again. Just because you're paying to stay somewhere doesn't mean you can trash the place. And when you're offered a free place to crash, take some kind of gift to show your appreciation.

Lodging can be one of the most expensive parts of touring. You can save a small fortune through finding discounts with reward points, getting places where you can crash for free, and maintaining the reputation that you're not the typical rockstar-hotel-room-destroyer type.

They know what you did last summer

Hotels or motels where you stay have the Internet now. Your reputation management is crucial if you want to not only come back to the place you stayed at, but stay at other places in their chains as well.

Many of these hotel chains are networked together and have a warning system for certain names; it can go both ways for you. You can receive both good reviews and bad reviews. Make them good ones by staying professional. When it comes to some of the family, friend, and fan houses where you crash, a good review or reference can go a long way to helping you get another night in another house or apartment for free.

Extra courteous steps take you far and get you invited back

For that reputation management, it's simple! Tidy up. Whether you're at someone's home or in a hotel room, bring the trash cans to the front of the room, or bunch all the used towels together in the bathroom. Don't leave wet towels on chairs, beds, or rugs. 'Might sound silly, but those simple acts show a great deal of respect.

In someone's home, ask if you should do a load of towel/sheet laundry in the morning. Get up that much earlier so that you can help to leave the place as you found it.

Be quiet, and be courteous to guests in the hotels or the people that live in the house. Realize not everyone is on your schedule and that some of the homes are in family neighborhoods.

In the cases of a fan house or a friend of a fan's house, bring a bottle of wine, some flowers, even some basic groceries to show your appreciation — along with some of your music and merchandise, of course.

Rewards, points, and sponsorships

Look to different rewards programs for hotels and motels, and think of how you can save a great deal of money over ten stays instead of worrying about getting the cheapest place for a single night. Look at touring from the angle of how to save as much as possible over the length of the tour, instead of how much you can save on a single day.

With reward programs, points for different stays, and an exclusivity to a certain brand or conglomerate of hotels that fall under the same chain, free stays, reduced costs, and heavy discounts can help. By staying true to a given brand, the ability to pitch for future sponsorships and support also becomes an option.

Sanity on the road

Spending a great deal of time on the road can suit some people very well, but it can wear on others. As fun as touring is, the constant change in locations, the different beds, long hours traveling, and nonstop pace can tax you both physically and mentally. By taking care of yourself both physically and mentally, your endurance and energy levels stay up as you keep the exhaustion and depression down.

As amazing as the highs of being on the road are, a great number of musicians on tour suffer intense depressions. You're on stage for one hour and rocking a crowd; a couple hours later you're in a hotel room planning out the next long day of driving and handling business issues. The see-saw of it all can be dramatic. Keep mentally fit to avoid mood swinging from a super high to a super low.

Phys ed for touring

You don't have to take four laps around a track, but if you're a runner, make the time to run. Even just walking and stretching every day can help keep your body in motion and a little more physically in check.

Even loading in gear each night can be a little bit of a workout with weights if you lift that tom tom case up and down a few times with each arm. I recommend adding at least a 30-minute walk in every day, whether it's on a treadmill in a hotel, around a city, or even if it's cold, doing one of those grandma mall walks inside a nearby shopping mall. (You can skip the awful yoga pant patterns and the shake weights, though.)

Bang your head — mental health on the road

Do you like the Quiet Riot reference? Good mental health is crucial for the road. Simple tricks like taking time alone and going for that walk by yourself can help. Try not to drink alcohol to a crazy excess, and avoid drinking, drugs, and other bad things to maintain the high you achieve from performing. External substances like that always lead to a crash.

Take time to do something completely non-music related, like going to a movie, playing a round of mini golf, reading a book in a coffee shop, or other things that have nothing to do with music. That separation — even if for a moment or a couple of hours, and at least once or twice a week — can make all the difference in the world to your mental health; it can also inspire your creativity and keep you fresh while on the road for those longer hauls.

Adding the physical fitness of sorts and the mental breaks into your busy schedule is just as important as scheduling all the work you have to do to promote, market, and sustain a tour. Just as you have to work to sustain and maintain your tour, it's crucial for you to take the time for you, so that you keep the endurance and energy to do what is required.

Before, During, and After the Show Checklists

Before/during/after-the-show checklists ensure that everything you need to handle is either being handled or is on the list to be handled. With all the different activities going on before, during, and after a show, it can be overwhelming to remember and track it all. Keep a little reminder sheet for each day and each show to help you remember to cross the Ts and dot the Is.

After you lock in the date

Refer to your database sheet (check out "Beginning your database — your tour data collection sheet" earlier in this chapter) for local media contacts. Reach out to your media sources and have a press release ready to go five weeks prior to your show. Then research that city or town for promotion options, cross-marketing with other bands, sponsorships, and ways to save on food and lodging.

4, 3, 2, 1 week out preparations

Start to follow up the press release at the five-week point with emails and calls to local media. See if you can get assistance in postering around town for the show. Make contacts more frequently as each date comes closer.

Show day and loading in

Arrive early to assist with some last-minute postering and potential pre-interviews before the load-in. As you arrive at the venue, get the gear inside, but also touch base with the other bands and the venue personnel. Make sure you know when and where you need to be as well as when sound check happens and what the exact show times are. Be cooperative with the venue and the staff. Play by their rules.

Da gig, da gig

As you take the stage and focus on the set, don't forget to include all the call-to-action elements in between the songs. This is easily forgotten but is also a core part in building your fan base and recognition. Set up a list on either your set list or next to your set list to remind you to

- ✔ Say the name of your band after each song.
- ✔ Give out website address and social media information throughout the show.
- ✔ Plug and pitch the merchandise and where it can be purchased.
- ✔ Recognize the venue, the other bands, and any sponsors involved in the show.
- ✔ Ask fans to sign up for your email list or join you on your social networks.
- ✔ Give something away from the stage to an audience member for free.
- ✔ Thank the venue, the other bands, the audience, and tell them where you'll be after the set if they want to talk.

Have the band or at least a few members present for the sets of the other bands. Regardless of whether you're the opener or they're opening for you, show that respect to build better networking and opportunities to play together again.

After-show administration

After the show is done and you're loading off the stage, the administrative follow-ups for getting paid, networking to see about getting a return gig down the line, and filing your set list with your performance rights organization are often overlooked. Collect all the information from other bands and local media, and ensure your agreement with the venue or the event producer is executed so that you're either paid that night or you know when to expect your check. If you're a band, have a couple members connect with the audience while another member double-checks with the venue and handles the administrative tasks to keep things from being missed.

Filing for royalties after a live show

Outside of being paid by the venue, the event producer, management, or booking agent, make sure to file your public performance statements with your affiliated performance rights organization. Yes, you can get royalties in the United States from a live venue for playing your music as long as that venue is paying their fees to one of the three U.S. organizations. (For more on performance rights organizations, check out Chapter 9.)

After the set is over, register your set list with ASCAP Onstage, BMI Live, or SESAC Live Performance Notification Systems. The legal venues pay royalties to allow live music in their clubs. By registering your set list, you receive royalties for your performance at that venue.

Follow-Ups

You may have moved on from your show in one particular town, but keep a list for follow-ups and check-ins. Add reminders to your calendar (whether it be on paper, on your computer, or in your phone) to touch base with the venue a week or so after your show as well as with the bands and others involved. Thank those who need to be thanked for a job well done, send links to any great pictures of the venue or other bands, and open up discussions for other shows in the future.

The follow-ups are almost as important as the show itself. As you stay engaged and connected with the bands, the staff, and the venues, you stay on their radar and in their mind for shows down the line.

By having a checklist of everything — from booking the club to booking the hotel on through sending a press release to promoting the show, then from the performance on stage to handling the administrative tasks afterwards — you build up your presence as you showcase your professionalism and see more opportunities coming your way.

Chapter 15

Securing Sponsorships and Endorsements

In This Chapter
▶ Knowing the right time to solicit for sponsorships or endorsements
▶ Understanding the different levels and requirements for an endorsement
▶ Soliciting and asking for a sponsorship or endorsement
▶ Representing and marketing your sponsorship or endorsement professionally

Many musicians see being endorsed as a level of success in their careers and almost more of an ego thing than the business transaction that's actually happening. Getting a sponsorship or an endorsement is much more than just a level of success or an ego boost. These can assist with certain costs as well as cover other elements. With instrument endorsements, you can receive a sense of security, support, and savings. With other large sponsorships, such as hotels, vehicles, or restaurants, you can reduce major touring costs as you represent that brand as you travel. Even smaller endorsements or sponsorships from local businesses that offer sponsorships for a particular show or a local newspaper that helps to cover promotional costs and postering from a show, can make a great difference.

All endorsements and sponsorships are two-way streets. Just as you receive gear, discounts, food, marketing, or more, you're responsible to "pay" for that endorsement through visibility, marketing, and the promotion.

Defining a Sponsorship or Endorsement

Imagine that a person or a company gives you a product for free or at a discount. In return, you use this product and tell as many people as possible how much you like, it to help increase the product's sales and recognition.

That's the basic definition of a sponsorship or endorsement — a mutually beneficial situation that helps you and those endorsing you.

Financial transaction of an endorsement

There needs to be a value, a level of exposure, and an opportunity for an endorsement or sponsoring party to make back what it costs them to give you a product or a discount. Understand that it costs a company money to give you something for free or let you have items at a discount because they're not seeing any revenue from those items. In fact, if they create customized items for you — say, for example, customized drumsticks for the drummer — this endorsement has just cost them even more. Add in the elements of shipping as well as any additional advertising they do to showcase you with their product, you can see that sponsorships and endorsements can be expensive. But the old adage "it takes money to make money" is prefect for this example.

With all sides considered, you can be the better endorsee and discuss with a particular company how you can make any endorsement or sponsorship worth their while. Talk with them about making back their investment in you, plus some.

Lay out a plan that includes the services and marketing that you can do to justify and balance out what's given to you from your sponsor. You can offer to wear their merchandise; highlight the product on your website and social media pages; include the product name on recordings; create content that showcases the gear; and tell fans why you use it and love it. By doing so, you build up a good reputation with a sponsor or endorser as someone with a true interest in their products. The next step is to outline the consistency of the marketing you do for that endorsement or sponsorship.

Truly stand behind the product you want to endorse. Don't just use something because you can get it for a discount or for free. Pitching companies by telling them you'll use their stuff if they give it to you for free won't work; this approach is rude as well as unprofessional.

Exclusivity and priority

How long you work with an endorser or sponsor can vary. Maybe till death do you part. Well, maybe not death, but at least the end of an agreement. And usually agreements spell out very clearly when you're to use their products.

If you endorse a drumstick, guitar, amp, guitar strings, or ukulele, and so on, and you signed to use this exclusively, don't use anything else. If you do, you're in violation of your agreement.

Commitment to that brand and no other

Your commitment to that brand, item, or product highlights you as that much more professional. Yes, you might have other guitars at home, but don't bring them out unless you clear it with the endorsing company. You might have other drumsticks in your bag, but if you're endorsing Regal Tip Drumsticks, then that's all anyone should see.

If you feel the need to play or use items from another company, or you're not happy with a given endorsement, you shouldn't work with or endorse them. In a way, it's like being an employee of that company, and you're paid in either a discount or free items. Use what you're advertising and follow through on stage, off stage, and in any type of videos and other content that's put out to the public.

Noncompetitive sponsorships

Having a radio station or local print shop sponsor you in one city and then having a completely different radio station or print shop sponsor you in another usually isn't an issue. Make sure, however, that the people and companies with which you're involved are okay with certain other competitive-type sponsorships. For example, if Subway sandwiches sponsors a show or event in one city with you and your band and then in another city you're offered similar marketing support from Quizno's, check with your contact at Subway before accepting the Quizno's sponsorship. Yes, they're franchise-owned, but that extra due diligence and double-checking can keep you on the up-and-up track of building larger-scale sponsorships and endorsements. Your exclusivity to Subway on a smaller or franchise level could lead you to sponsorship options on a larger level. Maybe your band could go on tour and become the Jarod of musicians eating only Subway on the road.

A sponsorship from Subway or another sandwich chain that allows you free lunches for a four-person band out on the road for 30 days at $7 a person can save you $840 in touring food costs. Just saying!

Determining whether you are ready

What? You think you're ready for an endorsement or sponsorship deal? How about you finish reading the book first! And then, if you feel you're ready, plan to go through a series of steps before going to the top of the mountain and screaming you deserve free stuff. The best and most humble way to determine if you're ready is to look at what you bring to a company's table and how your endorsement of their products can benefit them.

Defining what you bring to the table

Endorsements go to those who have the ability to expand on the visibility of their products, company, or services. Telling a company you have 100,000 followers on Twitter is not going to cut it. Share about the tour that you're doing, and showcase your existing online fan engagement as well as posts, pictures, videos, or audios that already involve or use their products to add an extra level of promotion.

Share information about being picked up by a label, a management group, or booking agency that can provide solid credentials, reviews, and press pieces about you. Think of it like a résumé showing what you've done, where you're at, and what's lined up for the future. These elements show that you're more serious and professional than many others.

Getting the ducks in a row and quacking in unison

Make sure that you've got a strong presence with your brand, marketing, and promotion regardless of your existing audience. Although larger-scale endorsements and the free stuff is set aside for the established, more-popular and higher-profile artists, those artists who are presenting the potential for much more down the line can begin to align with sponsorships and endorsements earlier on. Chapter 7 discusses more about the brand, whereas Chapter 11 covers more about preparing your marketing.

Highlight what you're doing right, even on the most grassroots level, to begin connections and relationships with different companies. You may only get your foot in the door, but it's a good first step. You can get set up for other options down the road by getting on a company's radar for being responsible and professional, even while you're still growing your fan base. Take this time to show how you use the gear you want to endorse, eat the sandwiches from the restaurant you want to sponsor you, and stay in the hotels from which you want support.

The best way to get your ducks in a row for endorsements and sponsorships is to start quacking, squawking, and talking about what you use, why you use it, and why others should use it, too. In a sense, this is the same stuff you'll do down the line when you are partially or fully endorsed.

 Start small and ask small when it comes to endorsements. Instead of requesting a free drum set, start with looking into drum sticks. Ask how you can help promote a specific brand of drumsticks as you explain your long-term interests of an endorsement, but clarify you want to take the right steps in beginning a long-term relationship. Most companies will love you for it because it's so rare to see that kind of interaction.

Looking at the best companies to ask first

Start at the shallow end of the pool when it comes to endorsements and sponsorships. This is a great way to get your feet wet, build experience, and highlight how you handle yourself with new business situations. As mentioned in the previous section, instead of a drum set, begin your solicitation by going after drum sticks. Instead of trying to get a guitar endorsement, start with guitar strings, and instead of a larger-scale restaurant sponsorship for a 45-day tour, approach a local restaurant franchise that can handle the food for a single show or event.

Starting with a smaller brand or service with a smaller ask

Start with the smaller endorsement, with a company that would be comfortable getting involved with you for a smaller cost and less risk. At the same time, if you're only asking for drum sticks, don't go in asking for your own customized stick and 20 boxes of them. Instead, follow up with the due diligence and do a search on the company's website about endorsement or sponsorship requirements.

Highlighting how you handle it to the bigger boys

Treating the smallest endorsements, such as getting some drum sticks for cost, like you're a top-rated endorsee, is a great way to build a long-term relationship. Showcasing how you market and promote those items on the smallest scale can give those endorsers an idea of how you would market and handle yourself with more.

When it comes to even the smallest and earliest endorsements, treat them like they are the biggest endorser and give you the most. The reputation you grow with this approach brings the starter and smaller endorsements up to higher levels as you are able to have that much more ammunition and experience to go after larger products, endorsers, and opportunities.

If you're able to find endorsement or sponsorship requirements on a website with instructions on how to apply, follow them to the tee. The first impression you make on many of these companies starts with how well you can follow directions. It's more than just making a good impression; it's showing an attention to detail that's missed by many.

Different Levels of Sponsorships and Endorsements

There is no such thing as just a single sponsorship or endorsement level. They all have a wide array of levels and options. Different companies offer different options. Having this understanding enables you to come to a conversation that much more educated and prepared to discuss options as well as how to negotiate deals and opportunities in the moment and for the long term. This section looks at a breakdown of the three major levels and sublevels for endorsements, sponsorships, and support.

Starting-out discounts

In some ways the Fisher Price endorsement (otherwise known as your first endorsement or sponsorship opportunity) builds a foundation for a long-term relationship with bigger options. Showing humility and an understanding as you start with your approach by asking for the starter discounts over requesting more highlights you as someone that people will want to work with, sponsor, and endorse.

For-cost deals

For-cost deals are the ground-floor entry-level endorsements. They enable you to make purchases at the "for cost" price. This means you get the items at the cost the dealer pays without any profit markup and gives you a shot while not costing the endorser any money. Think of it as breaking even for the endorser. Some companies give you for-cost but ask for you to pay shipping. Don't get cocky; do this. You're in on the ground floor and getting the chance to build a reputation, a relationship, and a real future with that product, company, or organization.

10 to 25 percent endorsement — and act now for free shipping

A small step for man, a large step for endorsement kind. Okay, it's not landing on the moon, but with this starting-out discount, you bypass cost, get a small discount off the price, and also the shipping fee is covered. This is one of those courting-type endorsements and is something to take seriously. Make sure you're marketing, promoting, and showing the endorser how you appreciate it through the way you spread the promotion, marketing, and love.

 Promoting a starting-level and starting-discount endorsement is about the endorsing company and not about the fact that you have an endorsement. Bragging to your fan base that you're endorsing a product or a company isn't good marketing. Posting content about the product, why you like it, how it helps you, and how everyone should get it is good marketing, good content, and exactly what your endorser wants to see.

Mid-level deals

Whether mid-level deals are offered in initial meetings or you work your way up to them from the smaller levels, these are where you get half off and usually get the shipping for free as well. This is also the point where you may get a few free items to see how things work, but no promises or guarantees for additional support, help, or assistance. In a way, this is that middle-of-the-road place where the eyes are on you to see what you're made of and what you can do.

Fifty percent off

Half off is twice as cool, but just as you want to shine with your promotion of a product through online content, events, and everywhere else, make sure you have a reminder and a checklist to promote the gear, company, or sponsor that's supporting you.

Lolly! Lolly! Lolly! Get your free gear here . . . or at least some free gear

Some companies, usually with smaller items, take a chance on an artist and give them a free product or a set of free products like a box of strings or a brick of drum sticks (a package of 16 to 24 pairs of sticks). As they do this, just like all the other levels before and after, they have an eye on you and what you do with the products. Make sure you're doing everything you can to promote them.

At this level, as you may be building sponsorship and endorsement connections with numerous companies, realize that they contact each other. Be that artist or band that builds up and has good references across the board from the smallest sponsorships to the largest-scale endorsements.

Top-notch and full-backing situations

The full ride and backing support endorsements are the highest levels you can get. These include a mixture of all the gear you need within reason as well as support for when things break down. These types of endorsements are for the highest-profile artists who enable the highest profiles of those products. It's not a good idea to approach companies for this kind of support right off the bat. Not only are they going to say no, but it hurts your chances further down the line if you ask again.

Full-ride endorsements

Most top-level endorsements enable the artist to get an allotted amount of items for free as well as a certain backup of those items available upon request. These endorsers also tend to be clinicians as well as musicians who can highlight, promote, and showcase the gear as well as their musical expertise on it. These also include the biggest touring acts that are seen by thousands of people per night — artists with major financial backing and yes, you guessed it, artists who might not even need the stuff for free.

Backing support

The highest echelon of endorsement support is that backing support for gear that's needed in a pinch. These are the musicians who break a cymbal and are able to have a cymbal dropped off from a local music store or FedEx'd out to the next show. Again, this is reserved for the highest-profile artists who allow for the most exposure and sale of a product.

Understand that in the music industry there are few people who are paid to play and use certain brands. It did occur at one point in time, but it's a thing of the past. Asking what a company plans to pay your to use their brand is not a good idea. Avoid that question at all costs!

With a clear understanding of the different levels as well as knowing what is expected of you, you're ready to either solicit for an endorsement or sponsorship, or cool your jets and get a few more things ready before you pitch.

Your delivery is everything as you begin to search out sponsorships and endorsements. From discussing on your own social media sites to videos, and from the eloquence in how you define the product to how you promote, make yourself a representative and create information that the endorser wants to market.

Preparing to Solicit for an Endorsement/Sponsorship

Your first experience, interaction, and impression with a potential endorser can make or break an opportunity. Whereas the usual focus is on larger-scale artists with higher profiles, it takes that extra professional and organized touch as well as how you communicate when you start to solicit. Having all the information together before you start to solicit gives you the best chances to exploit an opportunity and begin to build a long-term relationship with a brand or company.

Crafting the right letter

Each letter you create for a potential sponsorship or endorsement should be individualized and personalized for the company or brand with which you want to connect. In your letter, and just like all other letters for solicitation, it's all about the bass . . . well, actually all about the who, what, when, where, why, and how. With compressed and condensed clarity comes correspondence. Or in other words, don't write a book — get right to the point.

Getting right to the point and clarifying your ask

A long-winded email or letter that covers the array of when you started to play music up to your most recent show will turn away people and get emails deleted. Humble, but assertive approaches that cut to the chase have the best chance of being read and considered.

This also includes the subject line of your email. A subject line that showcases professionalism is key. Avoid opening with following statements:

- Endorse a great up and coming guitarist
- Wait 'til you hear what I can do on your gear
- If you give me a couple guitars, I will start using your brand
- I could be the best player on your roster of artists
- With me playing your products, the exposure will be through the roof

These are all real subject lines that were sent to a series of different companies, and not a single one of these people got a single thing. Open with a simple professional header such as:

- Query for potential endorsement and relationship with X brand
- For consideration of an entry-level endorsement from X brand
- Request for best steps to begin a relationship with X brand

All of these are much more professional openers and much more inviting for someone to read. These also start you off on the right foot with the subject line the start of a good first impression.

As you continue to the pitch or solicitation, keep it brief, and remember the who, what, where, when, why, and how of what you want, all while crafting brief sentences designed to intrigue the recipient and make them to want move. Do not overshare; you're looking for an endorsement, not telling your life story.

Following the requested formats to the letter in your letter

Do your due diligence and research how particular sponsors or endorsers prefer to receive information. Find out what they want to see and have in place before you contact them. And if you don't have that stuff, don't contact them. That's simple, isn't it? Many music business professionals and companies look very highly on the ability to follow instructions.

These same companies are inundated with requests every single day. Stand out and get read by considering the requirements of a brand or sponsor. Look at the requirements, and save that information for future use.

As you research the various requirements from different companies and sponsors, don't just keep searching till you find someone who accepts you. If you like a product and you begin to see a theme or set of requirements, such as proving sales, showcasing reviews or press, show events and exposure opportunities, and so on, take the time to build up those elements and don't rush to pitch for an endorsement. The more you have in line and up to the levels these companies like, the more doors open for you.

Don't come off bigger than you actually are. Don't fluff the numbers, over-exaggerate or hype where you are at beyond where you really are. Especially in the day of the Internet and social media, people find out and catch on as you are branded a liar. Your honesty serves you a great deal better than trying to pull one over on a company.

Organizing the most professional materials

Whether it's a summary in your pitch letter or having links and basic information added or ready to send upon request, have your best and most professional promotional materials ready to go. Whether they are direct website links to easy-to-understand pages (such as `http://kittylikesavocado.com/reviewsheet.pdf`), or a short link with a description for that link (such as Kitty Likes Avocado Review Sheet Link — `http://geni.us/KLAreviews`), have all your materials easily accessible with simple links or descriptive links so that people know exactly where they're going and what they should expect to see when they land there.

Ask your website designer about re-direct links and vanity URLs for your promotional items. With these, you can give simple links in endorsement pitches as well as booking and a number of other promotional items, song links, reviews, and other marketing materials. There are also websites like `www.goo.gl`, the Google URL shortener, that can shorten an existing link for you and enable you to track how many people clicked through it.

Samples, footage, promo items, press, and reviews

Many of the same materials for booking, reviews, and other solicitations can be used for potential endorsers and sponsors. Never give someone a website or a social media page unless that's all they ask for. Give them the links to the key information in the website that they want to see or a direct link to a video that showcases a great live performance rather than giving someone your YouTube channel and saying is the video's on there.

Not every company requests it, but have the following materials prepared as well as the links to these materials readily and easily available:

- ✔ Audio samples to your songs both from recordings and live
- ✔ Video samples of your shows and other promo videos
- ✔ Press kit samples including links to your promotional materials
- ✔ Reviews and press links to stories, interviews, and articles about you

This helps a potential endorser or sponsor get a better idea about what you do and how they can benefit by aligning with you.

Testimonials, professional bullets, and achievements

The next bits of useful information are testimonials from former sponsors and other endorsers, if you have them. Testimonials from management, booking agents, venue owners, as well as festival producers and larger-scale acts that you may have worked with are also helpful. This isn't material that you'd use online to promote to fans; this is more the type of material used specifically for potential endorsers, sponsors, and even investors. In a sense, it's sharing about the way you practice business over the way you practice and showcase the creative. If you don't have these types of testimonials, start asking for and collecting them now.

Achievements can include big opening-act spots, features on TV shows, radio programs, and other larger-scale media. They can also include tours you've been on and even the list of students you teach, or presentations for schools or music programs. It might not seem very rock-star-like, but certain teachers, both online and in music programs, can find lower-level endorsements because companies cater to students who could in turn buy the same equipment they use in class.

Sharing your total sales of music both online and off as well as other numbers including Alexa Rankings from your website can help showcase both your sales and visibility. Your Alexa ranking can tell just how often your website is being visited and its number in popularity of all the websites out there. Check out more information about Alexa Rankings in Chapter 17. You can find the Alexa ranking for your website by downloading the SEO Tool from Google Chrome. This also easily allows you to see the rankings for others sites.

Backlinks for Google as well as your Google page rank can give potential partners a real sense of how many people see you on a given day. The number is more reputable than Twitter figures because you can buy followers on Twitter. You can't buy your Alexa ranking or your Google Page ranking. Those have to be earned when people actually go to your pages.

Companies. They've heard it all before and they hear it every day. Stay away from coming off too arrogant and avoid claiming how you're new, unique, different, innovative, changing the game, and other overused words and phrases. These are good ways to turn off those who want to help you.

A clear and present danger presentation

Well, maybe not a dangerous presentation, but be both clear and in the present when you discuss what you've done and what you want to do. By showcasing your pitch in an email as well as revealing how you handle yourself on a phone call and in person, you display the type of vibe and professionalism that comes with these companies or products backing you.

Selling, supporting, and standing strong

The way you talk, walk, act, and even your posture can affect a potential endorsement or sponsorship. Whereas you may have seen very large and famous artists act like they couldn't care less about a product that sponsors them, they have money, fame, and luxury backing them up. As a starting artist or artist without anywhere near that level of popularity or reach, you need to be a better salesperson.

Find ways to describe, showcase, or use a product in a manner that's not been done before. This helps not only with your sell and promotion of the product or gear, but it also helps build interest the company's interest in you. They may want to advertise or highlight you that much more because you bring something to the table that others don't.

Using a guitar pedal as an effect with a keyboard or other less-practiced but cool types of uses for a product helps promote the product while also promoting you.

Describing the products

Be eloquent and descriptive for both the pitch and your representation of the product. Vague, overused phrases such as the following won't get you considered for an endorsement or sponsorship:

- ✔ I swear by this product!
- ✔ It's a great product!

✔ It's the only (insert product type) I use!

✔ It's the best!

✔ I've never used anything this good!

✔ I love this product!

These six incredibly oversaturated phrases don't help you. Although you may hear superstars use these exact phrases, you aren't a superstar. So to draw the interest at your level, dig a little deeper with your descriptions.

Give the potential endorser a true idea of not just why you want an endorsement but also why you play their product and what you like about it. Think of adding a short quote or pitch that could help you get that endorsement and also be used by the endorser to advertise their product in a different way.

For example, DW drum pedals are a very popular pedal, and a lot of drummers have sworn and continue to swear by them, but by digging in a little deeper and saying something like: "DW drum pedals have a great balance and sensitivity for your foot. Durable, strong, but easy to control, DW makes my feet that much better when I play on their pedals." In that quote, from yours truly (and I truly love DW pedals), I give a little more description, more detail, and showcase a quote that doesn't say the exact same thing as most others are saying.

No one would buy DW pedals because I played them. I was a session drummer and never a big name, but with a quote like that, I may entice someone to take a look if I was endorsing them.

The biggest difference between a celebrity or higher-profile musician endorsing a product and you is that their name and fame can be enough to draw people to buy, emulate, and copy the people they look up to. As you work to build up your name and presence, realize the more you market the products functions, features, and usability, the more doors you open for endorsement potential. Share what's good about a product, why others should use it, and how having that item makes work and play better for you.

Delivering your best pitch

Your delivery, tactics, and tact are some of the last pieces of the endorsement presentation. Do what you can to reduce the uses of the ums, uhs, and other verbal stutters while you work to avoid stuttering altogether. The assertiveness in your voice, your tone, and your physical presence should relay confidence, comfort, and charisma.

You wouldn't want someone who seemed depressed or morose with a stutter or slur to officially talk about your new song or promote a show, right? Well, these companies don't want that, either. Work on your enunciation, stay aware of the volume and dynamics in your voice, and don't talk too fast or too slow. It's not about turning into a radio or game show announcer, but you need to find that happy medium to be able to speak highly of an endorser or sponsor and being able to speak well for them.

Actually playing the products and having a great deal of experience with them is world's better than hopping from company to company and ask to ask. Having a trail of pictures, videos, and even plugs about that gear going way back helps you shine that much stronger for consideration.

Showcasing the Benefit to Endorsers

As you make your connections for sponsorships and endorsements, one of the biggest hurdles is proving and justifying the benefits of them helping you. Don't ever forget that they're doing you a favor, and your attitude can create more opportunities down the line.

Following best practices and promises

The majority of larger endorsements come with a contract, whereas smaller endorsement may be a little more loosey-goosey. Before you lock in an agreement, always plan to follow through on your word. If you have the slightest inkling that you can't do what's expected, don't do the deal.

Honor in the music business (in any business, really) is in short supply these days. It might sound a bit insane, but those who follow through and deliver on the deliverables create the best reputations for themselves. From taking care of the equipment to creating different marketing approaches to expanding the exposure, your attention to detail and effort enables you to shine in a world full of dull promises and lack of follow-through.

Learning more about the company and the competitors

Take the initiative to learn about the products you want to endorse as well as the companies behind them. This helps you both for your pitch and solicitation as well as your knowledge and ability to speak intelligently about that product and that company, if you get the opportunity to work with them.

An endorsement is going to be much more than just telling people that you use a product and that they should, too. Those types of endorsements are for much bigger names that have the name recognition. Most endorsements and sponsorship requirements for lower-profile artists include requests to showcase, market, promote, and create content as well as educate those you can reach. Knowing the company's history, cool bullet points, facts about the products, and even information of other people who use or used their gear, gives you an extra marketing edge.

By learning about the competition, you arm yourself with a better pitch as well as know what others are doing. This isn't about bashing the other company. Stay away from saying "use this, 'cause that sucks." It's unprofessional. You represent the company and the product, and most companies want to stay positive about their own products.

Keep gear in top-notch condition

One of the best ways to represent a product is to make that product shine . . . literally. From the gear you use to a stage that's sponsored by a company, make it look all sorts of "purty." Whether you're promoting a sponsored drum stick or a vehicle, make it all look good, sharp, pretty, and clean. And shiny. Always remember shiny.

From wiping down a guitar, to washing a car, cleaning up a sponsored stage to turning the logo of the drumsticks outward and visible for that picture, the small stuff can make a big difference. Allow that product you're representing or want to represent to look as good as possible. Showcase just how good you can make a musical product sound as you showcase just how good it looks.

The same goes for other sponsorships and endorsements outside of music. If someone is going to sponsor some ads or print posters for you, make sure to get those posters and ads designed in a way that looks top notch, and clearly add the sponsor or event sponsors' names with their logos and their fonts.

With any endorsements or sponsorships, make sure to get the company's permission to use their logos, fonts, and branding as part of your promotional materials. From posters to post cards, websites to social media, show how the combination of your branding and promotion helps promote a brand and products.

Going the distance for the long run

Most sponsors, especially product sponsors, want to see how relationships can work in the long run and not just a simple transaction lasting for a brief moment. Show your desired involvement with the company and what you can do to help market and promote. Many just look to get an endorsement and then brag about it. When you can show that you want to go the distance and plan for a long-term relationship, you become a much more attractive endorsee.

Ongoing marketing and commitment

Creating reminders in your marketing schedule or editorial calendars with your marketing of a product is a helpful way to remember to continue to market for the long term and keep up good engagement for the products or companies that you are pushing. Just as you work to create fresh and new content for marketing your music, your brand, and so on, schedule different ways to promote your sponsors and their gear to keep things fresh, consistent, and ongoing.

For example, set up a calendar of different ideas to pitch to a potential endorser. Use the various media formats like blogs, videos, audios, and images over a series of posts that cover topics such as tips, tricks, showcasing, testimonials, and links to their stores or where their products can be bought.

Enduring marketing with endurance

As you create a proposal of content, or as you begin to build up the content to promote your endorsement, don't toss it all out there all at once. You don't need to wear a T-shirt or a hat every day, yet wear that hat or that shirt at least twice a month and at shows. Make sure the logos of the endorsers are prominent on the posters, and save copies of each promotional item that showcases their logo and their information.

With different posts from videos to pictures to blogs directly related to the product, spread them out to go up at least once a month, instead of them all going up at one time. Just as the endurance for marketing you, your music, and your products has to expand and stretch over time, the marketing of your endorsers and sponsorships should as well. Laying this out in a proposal helps your chances exponentially. Think of it this way — would you want someone to shout from the mountain tops about you for one week, or for years and years to promote your music and you? I'd prefer the ongoing town crier over the mountain yeller.

Look at what other lower-level endorsers do to promote products from the company you want an endorsement from and ask them what they would like to see more of or areas and elements they want to promote. In just asking how you can help promote and market their company or product, you showcase your willingness to help and desire to go above and beyond.

Tying in outside influences and promo

There's a lot about you, your band, and your life that comes from outside of music and the products you use to create music. The elements, inspirations, influences, and stories that brought your band together can become a marketing point to reach a wider audience. You may not have the highest profile in the music industry, but elements of your personal story, individual experiences, and other aspects of your life outside of music that you have overcome and had to go through can help give you a higher profile in the media. This, in turn, could be a deciding factor in sponsorship, endorsements, and support.

Looking at companies outside of music

Think of the items you use, support, and like outside of music for additional endorsement and sponsorship options. From gel you use to style your hair to deodorant you use for perspiration, these are just two types of products and companies that you may be able to align with for support. For example, aligning with schools or alumni to represent their programs can open doors for a sponsorship. Tying in aspects of a local branch of a national company you worked for at one point and could promote on the side of your car and on stage on a banner and on posters could also be the starting point of a sponsorship.

Maybe the whole band wears a certain clothing or shoe brand that you can approach for additional support. From Converse to Nike, Adidas to Reebok, put your foot down there and try for some support. One of your favorite foods, snacks, or even drinks might have a sponsorship or endorsement option and a place to solicit on their website.

It's worth a look outside of music at companies and products that you like, have used, and have stories about. From the largest-scale items such as the car you drive to mom-and-pop print shops in towns you play, brainstorm and play with all kinds of different options. And then give them a try. The worst you can hear is "no."

Search sponsorships and endorsers online. There's a great deal of both new and innovative businesses as well as older and more established companies looking for different ways to connect with different audiences. Just as you have your daily to-do list of researching and contacting booking agents, venues, bands, reviewers, and other media, add your search for sponsorships and endorsements to your list. Even if you research and send three emails a week, you're reaching out that much further and connecting that much more.

Using the human-interest angle

It's not about exploiting a tragedy or sharing something too personal. Your life is your life, and you can always choose what you want to and don't want to share. This is also an area where you might find sponsorship a little easier. Think about all those morning and afternoon shows as well as any of those talk shows and now, all the reality shows. Someone is overcoming this sickness or this situation, and the viewers connect with it for the drama, entertainment, or familiarity. From humor to heartbreak, from trivial to strife and everywhere in between, sharing these experiences and angles can enable you with that many more options with both products inside and outside of music. You probably won't get your own reality show, but you can draw the interest in potential endorsements or sponsors with your story.

The core idea of this kind of sponsorship or endorsement is that while you might not have the reputation or recognition for your music, the higher-level exposure of your story or potential story can allow you a higher profile to companies based on your story and not on your current profile in music.

Learning your representative's birthday, the company's anniversary, and other personal style dates is not just kind; it exemplifies an additional attention to detail and helps to keep you on the radar.

Those courteous courtesies

Manners can make the man or woman. The courtesy and respect you show to those who are helping and working with you allows you to be seen with a higher level of professionalism.

Checkups, check-ins, and updates

Even before you lock up an endorsement, offer up an update plan of how you will stay in touch and update your endorser. Discuss a plan about how you plan to market them, what you can do for them, and how you plan to keep them up to date on the music and band.

From hiring a full-time publicist to getting a tour to a big article coming out, these are exactly the types of events those who endorse and sponsor you want to know about, both to see that you're growing and building more momentum and are able to reach a wider audience for their product to be seen.

After getting that endorsement, let your sponsor or endorser know when you put out a press release or do an interview on a larger scale. It's not just about listing them in certain press materials; they may counter your story, interview, or announcements with some additional promotion themselves.

For example, imagine you're the drummer in a band. You have a partial endorsement from Regal Tip drum sticks, and you're going to be featured in a Modern Drummer article with some other drummers. Be sure to give Regal

Tip the advanced notice so they can include you in one of their advertise-ments for the month you are being interviewed.

Those checkups and updates not only show that you continue to represent the products and companies in the best way, but also offer them the chance to reinforce on their end and supplement that media to both promote them-selves and you.

Giving updates to your sponsors and endorsers

There's a lot going on when you're on tour. From the traveling to the market-ing, the crazy schedules, and juggling a thousand things, it can be easy to let certain things slip. Think of your endorsers as part of the fuel that keeps you running, from the people helping you with gear to marketing support and everything in between. Make sure they are part of any media sheets going out, added into press releases, and brought up in interviews whenever possible.

While different media outlets may not include it in their stories, it's still your responsibility to always represent and not forget about those who work with and help you. From endorsers to sponsors to friends, stay in touch with those who make the difference for you and your career.

Again, this isn't only good to discuss in solicitations for endorsements as well as practicing these things when you get them, but it also highlights and show-cases you to other companies as well as helps to raise your support level or sponsor level in time with the endorsers you currently have.

Send out those thank you cards, not thank you emails. Thank you cards still go a long way, leave a strong impression, and show the effort of someone that companies want to know and be involved with. Every extra step you take is one more than most and keeps you moving beyond and above many others.

Promoting Endorsements and Products

After you lock in an endorsement or sponsorship and begin to receive the benefits through support, gear, or promotion, it's your turn to return that favor. From a mixture of both online and physical ideas that allow you to promote the product or company to marketing posts and testimonials, keep sharing — share the word, the products, and the information on a regular basis without spamming. That fine balance enables you to reach farther and wider as you don't overwhelm your existing fan base. Don't overdo the adver-tising bumper stickers.

Online endorsement promotion techniques

Online is a great place to promote your endorsements while continuing to market the music, yourself, and your information. When you take an approach of sharing information that people can relate to while highlighting a product, it comes off a lot less pitchy and more engaging.

Linking directly to the products and companies

Hey buddy!! Get your promo links here! Fill in your website and social media pages with links as well as descriptions to where those links are going. On your website and in the About sections of your social media sites, add a short description and the appropriate links.

For example, if you're endorsed by Pearl drums, add a link at the bottom of your bio that includes: *The drums we use in the studio and on tour: Pearl Drums*–http://pearldrum.com/.

List the endorsers and links on a web page, as well as some content and a testimonial that states what you like about the company and their products. This helps lead people to click through to those sites.

On that endorsement page or link page, don't just put up *Click here for Pearl Drums Website.* Instead, represent them well. Add their logo, font, and links to their website, as well as a few of their key social media sites. Include descriptions from you or the band like this: *Pearl drums are the only drums that Kitty Likes Avocado uses in the studio and on tour. The tone, the ability to easily tune, and the durability are just three of the reasons we love these drums as well as why they are the Best Reason to Play Drums. Here are the links to the Pearl drums website, Facebook, Twitter, and Instagram.*

This gives Pearl direct promotion on a page, along with a testimonial from you that includes their tagline (Best Reason to Play Drums).

Also, on the front page of your website, add those simple graphic-based links on the bottom of the page or running down the side. Let people know what you use and who supports you.

Per endorsement and company, put up a blog that highlights all the links to them, pictures of you with the endorsed gear, why you use it, why you like it, and why it's the best, in your opinion.

Using existing content from others as you create that much more

After you add the links and post a key blog as well as an announcement or press release about the endorsement, continue to add content in different formats over extended periods of time. This helps maintain regular engagement and promotion.

The idea is not to constantly be in a selling mode, just like you shouldn't constantly sell your music. The idea is to create engagement with a series of posts that come directly from you as well as posting headlines and linking to existing posts or content on other sites that represent the brand you endorse.

Here are five different examples of existing content and creating new content to promote an endorser while not pushing the sale too hard but keeping the message and marketing alive:

- ✔ Add a headline to a link of someone playing the same products that people might like to watch and mention what's cool about it.

- ✔ Add a headline to a link to a cool picture of a higher-profile artist playing on the same product.

- ✔ Share an audio link from another group with a headline that mentions the endorser or product.

- ✔ Record a short video that showcases a given endorsed item. Think along the lines of a video for Latin Percussion; their cowbells could be funny if you jump around like that Saturday Night Live skit saying "more cowbell."

- ✔ Share a video link from another group with a headline that mentions the endorser or product.

Here's an example of a leading headline that uses a video idea and promotes Evans drum heads: *Steely Dan Live drum solo with Keith Carlock burning on the song "Josie" live from a few years back. Cool solo whether you are a drummer or not. Keith also endorses Evans drum heads - https://youtu.be/ uqUq7oFIjRM.*

This highlights a band a lot of people know, mentions Keith's name, promotes Evans, and creates engagement for your fans, too!

Physical and in-person sponsor promotion techniques

There's nothing better in showcasing or promoting a product than watching it or trying it out for yourself, from test-driving a car to having a certain guitar in your hands to feel exactly how it plays for you. At the same time, seeing something in person and watching how others experience it can help, too. Experiencing a product for yourself, seeing someone in person with it, or just seeing the brand or the information somewhere else and not just online can help promote and is something you want to do for your endorsers and endorsements.

Using stickers and signage for marketing

Your signage is wonderful when it comes to your brand; the same goes for the brand you use and especially the brands that endorse you. From adding simple stickers to drum and guitar cases, and even your vehicles, you help further the visibility of a brand.

With companies like Carsticker.com, Vistaprint, and other decal companies, you can easily highlight endorsers on your vehicle as it spends the bulk of its days out on the road carrying you from gig to gig. Artists who spend a lot of time on the road are more likely to get endorsements over the artists who play only within a limited radius.

With very affordable and easy-to- remove stickers — and even car magnets — you create a great level of visibility to all those driving by you . . . or if you're a fast driver, driving by them.

Adding smaller stickers to your gear cases and even your luggage again is a great way to keep a brand that much more visible and seen by that many more people. As you add stickers, magnets, and other logos to your vehicle, your car, and your cases, make sure your name, logo, and website URL are always large and prevalent. Although you are endorsed by a company and need to be promoting them, the reason you are out there is you, and the main focus of marketing is getting you out there the most.

If you go this promotion route for use on cars, cases, and luggage, realize that while you're branding your name, website, and endorser's information on to these items, you're also in a way branding that you have expensive stuff. Especially with smaller vehicles, bring in all your gear. Make sure it looks like an empty vehicle in a hotel parking lot, and try to park in well-lit areas to avoid tempting potential thieves even more. Chapter 9 discusses more about insurance.

On the stage and in the studio

From setting up to sound check, you often deal with people who can directly benefit from your endorsed product and be potential purchasers. From the sound guy to the monitor guy who loves it and can further recommend an endorsed item to another band, this is where you can have a great representation effect.

From other musicians to musicians in the crowd during the show, showcase that gear in the best way possible to draw as much interest from others as you can. Invite other musicians to give the gear a test drive during sound check if they show a real interest in an item. Your endorsing company will love you for it.

Everyone has different tastes. In showing a type of effect pedal or set of pedals that you love, use, and are endorsed by, don't get all riled up if someone says they suck or that something else is better. It makes you look foolish and the company you represent look less than professional. Stand strong behind the gear you use but don't be that headstrong to have to get in an argument or a screaming match about which product is better and why. Pointless.

Wear it proudly, literally

Many endorsing companies have a great deal of promotional merchandise or swag that includes T-shirts, hats, jackets, raincoats, coffee mugs, and so on. Ask for some of these items to help the promotion of the brand or company that's supporting you.

Make sure to wear these items in a regular rotation when on the road or just in normal life to help to push and promote. This isn't about wearing a T-shirt every day, but rather wearing an endorser's shirt on a day when you're doing interviews or on a road day when you're traveling.

You don't have to wear it on stage, and a promotional shirt doesn't have to mess with your whole vibe or image, but show some extra support by donning that shirt or hat at least once a month and strive to get more people to see you and the brand standing behind you.

Promoting Localized Sponsorships

The local support channels such as mom-and-pop-type businesses, local restaurants, or franchise-owned places as well as radio stations, printing companies, and other local organizations can be helpful. It's a different type of promotion because these local sponsors are usually involved for only one show in their community. Your focus and approach to these local sponsors showcases to other potential sponsors what you're able to do for the local markets.

Short-term and single-event sponsors

For the sponsors that may be involved for only a single event in a single location, put a focus on a closer radius of that location. Give them a little more of your physical product and swag to use as a giveaway, and highlight them in the posters you create for that specific area.

Don't forget to make noise and make references to those local sponsors during the show. This is more important than shouting out that you use this guitar or that drum set. Giving that extra thanks verbally means that much more to the local business and local crowd.

The same goes for wearing a local radio station's shirt or seeing what you can do to cross-promote or tie into the local sponsor support. Whereas it may be a little more linear and centralized, your efforts to cross-promote on more of a local level are exactly what those local businesses are looking for and a part of the reason why they're potentially sponsoring you.

The smallest support can translate into the best promotion. Work for the regional as you still chase the international. The collection and collaboration of the biggest and smallest allot the best results and support.

Laying the foundation for future local opportunities

Even when it's a sponsorship for a single place and a single event, realize that done right, this can amount to future opportunities and assistance in that location. Just as you want to build up your support with larger scale endorsements, don't forget about the local yokels. Your effort and support of those who support you in a region or single city or town can continue to grow as you build a relationship.

Never lose site that every single town, city, or college cannot only help to build a longer-term relationship with that location, but can also showcase how you handle smaller-level sponsorships in smaller towns. Your attention to detail for the smaller and more localized regions can help to compound and grow in many more places for you.

Chapter 16

Considering Additional Opportunities

In This Chapter

▶ Researching every option available for exposure and profit

▶ Narrowing the best options and opportunities for you

▶ Working with the right people to create the right results

▶ Fact-checking and double-checking to ensure the right choices

Many look to the music business with a goal to win a Grammy, play in front of thousands, and become famous, but many forget that an expanded view can offer a lot more options and opportunities that enable success. By considering all the different opportunities for your music and your career, you up the chances of success. From licensing songs to being the support band for another act to performing at weddings, your ability to organize as many avenues of revenue as possible for your music allows for more options to be profitable for you.

There's a better chance to make a million dollars from ten different sources than to make it from just one source in the music business. By creating more options that might pay a little less, the sum of profits are greater as well as more likely to happen.

Making the Most Out of All Opportunities

For every gig, contact, sale, and opportunity, always look at it from the standpoint of how more things can come later from it. Use and develop it all. That one single show you did with a band that had an amazing draw and helped to sell a whole bunch of product and connect with new fans afterwards made for a successful night. Still, by utilizing the best way to create future opportunities, make sure you stay in touch with that band, cross-market that venue, and talk to them, their management, or booking agent about setting up another show down the line. It's all about compounding for conversion from every event, promotion, advertisement, or product sale that went well for you.

Buying in, not selling out

There is a negative connotation with going after numerous opportunities outside of just performance and selling products, which some people claim is selling out. You're not selling out when you look for more opportunities; you're buying into the business by creating the most opportunities for profit and success.

Look at every option available to create, build, support, and sustain success for your music and your career as you continue to grow your exposure, expand your brand, and reach wider audiences around the world. A linear focus on touring and sales of your product as a whole puts you at a much greater risk of not being able to sustain your success. While looking into other opportunities from licensing to sponsorships, endorsements to different products, and applying a broader approach to your marketing, you buy into a much larger level of visibility.

Preparing for all the avenues of revenue possible

As you look to all the different options and avenues of revenue as covered in a detailed list in Chapter 4, the more you create for more uses, the more profit can be made.

A song that's recorded for an album or EP and mastered with a no vocal track could be used in a TV show. It could also have a loop section of something that can be used for a sampling track for another song. And a translation version of either the vocalist or someone else singing that tune in another language offers another option. So from one song, you get five different avenues of revenue:

✔ The single download of the track

✔ Part of the body of work of an album or EP

✔ The sync licensing profits of the no-vocals track used for a TV show

✔ A sampling license from someone else using your sample in their song

✔ Foreign rights licensing of that song being played in another country or sung by someone else

Expanding your options for opportunities early on allow for that much more to happen for you later down the line. The same goes for the early branding stage when you're creating your bio, logo, and initial marketing.

By creating a bio and then translating it into a series of different languages, you open up for more opportunities to market to more countries that much faster. Also by translating early on, if you receive a request or a connection from someone who speaks that language or is from that country, after finding a translator who can help you, you can get that information right back to them, showing how prepared you are.

With your logos being formatted for posters, stickers, flyers, and various merchandise, it's that much faster to create all these items and get them out to the public.

With your publishing in place by having all your copyrights in order as well as all basic agreements ready to go on a moment's notice along with tracks that are zipped up and ready to send upon request and contract, it's easier for a music publisher to help you with licensing opportunities as you search out more options yourself.

Your array of preparation and solicitation of options also helps when life throws you a curve. If you're counting on performance money from a tour, and a major snowstorm cancels shows for four days, you don't play and don't get paid. With more options, however, you have more revenue to fall back on.

By getting away from a singular focus and diversifying your music business portfolio to include performance, downloads, subscriptions, merchandise, sampling, songs going into or pitched to TV, movies and so on, you are building a better foundation to profit from. This also can include backing other bands, playing certain general business-type shows like weddings, and working on your online affiliate programs and advertising programs to generate additional revenues as well. With these elements in place, you create numerous options and allow for the most events to happen. On top of that, you no longer need to put all your eggs in one basket to rely on only one area.

The more streams and options you have for different revenues, the more profit can flow for you and enable you to make that much more in your career.

Tapping Into Various Events, Experts, Deals, and Options

Networking is a big part of connecting with others in the industry and other opportunities. From conferences to festivals, award shows to contests, and consultants to coaches, there's a great deal of networking, connections, and opportunities that can come from tapping into these events and resources. Still, watch out and do the research on what actually is happening and if these events, people, and deals are worth your time and energy.

Music conferences

From the largest conference such as The ASCAP Expo in Hollywood to smaller and more localized conferences like Millennium Music Conference in Harrisburg, Pennsylvania, there are so many events around the United States that you could pretty much hit a different one every weekend.

Effectively tapping into the right music conferences for you comes down to research and being realistic as well as frugal with your funds. These are events that are part of businesses to make money. If you sign up for every single one and travel to each along with paying for food, gas, and hotels, you will be broke pretty quickly.

For every music conference that you hear about, try to find out what other bands are going to be there as well as booking agents, publishers, and speakers. Look to the events not for what they promise but rather to find out how to connect with music supervisors, branding, marketing, and promoting as well as the number one reason to go to — to connect with other bands.

Yes, it can be cool to get a showcase at a music conference, but just being able to go, even if you're not playing, to connect with artists and bands from all over the country or world is an opportunity to build relationships and find new artists that you can open for in their stronger areas as they can open for you in yours.

Approach music conferences as a chance to meet and greet with as many different bands as possible, as well as with industry professionals. Don't get all caught up in a showcase or waste time at the bar. Use your time wisely and develop the opportunity to connect, network, and lay the foundation for future opportunities. Have your fun, but make it work for you for the future.

Check out conferences like the National Association for Campus Activities (NACA) or other booking agent showcase-type events. These kinds of conferences can create the highest conversions to gigs and future opportunities. Find out more at www.naca.org.

Music festivals

Festivals like SXSW (South by Southwest), Canadian Music Week, NXNW (North by Northwest), and Bumbershoot, to name a few, mix up national-scale acts with locals, regionals, and independents. Attending these festivals can be great networking events to meet up as well as be around so many different artists.

Even if you're not playing, many doors can open to connect with bands from all over the country and all over the world. You more than likely can't meet some of the larger acts, but you can talk to their crew to find out about options for connecting with them, their management, or others who can help with the networking.

While you're there, don't make it a time of solicitation, and don't be that person carrying around CDs or promotional packages. If anything, have a download card or business card available upon request, but don't be pushy and overly promoting. You'll see a lot of others doing that, but stand out with professionalism and don't do it yourself. Look at the festivals as a place to expand your connections as you research, and talk with groups about cities or venues that are up and coming, reviewers or magazines that help them out as well as people to watch out for and places to avoid.

You can buy every guide and database, visit tons of websites, but the best up-to-date information is what you get from the people who have been there and done that.

It's much more than just finding bands you might be able to play with; it's about learning what bandmates experience first-hand.

Again, just like conferences, enjoy the shows but make sure you're getting the most out of the opportunities being presented. Taking a business and research approach to music festivals can enable you to both create and explore many more opportunities.

Award shows and music contests

Awards shows can be a chance to network and meet a number of people, but just as in music conferences, you can find a lot of scams going on. I'm not a fan of a pay-to-be-nominated situation. Those are the type of events where artists are asked to pay a fee to be nominated for an award in the show. It's a money-making event for the producers and promoters, and it doesn't really help the artists. That said, however, if there's a nearby and affordable awards show, you might meet more artists as well as learn about companies that sponsor these types of events. Use these opportunities wisely, and don't get sucked into the pay-to-get-nominated situations.

Music contests can be similar in formats to award shows. There are certain legitimate contests that require admission payment and offer opening spots and opportunities to play for certain shows. Check them out and, of course, do your research.

Don't spend the cash to travel to awards shows; find ones that are close by. They don't all have to be about music, either. Many awards shows have event producers, publicists, and other entertainment professionals along with sponsors that might be useful connections for you. Events outside of music can still pertain to music opportunities. Fashion and runway shows, food shows, and even local business-type events can connect you with those event producers, publicists, and possible opportunities to be involved with those shows in the future.

Always double-check to see who's involved with awards shows and who's planning to be there to see if it's worth your time and money. Look into the contests and check their validity as well as what opportunities they offer. Do this research by contacting former winners, losers, and sponsors. They can give you a much better sense of what's going on over the self-and direct-hype of the website or advertisement.

Music business consultants, and advisors

At many conferences and festivals as well as online, you find music business consultants, coaches, speakers, and advisors who can potentially assist you with where you are with your career and help organize and plan your next best steps. A true professional with a proven track record can help expand on your current opportunities as well as create additional ones for your future.

After doing your research and due diligence, working with a consultant, coach, or advisor can serve as one of the best ways to tap into more opportunities.

They serve as independent contractors to help you create and choose the best paths without taking percentages or creating situations for their own self-interest. This is a much better route before signing with a record label, a management group, or an agent that may only be looking to a deal that benefits them, not you. In turn, it could squash opportunities by being stuck in deals that tie your hands and options.

The down side is the fakes who waste your time and cost you money as well as opportunities. These are the types who sell hype and are only looking to make a buck. Dig in with research and due diligence for the consultants, speakers, or any professional you choose to listen to before you commit to the time and money, or take the advice.

Entertainment lawyers and music publishers

One of your best investments, which allows for the greatest returns opportunities than almost anything else, is when you have all your legal ducks in a row and quacking in unison. A lawyer can help you format internal agreements as well as review and educate you about deals, contracts, and options. You can learn more about the legal crew in Chapter 9.

The more you have your fundamentals organized, down on paper, and signed, the more seriously you're viewed and the more opportunities can follow because your foundation is already in place.

Same thing goes for songs, especially for licensing. Connecting with a music publisher doesn't always have to be about publishing your music with them. There are music publishing companies out there that can help get your copyrights, template contracts, set up musician releases and song split agreements, and review publishing agreements. One of the best companies for this is SSA Music Publishing. Check out more information about them at www.ssamusicpublishing.com. Find out more about the copyrights, publishing, and licensing in Chapter 9.

Having all your music in order and legally set up allows for easier transitions to licensing deals and publishing opportunities. This helps you to avoid hassle if a song is picked up for use as well as other deals presenting themselves too soon. With the legal aspects of you, your music, your copyrights, and your publishing in order, you up the opportunities while reducing the problems or chances of being taken advantage of.

Hiring a music publisher for consulting or a lawyer who's not part of a record label or management company gives you a disinterested third party who works for your best interests. Working with internal publishers and lawyers who are directly involved with the companies that offer potential deals and contracts can get you in worlds of trouble.

Management and record label deals

The right deals with the right teams can include managers, booking agents, or record labels and can advance careers and compound opportunities. Pay attention, however, to exactly what they offer and what they don't. Artists who connect with that entertainment lawyer (mentioned earlier in this chapter as well as in Chapter 9) to review contracts and clearly understand what's covered and what isn't see the best results.

A deal is only as good as the details of that deal and the execution of the right contract. It's no longer about getting a manager or a record label. It's about getting the right manager who can help build those opportunities or connect with the right label that handles the details from recording to promotion to touring to publicity. Otherwise, it's a better approach to take a more independent route and find the people who can cover all the business plan line items that have to be executed to create opportunities and options for success in music.

Buying in bulk

By buying promotional merchandise in larger qualities, you pay less for the items. You can sell more for less and still see a generous profit.

This also enables you to give away more on a promotional level without taking as much of a loss. Whether CDs, T-shirts, hats, cups, or anything else, buy in bulk to achieve the highest profits as you create the lowest prices to draw the most interest for the sale.

Schools, education, and yes, military

There are many schools and music programs that you can take part in to expand your abilities, grow, and network with other students and teachers. Learning your instrument to studying another instrument, or taking courses for engineering, music business, and other business courses expanding your knowledge, experience, and technique helps every facet of your career.

Furthering your knowledge, technique, and abilities while meeting with other musicians not only helps you on your path, but may help you find band mates and others with whom you want to work. Don't rush a career; with so much competition out there, the better the musician you can be, the more opportunities will come.

There are options in the military for your music career. Although it might sound outlandish, joining the military can enable you to work with musicians in a full-time capacity as you grow your abilities. Yes, it might be for a couple of years, but it can help you work on your skills with three squares a day plus room and board while being paid. And then there are the military benefits when you leave the service, but this is a discussion for another day . . . or another book!

Supplementing Opportunities Outside of Music

Musicians can get pulled into the all-or-nothing mindset, which can hold you back from career-forwarding opportunities. Although opportunities outside of music might not be perfect, they can supplement your income and enable you to spend more time playing and living your dream.

Online work

If you have a day job that can be done with a computer and an Internet connection, you may be able to work from the road. Although not being completely self-sufficient with music, doing work online can enable you to be out on the road playing and promoting your music.

Make sure that you can work from the road, both physically and professionally. Discuss with a boss what you're doing as well as test out how you can work on the road or in hotel rooms and complete the required tasks.

Part-time and bulk work

Another way to supplement income and have more time on the road is with part-time jobs that enable you to work fewer hours and fewer days or shifts. These jobs give you the time to come closer to being a full professional, but not quitting that day job quite yet. A better situation can be a bulk-work job. These can be the type of jobs where you work very intensely for a few weeks or a month at a time and then have a series of months off. This can include certain serving jobs at resorts, work on cruise ships (not just in being a musician; I cover that in the next section), or certain farm labor jobs. The Christmas holidays are rife with temporary sales and warehouse gigs that offer decent pay and as many hours as you want to work.

Farm labor jobs are not the most glamorous, and the work can be hard, but you can save a bunch of money, giving you that much more time to be out on a full tour where a regular type of job wouldn't let you be gone for so long.

Supporting Your Music with Music

There are ways to work inside of the music business with others outside of your music. Look at options where you can work with other artists as either a sideman or even with your band as a backing band for another artist. Another option is to give music lessons either in person or online. There are other options that can help you supplement revenues for your career as you help others with theirs.

Session, substitute, backing musician, or band work

Supporting other musicians as a session artist and substituting for musicians who are sick or unable to make a show or recording session are a couple options that can help you pay the bills as you make connections and look for more opportunities for you and your music.

Having your group work as the backing band for a single artist who might be coming to town without other musicians can create more revenue and exposure for your group. too. These are all options that keep you inside of the music realm, making money and making more connections.

Other band work-type situations can include cruise ship work and general business-style bands like wedding or cover bands. It might not seem like the route to rock stardom, but as you get better technically and market to people who see you perform, you're working your way to the place you want to be.

Teaching and giving lessons

Offering lessons with students and groups brings income. With many amazing online platforms like Lesson Face, The ZOEN, and Take Lessons, you can give lessons online from practically anywhere. These can be lessons based on music instruments but also can be lessons in regular school subjects such as math, science, and English.

If you don't know how to teach, please don't! Make sure you can teach and be kind and helpful to your students. Don't do it only for the money.

Considering the Cost of the Conversion for Every Opportunity

It would be amazing if you had millions of dollars and could afford to test out every option and explore every opportunity. Sadly, that isn't possible, so it's crucial to look at the potential costs and the possible conversions of those costs for every opportunity.

All the costs have to be weighed out not just for the opportunity, but also for where you're at in your career, what you need, and what you want to try. There's no exact formula, but looking at the best steps for you can include saving money to go to a conference that's only 100 miles away rather than attending one on the other side of the country. The same goes with festivals as far as distance, too.

The main point to keep in the front of your mind is how every opportunity converts to enable for more opportunities as they each support you career-wise and convert to exposure that prompts sales, marketing that ups attendance, and networking that creates more shows, tours, and music.

Defining conversions

There's a great deal of confusion about what a conversion is and how it allows for growth, success, and revenue. True conversions mean that you have put time, effort, or investment into something that's garnering actual benefits of more shows and fans who are buying music, merchandise, or attending shows. These conversions also come in the shape of connecting you with real investors, music industry professionals, publishers, and booking agents who assist and execute in furthering your career.

A conversion is not spending thousands of dollars on a radio campaign to achieve a chart placement or a certain number of plays that don't create any sales, opportunities, or profit. The same goes for a social media campaign where thousands of new Twitter followers are added, but barely a one came to a show, bought a download, or became engaged with you. These are expenses, actions, and opportunities that end up dead ending.

The biggest problem is that many get suckered into thinking it'll work and just needs more time and more money. By considering every step with even the smallest conversion that you look for, hope for, or expect, it makes it much easier to see what's working, what isn't, what needs to be changed, and what needs to be stopped altogether.

Look before you leap, and watch before you spend. When you're promised results for a service, an opportunity, or anything else, make those calls and send those emails to find out if they actually worked out for others.

Tracking the outgoing checks and incoming balances

The best way to stay on top of what's working and what isn't is by tracking how actions and events can create the conversions you need from start to finish. The more you know, understand, and track the details that create the results, good or bad, the better information you have to keep things on the right track, fix them, or change them altogether.

For example, maintain a weekly and monthly tracking sheet that includes the following basic eight categories:

✔ Sales from digital downloads directly from your stores

✔ Distribution sales from stores like iTunes and Amazon

✔ Payments from performances

✔ Sales of physical merchandise and apparel

✔ Number of shows booked

✔ Number of Shows played

✔ Number of connections on the core social media channels

✔ Number of licensing opportunities

This list enables you to see the effects of your efforts. From promoting posts on Facebook, you can see not only how many people clicked through or added you, but you can also look to the bump in sales, opportunities, or exposure.

You don't have to be an accountant or a financial guru. If one month you pay for a certain advertisement or promotion and you see solid conversions across the board, then extend that advertisement, or expand and change the location and try it somewhere else.

As you test out different options, such as advertisements along with attending different conferences and festivals or working with different music professionals, spread out these elements so that you can really see what's working and what isn't. If you run four different types of promotions or ads, it's harder to know exactly which one worked best and which one didn't work at all.

If you practice with a short promotion for a week and then stop for a week, you get a clearer sense of its success. In turn, by extending and expanding different ad campaigns, visiting different conferences, and investing in other opportunities, you provide yourself with more clarity for exactly what works for you.

Due Diligence and Fact-Checking the Opportunities

Just as you want the highest rate of conversions to sales and other profitable opportunities, it's crucial to practice your due diligence and fact-checking to make sure those opportunities are worth your time, investment, or effort. When considering other opportunities as you get close to something, do that double-checking, that fact-checking, and that follow-up on references to make sure you aren't losing out on one opportunity because you mistakenly took a chance on another that ended up to be scam.

Finding out all you can first

From signing with a music publisher to signing with a label, from hiring a music business consultant to attending a music conference, find out all you can. Get your information from others, not the website or social media pages promoted by those with whom you're considering a relationship.

Check references, referrals, and testimonials on the people, company, or event. Go to websites like Rip Off Report (www.ripoffreport.com) to see if there are any outstanding issues. Make sure a business is actually a business by searching for its legitimacy online. Connect with former clients, attendees, or others who were involved in the past to see if the fit is right for you. All these extra steps make for a wise decision — and while nothing is foolproof, the chances of you getting fooled are a great deal less.

Watch out for the outlandish promises, the success overnight, the guarantees of the finish line without explaining how to prepare or run the race. Throw a red flag when you hear vague responses to detailed questions or get a sense of tension from the person you're asking. If it seems too good to be true, then it's pretty safe to bet that it is. And if you can't find examples, proof of concept, or the execution of others doing it, then more than likely it can't be done.

Keep an eye out for people who discuss models that worked years ago, but aren't able to show a single example of them working in recent times. The same goes for the people who have a résumé of success that's dated and are unable to show anything more recent. These steps help keep you in step and avoid so many problems that you don't need to have.

When it comes to consultants, labels, managers, or anyone else claiming to have a business, a simple way to check on them is to look online. Another option is your local Better Business Bureau (BBB) website. Know that the BBB has sites for hundreds of cities across the United States, so you can check on a business in other locations.

Taking calculated risks

As you look into opportunities that might not have as long a track record or are based on newer models, these can be times when a good calculated risk can work in your favor. Realistically, anything you do in entertainment is a risk, but by doing the research and calculating the risk with information, something that might not be completely in line could still work very well for you.

Think of certain risks like math problems and equations. If someone can give you a great deal of information that comes from good sources to create the right equation, you're on the right track to a less-risky choice. If they can also help you with rational justifications and reasons as to why they think something may be the next trend, may work in the near future, or how many other aspects show that the direction is leading there it just might be something to try. From new products to new distribution to new methods of payment and even management, look with a set of calculating and even doubting eyes to see if it seems to balance out. If it makes sense, though, it might be worth a shot.

Everything is a risk, but the more you dig in, learn all you can, and do the double-checking and detailed due diligence regarding any opportunity, the less the risk is in the end, in most cases.

The more you dig into the different options and opportunities for your career, the more chances you allow for a better career. Look at your career as an array of different elements that can combine and give you that steady stream to live your dream. The wider you can view the world of the music business, the more opportunities there are for a great career.

Chapter 17

Tracking and Analyzing Your Progress

*T*he more you understand the root, reaction, and results of your activity, the more progress you can make in your career. Sometimes failure and issues are helpful. They enable you to problem-solve, resolve, and move forward with a greater understanding and more confidence than if events and situations come off without a hitch. You could just track your progress, but all and all, it's more informative to track and *analyze* your progress to continue and sustain success.

Detailing Your Detailed Account

Setting up automated tracking systems for social media and certain sales systems is a smart idea, but take it one step further and make sure you're reviewing the details and have a clear understanding of what they mean. All too often, data can come off overwhelming, especially when presented in bars, graphics, charts, and candlestick setups.

In reality, however, it's not that complex. Instead of getting consumed in crazy formatting, the idea is to clearly see what you spend, what the results of that expenditure are, and how much if any profit you make from it. A simple Excel spreadsheet or Word document into which you can enter dates, profits, revenues, and other information gives you an easy guide to understanding the details.

Leverage your experience. Imagine you're nine years old and on the playground. You're playing kickball and you just watched four kids kick to one area of the field that never seems to get covered by the other team. If you saw three kids kick to a kid or area where someone caught the ball and got people out, you wouldn't want to kick there. It really is that simple.

If you put up a Facebook promotional ad in a focused area and you see downloads, online sales, and requests to play that area as well as a growth in fan base there, you kicked the ball to the right place. If you hire a manager who helps get you a series of shows around a certain region and they all pay, again you kicked the ball into the right place.

If you spend money on a Twitter campaign that adds a couple hundred followers but doesn't bring any type of conversion to sales, gigs, or exposure, you kicked the ball into the wrong place on the field. If you hire a promoter who promises to get you interviews with connections to bloggers on websites, radio, and magazines but you don't see a single result, then you kicked the ball in the wrong place again.

It really is that simple. Look at your activities, the money you spend, the content that you market, the people you connect with, and the actions you take. Then balance them against the conversions and the results. This gives you a front row seat to what works and what doesn't right down to the nail with every detail.

Understanding Your Strengths, Weaknesses, Opportunities, and Threats

When investors look at business plans, they check out the expenses and the revenues, and then go directly to the SWOT —strengths, weaknesses, opportunities, and threats. This gives an investor an overview of how a project can work and how it can fail. Take a humble look at yourself and all those elements to see which ones might need a little reinforcement and which ones are firmly in place.

✔ **Strengths:** Your strengths are just what you think they are — they're your gifts, your assets, and your strong suits. Yes, living at home can be a kind of strength in your career, because you don't have rent, a mortgage, or utilities to pay. Although your mom and dad might find this to be a little annoying, it enables you to need that much less to be able to stay out on the road and reach that many more people.

- ✔ **Weakness:** If you have a full-time law career, this can be a weakness. It's not weak that you have a degree or a professional job. It's viewed as a weakness that you need more money to sustain your business and life-style. Weaknesses can also include lack of marketing support, egos, and even listing if a key member were to die.

- ✔ **Opportunity:** Opportunities include existing promotions or elements already in place as revenue generators, as discussed in Chapter 16. Deals that are in the making, marketing that's occurring, a tour that's starting, even if there's a certain amount of money available for use for the recording or marketing, can be considered opportunities.

- ✔ **Threat:** Threats include debts, bad contracts, exclusive agreements that prevent opportunities, band member illness, egos, and anything else that can hurt the project or profits as a whole.

When everything is considered from the good to the bad, from what you bring to the table and what can make projects a little more challenging or problematic, you have the best data to make the best decisions about what works for you.

Don't rush the decisions for your career, and don't rush the process. The information you collect and track matched with the opportunities that present themselves deliver the most clarity.

Look at your SWOT for every process and every expense, to make the best decision and protect your best interest in moving forward regardless of what you are doing. By analyzing the strengths, weaknesses, opportunities, and threats for every opportunity or expense, you can make much better choices.

Tracking to Showcase All Things at All Levels

The tracking isn't just for you. It's also for investors, record labels, booking agents, and promoters as well as sponsors and endorsers. Showing growth and progress to people who may want to work with, support, or stand behind you with investment and opportunities increases their faith and belief in you. These people and companies are going to be interested in knowing how you got to those numbers.

Saying that you had a certain number of shows last year doesn't give an idea of how you grew the numbers of shows. Telling people you made a certain amount from downloads last year doesn't showcase when sales were high or when sales were flat. By expanding the fields by the month and filling in the all the fields, you help explain what happened at what point. You also showcase where you're going strong and where assistance could help move you forward faster.

Doing monthly and yearly reports

Creating and filling in the numbers for your sales of music, merchandise, and products both online and physical each month helps others to see your success, but it can also show you where money is coming in versus money going out. These reports also include expenses from gas to tolls, gear to copyrighting fees, and physical to online advertising as well.

These reports include all the numbers that come in on a monthly basis but also can stretch out over the year as well. The following is a sample list of expenses. This isn't a definitive or complete list, and there are other costs that may come up as well. All these costs should be added as line items across each month. In the first set are the basic costs:

Copyrights/publishing fees	Merchandise ordering
Legal/lawyer fees	Web hosting/domain costs
Business/corporate fees	Graphics
Payments to band	Accounting/taxes
Recording costs	Website build costs
Gear cost	Photography/videography
Printing/mailing	Publicist

The next set of costs is tied into the operational, marketing, and promotional elements:

Physical promotion/promotional items	Solicitation mailers
Online promotion	Gas/ parking
Radio promotion	Food
Memberships	Clothing
Manager	Hygiene items
Vehicles/car maintenance	Makeup
Banners	Laundry
Rehearsal space rent	Hotels

Breaking down the online promotion even further, add subcategories for promoted posts on Facebook and on Twitter, as well as advertising for those sites and others. The key point is to break down what's going out just as you track what's coming in to give the best look at what's being spent and how it's coming back. In turn, this gives much more detail than just summarized numbers for an extended period of time.

Even if a line item, such as annual memberships, reflects $0 for 12 months, you still need to list all the zeroes. Should an investor see the tracking and the detail put into it, they have a better idea of exactly the costs to know how to make profits, growth, and exposure better.

Tracking sections for solicitations, sponsorships, and investors

Online programs in Excel as well as certain financial programs can help organize your data and keep it looking a little cleaner for presentation. Those extra steps that give the details in the numbers but also clean them up and make them a little prettier can help with sponsors and potential investors. The more streamlined the information, the easier it is to take in.

The tracking part of your presentation comes after the main pitch and all the pretty stuff; don't lead with it. Give the basics on you, your plan, and why you want to have a potential sponsor or investor involved. Showcase the brand, the ask, and the marketing plan first; then bring in the tracking sections as the cherry on top to show what you've been able to do in the past number of months, years, or other specific time period.

It's okay to do summary sheets that then lead to more of the details, but have those details and extra sheets ready. Prepare all the materials, but give a simple summary page of the key numbers first.

Tracking Website Traffic and Social Media

Just as you track the financials, tracking all the aspects of your website traffic and social media helps define where the online marketing elements are and where they can go. Just like expenses and revenues, a simple monthly summary of this data allows for a better understanding of your process, marketing, and online growth. Now that it's easier than ever to buy views, friends, and followers, your monthly numbers can help justify your growth with more realistic and legitimate numbers.

Alexa traffic rankings

The Alexa ranking is easy to get from a free toolbar download available on Google Chrome or any browser. The Alexa traffic rankings count down the most highly visited websites in the world. Tracking your Alexa ranking isn't about trying to have the lowest ranking, but it can show just how much traffic comes through your site. If you are under the five million mark, you have some attention going, and of course realize sites like Twitter and Facebook are often numbers 1 and 2. This is also covered in Chapter 15.

Again, it's not about being number one, but more about showing a dropping Alexa ranking each month to show a rise in website engagement for you and your music. Too many tell very tall tales about how a website is doing. The proof is in the numbers and the spreading out of those numbers over time to give much better data.

Subscriptions

On your website or through your blogs or mailing list sign-up, track the growth by the month. Just like many of the other elements you're tracking, show the growth over time of subscriptions and the engagement of fans that are signing up and staying connected with your updates. This data spread out over time gives a potential sponsor or investor a sense of your growth tempo that can be adjusted to a marketing budget. If investors see a certain number of subscriptions and then see the money you put into marketing, even at the smallest amount, it can give them some sense of what to spend to make that same growth happen on a larger scale.

There are numerous mailing list and subscription software programs and tools like Mail Chimp that cannot only help track your list but also give you extra data, including who's opening that mail, too.

Backlinks

Although backlinks don't necessarily equate to profits, keeping a list of backlinks and the growth of those that are pointing back to your site shows the work that's being done to expand your website out and connect it with others sites that can lead back to you. The more backlinks you have coming to your site can equate to the popularity of your website. It also is highly looked upon by search engines like Google, which gives more credit and visibility to a site that has more or growing backlinks by seeing that site as more relevant. Tracking these backlinks and their growth shows that your popularity is growing, even if it's just page by page. This information can be found by using the Open Stat SEO plug-in on Google Chrome.

Pages indexed by Google

This line item checked once a month and added to the list covers the number of pages Google has indexed from your site into its search engine. These indexed pages show up in searches that much more and help your website as a whole to show up more often in Google searches related to music.

More pages are indexed by Google and other search engines if the pages are correctly laid out and SEO friendly. Check out *Search Engine Optimization For Dummies* by Peter Kent (Wiley and Sons, Inc.) for a series of great tips to format a web page so it can be indexed that much better.

All social media sites

This is where you show true growth on social media over time. Saying you have a hundred thousand followers on Twitter in a year can sound like you may have just paid for those followers and they all magically came in to play. From being able to buy views, to followers, to friends and likes, social media numbers and growth, while very crucial, have become that much more scrutinized.

A much easier way to get around those doubts, highlight your professionalism, and prove the truth behind your numbers is to simply track those numbers at the top of every month to show a longer and more realistic pattern.

With months that have larger jumps, you can look across your numbers to have a better understanding of where your conversions and profits came from. Not only does this give you great information to help determine what's working and why, it also sets up a simple sheet that can be used as excellent ammunition and proof to sponsors and investors as well.

Set up a list of your social media sites starting at the first of the month, and collect the following information that's added in column to look like Table 17-1.

This part of the list shows only five months of data and four key social networking sites, but tracking all social media sites for a full year is a good idea. It's an easy system to track after you set it up, and it can be done on a simple spreadsheet. Again, it's less about the total numbers and more about showing how your numbers grow in order to grow the opportunities.

Table 17-1	Monthly Results of Social Media				
Site	*January*	*February*	*March*	*April*	*May*
Facebook (Likes)	3293	3801	4711	5733	7129
Twitter (Followers)	1049	1500	2148	2988	3901
YouTube (Subscribers)	201	380	693	822	944
Google+ (Followers)	233	289	301	336	298
Other sites here					

This type of tracking helps build confidence in people you connect with down the line as you build up that fan base and those numbers over time.

People who track your growth can easily go into sites like Twitter and scroll through your followers to see if they're even real. It's not that they can easily catch you by pinpointing and checking a series of profiles. Whereas fake profiles slip into everyone's accounts, if you have too many, it makes it look like you bought them, and it could turn away potential investors.

YouTube, including views per video

Along with tracking the monthly numbers of subscribers on your YouTube page, create a second page and track the video views. Sounds a little nuts, but by tracking the rise in views, you can learn what videos are most popular as well as keep track of video titles to make sure you don't repeat them.

Set up a simple list as follows:

Name of Video	*Date Uploaded*	*Jan*	*Feb*	*Mar*	*Apr*
Fifty ways to sing a polka	1/1/15	2	2432	2893	2901
Cat ate my homework	2/4/15	X	X	4601	8730
Live at Orchid Island Brewery	2/17/15	X	X	201	300

It's not just tracking numbers; it's understanding the process that works best for you. For example, the cat video did much better than the other two, so that could mean more cat videos might help. Live at Orchid Island was the worst of the three, so it's safe to assume that titling a video named "Live at" is an overused search.

Tracking Physical and Digital Revenues

You can easily keep track of digital revenues from your downloads to your online sales and distribution. Simply use the reports from Amazon, iTunes, your distributors, or even your own direct stores that you set up with PayPal or Square.

It can be a little more challenging when a fan pays cash for a T-shirt, a CD, or download card at a gig. But make sure you mark it all down and are able to show all revenues across the board. Both for the legal purposes of taxes as well as the tracking purposes of knowing what is working and what isn't as far as conversions, every revenue has to be tracked. By tracking all the information for every dollar made, you get the best sense of conversions possible.

Music and merchandise direct

Tracking your music and merchandise can be a little more challenging if you don't organize and track your inventory. Make sure to always cover what you bring to a show, give away, sell at the set prices, and sell at a discount.

Track it, regardless if it's cash or not. Make sure you have some kind of tracking in place. Whether you enter it into a spreadsheet or you have a financial program like QuickBooks, every sale has to be registered.

It might seem like it's easier on a cash sale to just pocket the money — but don't. Musicians and artists are some of the most audited people out there when it comes to taxes. And you want to show as much in sales as possible and as much growth to those who look at you for sponsorships and investment. Your ability to track, share, and identify what you made and where you made it as well as show every dollar that goes out and every dollar that has come back showcases your organization and makes you appear as a better investment with less risk.

With certain merchant applications like Square, you can make a sale from cash that registers in your Square account and issues a receipt to the email of the customer. This is a great merchandising tool to investigate.

Music and merchandise distributed

Tracking distributed products is easier because through all distribution channels, at least the legitimate ones, you see reports on what sold as well as the percentage you're getting. From Amazon to iTunes, Reverbnation, and the rest, there's a contract that clearly lays out what's being sold, what percentage the distributor gets, and when you get your agreed-upon percentage.

As all this goes into the tracking, there's one more step you can take to make sure everything that comes from distributed sales is being tracked correctly. Test it yourself. Go through every channel where you have a download, a CD, or any type of merchandise, and with a guest account, a friend's account, or even a testing account for the given store, buy your own stuff. This is a great way to truly track every step from the click-through to the payout. It also ensures that your distribution agreement is really being followed down to the T.

Tracking your Publishing from A to Z

Tracking your publishing from the copyright to the solicitation to the pitching, placing, tracking, and collecting is a full-time job. This comes down to more than setting up a few spreadsheets and filling them in every month. It's also a big reason why for most it can be a very good idea to work with a music publisher over trying to track everything yourself.

Preparing for publishing

A song that's going to be published has to have all of its fundamentals in order to allow the song to be profitable. Make sure that everyone is on the same page with who owns what and who gets what. Before the publishing agreements are set, the song splits agreements as to who gets what, the producer rights agreements, musician releases, copyrights, and performing rights organization registrations have to take place. Check out more about publishing in Chapter 9.

Pitching and placing

The music publisher (or you, if you're your own publisher) has to research the options and send the pitches for your music to music supervisors, film, TV, and other music producers. These pitches and potential placements are also run through video game creators, music industry executives, advertising executives, and artist management and representation. A great deal of the pitching phase means tracking current trends, tracking the new people coming into music supervision, and maintaining the older contacts. You can find more details about placement in in Chapter 9.

Tracking, collecting, and paying

After a song is placed or en route, the music publisher has to secure the licenses and the cue sheets for the song as well as start to track the data on the plays and use of the song as well as keeping an ear out for copyright infringement issues.

Lastly, collect and distribute profits and royalties to everyone involved as the agreements in the preparations phase were set up. These include the six major royalty payments covered more in depth in Chapter 9.

With all the time and craziness that it takes to handle, track, and make publishing work to the best of its abilities, bring in a professional music publisher to handle at least some of your catalog. It makes all the difference.

Performance Tracking

Venues, locations, audiences, and connections are all around you and with every show that you're a part of. A number of the connections that are made through performances are often forgotten because people just get on to the next event. Yet, performance tracking and noting all the details of a show allow you to showcase to potential backers, labels, and managers a few more details than just you played at Orchid Island Brewery on this date. Digging in deeper and easily by tracking and writing down the basic information about a show, right after that show, helps you build a great deal of useful data.

Narrowing the numbers

Not every place is going to give you a head count of how many people showed up to a gig or help you with all the information you want to find out. Estimates and best guesses are fine with some of these numbers. Again, all the information you're able to compile from the performance tracking can be used for booking and shown to investors. It also gives you an idea of what kind of promotional budgets you need in specific areas.

The following is a list of all the trackable performance basics:

- ✔ Date
- ✔ Event type (opening slot, headlining slot, festival, or other type of event)
- ✔ Address, city, and state

- ✔ Venue — capacity and attendance
- ✔ Booked by
- ✔ Pay and pay equation (flat fee, percentage of door, bonus of bar percentage)
- ✔ Signed up for the mailing list
- ✔ Product and merchandise sold
- ✔ Other acts on the bill
- ✔ Point of contact for the venue
- ✔ Advertising or marketing spent by you for promotion
- ✔ Issues, pay problems, management problems

With this list it's easier to fill out the basics the day of rather than trying to remember back to an exact show when you have been on the road for a month. Having all this data helps you with future bookings and reminds you about places and people with whom you had issues.

The more numbers and data you have available for investors, sponsors, management, and other music industry professionals who may want that additional information, the more research and the information you have ready and accessible about you to give you the best shot at support.

The other set list

From jotting down on your music set list or another piece of paper on stage how big the crowd is to getting an overall vibe of how you are being received, take down the notes before and after the show. Stay tuned into everything that's going on around you without being too distracted from making the music and connecting with the audience.

Think of all that data as your other set list to use when you get home as you make plans to return. The more you track, the more you understand every place you go and how the people react to you as well as the business that's being done well or, in many cases, not being done correctly. This data enables you to make better decisions regarding where and when to play, who to play with, and how to make every booking and event stronger, more effective, and more profitable.

This information is also useful for your booking spreadsheets that you build as you visit venues and work in different cities. It's duplicate info in some ways that can be used in different areas to help your career.

Tracking Expenses Breakdown

While you organize the expenses for a music business plan or solicitation proposal for monies you don't have and want to spend, organize for the short term, too. Also realize that it's important on a series of different levels to track all the existing expenses in a breakdown to showcase what your music as a business is worth and what's been put into it.

Making an out-of-thin-air guess that you've put in "like, thousands of dollars" isn't going to help you solidify the worth of your music. It's a hard and humble thing to do to first turn that passion to a business and then put a price tag or net worth on that passion. Organizing your business, however, brings you that much more business and in turn many more opportunities and support.

As you showcase the expenses broken down into the following categories, it helps give a solid idea on what you've spent and where you've spent it as well as highlighting you're working within your budget as you seek help or investments. This shows you're investing in you and creating a business that needs help getting to the next level as opposed to building from the ground up.

Studio and recording

Track every cost in the studio, not just what you pay for the studio time and a producer. This includes food and snacks in the studio, and gas and mileage to and from the studio. Also track additional musicians you pay for backing tracks or help in the studio as well as any strings, drumsticks, drumheads, reeds, or gear you purchase for that session.

Track those studio hours as well. It's a three-fold advantage. You can write off the studio time on your taxes; you can define to investors exactly what it costs for you to complete recordings and music from start to finish and set up to final mix; and you can showcase the investment on your part and what you've put in already to your music and your business.

Promotion and marketing

Tracking the best results of the money you spent on marketing as well as the money that wasn't effective gives you a better understanding of how to spend. Applying this information to future costs ups the effective expenses and reduces the bad results.

Tracking every dollar spent — from the graphic design of a sticker to the shipping of those stickers to mailing out some of those stickers for different people to post in different places — helps you know what's working and what isn't. Also, you track every aspect for tax purposes as well as presentations to investors, sponsors, and other music industry professionals.

It isn't about showcasing massive and amazing numbers or trying to doctor them to look prettier. It's only ratios and conversions. If you invest $100 in some kind of marketing and promotional campaign that helps to convert to $200 in sales of product and exposure, while small, it can show that someone's investment of $100,000 in a similar method could return $200,000.

Doctoring up your numbers, lying about facts, or making yourself out to be doing a great deal better than you actually are makes investors question why you need help in the first place. Too, no one can trust a liar, and you will be hard pressed to find anyone who will want to work with you.

Online and social media advertising

As in the previous section, the same goes for online and social media advertising as it does for promotion and marketing. The cool thing about online advertising is that all the tracking and details based around the campaigns often come with the analytics and details already well organized in an easy-to-present spreadsheet and downloadable format.

Again, you don't have to show out-of-the-world numbers or crazy and amazing growth. The key is to show the investment and the money you put into these ads and the results and conversions that follow.

With the information easily available for download mixed with the other tracking information you have from your social media growth to show to sales in a given period, you allow the investor to obtain a better sense of how and where your conversions come from.

Website and SEO

Tracking the costs and investment you've put into creating your website, which in many ways is the root of your web presence and a home base, shows that you're keeping up on your digital housekeeping as well as making that primary site set up with the strongest foundation.

From showing the work that was done from design to coding, graphics to layouts, SEO implementation to content management, you deliver the numbers that show you're making your home base a truly sturdy home.

These numbers can include consulting fees, or costs for webmasters to make your site load faster, optimize easier, and streamline for search engines to pick up. You find more in Chapter 10.

These are costs that you need to pay for. While investors can help build up your site, you need to own your domain names. You need to own your hosting and have the administrative rights to every social media page out there. You can assign management access to others, but this is a place where you personally need to pay for this to ensure the right control for the long run.

Touring and performing

The touring and performing category shows where you can save money and showcase yourself or band as a good investment to put out on the road. This can show how you can save on touring and performing costs, which enables investors to spend less while getting you to more places with more dates for a longer period of time.

This requires you to combine information you've already tracked to show that you know how to save, how to make the most out of the road on the most grassroots level, and that you're a smart investment.

This is one of the most important places to showcase you know-how to spend wisely and save as much as possible. Showing your ability to be out on the road and stay out on the road for the least amount of money enables a higher-level budget for marketing and promotions as you keep things a little more frugal on the road.

It's not as much work as it seems

Tracking and building basic spreadsheets for everything going out, coming back in, and everything in between may seem a little overwhelming. The organization that you create, however, makes the entire process take only seconds.

Don't get caught up in trying to collect too much back information. That can be a massive headache and take hours and hours to complete. Although information about specific venues, people, and companies can be good to organize and slide into your tracking, when it comes to tracking your older expenses, basic summaries can still work. Simply explain that you started to fully track and showcase the exact numbers from a specific date forward.

After you set up the basic spreadsheets for data collection, tracking and posting become simpler daily and monthly tasks. As numbers come in, whether it be a sale, a receipt, or any piece of information, add it to the appropriate list or email yourself a reminder as to where to add it. The biggest task is to organize the lists for all the information; after that, you're home free. Check out more about record keeping in Chapter 4.

Chapter 18

Persevering, Problem-Solving, and Retiring

In This Chapter

▶ Staying up to date on recent changes and changing with the times

▶ Continuing to expand your reach to more fans and opportunities

▶ Streamlining and simplifying the workload for the long haul

▶ Knowing when to call it a career or when to stop

wo of the biggest and most crucial traits to practice for success in the music business are perseverance and problem-solving. By persevering with a steadfast work ethic while combining attention to detail and drive in the good times, and practicing creative problem-solving in the bad times, you can sustain successes and contain problems.

Keeping on when the going is good . . . or bad

Perseverance is really all about tenacity, staying power, and determination in the worst of times, but even more so in the best of times. The ability to keep on keeping on when the rough times hit, but maintain a solid mindset of pushing even when things are good separates the long-term successful musicians from the flashes in the pan. Think of it as reinforcing the good stuff to make those good times last longer. Often when things are going well, and your profile and overall promotion are at a higher level, is the perfect time to reach out to that many more people and music business professionals who can see how well you're doing and will likely be that much more receptive to working with you.

Enduring for the long term

Your musical, marketing, and networking endurance in both fast and slow times helps to keep a busy booking schedule and other opportunities coming. Even if you booked out the next six months, it's still the perfect time to push for the six months after that. Using the momentum to entice further bookings, opportunities, interviews, or exposure down the line is easier when you can showcase how busy you are. In turn, your busy schedule makes others want to get on the bandwagon to book, promote, or help you.

When you start to make waves, use the momentum to make them even bigger. It's easier to create more powerful motion when you're already in motion.

Changing gears when momentum shifts

As you feel a lull, a pull, or shift when you track your shows, contacts, sales, or fan reach, or when you see reductions and problems arising, get right on researching and analyzing to determine what's going wrong and figure out how to solve it. By tracking and analyzing your results, you can see when issues arise and when profits or opportunities drop. Changing gears and testing different approaches when things aren't flowing can help get you shifted back into the right gear.

For example, if there's a decrease in the number of social media followers on Twitter and conversions begin to fall, consider shifting some of your budget to a Twitter advertisement and attacking a different area. If you're getting fewer bookings in a certain market, look to booking agents in that area or promoters who might be able to help. It's all about problem-solving and shifting gears when momentum shifts in order to keep the forward motion going.

Don't just sit back when there's a momentum shift and watch it happen. Stay connected, and look at what can be done to correct it. Sitting back and staying on the same course when the direction is leading you off a cliff is only going to set you up for a long fall.

Staying Aware of Trends and Changes

With all the changes and trends in the music business, what you might think is the golden rule one moment could become obsolete and wrong the next. The majority of the concepts regarding business practices, approaches, and habits have stayed true and strong for years, but just as vinyl gave way to tape, tape gave way to CDs, CDs to downloads and so on, a keen awareness and being a constant student of the music industry can help you stay on top — and even ahead — of the changes that you need to consider and make.

Finding your pulse and learning your pace

Every day there's a different article about how someone is the next big thing, how this is the new product everyone needs, or how there's no reason to use this social media site, and so on. The truth is that in the middle of all the fast headline statements, before listening to everyone else, the best approach is listening to the pulse around you.

The pulse around you beats with other groups that have similar budgets, similar sounds, and comparable audiences. This information can guide you to knowing the best pace for you for the decisions to make and the changes to take.

For example, if a major artist with a multi-million-dollar budget and a great deal of fame says that download cards are worthless this doesn't mean you should drop your download cards, especially if an artist that's closer to your sound and budget with a similar or closer-sized audience sold 500 of them last month.

Each decision you make in keeping your pace, staying with certain items, and changing with others should be based in what's working for those on the same level and a few levels above you. Following the trends and making the changes of the largest-scale artists without taking into consideration how they affect you could send you off in a more hurtful than helpful direction.

Tracking the trends, analyzing what others are doing, and looking at the genuine results over the marketed hype puts you in the best place to make the best choices for you.

Changing horses midstream

Sometimes things go wrong. The old Tower of Power song says not to change horses in the middle of a stream, but if you can call for another horse that gets you back on a better path and out of deeper water that much quicker, well, Hi Ho Silver . . . Away!

Take a serious look at what's going wrong, and if the best fix is a change, determine what kind of change you need to make. Be careful about plugging cracks — they can lead to larger problems down the line. For example, if you find that you're working with a bad manager who's doing next to nothing and hurting your forward motion, get out of the agreement and move on. Just do it.

Staying with people, practices, and processes that are working against you for longer than you should creates more and more damage. Identifying issues and seeing if problem-solving is possible for them as you work to remedy what is wrong is a great approach. Still, if you're avoiding the inevitable because of passive-aggressive behavior, fear, or delusion, it can only get worse. Plan the change, execute the action, and take the motions necessary to move back onto a better path for you. This is one time where it's all good to change horses in the middle of the stream.

Realize that certain actions need to be implemented and remain consistent for some time before you see the conversions you want. Make sure you're not impatiently switching up something that hasn't had the time to develop correctly.

Finding the New Fan While Keeping the Old One Interested

The number one thing in the root of all your marketing and promotion is to engage the existing fan, keep them in touch, in tune, connected, and interested as you simultaneously reach out to build a larger base with new fans. This is one of the biggest struggles both artists and businesses face every day. The content, creativity, and call to action that draw the interest of someone new as they retain the interest of an old fan is a true balancing act.

Constant craving from quality content

To continually push the sell, the existing products, and the requests to add here, buy this, share that, follow here, and every other aggressive push may reach a number of people. After they've engaged, however, and after they've seen a show, bought an album, and ordered a T-shirt, they might get a little tired of being told to do what they've already done. Worse yet, they may lose interest in your selling and disconnect from you.

Think of it like buying an entire wardrobe from your favorite clothing store. Imagine you have everything you need — from dress shirts, to short sleeve shirts, from pants to jackets, ties to hats, and so on. At this point, you have what you need, but you're still bashed over the head on a daily basis to

✔ Check out a jacket you already bought

✔ Try on a pair of pants you already own

✔ Order a shirt you already have

✔ Follow a page you already follow

✔ Donate money to a kickstarter campaign so they can create a new kind of suit

It would get old, and it would make you lose interest. This is exactly what's happening with a great deal of musicians out there who only push the sell and stop considering the ways to market to maintain their new fans as well as their older ones.

Make new and old fans crave your content and look for information by adjusting and adapting content and even the sales pitch content. For example, if you push a new single on Amazon one week, add in something interesting or funny about the song, like "See if you can hear the drummer sneeze in the song, tell us where and we'll send you a free download of another song." The next week, point them to the Amazon store where that song is available and tell a different story to draw new interest from everyone, whether they bought it or not. It's still selling the song, but you're putting out the kind of content that people crave and want to connect with.

Watch the tempo of your marketing, especially on social media sites like Twitter. Whereas there are tools to help automatically post every hour on the hour to be seen in as many feeds as possible, it's important to realize many fans and followers are following fewer people than you. In turn, it makes you come off like spamming as they constantly see you all over their feed all day.

Engage first, sell second

Creating content that people crave consists of interesting posts, blogs, videos, pictures, audios, and links that engage anyone. This means not starting with the sell, but with information that both a new person finds appealing as well as someone who's been a fan for years.

The close is the call to action. (For more on the call to action, check out Chapter 11, "Planning for Content Marketing throughout the Year.") Your ability to engage across the board keeps the respect going with the person who just heard of you as well as the person who's known about you for years. The direct sell posts and marketing are fine, but limit them to once a week at most. With content that's set up to draw people in as well as maintain people with a call to action that tells them where to get more of you or where to buy this product or see that show, you maintain a much greater interest.

Content that respects, interacts, engages, and connects with both the new fan and the old friend is the most important element of marketing, hands down. Maintaining and sustaining fans as you reach out at the same time and obtain more is the foundation and blueprint of the most successful marketing plans.

Testing New Products and New Methods

New products come on the market at a very fast rate. From customizable golf balls to sunglasses with your logo on them, computer skins to phone covers, there are new options popping up for merchandise and promotional items every day. The same goes with different methods of promotion and technology, such as programs that post for you on Twitter every 30 minutes (don't use this tool; it's too much and honks off fans) to electronic and digital resource tools for touring and new social media sites.

Although primarily sticking to a solidified and well-organized plan is best, a truly solid and professional plan leaves room for the new options and approaches to come. The best ways to approach new methods, technology, gear, websites, and anything else is to keep steady on the track as you test the waters in the shallow end and don't get sucked into a rip tide of change that can pull you and your career under.

It's new, shiny, fun, and neato!

Take heavy steps around the latest product or the newest social media site, sales site, or opportunity. It's easy to get caught up in an ADHD-type of madness where you drop everything you're working on and continue to chase, invest in, or try out the next new thing. In most cases, this sets you up for failure.

This goes for approaches, too. To start a marketing campaign with a set plan and then change up a dozen times in a two-month period doesn't help you at all. Instead, work with a sense of multitasking when it comes to something new. Stand by your plan, and follow through as you test a new idea in one area without shifting everything all at once.

Try to stay away from the wooing lights and hype excitement of doing something too quickly that might not work and just might hurt what you already have in place. Take the time to do your research, and try to avoid jumping the gun before you know whether or not there's a bullet in the barrel.

Small chances with small risk to gain reward

Take small steps with new ideas to reduce the risk and test the reward. From joining a new site to testing a new product, give everything a fair chance but don't gamble all your budget on something that hasn't proven if it can work for you.

From a new merchandise item to a new promotion campaign to a new way to sell your music or sell your merchandise, test the waters to see what works. If things go well, then up the ante; if things don't, then go back to where you were before.

As new social media sites comes into play on a monthly basis, don't get wrapped up in the idea of shutting down your MySpace or no longer using Google+ or another site. With many site aggregators, there are ways to share information and posts to these less-popular sites, but why remove a page when it's one more place you can be found? When it comes to new pages and sites, sign up for all of them, even if you aren't posting on them. At least no one else can take your name!

Working to Streamline the Workload

With the array of tasks that need to be done (the lists, the action items, the marketing, content creation, shows, traveling, and yes, we can keep going, but let's stop here . . .) in the mix of everything that's happening on any given day, the ability to streamline and simplify your workload is key to enabling you to accomplish important duties.

Building and implementing elements and tools that streamline work may seem like yet another task that need to be done. But by doing so, you save time, energy, and stress as you get that much more completed in much less time.

To-do lists are great ways to organize and look at the broader scope of what needs to be done in a given time period. From the researching phase to the tracking phase, the soliciting phase to the marketing phase, all of these need to work in harmony. If you don't have the time to do every task each day, assign specific days to make it easier. However, if you're a solo artist or a band that doesn't have a great deal of time, putting in shorter spurts of time more often can open up a lot more doors over spending bulk hours on single items.

Simply broken down, the following are the ten key areas of music business productivity:

- ✔ **Practicing and creating:** Dedicate time every day to practice different aspects of your job — from practicing your instrument, to practicing stage presence, to practicing how you sound on a phone call, or how you come off when asking for a booking, an endorsement, support, an interview. And whether you craft marketing content, solicitation packages, photos, videos, blogs, or songs, make sure there's always time in the day to create.

✔ **Performing and maintenance:** Most musicians want to perform, whether on stage or in a recording studio. Keeping up the ability to perform from your personal well-being to keeping your instrument in performance shape allows for the continuity required for the stage and studio. Other parts of the business that require maintenance include the vehicles you drive, the bills you pay, the computers you use, the website you update, the hardware, software, and even food and rent.

✔ **Researching, soliciting, and networking:** Always do your research on managers, investors, booking agents, venues, festivals, cities, labels, publishers, and talent buyers as well as other bands you can work with. After you complete your research, you can decide which ones to reach out and solicit to. This is also the same list of contacts with whom you can network as well as add to social networks and connect with on and offline.

✔ **Tracking:** Track the results of your sales, marketing, networking and conversion efforts. You might find this fairly easy, because you just add the data and results that occur from your actions. For more on tracking, check out Chapter 5, "Writing, Rehearsing, Recording, and Performing."

✔ **Follow up:** Follow up with every person, company, and event that was a positive. From booking agents you worked with for a great show, to a band you played with to a magazine that interviewed you to the fans that reach out to you, your follow-up and follow-through actions can give you the greatest benefits.

✔ **Educating:** Take the time to read up, learn up, and stay up to date on the changes in the music business and in the law. Learn about what's happening around you, for you, and against you. Taking those moments each day helps you grow your career by having a better grasp on current and correct information on which you can make better decisions.

Each of these tasks can be color-coded and assigned to numerous members. By understanding the details of all these basic elements that have to be done, it not only makes it easier to break out the responsibilities, but also to have a better idea what to ask for when you look for help from others.

Outlining all the information that you need to track as well as setting up calendars for what you need to post, who you need to call, where you need to be, and what you need to research can make life much easier. A simple checklist can serve as a reminder to handle all the line items that need to be covered.

It's a great deal of stuff, but broken down, spread out, and checked off, you can make it much more manageable when you see it in small, simple pieces. Then as you look down the line at the bigger picture, you can see just how effective you are both on stage and off.

Staying in Control and Watching Others Who Share Control

As you look for help from others or align with everyone from publishers to consultants, labels to managers, promoters, investors, social media experts, and so on, many of these people look to help you but also look to benefit themselves. As people invest time, work, and effort, they look for a level of control — some with the best intentions and others to maintain a bargaining chip.

You have to share percentages and control with those who help, invest in, and create a business with you; however, a clear understanding of what you have to share helps avoid problems. Knowing exactly what you're able to retain complete control over, where you're sharing control, and having access to be able to watch the control others take keeps you from being blindsided or taken advantage of.

Keeping your fingers in everything

Many artists dream of having others take care of all the business aspects so they can focus only on the music and nothing else. The problem is when no one is watching, anything can happen, and those happenings can include someone taking over a social media account to someone commandeering a bank account and finances, leaving you with no control. If you don't keep an eye on the business side, you can also lose control of your right to sign contracts as well as the percentage amount to which you agreed.

Working with a disinterested lawyer, one who's not tied directly to a label, an investor, or anyone with whom you're working, ensures that you have rights to all statements and transactions legal, contractual, or financial. Going over your publishing with a music publisher that organizes contracts can help, too. Learn more about lawyers in Chapter 9, "Securing Your Music and Brand."

Your attention to detail and perseverance to both maintain access as well as allow a third party to have access to the money coming in and money going out keeps you that much more in the loop. The third party can help you review, explain or look out for abnormalities or patterns that could be potential problems. No one should have a problem with you asking to see your own books and contract. If they do, you could be the victim of a scam.

Ask your attorney to draw up legal documents that outline the roles each person plays and what rights they have within your organization as well as the access they can have to the organizations working with you. Consider when creating these legal documents that a section is added to keep you updated on a regular basis about what's coming in, what's going out, what's on track, and what's changing.

Make sure when you're given an update regarding finances, contracts, or any type of information that you can also access your bank statements as well as documentation from iTunes, distributors, and other merchants. Anyone can prepare a beautiful report that looks all happy and hide profits and revenues from you.

It's not a question of how good or honest people are when they're held accountable. It comes down to what they do when no one is looking. By keeping an eye on things and adding additional updates and review measures, it gives you a better chance to keep all records in order, in line, and above board.

Defining the roles and the access online

Another common dream is for others to handle all your social media for you, so you can focus on just the music. Know, however, that this can be very dangerous. A great deal of your engagement and promotion is derived from sites like Facebook, Twitter, YouTube, and Instagram.

It's key to have an agreement in place about who has access to what when it comes to your website, your social media pages and your distribution and sales sites. Your lack of access or control can make it more challenging when it comes to removing spam posts and other postings you don't want to have on your pages. These agreements should also give you the clear ownership of the social media pages, domain names, and hosting for your website.

As you define the roles, it's also key to have access to reports coming from advertising campaigns as well as sales reports from Amazon and other online merchant sites. The clarity and definition of your continued involvement and access to these sites enable others to help you and work those sites, but allow you to know what is going on when you want to.

There are too many horror stories about artists who accidently and ignorantly gave up their rights to their websites and social media sites, and had to go as far as suing to gain access to them. The biggest problem is that these artists signed away their rights when they signed many of their contracts. Know your role, define others' roles, and clarify the access for everyone to protect you, your business, and everyone around you.

Take the initiative to set up all your social media sites yourself as owner and admin. Then assign management to others who update and work on the sites. This can help ensure you maintain access and control of your social media pages.

Clarifying the Financial Channels and Return on Investment

Whether you receive sponsorship support, funding, a label deal, or any kind of support money to move your products, touring, and career forward, the understanding of how that money is being paid back, what percentages are being made, and at what point you get to see the greater amounts of it are crucial.

I've heard horror stories that stem from people not paying attention to or having a clear idea of exactly what was spent, what's due, and when a debt is paid in full. With every dollar of support and every opportunity that comes in, before you sign anything, make sure you have a clear understanding that's down on paper as well as reviewed by a lawyer or accountant making it crystal clear how the waters flow and how they flow to you.

Debts going past the original payback

When people or companies invest in artists, they look not only to make back their initial investment; they want to make money. These labels, investors, and agents take an enormous risk that's often reflected in the payback they receive.

From demanding a high interest rate to a longer-term percentage afterward, the debts you accrue, especially early on, are with you well past the initial payback. Many artists are so desperate that they sign deals on the front side that don't sting until well down the road. For example, a high-interest deal where the investor is continually spending money on the artist will keep you in debt.

It comes down to those label-hosted super expensive dinners after a deal or a show. It also rings true when a label or investor ups the hotel room to something nicer than needed. These are all costs that have to be repaid by you with interest on top. Although these amounts might seem frivolous when things are good, a few years down the line when popularity as well as profits fade, that higher percentage can be a career killer.

Say you're making less than 20 percent of millions and millions of dollars in that top percentage. In the moment of millions, it seems fine, but when times get tighter, and you only make a small percentage on hundreds of thousands, it can be devastating. This scenario happens on a regular basis.

To avoid it, look to lawyers and accountants to help you keep an eye on your finances and carefully explain what you sign on to as well as what it means in the long run. Look to persevere with your investors to allow them the returns they're looking for while still allowing you to regain more control and pay for necessities without adding interest.

Get those debts paid back as fast as you can, so you're able to realize more cash in your pocket. Work to take over the costs of items needed as you make money instead of looking to an investor or label for continued support, even when you no longer require the support. Persevere with the most responsible financial actions to achieve the most financial control of your career.

There are only so many ways you can split up a dollar bill. Keep that in mind as you assign percentages. Looking at how it affects you now, in a month, a year, and then five years helps you not only persevere, but also sign the best contracts for the best chances for you.

Taking the reins of your financial future

As you move forward in your career, look to become your own label and own investor as opposed to looking to another investor, another deal, or another option that keeps you in a vicious circle of debt.

As the music industry has changed, so have the options. It's no longer about needing a record label; it's about needing all the different elements and pieces a label brings to the table. With a strong music business plan that covers all the elements, services, and requirements that a label provides, you're on the right track. By creating your music business plan with investors outside of a record label, there's a greater chance you won't be stuck paying high interest or losing as much ownership and percentages of profits as you would with a larger label.

If you achieve success with an investor or label and can take control, don't just look to another deal to make the next record or find an investor to pay for everything. Cover what you can with what you have and look for support with a bank or other types of loans to help with the rest. Keep as much of the control, percentages, and revenues coming to you over going to others.

With the ability to connect directly with all the different sources, services, and resources needed for success and sustainability in music today, work to find those outlets and make as many direct contacts and connections as you can. It works to your favor over someone else being a middle man who's taking one more piece of the pie that doesn't need to be fed to anyone else.

Knowing When It's Time to Stop or Change Careers

As you journey through a career in music, regardless of the best of times, the worst of times, and every experience that you have in between, there comes a time when it is time to stop. Whether it's viewed as retiring, quitting, or changing paths, knowing that in your heart you are always a musician is fine. But keeping the consideration out there that you can't do this forever helps you for plan for the future even as you're in the present still planning on how to build your career.

It's not about being negative; it's about thinking in the long term. You can maintain a career for the length of your life, or have an understanding of when to call it a day.

It's okay to not make it full-time

It's okay to not be able to make music a full-time gig, just as it's okay to switch careers to something else or take more of the hobby approach. In many cases, it might make you a happier person in the end.

Going part time or taking the hobby approach doesn't mean failure. Most musicians who aren't able to make it to the levels that they dreamed of end up sacrificing way too much, and lose it all. They end up in a dead-end job as they struggle with debts, bankruptcies, and other issues.

This isn't meant to scare you. This is meant to make you think — regardless how well or how bad things go on your journey, be prepared while planning and persevering for the best and the worst. The end result of that kind of advanced problem-solving and planning allows for transitions to be that much easier to handle.

Don't get caught up in the make-or-break scenarios, especially if you have a family or children. There are musicians who not only are unable to reach that next level, but as they forget and forgo family responsibilities, they end up hurting those they love. Don't allow for any situation or any opportunity to break you, especially if you have people counting on you.

Hard challenges becoming impossible tasks and other signs its time to change

Although much of this chapter and book can feel overwhelming, as you see in every section, it's doable and you can do it, every step. The answers are here, as well as what it takes to build the foundation for the next step and the step after that.

At times those simple steps and directions that you know how to do will feel more challenging. Other times they become confusing, but there is still that fire to push onward. When that fires starts to go out, that's when it's time to think about transitioning, changing, or retiring. Your ability to look at back up plans you organize along the way mixed with a simple list of your stopping points can make a transition easier.

These stopping points are made up of a personal list that you create stating if certain things aren't happening by a certain point, if a certain amount of money has been spent, a defined amount of debt has been reached, and so on, that it's time to change gears.

Just as you layer out the goals in your music business plan to showcase the marks you want to hit and how you plan to hit them, this list may also show up as part of your failure analysis (discussed in Chapter 4, "Creating a Music Business Plan") showing that if certain events occur, the positive results or expectations may not happen.

After the love has gone

You never lose the love, and if you're able to plan an exit or a retirement from music at the right time for you, those memories, that joy, and that love can stay with you a long time. Don't resent the career you might have had; enjoy all that you've done and what you did have. It's okay to lose the love for the business side of music — and many do — but always keep that love for the music itself, regardless of where you go or what you do in life.

You're in the music business because it is your dream. If your dream changes or you lose the desire for that dream, look at whether it's a bump in the road or if it's time to start down a new road. Don't neglect your happiness for pride or ego.

Part V
The Part of Tens

Visit www.dummies.com/extras/musicbusiness to find more important info.

In This Part . . .

✔ Learn how to increase the odds of building lasting connections and opportunities.

✔ Discover the ten core tips for presenting the most professional-looking you.

Chapter 19

Ten Habits of Successful Musicians

▶ Taking the best approaches to your career using the best traits

▶ Increasing the odds of building your connections and opportunities

*T*here's a saying that if you do something 30 times for 30 days straight, it becomes a habit. By practicing and having certain habits and traits become part of you and your approach to the music business, you have a much better chance at succeeding as well as sustaining that success for a long time to come. In this chapter, you get ten of the best habits to learn and practice on a daily basis.

Humility

Being able to exhibit genuine humility is a challenge as you may find yourself in a world of ego with many different genres. Being the greatest, the best, above the rest, and better become commonplace, especially in the media. At the same time, however, that arrogance, ego, or excess of confidence can close many doors, kill opportunities, and destroy connections.

Be confident and be assertive, but take a down-to-earth, humble and respectful approach to not just those who are above you or where you want to be, but also with the people on the same level — even with those not as far along as you. From allowing your opinion to be voiced as your opinion and not fact to describing your sound the same way to a fan as you would to one of your heroes, a consistency in confidence without arrogance makes people remember you. Humility is one of the best habits to practice and one of the greatest traits to have as you journey into a world that's incredibly lacking in it.

Art is opinion. Music is opinion, and no one person's opinion is better than another's. When you're asked who you think is the best this or the best that, showcase respect and humility by sharing it as your opinion and not as fact.

Excellent Social Respect Skills

As simple as it sounds, many artists lack solid social skills and basic respect. From shaking a hand and looking someone in the eye, to saying "please" and "thank you," these basic *come on do we really need to go over them* type items need to be covered and are missed by many. From interpersonal to good communication to your awareness for others around you, it's not only something that's going to get you better interactions on both personal and professional levels, it may also be something that industry professionals might look at to see how you act and how you operate.

The difference between "let's see, I need a burger, gimmie a medium fry, and I guess a small Coke" to "may I have a burger, a medium fry, and a small coke, please?" makes a world of difference in how someone *wants* or someone *has* to help you.

The same goes for other scenarios, such as screaming at someone in an airport because your flight was cancelled by weather. Choose to remain calm and polite to those who have no control over a situation, such as a blizzard and a 747.

Attention to Detail

Reading every line of that contract and bringing it to a lawyer or consultant if something doesn't make sense before signing it is just one part of the attention-to-detail habits you need to practice every day. Most musicians who run in to trouble, have problems, or find themselves in the worst scenarios tend to end up there from a lack of attention to detail. Many times what was presented right in front of them could have been identified and squashed before they turned into monster-size issues. If only the musician had that attention to detail in place, in check, and active, much heartache could be avoided.

From the contracts to the research, from tracking and analyzing what's working and what isn't, to making sure that you format a marketing post the right way, keep yourself in check as you double-check everything.

Acting Like a Student of Science

The science student has to look at the world in a way that can show proof. In another sense, it's like being a detective. In a world where so many people put out so much information on how to do this and how to do that with so much of it not being true, a great habit to get into is being that detective or scientist who does the research and looks for the proof instead of just buying into the theory or a meme.

The music business is filled with theories, false claims, and flat-out lies that too many follow and then find themselves in a place where they wasted time, money, or signed a contract they shouldn't have. Finding all the proof to support a theory, and looking at other examples of what worked or didn't work enables you to make more informed decisions.

Prove the theories with the research and the backup information of the steps, methods, and approaches you want to take. Be the scientist yearning to see the equation and the elements that make the results facts instead of being the child believing the magic of the desired end result without knowing exactly how to get there.

Problem-Solving

Problems are going to arise regardless of how great the plan and how much you have in place. It's inevitable. It's the music industry! Your ability to run toward a problem as soon as it's a evident with the intention to fix it and prevent it from occurring again gives you a serious leg up on those who run away and hide from snags and glitches. Those problems generally end growing larger and more problematic when left alone or ignored.

Your immediate attention and effort to solving a problem as soon as you are aware of it gives you the type of reputation that others can feel confident in and trust. There are a lot of people who can do a fine job when everything is on course and on track. It's a much-reduced number of those who can be trusted to work through problems, stormy waters, and issues when they arise.

Also understanding (and this is adding in that habit of humility here) when you need help and can't do it all on your own is a major factor for a productive and effective problem solver. Continually trying to fix a problem that you can't handle or haven't been able to fix doesn't make you a good problem solver; it makes you a part of the problem that's more than likely getting worse.

Worry less about putting blame on someone, and focus your energy on problem solving to fix the problem. Then you can work to put the measures in place for that problem not to occur again. Assigning blame does nothing to get you to a solution. Yes, if someone is constantly a problem or creating problems, they may need to be removed from the equation, but if you were on a ship with a hole in it and starting to sink, you wouldn't want to watch people pointing fingers at each other. You'd want to get everyone together to plug the hole and get to dry land.

Honor

That whole "do unto others as you would want them to do unto you" is a little more than just the Golden Rule. In some ways it's a silver coin of the distant past. Many musicians step on the backs of others to get ahead. They lie, cheat, steal, and take any available step to get a step further. At the same time, many music industry professionals, companies, and con artists play the same game of shame and deception.

Get into the habit and have the reputation of someone who stands by their words and their actions all the time. This is a good reputation to have. Being seen as the person who can stand by their words and their actions when no one is looking and no one is holding you accountable is even better, even when no one else is doing it.

Trust is earned over time and not given overnight. Avoid telling people how honorable and trustworthy you are. Stay away from telling people to trust you. Rather, show them they can trust you by your honorable actions over time as you do the right thing when the spotlight is both on you and when no one is looking.

Wearing a Thick Skin

It's all the fashion craze this year; that thicker skin is soooo in! All joking aside, if you're in the music business or any type of artistic or creative venture, anything less than a thick skin is going to make it a rougher experience as a whole. Especially as you get more popular and more recognized, the critics, haters, complainers, and just all-around mean people will show their heads.

Engage those with whom you can build connections, instead of focusing time, energy, and effort on those who will never be fans.

There's always that sting that comes along when someone doesn't like you. Still, your ability to brush it off, take it as an opinion, and not engage in a way to further cause friction makes you a happier person and in many cases disarms a cruel attacker. Avoiding retaliation is best; however, responding on a calmer level can sometimes diffuse the attacker or bully. But stay nice even when they aren't.

Wear your thick skin on the stage as well. You may get people who boo. You may hear the cat calls of "You suck" and "stop playing." Take it in, make a light-hearted joke, if you can, and keep on with the set. Play for the people who want to hear you and are there for you instead of fighting with the people who don't like you and couldn't care less about you.

It's still good to take constructive criticism, so while building up a thicker skin and ignoring some critics is a good thing, have the ability to handle constructive criticism to make your music, your branding, your marketing, or your business that much better.

Frugal Penny Pincher

Get into the habit of being the penny pincher and money saver. In the best of times when money and profit starts coming in, that's the best time to put away, save, and invest it. If you're out on the road with most expenses being covered and profits begin to rise, keep them going upward instead of balancing them out by staying in nicer hotels. The frugal penny-pincher approach gets investments and interest paid off that much faster as you begin to not only save for the next tour or the next album, but also for your long-term future.

There's a major tendency when artists start to see money coming in to spend it and enjoy it. Now, it's fine to enjoy things, but when you begin to see more revenues and profits, but you continue to work and budget as if you aren't there yet, you begin to build up the foundation for future stages that don't require other people to invest in you, which in turn allows for more money to be made that goes directly back to you.

Practice the habits of a frugal penny pincher as you grow your career, and see your savings, your opportunities, and your bank account grow right along side of them.

Think of what and where you can save, even when others are paying for it. By spending less of their money, you owe less back to them, and you won't have to pay additional interest on the money spent on you.

Endurance

The trait and habit of endurance is what brings it all together in the music business. To have the energy to do the work over the long haul at the same effort level, with the same drive, and the same professionalism is one of the biggest challenges. Endurance to do all the work that has to be done and take on the small steps each day is key. In a way, a habit or the execution and practicing of that habit defines the meaning of endurance.

There are many who can get on a roll and do a lot of work in a short period of time, but those blast efforts tend to be just that — blasts of efforts that help in the moment, but don't plant the seeds or build the foundation for the long term.

The people who can do it even when they don't want to, from practicing their instrument to researching a new venue, to creating new marketing content, to soliciting a review, an investor, or a gig every day are the ones who thrive.

Patience

It all comes together with the patience. All the other nine habits are glued together with the patience to do things the right way, at the right time, to cultivate the right results. Just as patience is a habit for the successful, impatience and rush are a recipe and habit for the very quick to fail. Your ability to take the time when time needs to be taken protects you, supports you, and helps you find the success you're looking for.

The patience you apply to your career to do things the right way in the right time with the right people allows for so many more events to go right over rushing, pushing, skipping, and jumping the gun when you aren't ready.

Chapter 20

Ten Tips on Presenting Yourself Professionally

In This Chapter

▶ Using the best methods to get the best from every presentation.

▶ Preparing and researching before presenting

A s you prepare your music, your business, and your plan, the last step comes down to your presentation. Whereas people invest in a business, in the arts, they also invest in the people. All the more reason it's important to have the ability to present and carry yourself well. A great deal of your career consists of presentations. Whether talking to investors, booking agents, potential endorsers, sponsors, managers, labels, or anyone else, your ability to present in a professional and personable way that engages, entices, and excites gives you that much more ammunition to get a project funded, done, booked, and more.

In this chapter, I cover the ten core fundamental tips to practice, learn, and execute the right way to achieve the best results.

Posture

You may have heard that phrase about chin up, shoulders back, chest out, and gut in. Many make fun of it, but don't realize that your physical presence is a key part of your entire presentation. A confident walk that carries a confident body makes all the positive difference in the world. One of the first things that people see is your posture and your walk when you go into a meeting, so make it count. Start off on the right foot with the right step and the solid posture to support it.

It doesn't matter if you're short or tall, fat or thin, and while it's good to present in clean and solid clothing, bad posture, slouching, and a passive walk can turn potential opportunities and connections off.

Simple stretching, a little bit of basic yoga, and attention to how you stand and even walk in front of the mirror can help you make simple adjustments that can yield the best results. Take the time and put in the effort to reinforce good posture techniques. Those first impressions are key, and the first thing others see is your body.

The tone of your voice can be altered in bad posture. When you stand straight with solid posture, even your voice has a cleaner tone. Don't underestimate the power of physical projection. It's one of the first things people see and one of the first things people judge before even hearing your first words.

Your Volume Speaks Volumes

Think of those people whose voices just annoy the daylights out of you. Think of those people who seem to be completely unaware of just how loud they are. Then think about the people who speak so softly, it's both annoying and challenging to try to hear them. Then the last type, those fluctuating between sounding as quiet as a mouse and then roaring like a lion. Now, here's that moment of truth and something to put you in check . . . make sure you aren't one of them.

The volume of your voice truly speaks volumes about your confidence and your ability to connect, project, and communicate. When you talk too loudly, it gives off a sense of fear and lack of confidence mixed with trying to over-compensate. When you speak too softly, it highlights the same fear in a different way and a passiveness that can turn people away.

Look at it like Goldilocks and the three bears. Not too loud, not too soft, project with your volume just right. Don't overcompensate or undercompensate; just deliver an even tone at a reasonable volume. Inflections are fine. You don't want to sound monotone or like that teacher from *Ferris Bueller's Day Off*. (I might be dating myself here. Bueller, Bueller, Bueller. Just YouTube Ferris Bueller teacher and you will see what I mean.)

The consistency of the volume of your voice subliminally presents a confident person delivering something solid. Be seen as someone who presents a well-equalized and decent volume in their voice.

As hard as it might be, record yourself. Whether on a phone voice memo program or some kind of audio or video application, listen to how you sound, how you fluctuate in volume and pitch. Addressing these tiny intricacies can help open the doors for the biggest results and benefits from your presentations.

Uhs, Ums, Ohs, and Stuttering

Sometimes space is a beautiful thing. There's this simplicity, a comfort, and a sense of relaxation in space and in silence. The space between a note in a song or the space and pause between words in speech can have a great impact, while at the same time add a sense of dominance, control, and confidence.

On the exact opposite side of the spectrum, add someone who is afraid of space and feels like silence or a pause is the enemy. Then, of course, compound that with fear, lack of confidence, and the almost allergic reaction and outbreak of uhs and ums and ohs and stuttering, and you've taken the best plan and destroyed any chance of it, right there in the presentation.

By rooting yourself in your belief and confidence in whatever project, concept, or idea you're pitching and feeling the security to allow for pauses, silence, and breaks, you can raise the assertiveness and project a much stronger foundation for your presentation and your ability to present that much more professionally.

Trust yourself and allow for spaces, a breath, and even silence to occur without feeling that the given space has to be filled. The security and confidence in what you say mixed with what you don't say can speak volumes and showcase a strength even in a moment of silence.

Education for the Presentation

This is one of those due diligence type of pieces to the puzzle of your overall presentation. You may have prepared and educated yourself on the pitch or solicitation, but make sure you know about the people you're talking to, the company you are pitching, or the history of those who can help you achieve the results you're looking for.

Showcasing personal and professional respect to the person, company, group, or product that you're pitching or presenting helps you out exponentially with your presentation. Stay confident, but keep the ego checked at the door.

With all the time that goes into preparing and building that rock-solid, impress-them-all presentation, leave the time to learn and educate yourself on the people, the companies, and the products that those people and companies put out. Educate yourself on the key names, history, and success of that company, person, or organization. Bringing this type of individualized knowledge, information, and preparation to your presentation builds up that much better of a concentration from the listening audience.

The more you go into a meeting, pitch, or presentation not only asking but also showcasing and sharing your knowledge and respect to the person or company you want to align with, you prove you did your homework and you're not just trying to repeat the same pitch to a series of different people, over and over again.

Pre-Production for Pre-Presentation

A week before a Skype or video call, a phone meeting, or a face-to-face meeting, take in a rehearsal or two. Think of it as pre-production or a cold rehearsal before you go into do the real thing. Try a role-play-type scenario and test the waters. Get a friend you trust or business person you know and ask them to play the role of a skeptical, doubting, but slightly interested person who has agreed to hear you out.

Ask them to be honest, critical, as well as doubtful and very apprehensive. This dry run can help you test out how you present as well as allow you feedback on how you came off from someone other than the person or people who you plan to approach.

This can help you to dial in last-minute issues and prepare for some unexpected questions that might arise. Still, understand that no amount of practice can prepare you for the real presentation, and the best take-away from your pre-production and rehearsals is to achieve a basic level of comfort and confidence to take whatever is thrown at you and have the ability to address it.

It isn't about preparation to have the answers for every single question. It's more about being comfortable and confident in fielding and handling all the questions, over having all those answers. No one has all the answers, but those who can handle the questioning while explaining how they get the answers are the ones who see a greater level of support, investment, and sponsorship.

While preparation is a good idea, don't take it to the extent of trying to learn lines or make it too rigid or sterile. Rehearsal and preparation are good things, but something too rehearsed, too contrived, and too planned has a big chance of backfiring.

Adapting, Improvising, and Resonating with a Room

Imagine you're a chameleon, able to shift to any color to fit the environment around you. Sounds almost like some superhero, but it's not. It's your responsibility to adapt, adjust, improvise, and resonate with those who you're meeting. Your ability to relate and reset to resonate with the people around you will help those people feel both comfortable with you and with the idea, investment, concept, or pitch you're sharing.

As much as you may have done your research and your due diligence, there's no way to know what a room is like when you walk in, just as there's no way to guess what type of mood a person is in when you talk to them. This is all the more reason why it's crucial to be prepared to change on the drop of a dime.

Preparing and executing a professional but more rigid business pitch when you walk into a room of investors who have their suits on and ties straightened is a better choice than walking in, putting your feet up on a conference table, and calling people "dude."

On the other side of the coin, there's no need to keep that more rigid approach when you sit down in a more relaxed environment with people who tell you to call them by their first names, are cracking jokes, and seem like the kind of people you'd hang out with. In that case, you can dial back the formality and adjust accordingly.

Plan for what you can and find out who you're meeting, and where and when you're meeting them. Even more so, though, be prepared to switch up your presentation and vibe to meet, match, and resonate with someone from whom you want something.

 Regardless of how formal or relaxed a situation is, adjust to the situation, but stay professional. Even if it shifts to a buddy-buddy type meeting, you're there for business. Don't forget that.

Other Side of the Coin: Empathy

Whereas you have the best sense of what you're looking for, why you want it, and what you plan to do with it, realize that the majority of people you meet as you present and solicit your pitch have heard it all before. And they've heard it a lot. A great element to practice is that of empathy and seeing things from the other side of the coin with the person or people you are talking to.

This relating and understanding of their point of view and their experience enables you to make the experience all the stronger for yourself and what you are asking for. Too many people go into presentations with a selfish and very linear view that what they're saying, doing, and planning is something that no one has ever seen. Your presentation should be personalized and individualized as you define the points about who you are and what you're doing, but it's crucial to add an element of empathy, understanding, and looking at the other side of the coin.

As you work to understand how the other side feels, look at how you can supplement your presentation by thinking of how your presentation would make you feel. As you look at yourself as the requesting party, make sure you come off like someone you'd want to invest in.

Work to understand the other person's view of you and your project. Even if it isn't true or completely correct, that understanding mixed with the efforts to present in a way where you've already scrutinized and analyzed allows you a better connection and resonation with you.

Confidence without Arrogance

Confidence and assertiveness in a presentation are two attributes that make any presentation that much better, but keep them in check and don't let them run out of control into arrogance and belligerence. Your ability to present in a way that excites, draws people in, and engages people comes from the confidence you have in your project and in yourself.

Regardless of how good the presentation is on paper, a great deal comes down to how confident you are in person. If someone senses you seem doubtful, questionable, or iffy on how you're presenting, that can translate for them that you're doubtful, questionable, or iffy on what you presenting.

Believe in yourself and in your presentation. Being a little nervous and a shaky before delivering a pitch is one thing, but if you don't have the core confidence to deliver a presentation, get someone else to deliver it or spend a little more time honing it so you can deliver with the confidence it requires.

Saying that you don't know something showcases a lot more confidence than lying about something you don't have an answer for. People are much more impressed by someone who can look them dead in the eyes and say, "I don't know, but I will go and find out."

The Little Things

Many times a series of little things can make the difference and add that extra embellishment to a presentation. At the same time those little things that are forgotten or skipped over can also take away from presentations and potential opportunities.

As much as you'd like it to be all about the plan, all about the business, and all about what's being presented, the way you present yourself and the different parts of you can make all the difference. The following is a simple checklist of the little things to address to add that extra punch of professionalism to your presentation:

- Shine those shoes or clean those sneakers. A little blackener on the sole of a dark shoe or a little bleach to the sole of a sneaker shows that attention to detail.

- Present your clothes as clean and well cared for. Regardless of what you're presenting in, iron garments that can use ironing. Avoid looking overly wrinkled or sloppy.

- Trim and clean your fingernails. Show that you put effort from tip to toe.

- Shower and relax on the cologne or perfume. Don't overwhelm and intimidate with good or bad smells.

- Clean your phone. Clean your keys. Clean your laptop. That shiny screen on a phone, on a laptop, or even a set of keys that look cared for as well as anything else that can be seen during a meeting or presentation shows that extra attention to detail.

All those little extra embellishments bring that much more for reinforcements to your presentation in what you're sharing and how you appear while sharing it.

Talking With, Not To or At, People

There's a big difference in talking *with* someone, talking *to* someone, and talking *at* someone. It might be seen like semantics, but it goes much further and that's why it's the last tip for presentations. Although you're doing a great deal of the talking in a given presentation, solicitation, or pitch, keep in mind *how* you're talking. This is a much more psychological aspect with much more subliminal-type connections. People who present as they're talking with someone create a much more comfortable experience with the people to whom they're presenting.

In talking with someone, it becomes that much more of an inviting presentation and comes off softer and more welcoming. Think of talking with someone in the sense that they could jump in and add a thought, ask a question, or become a part of the presentation themselves, even though you're the presenter.

Steer clear of talking *at* someone, which usually brings the sense of being almost looked down on. Dominating a talk, not allowing for others to interject, and making it more like a speech over a conversation between two parties is a good way to alienate your audience and come off as condescending. Even the phrase of talking *to* someone has many of those aggressive elements as well.

Keep in mind that you're presenting by talking *with* someone or talking *with* a group of people, not just talking *at* them. Even if no one else says a word, giving off the two-way vibe of talking *with* someone creates a more inviting, engaging atmosphere for your presentation. In turn, it has that much more of an effect because you make everyone part of the conversation.

No one has a better understanding of what you want than you. Take every step, use every tool in your toolbox, and every tip in this chapter to bring across the strength of your presentation and your pitch. Even more so, present the best of you. You're the maker of your music, the foundation of your business. The plan and elements are detailed, defined, and organized, but the final piece comes back to you and your delivery.

Index

About the Author

Music business advisor, speaker and author Loren Weisman organizes, optimizes, and implements individualized branding, marketing, and content plans for musicians, managers, record labels, authors, and other entertainment businesses. Basically, he's the guy behind the guy . . . or girl.

Loren has worked on hundreds of albums as a drummer and music producer. He also maintains TV productions credits for three major networks as well as serves as a media consultant for many businesses in and out of the arts and entertainment fields. Loren has seen and stayed up to date with the constant changes in both the music and television industries over the past two decades as well as kept up with the pulse and motion of marketing, promotion, and social media in today's world.

For more information about Loren Weisman, or to book him for a speaking engagement or consulting packages, go to

```
http://lorenweisman.com/
http://facebook.com/lorenweisman/
http://youtube.com/lorenweisman/
http://linkedin.com/in/lorenweisman
http://instagram.com/lorenweisman/
http://twitter.com/lorenweisman/
```

Dedication

This book is dedicated to Olivia. Your inspiration is so big while at the same time, you make me see and feel all the little things that much clearer.

Acknowledgements

Sue Hobbs, David Lutton, Melisa Duffy, and everyone at Wiley and Sons; Maciej Jasinski, Rebecca Larkin, Barbara Brown, Phil Gent, Brandon Powers, Peggy Hazlett, Steve Moreau, Ed Verner, Paula Savastano, Nick Carr, Adam Metzger, Roy Wells, Triad Strategies, Thom Lemmons, Edyta Palenica, Jean D Zana, Gigi and Char Coggin-Davis, Elliott Randall, Peter Fernandez, John Voshell, Joel Ryan, Kyra Hagan, Kurt Hilborn, Christopher Laird Simmons, Mike Sinkula, Michelle Calato, Matthew Carrier, Scott Payne, Brian Ulery, Jana Pelinga, Corrine Bonneau, Margaret Hoelzer, Jim and Andrea Vidmar, Elizabeth Larkin, Steve Ceragno, Johnny Lee Lane, Cole Lakes, Jason Rubal, Vikki Hein, Elizabeth Larkin, Erin Mullen, Rosemary Caine, Roger Wallace, Rick Gibson, Sheri Fretwell, and Auggie!

Special thanks to Pam and Peter Hoagland, Tommy and Kathy Trufa, Cal and Anne Potter, Mike and Kathryn Kenney, Pat and Beth Pritchett, Sarah Nichols, Joanne and Ernie Hatt; also Madalyne Ann Crane Menzies and Judy!

An additional thanks to Regal Tip Drum Sticks, DropCards, Hilton Hotels, Qick Pick, GeoRiot, Wells Fargo, Remo Drum Heads, Prestige Hotel (especially Justin), Einstein's Bagels, Domino's Pizza, and Jeep.

This book was written, edited, and reviewed exclusively in Vero Beach, Florida, in 261 hours, and 39 minutes, in 91 days in my apartment affectionately referred to as the Sand Dune Cottage, the beach, Di Mare, Mulligan's Waldo's, Orchid Island Brewing Company, Starbucks at 1235 US Highway 1, Vero Beach, Cravings, as well as Grind and Grape.

Publisher's Acknowledgments Page

Acquisitions Editor: David Lutton and
Tracy Boggier

Project Editor: Susan Hobbs

Copy Editor: Susan Hobbs

Technical Editors: Steve Gerardi

Art Coordinator: Alicia B. South

Project Manager: Jennifer Ehrlich

Cover Image: Loren Weisman

Apple & Mac

iPad For Dummies,
5th Edition
978-1-118-72306-7

iPhone For Dummies,
7th Edition
978-1-118-69083-3

Macs All-in-One
For Dummies, 4th Edition
978-1-118-82210-4

OS X Mavericks
For Dummies
978-1-118-69188-5

Blogging & Social Media

Facebook For Dummies,
5th Edition
978-1-118-63312-0

Social Media Engagement
For Dummies
978-1-118-53019-1

WordPress For Dummies,
5th Edition
978-1-118-79161-5

Business

Stock Investing
For Dummies, 4th Edition
978-1-118-37678-2

Investing For Dummies,
6th Edition
978-0-470-90545-6

Personal Finance
For Dummies, 7th Edition
978-1-118-11785-9

QuickBooks 2014
For Dummies
978-1-118-72005-9

Small Business Marketing
Kit For Dummies,
3rd Edition
978-1-118-31183-7

Careers

Job Interviews
For Dummies, 4th Edition
978-1-118-11290-8

Job Searching with Social
Media For Dummies,
2nd Edition
978-1-118-67856-5

Personal Branding
For Dummies
978-1-118-11792-7

Resumes For Dummies,
6th Edition
978-0-470-87361-8

Starting an Etsy Business
For Dummies, 2nd Edition
978-1-118-59024-9

Diet & Nutrition

Belly Fat Diet For Dummies
978-1-118-34585-6

Mediterranean Diet
For Dummies
978-1-118-71525-3

Nutrition For Dummies,
5th Edition
978-0-470-93231-5

Digital Photography

Digital SLR Photography
All-in-One For Dummies,
2nd Edition
978-1-118-59082-9

Digital SLR Video &
Filmmaking For Dummies
978-1-118-36598-4

Photoshop Elements 12
For Dummies
978-1-118-72714-0

Gardening

Herb Gardening
For Dummies, 2nd Edition
978-0-470-61778-6

Gardening with Free-Range
Chickens For Dummies
978-1-118-54754-0

Health

Boosting Your Immunity
For Dummies
978-1-118-40200-9

Diabetes For Dummies,
4th Edition
978-1-118-29447-5

Living Paleo For Dummies
978-1-118-29405-5

Big Data

Big Data For Dummies
978-1-118-50422-2

Data Visualization
For Dummies
978-1-118-50289-1

Hadoop For Dummies
978-1-118-60755-8

Language &
Foreign Language

500 Spanish Verbs
For Dummies
978-1-118-02382-2

English Grammar
For Dummies, 2nd Edition
978-0-470-54664-2

French All-in-One
For Dummies
978-1-118-22815-9

German Essentials
For Dummies
978-1-118-18422-6

Italian For Dummies,
2nd Edition
978-1-118-00465-4

e Available in print and e-book formats.

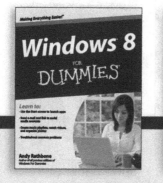

Math & Science

Algebra I For Dummies,
2nd Edition
978-0-470-55964-2

Anatomy and Physiology
For Dummies, 2nd Edition
978-0-470-92326-9

Astronomy For Dummies,
3rd Edition
978-1-118-37697-3

Biology For Dummies,
2nd Edition
978-0-470-59875-7

Chemistry For Dummies,
2nd Edition
978-1-118-00730-3

1001 Algebra II Practice
Problems For Dummies
978-1-118-44662-1

Microsoft Office

Excel 2013 For Dummies
978-1-118-51012-4

Office 2013 All-in-One
For Dummies
978-1-118-51636-2

PowerPoint 2013
For Dummies
978-1-118-50253-2

Word 2013 For Dummies
978-1-118-49123-2

Music

Blues Harmonica
For Dummies
978-1-118-25269-7

Guitar For Dummies,
3rd Edition
978-1-118-11554-1

iPod & iTunes
For Dummies, 10th Edition
978-1-118-50864-0

Programming

Beginning Programming
with C For Dummies
978-1-118-73763-7

Excel VBA Programming
For Dummies, 3rd Edition
978-1-118-49037-2

Java For Dummies,
6th Edition
978-1-118-40780-6

Religion & Inspiration

The Bible For Dummies
978-0-7645-5296-0

Buddhism For Dummies,
2nd Edition
978-1-118-02379-2

Catholicism For Dummies,
2nd Edition
978-1-118-07778-8

Self-Help & Relationships

Beating Sugar Addiction
For Dummies
978-1-118-54645-1

Meditation For Dummies,
3rd Edition
978-1-118-29144-3

Seniors

Laptops For Seniors
For Dummies, 3rd Edition
978-1-118-71105-7

Computers For Seniors
For Dummies, 3rd Edition
978-1-118-11553-4

iPad For Seniors
For Dummies, 6th Edition
978-1-118-72826-0

Social Security
For Dummies
978-1-118-20573-0

Smartphones & Tablets

Android Phones
For Dummies, 2nd Edition
978-1-118-72030-1

Nexus Tablets
For Dummies
978-1-118-77243-0

Samsung Galaxy S 4
For Dummies
978-1-118-64222-1

Samsung Galaxy Tabs
For Dummies
978-1-118-77294-2

Test Prep

ACT For Dummies,
5th Edition
978-1-118-01259-8

ASVAB For Dummies,
3rd Edition
978-0-470-63760-9

GRE For Dummies,
7th Edition
978-0-470-88921-3

Officer Candidate Tests
For Dummies
978-0-470-59876-4

Physician's Assistant Exam
For Dummies
978-1-118-11556-5

Series 7 Exam For Dummies
978-0-470-09932-2

Windows 8

Windows 8.1 All-in-One
For Dummies
978-1-118-82087-2

Windows 8.1 For Dummies
978-1-118-82121-3

Windows 8.1 For Dummies,
Book + DVD Bundle
978-1-118-82107-7

e Available in print and e-book formats.